AF334566

THE WORLD SERIES

THE WORLD SERIES:
The Statistical Record

Revised Edition

HAROLD R. PARETCHAN

South Brunswick and New York:
A. S. Barnes and Company
London: Thomas Yoseloff Ltd

A. S. Barnes and Co., Inc.
Cranbury, New Jersey 08512

Thomas Yoseloff Ltd
108 New Bond Street
London W1Y OQX, England

ISBN 0-498-01303-0
Printed in the United States of America

To the late Tommy Marino of Foxboro, Massachusetts —a dear friend
and a great sports fan who knew baseball well

Contents

Acknowledgments

I wish to extend a special word of thanks to three members of the Boston Globe who over the years gave me encouragement and purpose: Harold Kaese, a sports writer with an analytical mind; Jerry Nason, always with the human side of all aspects of sports; and Jack Barry, a truly wonderful person.

Introduction

Since the dawn of the World Series, in the early nineteen hundreds, to the present time, the World Series has been a dream for all baseball players. There have been about ten thousand or more ballplayers participating in this sport, but only a relative number have been fortunate enough to have a dream become a reality. From the days of Ty Cobb and Hans Wagner through Babe Ruth, Frankie Frisch, Lou Gehrig, Joe DiMaggio, and Ted Williams, to the present superstars, such as Mickey Mantle, Willie Mays, and Hank Aaron, the World Series has been the ultimate display of talent, courage, and pressure.

The purpose of this book is to give baseball fans a clearer and more concise picture of the **World Series.** The book is divided into three sections, dwelling upon individual performance during each World Series game. The first section shows the contributions of each individual ballplayer in deciding the outcome of each World Series game by either driving in the winning run or decisive run of victory. The second section deals with Individual Offensive Records for all World Series games, consisting of fourteen offensive departments. The third section pertains to individual ballplayers who have hit home runs in World Series competition and other relative pertinent facts.

Many of the super baseball stars have been great during the regular season but have become lesser stars in the World Series. On the other hand, average journeymen ballplayers playing during the regular season have displayed outstanding ability in the all-important World Series. For instance, Gerry Coleman was a good average ballplayer throughout his career, but whenever participating in the World Series, he ascended a plateau of brilliance, particularly in the World Series games of 1949 and 1950.

In the 1949 World Series, Coleman won the third game in the ninth inning with a single. In the fifth and last of the 1949 World Series, he drove in the deciding run in the fifth inning on a ground out. In the 1950 World Series, Coleman arose to the occasion and won the first game, driving in the only run of the game. Once more, Gerry Coleman drove in the winning run in the third game of the World Series with a single in the ninth inning.

In regards to the home run, which in the baseball annuals is considered by many the most outstanding achievement, both Mickey Mantle and Babe Ruth head the list. Between them, these two fine athletes have hit thirty-three home runs in World Series competition, with Micky Mantle hitting eighteen and Babe Ruth hitting fifteen. Of the eighteen home runs hit by Mickey Mantle, six of them accounted for the margin of victory. Despite hitting three home runs in a game twice in 1926 and 1928, Babe Ruth only won one ball game in the World Series games, and that was by a single in the 1921 World Series. However, the same Babe Ruth lead all other baseball players in the Individual Offensive Records department with a total of thirty times.

Throughout this book baseball fans will find other notable facts that should be most interesting and informative.

Abbreviations

AL	American League	LAD	Los Angeles Dodgers
BA	Batting Average	LH	Long Hit
Balt.	Baltimore Orioles	M	Minnesota Twins
BB	Bases on Balls	Mil.	Milwaukee Braves
BBR	Boston Braves	NL	National League
Br.	Brooklyn Dodgers	NYG	New York Giants
BRS	Boston Red Sox	NYM	New York Metropolitans
ChC	Chicago Cubs	NYY	New York Yankees
ChW	Chicago White Sox	1B	Single
Cin.	Cincinnati Reds	OAK	Oakland Athletics
CL	Cleveland Indians	PB	Passed Ball
D	Detroit Tigers	PhA	Philadelphia Athletics
EBLH	Extra Bases on Long Hit	PhP	Philadelphia Phillies
ER	Error	PP	Pittsburgh Pirates
FC	Fielder's Choice	R	Run
G	Games	RBI	Run Batted In
GO	Grounded Out	SB	Stolen Base
H	Hits	SF	Sacrifice Fly
HR	Home Run	SFG	San Francisco Giants

SH	Sacrifice Hit		3B	Triple
StLB	St. Louis Browns		2B	Double
StLC	St. Louis Cardinals		W	Washington Senators
TAB	Times at Bat		WP	Wild Pitch
TB	Total Bases			

THE WORLD SERIES

Part One: World Series Records: Players Driving in Winning or Decisive Runs

1

Players Driving in Winning or Decisive Runs from 1903 to 1973, except 1904

Overall W.S. Game	Year	Game	Score	Player	Inn	Type of Hit	Remarks
1	1903	1	PP 7 BRS 3	J. Sebring	1st	1B	Driving in 2 Runs
2	1903	2	BRS 3 PP 0	P. Dougherty	1st	HR	Driving in 1st Run of Game
3	1903	3	PP 4 BRS 2	J. Sebring	3rd	F. C.	Attempting to catch Wagner going to 3B. Leach scored from 3B.
4	1903	4	PP 5 BRS 4	H. Wagner	7th	1B	Driving in 1 Run
5	1903	5	BRS 11 PP 2	Error	6th	ER	3rd Run Scored on Shortstop's Error
6	1903	6	BRS 6 PP 3	B. Freeman	5th	SF	Driving in 1 Run
7	1903	7	BRS 7 PP 3	F. Parent	4th	1B	Driving in 1 Run
8	1903	8	BRS 3 PP 0	H. Ferriss	4th	1B	Driving in 1st 2 Runs of the Game
9	1905	1	NYG 3 PhA 0	Error	5th	ER	2 Runs Scored on Catcher's Error
10	1905	2	PhA 3 NYG 0	B. Lord	3rd	1B	Driving in 1st Run of the Game
11	1905	3	NYG 9 PhA 0	D. McGann	1st	1B	Driving in 1st Run of the Game

23

<table>
<thead>
<tr><th>Overall
W.S.
Game</th><th>Year</th><th>Game</th><th>Score</th><th>Player</th><th>Inn</th><th>Type
of Hit</th><th>Remarks</th></tr>
</thead>
<tbody>
<tr><td>12</td><td>1905</td><td>4</td><td>NYG 1 PhA 0</td><td>Error</td><td>4th</td><td>ER</td><td>Only Run Scored on Shortstop's Error</td></tr>
<tr><td>13</td><td>1905</td><td>5</td><td>NYG 2 PhA 0</td><td>B. Gilbert</td><td>5th</td><td>1B</td><td>Driving in 1st Run of the Game</td></tr>
<tr><td>14</td><td>1906</td><td>1</td><td>ChW 2 ChC 1</td><td>F. Isbeli</td><td>6th</td><td>2B</td><td>Driving in 1 Run</td></tr>
<tr><td>15</td><td>1906</td><td>2</td><td>ChC 7 ChW 1</td><td>E. Reulbach</td><td>2nd</td><td>SH</td><td>S.H. allowing 2nd Run to Score</td></tr>
<tr><td>16</td><td>1906</td><td>3</td><td>ChW 3 ChC 0</td><td>G. Rohe</td><td>6th</td><td>3B</td><td>Driving in all Runs of the Game</td></tr>
<tr><td>17</td><td>1906</td><td>4</td><td>ChC 1 ChW 0</td><td>J. Evers</td><td>7th</td><td>1B</td><td>Driving in only Run of the Game</td></tr>
<tr><td>18</td><td>1906</td><td>5</td><td>ChW 8 ChC 6</td><td>J. Donahue</td><td>4th</td><td>2B</td><td>Driving in 1 Run</td></tr>
<tr><td>19</td><td>1906</td><td>6</td><td>ChW 8 ChC 3</td><td>Geo. S. Davis</td><td>2nd</td><td>1B</td><td>Driving in 1 Run</td></tr>
<tr><td>20</td><td>1907</td><td>1</td><td>ChC 3 D 3</td><td>Tied Game</td><td></td><td></td><td>Tied Game</td></tr>
<tr><td>21</td><td>1907</td><td>2</td><td>ChC 3 D 1</td><td>J. Slagle</td><td>4th</td><td>1B</td><td>Driving in 1 Run</td></tr>
<tr><td>22</td><td>1907</td><td>3</td><td>ChC 5 D 1</td><td>Frank Schulte</td><td>4th</td><td>1B</td><td>Driving in 1 Run</td></tr>
<tr><td>23</td><td>1907</td><td>4</td><td>ChC 6 D 1</td><td>J. Slagle</td><td>5th</td><td>1B</td><td>Driving in 1 Run</td></tr>
<tr><td>24</td><td>1907</td><td>5</td><td>ChC 2 D 0</td><td>H. Steinfeldt</td><td>1st</td><td>3B</td><td>Driving in 1st Run</td></tr>
<tr><td>25</td><td>1908</td><td>1</td><td>ChC 10 D 6</td><td>S. Hofman</td><td>9th</td><td>1B</td><td>Driving in 1 Run</td></tr>
<tr><td>26</td><td>1908</td><td>2</td><td>ChC 6 D 1</td><td>J. Tinker</td><td>8th</td><td>HR</td><td>Driving in 2 Runs</td></tr>
<tr><td>27</td><td>1908</td><td>3</td><td>D 8 ChC 3</td><td>C. Rossman</td><td>6th</td><td>1B</td><td>Driving in 2 Runs</td></tr>
<tr><td>28</td><td>1908</td><td>4</td><td>ChC 3 D 0</td><td>H. Steinfeldt</td><td>3rd</td><td>1B</td><td>Driving in 1st Run</td></tr>
<tr><td>29</td><td>1908</td><td>5</td><td>ChC 2 D 0</td><td>F. Chance</td><td>1st</td><td>1B</td><td>Driving in 1st Run</td></tr>
<tr><td>30</td><td>1909</td><td>1</td><td>PP 4 D 1</td><td>G. Gibson</td><td>5th</td><td>2B</td><td>Driving 1 Run</td></tr>
<tr><td>31</td><td>1909</td><td>2</td><td>D 7 PP 2</td><td>J. Delahanty</td><td>3rd</td><td>1B</td><td>Driving in 2 Runs</td></tr>
<tr><td>32</td><td>1909</td><td>3</td><td>PP 8 D 6</td><td>F. Clarke</td><td>9th</td><td>SF</td><td>Driving in 1 Run</td></tr>
<tr><td>33</td><td>1909</td><td>4</td><td>D 5 PP 0</td><td>O. Stanage</td><td>2nd</td><td>1B</td><td>Driving in 1st 2 Runs</td></tr>
<tr><td>34</td><td>1909</td><td>5</td><td>PP 8 D 4</td><td>F. Clarke</td><td>7th</td><td>HR</td><td>Driving in 3 Runs</td></tr>
<tr><td>35</td><td>1909</td><td>6</td><td>D 5 PP 4</td><td>T. Cobb</td><td>6th</td><td>2B</td><td>Driving in 1 Run</td></tr>
<tr><td>36</td><td>1909</td><td>7</td><td>PP 8 D 0</td><td>R. Hyatt</td><td>2nd</td><td>SF</td><td>Driving in 1st Run</td></tr>
<tr><td>37</td><td>1910</td><td>1</td><td>PhA 4 ChC 1</td><td>C. Bender</td><td>2nd</td><td>1B</td><td>Driving in 1 Run</td></tr>
<tr><td>38</td><td>1910</td><td>2</td><td>PhA 9 ChC 3</td><td>H. Davis</td><td>7th</td><td>1B</td><td>Driving in 1 Run</td></tr>
<tr><td>39</td><td>1910</td><td>3</td><td>PhA 12 ChC 5</td><td>D. Murphy</td><td>3rd</td><td>HR</td><td>Driving in 3 Runs</td></tr>
<tr><td>40</td><td>1910</td><td>4</td><td>ChC 4 PhA 3</td><td>J. Sheckard</td><td>10th</td><td>1B</td><td>Driving in Winning Run</td></tr>
<tr><td>41</td><td>1910</td><td>5</td><td>PhA 7 ChC 2</td><td>B. Lord</td><td>8th</td><td>2B</td><td>Driving in 1 Run</td></tr>
</tbody>
</table>

Overall W.S. Game	Year	Game	Score	Player	Inn	Type of Hit	Remarks
42	1911	1	NYG 2 PhA 1	J. Devore	7th	2B	Driving in 1 Run
43	1911	2	PhA 3 NYG 1	J. F. Baker	7th	HR	Driving in 2 Runs
44	1911	3	PhA 3 NYG 2	H. Davis	11th	1B	Driving in Winning Run
45	1911	4	PhA 4 NYG 2	I. Thomas	4th	SF	Driving in 1 Run
46	1911	5	NYG 4 PhA 3	F. Merkle	10th	SF	Driving in Winning Run
47	1911	6	PhA 13 NYG 2	Error	4th	ER	3rd Philadelphia Run Scored on Outfielder's Throwing error.
48	1912	1	BRS 4 NYG 3	S. Yerkes	7th	1B	Driving in 1 Run
49	1912	2	BRS 6 NYG 6	Tied Game			Tied Game
50	1912	3	NYG 2 BRS 1	A. Fletcher	5th	1B	Driving in 1 Run
51	1912	4	BRS 3 NYG 1	F. Cady	4th	1B	Driving in 1 Run
52	1912	5	BRS 2 NYG 1	T. Speaker	3rd	1B	Driving in 1 Run
53	1912	6	NYG 5 BRS 2	B. Herzog	1st	2B	Driving in 1 Run
54	1912	7	NYG 11 BRS 4	A. Fletcher	1st	2B	Driving in 1 Run
55	1912	8	BRS 3 NYG 2	L. Gardner	10th	SF	Driving in Winning Run
56	1913	1	PhA 6 NYG 4	J. F. Baker	5th	HR	Driving in 2 Runs
57	1913	2	NYG 3 PhA 0	C. Mathewson	10th	1B	Driving in 1st Run of the Game
58	1913	3	PhA 8 NYG 2	Error	1st	ER	2 Runs Scored on Throwing Error by Shortstop
59	1913	4	PhA 6 NYG 5	W. Schang	5th	1B	Driving in 2 Runs
60	1913	5	PhA 3 NYG 1	J. F. Baker	3rd	FC	1st Baseman Missed Runner going to 1B, then threw home, but Runner Scored
61	1914	1	BB 7 PhA 1	R. Maranville	2nd	1B	Driving in 1 Run
62	1914	2	BB 1 PhA 0	L. Mann	9th	1B	Driving in 1 Run
63	1914	3	BB 5 PhA 4	Error	12th	ER	Pitcher's Error Allowing 1 Run to Score
64	1914	4	BB 3 PhA 1	J. Evers	5th	1B	Driving in 2 Runs
65	1915	1	PhP 3 BRS 1	C. Cravath	8th	GO	Driving in 1 Run
66	1915	2	BRS 2 PhP 1	G. Foster	9th	1B	Driving in Winning Run
67	1915	3	BRS 2 PhP 1	D. Lewis	9th	1B	Driving in Winning Run
68	1915	4	BRS 2 PhP 1	D. Lewis	6th	2B	Driving in 1 Run
69	1915	5	BRS 5 PhP 4	H. Hooper	9th	HR	Driving in Winning Run With 2nd HR of Game

Overall W.S. Game	Year	Game	Score	Player	Inn	Type of Hit	Remarks
70	1916	1	BRS 6 BR 5	Error	8th	ER	Run Scored on Outfielder's Throwing Error
71	1916	2	BRS 2 BR 1	D. Gainor	14th	1B	Driving in Winning Run
72	1916	3	BR 4 BRS 3	I. Olsen	5th	3B	Driving in 2 Runs
73	1916	4	BRS 6 BR 2	L. Gardner	2nd	HR	Hit 3 Run Home Run
74	1916	5	BRS 4 BR 1	Error	3rd	ER	Throwing Error by Shortstop Allowing 1 Run
75	1917	1	ChW 2 NYG 1	O. Felsch	4th	HR	Driving in 1 Run
76	1917	2	ChW 7 NYG 2	H. Leibold	4th	1B	Driving in 1 Run
77	1917	3	NYG 2 ChW 0	W. Holke	4th	2B	Driving in 1st Run of Game
78	1917	4	NYG 5 ChW 0	B. Kauff	4th	HR	Driving in 1st Run Longest Home Run of the Season in Polo Grds.
79	1917	5	ChW 8 NYG 5	E. Collins	8th	1B	Driving in 1 Run
80	1917	6	ChW 4 NYG 2	C. Gandil	4th	1B	Driving in 2 Runs
81	1918	1	BRS 1 ChC 0	S. McInnis	4th	1B	Driving in only Run of the Game
82	1918	2	ChC 3 BRS 1	G. Tyler	2nd	1B	Driving in 2 Runs
83	1918	3	BRS 2 ChC 1	E. Scott	4th	1B	Driving in 1 Run
84	1918	4	BRS 3 ChC 2	Error	8th	ER	Winning Run Scored on Wild Throw by Pitcher
85	1918	5	ChC 3 BRS 0	L. Mann	3rd	2B	Driving in 1st Run of the Game
86	1918	6	BRS 2 ChC 1	Error	3rd	ER	2 Runs Scored on Outfielder's Error
87	1919	1	Cin 9 ChW 1	I. Wingo	4th	1B	Driving in 1 Run
88	1919	2	Cin 4 ChW 2	W. Kopf	4th	3B	Tripled Driving in 2 Runs
89	1919	3	ChW 3 Cin 0	C. Gandil	2nd	1B	Driving in 2 Runs
90	1919	4	Cin 2 ChW 0	Error	5th	ER	1st Run Scored on Pitcher's Error
91	1919	5	Cin 5 ChW 0	M. Rath	6th	1B	Driving in 1st Run of Game
92	1919	6	ChW 5 Cin 4	C. Gandil	10th	1B	Driving in Winning Run
93	1919	7	ChW 4 Cin 1	J. Jackson	3rd	1B	Driving in 1 Run
94	1919	8	Cin 10 ChW 5	G. Neale	5th	1B	Driving in 1 Run
95	1920	1	CL 3 BR 1	S. O'Neill	2nd	2B	Driving in 1 Run
96	1920	2	BR 3 CL 0	Z. Wheat	1st	2B	Driving in 1st Run of the Game
97	1920	3	BR 2 CL 1	H. Myers	1st	1B	Driving in 1 Run
98	1920	4	CL 5 BR 1	L. Gardner	1st	SF	Driving in 1 Run

Overall W.S. Game	Year	Game	Score	Player	Inn	Type of Hit	Remarks
99	1920	5	CL 8 BR 1	E. Smith	1st	HR	Hitting 1st Grand Slam in World Series History
100	1920	6	CL 1 BR 0	G. H. Burns	6th	2B	Driving in only Run of the Game
101	1920	7	CL 3 BR 0	Error	4th	ER	1st Run Scored on Pitcher's Error
102	1921	1	NYY 3 NYG 0	B. Ruth	1st	1B	Driving in 1st Run of Game
103	1921	2	NYY 3 NYG 0	W. Hoyt	4th	GO	Run Scored as Hoyt Grounded Out
104	1921	3	NYG 13 NYY 5	E. Meusel	7th	2B	Driving in 2 Runs
105	1921	4	NYG 4 NYY 2	G. J. Burns	8th	2B	Driving in 2 Runs
106	1921	5	NYY 3 NYG 1	R. Meusel	4th	2B	Driving in 1 Run
107	1921	6	NYG 8 NYY 5	G. Kelly	4th	1B	Driving in 2 Runs
108	1921	7	NYG 2 NYY 1	F. Snyder	7th	2B	Driving in 1 Run
109	1921	8	NYG 1 NYY 0	Error	1st	ER	Run Scored on Shortstop's Error
110	1922	1	NYG 3 NYY 2	R. Youngs	8th	SF	Driving in Winning Run
111	1922	2	NYG 3 NYY 3	Tied Game			Tied Game
112	1922	3	NYG 3 NYY 0	F. Frisch	3rd	SF	Driving in 1st Run of the Game
113	1922	4	NYG 4 NYY 3	R. Youngs	5th	1B	Driving in 1 Run
114	1922	5	NYG 5 NYY 3	G. Kelly	8th	1B	Driving in 2 Runs
115	1923	1	NYG 5 NYY 4	C. Stengel	9th	HR	Driving in Winning Run
116	1923	2	NYY 4 NYG 2	E. Scott	4th	1B	Driving in 1 Run
117	1923	3	NYG 1 NYY 0	C. Stengel	7th	HR	Driving in Only Run of the Game
118	1923	4	NYY 8 NYG 4	R. Meusel	2nd	3B	Driving in 2 Runs
119	1923	5	NYY 8 NYG 1	R. Meusel	1st	3B	Driving in 2 Runs
120	1923	6	NYY 6 NYG 4	R. Meusel	8th	1B	Driving in Tying and Winning Runs
121	1924	1	NYG 4 W 3	G. Kelly	12th	SF	Driving in Winning Run
122	1924	2	W 4 NYG 3	R. Peckinpaugh	9th	1B	Driving in Winning Run
123	1924	3	NYG 6 W 4	F. Lindstrom	6th	1B	Driving in 1 Run
124	1924	4	W 7 NYG 4	G. Goslin	5th	1B	Driving in 2 Runs
125	1924	5	NYG 6 W 2	J. Bentley	5th	HR	Driving in 2 Runs

126	1924	6	W 2 NYG 1	S. Harris	5th	2B	Driving in Tying and Winning Runs
127	1924	7	W 4 NYG 3	E. McNeeley	12th	1B	Driving in Winning Run
128	1925	1	W 4 PP 1	S. Rice	5th	1B	Driving in 2 Runs
129	1925	2	PP 3 W 2	K. Cuyler	8th	HR	Driving in 2 Runs
130	1925	3	W 4 PP 3	J. Harris	7th	1B	Driving in 1 Run
131	1925	4	W 4 PP 0	G. Goslin	3rd	HR	Driving in 3 Runs
132	1925	5	PP 6 W 3	C. Barnhart	7th	1B	Driving in 1 Run
133	1925	6	PP 3 W 2	Grant Moore	5th	HR	Driving in 1 Run
134	1925	7	PP 9 W 7	K. Cuyler	8th	2B	Driving in 2 Runs
135	1926	1	NYY 2 StLC 1	L. Gehrig	6th	1B	Driving in 1 Run
136	1926	2	StLC 6 NYY 2	B. Southworth	7th	HR	Driving in 3 Runs
137	1926	3	StLC 4 NYY 0	Error	4th	ER	1st Run Scored on Shortstop's Error
138	1926	4	NYY 10 StLC 5	T. Lazzeri	5th	SF	Driving in 1 Run
139	1926	5	NYY 3 StLC 2	T. Lazzeri	10th	SF	Driving in 1 Run
140	1926	6	StLC 10 NYY 2	L. Bell	1st	1B	Driving in 2 Runs
141	1926	7	StLC 3 NYY 2	T. Thevenow	4th	1B	Driving in 2 Runs
142	1927	1	NYY 5 PP 4	L. Gehrig	5th	SF	Driving in 1 Run
143	1927	2	NYY 6 PP 2	T. Lazzeri	3rd	SF	Driving in 1 Run
144	1927	3	NYY 8 PP 1	L. Gehrig	1st	3B	Driving in 2 Runs
145	1927	4	NYY 4 PP 3	Wild Pitch	9th	WP	Pitcher Wild Pitched Run Home
146	1928	1	NYY 4 StLC 1	R. Meusel	4th	HR	Driving in 2 Runs
147	1928	2	NYY 9 StLC 3	C. Durst	2nd	1B	Driving in 1 Run
148	1928	3	NYY 7 StLC 3	Error	6th	ER	B. Ruth Scored on a Double Error
149	1928	4	NYY 7 StLC 3	T. Lazzeri	7th	2B	Driving in 1 Run
150	1929	1	PhA 3 ChC 1	Bing Miller	9th	1B	Driving in 2 Runs
151	1929	2	PhA 9 ChC 3	M. Haas	4th	FC	Run Scored on Attempted Double Play One Run Scored
152	1929	3	ChC 3 PhA 1	K. Cuyler	6th	1B	Driving in 2 Runs
153	1929	4	PhA 10 ChC 8	J. Dykes	7th	2B	Driving in 2 Runs
154	1929	5	PhA 3 ChC 2	Bing Miller	9th	1B	Driving in 1 Run

| --- | --- | --- | --- | --- | --- | --- | --- |
155	1930	1	PhA 5 StLC 2	J. Dykes	6th	2B	Driving in 1 Run
156	1930	2	PhA 6 StLC 1	J. Foxx	1st	2B	Driving in 1 Run
157	1930	3	StLC 5 PhA 0	T. Douthit	4th	HR	Driving in 1st Run of the Game
158	1930	4	StLC 3 PhA 1	Error	4th	ER	Run Scored on Third Baseman's Error
159	1930	5	PhA 2 StLC 0	J. Foxx	9th	HR	Driving in the only 2 Runs
160	1930	6	PhA 7 StLC 1	Bing Miller	1st	2B	Driving in 1 Run
161	1931	1	PhA 6 StLC 2	J. Foxx	3rd	1B	Driving in 2 Runs
162	1931	2	StLC 2 PhA 0	James Wilson	2nd	SF	Driving in 1st Run of the Game
163	1931	3	StLC 5 PhA 2	P. Martin	4th	2B	Driving in 1 Run
164	1931	4	PhA 3 StLC 0	A. Simmons	1st	2B	Driving in 1st Run of the Game
165	1931	5	StLC 5 PhA 1	P. Martin	6th	HR	Driving in 2 Runs
166	1931	6	PhA 8 StLC 1	M. Haas	5th	BB	Walked with Bases Full
167	1931	7	StLC 4 PhA 2	G. Watkins	4th	HR	Driving in 2 Runs
168	1932	1	NYY 12 ChC 6	E. Combs	6th	1B	Driving in 2 Runs
169	1932	2	NYY 5 ChC 2	B. Chapman	3rd	1B	Driving in 2 Runs
170	1932	3	NYY 7 ChC 5	L. Gehrig	5th	HR	Driving in 1 Run
171	1932	4	NYY 13 ChC 6	J. Sewell	7th	1B	Driving in 2 Runs
172	1933	1	NYG 4 W 2	M. Ott	3rd	1B	Driving in 1 Run
173	1933	2	NYG 6 W 1	F. O'Doul	6th	1B	Driving in 2 Runs
174	1933	3	W 4 NYG 0	J. Cronin	1st	GO	Batter Thrown out at First, Run Scoring From Third Base
175	1933	4	NYG 2 W 1	B. Ryan	11th	1B	Driving in 1 Run
176	1933	5	NYG 4 W 3	M. Ott	10th	HR	Driving in Winning plus Last Run of the 1933 Series
177	1934	1	StLC 8 D 3	J. Medwick	5th	HR	Driving in 1 Run
178	1934	2	D 3 StLC 2	G. Goslin	12th	1B	Driving in Winning Run
179	1934	3	StLC 4 D 1	P. Dean	2nd	SF	Driving in 1 Run
180	1934	4	D 10 StLC 4	H. Greenberg	7th	2B	Driving in 1 Run
181	1934	5	D 3 StLC 1	C. Gehringer	6th	HR	Driving in 1 Run
182	1934	6	StLC 4 D 3	P. Dean	7th	1B	Driving in 1 Run
183	1934	7	StLC 11 D 0	F. Frisch	3rd	2B	Doubled, Driving in 3 Runs

Overall W. S. Game	Year	Game	Score	Player	Inn	Type of Hit	Remarks
184	1935	1	ChC 3 D 0	Error	1st	ER	Run Scored on Pitcher's Error
185	1935	2	D 8 ChC 3	H. Greenberg	1st	HR	Driving in 2 Runs
186	1935	3	D 6 ChC 5	JO JO White	11th	1B	Driving in Winning Run
187	1935	4	D 2 ChC 1	Error	6th	ER	Run Scored on Shortstop's Error
188	1935	5	ChC 3 D 1	C. Klein	3rd	HR	Driving in 2 Runs
189	1935	6	D 4 ChC 3	G. Goslin	9th	1B	Driving in Winning Run
190	1936	1	NYG 6 NYY 1	G. Mancuso	6th	1B	Driving in 1 Run
191	1936	2	NYY 18 NYG 4	B. Dickey	3rd	1B	Driving in 1 Run
192	1936	3	NYY 2 NYG 1	F. Crosetti	8th	1B	Driving in 1 Run
193	1936	4	NYY 5 NYG 2	L. Gehrig	3rd	HR	Driving in 2 Runs
194	1936	5	NYG 5 NYY 4	B. Terry	10th	SF	Driving in 1 Run
195	1936	6	NYY 13 NYG 5	T. Lazzeri	8th	1B	Driving in 1 Run
196	1937	1	NYY 8 NYG 1	J. DiMaggio	6th	1B	Driving in 2 Runs
197	1937	2	NYY 8 NYG 1	C. Ruffing	5th	1B	Driving in 1 Run
198	1937	3	NYY 5 NYG 1	B. Dickey	3rd	3B	Driving in 1 Run
199	1937	4	NYG 7 NYY 3	D. Bartell	2nd	1B	Driving in 1 Run
200	1937	5	NYY 4 NYG 2	L. Gomez	5th	1B	Driving in 1 Run
201	1938	1	NYY 3 ChC 1	J. Gordon	2nd	1B	Driving in 1 Run
202	1938	2	NYY 6 ChC 3	F. Crosetti	8th	HR	Driving in 2 Runs
203	1938	3	NYY 5 ChC 2	J. Gordon	6th	1B	Driving in 2 Runs
204	1938	4	NYY 8 ChC 3	T. Henrich	6th	HR	Driving in 1 Run
205	1939	1	NYY 2 Cin 1	B. Dickey	9th	1B	Driving in Winning Run
206	1939	2	NYY 4 Cin 0	F. Crosetti	3rd	GO	Driving in 1 Run
207	1939	3	NYY 7 Cin 3	J. DiMaggio	3rd	HR	Driving in 2 Runs
208	1939	4	NYY 7 Cin 4	J. DiMaggio	10th	1B	Driving in 1 Run
209	1940	1	D 7 Cin 2	D. Bartell	2nd	1B	Driving in 2 Runs
210	1940	2	Cin 5 D 3	J. Ripple	3rd	HR	Driving in 2 Runs
211	1940	3	D 7 Cin 4	M. Higgins	7th	HR	Driving in 2 Runs
212	1940	4	Cin 5 D 2	J. Ripple	3rd	2B	Driving in 2 Runs
213	1940	5	D 8 Cin 0	H. Greenberg	3rd	HR	Driving in the 1st 3 Runs
214	1940	6	Cin 4 D 0	Ival Goodman	1st	1B	Driving in 1st Run of Game
215	1940	7	Cin 2 D 1	B. Myers	7th	SF	Driving in 1 Run

Overall W.S. Game	Year	Game	Score	Player	Inn	Type of Hit	Remarks
216	1941	1	NYY 3 BR 2	J. Gordon	6th	1B	Driving in 1 Run
217	1941	2	BR 3 NYY 2	D. Camilli	6th	1B	Driving in 1 Run
218	1941	3	NYY 2 BR 1	C. Keller	8th	1B	Driving in 1 Run
219	1941	4	NYY 7 BR 4	C. Keller	9th	2B	Driving in 2 Runs
220	1941	5	NYY 3 BR 1	J. Gordon	2nd	1B	Driving in 1 Run
221	1942	1	NYY7 StLC4	Error	8th	ER	Outfielder's Error on Fly Ball Allows 2 Runs to Score
222	1942	2	StLC 4 NYY 3	S. Musial	8th	1B	Driving in 1 Run
223	1942	3	StLC 2 NYY 0	J. Brown	3rd	GO	Driving in 1 Run
224	1942	4	StLC 9 NYY 6	W. Cooper	7th	1B	Driving in 1 Run
225	1942	5	StLC 4 NYY 2	G. Kurowski	9th	HR	Driving in 2 Runs
226	1943	1	NYY 4 StLC 2	Wild Pitch	6th	WP	Pitcher's Wild Pitch Allows Runner to Score from Third Base
227	1943	2	StLC 4 NYY 3	R. Sanders	4th	HR	Driving in 2 Runs
228	1943	3	NYY 6 StLC 2	B. Johnson	8th	3B	Driving in 3 Runs
229	1943	4	NYY 2 StLC 1	F. Crosetti	8th	SF	Driving in 1 Run
230	1943	5	NYY 2 StLC 0	B. Dickey	6th	HR	Driving in the only 2 Runs **of the Game**
231	1944	1	StLB 2 StLC 1	G. McQuinn	4th	HR	Driving in 2 Runs
232	1944	2	StLC 3 StLB 2	K. O'Dea	11th	1B	Driving in 1 Run
233	1944	3	StLB 6 StLC 2	M. Christman	3rd	1B	Driving in 1 Run
234	1944	4	StLC 5 StLB 1	S. Musial	1st	HR	Driving in 2 Runs
235	1944	5	StLC 2 StLB 0	R. Sanders	6th	HR	Driving in 1 Run
236	1944	6	StLC 3 StLB 1	E. Verban	4th	1B	Driving in 1 Run
237	1945	1	ChC 9 D 0	Passed Ball	1st	PB	1st Run of Game Scored on Passed Ball
238	1945	2	D 4 ChC 1	H. Greenberg	5th	HR	Driving in 3 Runs
239	1945	3	ChC 3 D 0	B. Nicholson	4th	1B	Driving in 1st Run of the Game
240	1945	4	D 4 ChC 1	R. Cullenbine	4th	2B	Driving in 1 Run
241	1945	5	D 8 ChC 4	J. Webb	6th	FC	Runner Scored on Fielder's Choice
242	1945	6	ChC 8 D 7	S. Hack	12th	2B	Driving in Winning Run
243	1945	7	D 9 ChC 3	P. Richards	1st	2B	Clearing the Bases With a Double

Overall W.S. Game	Year	Game	Score	Player	Inn	Type of Hit	Remarks
244	1946	1	BRS 3 StLC 2	R. York	10th	HR	Driving in Winning Run
245	1946	2	StLC 3 BRS 0	H. Brecheen	3rd	1B	Driving in 1st Run of the Game
246	1946	3	BRS 4 StLC 0	R. York	1st	HR	Driving in the 1st 3 Runs
247	1946	4	StLC 12 BRS 3	S. Musial	3rd	2B	Driving in 2 Runs
248	1946	5	BRS 6 StLC 3	M. Higgins	7th	2B	Driving in 1 Run
249	1946	6	StLC 4 BRS 1	G. Kurowski	3rd	1B	Driving in 1 Run
250	1946	7	StLC 4 BRS 3	H. Walker	8th	2B	Driving in Runner Racing from 1st Base
251	1947	1	NYY 5 BR 3	T. Henrich	5th	1B	Driving in 2 Runs
252	1947	2	NYY 10 BR 3	T. Henrich	5th	HR	Driving in 1 Run
253	1947	3	BR 9 NYY 8	G. Hermanski	4th	1B	Driving in 1 Run
254	1947	4	BR 3 NYY 2	C. Lavagetto	9th	2B	Driving in 2 Runs with the Only Hit Bevens Allowed.
255	1947	5	NYY 2 BR 1	J. DiMaggio	5th	HR	Driving in 1 Run
256	1947	6	BR 8 NYY 6	P. Reese	6th	1B	Driving in 2 Runs
257	1947	7	NYY 5 BR 2	T. Henrich	4th	1B	Driving in 1 Run
258	1948	1	BB 1 CL 0	T. Holmes	8th	1B	Driving in the only Run
259	1948	2	CL 4 BB 1	L. Doby	4th	1B	Driving in 1 Run
260	1948	3	CL 2 BB 0	Error	3rd	ER	Shortstop's Error Allowed 1st Run to Score
261	1948	4	CL 2 BB 1	L. Doby	3rd	HR	Driving in 1 Run
262	1948	5	BB 11 CL 5	E. Torgeson	7th	1B	Driving in 1 Run
263	1948	6	CL 4 BB 3	E. Robinson	8th	1B	Driving in 1 Run
264	1949	1	NYY 1 BR 0	T. Henrich	9th	HR	Driving in Winning and Only Run
265	1949	2	BR 1 NYY 0	G. Hodges	2nd	1B	Driving in only Run
266	1949	3	NYY 4 BR 3	G. Coleman	9th	1B	Driving in 1 Run
267	1949	4	NYY 6 BR 4	B. Brown	5th	3B	Driving in 3 Runs
268	1949	5	NYY 10 BR 6	G. Coleman	5th	GO	Driving in 1 Run
269	1950	1	NYY 1 PhP 0	G. Coleman	4th	SF	Driving in Only Run
270	1950	2	NYY 2 PhP 1	J. DiMaggio	10th	HR	Driving in Winning Run
271	1950	3	NYY 3 PhP 2	G. Coleman	9th	1B	Driving in Winning Run
272	1950	4	NYY 5 PhP 2	Y. Berra	6th	HR	Driving in 1 Run

Overall W.S. Game	Year	Game	Score	Player	Inn	Type of Hit	Remarks
273	1951	1	NYG 5 NYY 1	M. Irvin	1st	SB	Stolen Base Scored 2nd Run of the Game
274	1951	2	NYY 3 NYG 1	J. Collins	2nd	HR	Driving in 1 Run
275	1951	3	NYG 6 NYY 2	Error	5th	ER	Run Scored on Catcher's Error
276	1951	4	NYY 6 NYG 2	J. DiMaggio	5th	HR	Driving in 2 Runs
277	1951	5	NYY 13 NYG 1	G. McDougald	3rd	GS HR	Hits Grand Slam Home Run
278	1951	6	NYY 4 NYG 3	H. Bauer	6th	3B	Tripled Driving in 3 Runs
279	1952	1	BR 4 NYY 2	D. Snider	6th	HR	Driving in 2 Runs
280	1952	2	NYY 7 BR 1	B. Martin	5th	1B	Driving in 1 Run
281	1952	3	BR 5 NYY 3	Passed Ball	9th	PB	2 Runs Scored on Passed Ball by Catcher
282	1952	4	NYY 2 BR 0	J. Mize	4th	HR	Driving in 1st Run of the Game
283	1952	5	BR 6 NYY 5	D. Snider	11th	2B	Driving in 1 Run
284	1952	6	NYY 3 BR 2	M. Mantle	8th	HR	Driving in 1 Run
285	1952	7	NYY 4 BR 2	M. Mantle	6th	HR	Driving in 1 Run
286	1953	1	NYY 9 BR 5	J. Collins	7th	HR	Driving in 1 Run
287	1953	2	NYY 4 BR 2	M. Mantle	8th	HR	Driving in 2 Runs
288	1953	3	BR 3 NYY 2	R. Campanella	8th	HR	Driving in 2 Runs
289	1953	4	BR 7 NYY 3	J. Gilliam	4th	2B	Driving in 1 Run
290	1953	5	NYY 11 BR 7	B. Martin	7th	HR	Driving in 2 Runs
291	1953	6	NYY 4 BR 3	B. Martin	9th	1B	Driving in Winning Run
292	1954	1	NYG 5 CL 2	J. Rhodes	10th	PH HR	Won Game With 3 Run Pitch Hit Home Run
293	1954	2	NYG 3 CL 1	J. Antonelli	5th	FC	Attempting a Double Play The Runner Scored from Third Base
294	1954	3	NYG 6 CL 2	J. Rhodes	4th	1B	Driving in 2 Runs
295	1954	4	NYG 7 CL 4	H. Thompson	5th	BB	Walked with the Bases Filled
296	1955	1	NYY 6 BR 5	J. Collins	6th	HR	Driving in 2 Runs
297	1955	2	NYY 4 BR 2	T. Byrne	4th	1B	Driving in 2 Runs
298	1955	3	BR 8 NYY 3	P. Reese	2nd	BB	Walked with Bases Filled

Overall W.S. Game	Year	Game	Score	Player	Inn	Type of Hit	Remarks
299	1955	4	BR 8 NYY 5	D. Snider	5th	HR	Driving in 3 Runs
300	1955	5	BR 5 NYY 3	D. Snider	5th	HR	Driving in 1 Run
301	1955	6	NYY 5 BR 1	H. Bauer	1st	1B	Driving in 1 Run
302	1955	7	BR 2 NYY 0	G. Hodges	4th	1B	Driving in 1st Run of the Game
303	1956	1	BR 6 NYY 3	G. Hodges	3rd	HR	Driving in 3 Runs
304	1956	2	BR 13 NYY 8	G. Hodges	4th	2B	Driving in 2 Runs
305	1956	3	NYY 5 BR 3	E. Slaughter	6th	HR	Driving in 3 Runs
306	1956	4	NYY 6 BR 2	G. McDougald	4th	SF	Driving in 1 Run
307	1956	5	NYY 2 BR 0	M. Mantle	4th	HR	Driving in the 1st Run of the Perfect Game by D. Larsen
308	1956	6	BR 1 NYY 0	J. Robinson	10th	1B	Driving in Only Run of the Game
309	1956	7	NYY 9 BR 0	Y. Berra	1st	HR	Driving in the 1st 2 Runs of the Game
310	1957	1	NYY 3 Mil 1	A. Carey	6th	1B	Driving in 1 Run
311	1957	2	Mil 4 NYY 2	W. Covington	4th	1B	Driving in 1 Run
312	1957	3	NYY 12 Mil 3	J. Lumpe	3rd	1B	Driving in 2 Runs
313	1957	4	Mil 7 NYY 5	E. Mathews	10th	HR	Driving in 2 Runs
314	1957	5	Mil 1 NYY 0	J. Adcock	6th	1B	Driving in only Run of the Game
315	1957	6	NYY 3 Mil 2	H. Bauer	7th	HR	Driving in 1 Run
316	1957	7	Mil 5 NYY 0	E. Mathews	3rd	2B	Driving in 2 Runs
317	1958	1	Mil 4 NYY 3	B. Bruton	10th	1B	Driving in the Winning Run
318	1958	2	Mil 13 NYY 5	L. Burdette	1st	HR	Driving in 3 Runs
319	1958	3	NYY 4 Mil 0	H. Bauer	5th	1B	Driving in 2 Runs
320	1958	4	Mil 3 NYY 0	Error	6th	ER	Runner Scored from Third Base due to Shortstop's Error
321	1958	5	NYY 7 Mil 0	G. McDougald	3rd	HR	Driving in the 1st Run of the Game
322	1958	6	NYY 4 Mil 3	B. Skowron	10th	1B	Driving in 1 Run
323	1958	7	NYY 6 Mil 2	E. Howard	8th	1B	Driving in 1 Run

Overall W.S. Game	Year	Game	Score	Player	Inn	Type of Hit	Remarks
324	1959	1	ChW 11 LAD 0	T. Kluszewski	1st	1B	Driving in 1st Run of the Game
325	1959	2	LAD 4 ChW 3	C. Neal	7th	HR	Driving in 2 Runs
326	1959	3	LAD 3 ChW 1	C. Furilio	7th	1B	Driving in 2 Runs
327	1959	4	LAD 5 ChW 4	G. Hodges	8th	HR	Driving in 1 Run
328	1959	5	ChW 1 LAD 0	Double Play	4th	DP	Run Scored as Batter Hit into Double Play
329	1959	6	LAD 9 ChW 3	J. Podres	4th	2B	Driving in 1 Run
330	1960	1	PP 6 NYY 4	B. Mazerowski	4th	HR	Driving in 2 Runs
331	1960	2	NYY 16 PP 3	M. Mantle	5th	HR	Driving in 2 Runs
332	1960	3	NYY 10 PP 0	B. Skowron	4th	1B	Driving in 1st Run of the Game
333	1960	4	PP 3 NYY 2	B. Virdon	5th	1B	Driving in 2 Runs
334	1960	5	PP 5 NYY 2	B. Mazerowski	2nd	1B	Driving in 2 Runs
335	1960	6	NYY 12 PP 0	W. Ford	2nd	1B	Driving in 1 Run
336	1960	7	PP 10 NYY 9	B. Mazerowski	9th	HR	Driving in Winning Run
337	1961	1	NYY 2 Cin 0	E. Howard	4th	HR	Driving in 1st Run
338	1961	2	Cin 6 NYY 2	Passed Ball	5th	PB	Run Scored on Passed Ball
339	1961	3	NYY 3 Cin 2	R. Maris	9th	HR	Driving in Winning Run
340	1961	4	NYY 7 Cin 0	Double Play	4th	DP	1st Run Scored on Double Play
341	1961	5	NYY 13 Cin 5	R. Maris	2nd	2B	Driving in 1 Run
342	1962	1	NYY 6 SF 2	C. Boyer	7th	HR	Driving in 1 Run
343	1962	2	SF 2 NYY 0	M. Alou	2nd	GO	Grounded out driving in 1 Run
344	1962	3	NYY 3 SF 2	C. Boyer	7th	FC	Driving in 1 Run Due to a Forced Play at one of the bases
345	1962	4	SF 7 NYY 3	C. Hiller	7th	GS HR	Hit Grand Slam Home Run Driving in 4 Runs
346	1962	5	NYY 5 SF 3	T. Tresh	8th	HR	Driving in 3 Runs
347	1962	6	SF 5 NYY 2	J. Davenport	4th	1B	Driving in 1 Run
348	1962	7	NYY 1 SF 0	Double Play	5th	DP	Only Run Scored on A Double Play

Overall W.S. Game	Year	Game	Score	Player	Inn	Type of Hit	Remarks
349	1963	1	LAD 5 NYY 2	J. Roseboro	2nd	HR	Driving in 3 Runs
350	1963	2	LAD 4 NYY 1	W. Davis	1st	2B	Driving in 2 Runs
351	1963	3	LAD 1 NYY 0	T. Davis	1st	1B	Driving in 1 Run
352	1963	4	LAD 2 NYY 1	W. Davis	7th	SF	Driving in 1 Run
353	1964	1	StLC 9 NYY 5	C. Flood	6th	3B	Driving in 1 Run
354	1964	2	NYY 8 StLC 3	M. Mantle	7th	GO	Driving in 1 Run
355	1964	3	NYY 2 StLC 1	M. Mantle	9th	HR	Driving in Winning Run
356	1964	4	StLC 4 NYY 3	K. Boyer	6th	GS	Grand Slam Home Run Driving in 4 Runs
357	1964	5	StLC 5 NYY 2	T. McCarver	10th	HR	Driving in 3 Runs
358	1964	6	NYY 8 StLC 3	E. Howard	8th	1B	Driving in 1 Run
359	1964	7	StLC 7 NYY 5	T. McCarver	7th	SF	Driving in 1 Run
360	1965	1	Minn 8 LAD 2	Z. Versalles	3rd	HR	Driving in 3 Runs
361	1965	2	Minn 5 LAD 1	H. Killebrew	6th	1B	Driving in 1 Run
362	1965	3	LAD 4 Minn 0	J. Roseboro	4th	1B	Driving in 1st 2 Runs
363	1965	4	LAD 7 Minn 2	W. Parker	4th	HR	Driving in 1 Run
364	1965	5	LAD 7 Minn 0	J. Gilliam	1st	1B	Driving in 1st Run of the Game
365	1965	6	Minn 5 LAD 1	B. Allison	4th	HR	Driving in 2 Runs
366	1965	7	LAD 2 Minn 0	L. Johnson	4th	HR	Driving in 1st Run of the Game
367	**1966**	1	Balt 5 LAD 2	B. Robinson	1st	**HR**	Driving in 1 Run
368	1966	2	Balt 6 LAD 0	Error	5th	ER	1st and 2nd Runs Scored on Center-fielder's 2nd Error of Inning
369	1966	3	Balt 1 LAD 0	P. Blair	5th	HR	Driving in Only Run of the Game With a 430 ft. HR
370	1966	4	Balt 1 LAD 0	F. Robinson	4th	HR	Driving in Only Run of the Game With a 410 ft. HR
371	1967	1	StLC 2 BRS 1	R. Maris	7th	GO	Driving in 1 Run
372	1967	2	BRS 5 StLC 0	C. Yastrzemski	4th	HR	Driving in 1st Run of Shutout
373	1967	3	StLC 5 BRS 2	M. Shannon	2nd	HR	Driving in 2 Runs
374	1967	4	StLC 6 BRS 0	R. Maris	1st	2B	Driving in 2 Runs

Overall W.S. Game	Year	Game	Score	Player	Inn	Type of Hit	Remarks
375	1967	5	BRS 3 StLC 1	E. Howard	9th	1B	Driving in 1 Run
376	1967	6	BRS 8 StLC 4	J. Foy	7th	2B	Driving in 1 Run
377	1967	7	StLC 7 BRS 2	B. Gibson	5th	HR	Driving in 1 Run
378	1968	1	StLC 4 D 0	M. Shannon	4th	1B	Driving in 1st Run of Game
379	1968	2	D 8 StLC 1	M. Lolich	3rd	HR	Driving in 1 Run
380	1968	3	StLC 7 D 3	T. McCarver	5th	HR	Driving in 3 Runs
381	1968	4	StLC 10 D 1	M. Shannon	1st	1B	Driving in 1 Run
382	1968	5	D 5 StLC 3	A. Kaline	7th	1B	Driving in 2 Runs
383	1968	6	D 13 StLC 1	B. Freehan	2nd	1B	Driving in 1 Run
384	1968	7	D 4 StLC 1	J. Northrup	7th	3B	Driving in 2 Runs
385	1969	1	Balt 4 NYM 1	M. Belanger	4th	1B	Driving in 1 Run
386	1969	2	NYM 2 Balt 1	A. Weis	9th	1B	Driving in Winning Run
387	1969	3	NYM 5 Balt 0	T. Agee	1st	HR	Driving in 1st Run of Shutout
388	1969	4	NYM 2 Balt 1	Error	10th	ER	Pitcher hits Batter as Runner Scores From Third Base
389	1969	5	NYM 5 Balt 3	R. Swoboda	8th	2B	Driving in 1 Run
390	1970	1	Balt 4 Cin 3	B. Robinson	7th	HR	Driving in Winning Run
391	1970	2	Balt 6 Cin 5	E. Hendricks	5th	2B	Driving in 2 Runs
392	1970	3	Balt 9 Cin 3	D. Buford	5th	HR	Driving in 1 Run
393	1970	4	Cin 6 Balt 5	L. May	8th	HR	Driving in 3 Runs
394	1970	5	Balt 9 Cinn 3	P. Blair	2nd	1B	Driving in 1 Run
395	1971	1	Balt 5 PP 3	M. Rettenmund	3rd	HR	Driving in 3 Runs
396	1971	2	Balt 11 PP 3	J. Palmer	4th	BB	Driving in 1 Run
397	1971	3	PP 5 Balt 1	J. Pagan	6th	1B	Driving in 1 Run
398	1971	4	PP 4 Balt 3	M. May	7th	1B	Driving in 1 Run
399	1971	5	PP 4 Balt 0	B. Robertson	2nd	HR	Driving in 1st Run
400	1971	6	Balt 3 PP 2	B. Robinson	10th	SF	Driving in 1 Run
401	1971	7	PP 2 Balt 1	J. Pagan	8th	2B	Driving in 1 Run
402	1972	1	Oak 3 Cin 2	G. Tenace	5th	HR	Driving in 1 Run
403	1972	2	Oak 2 Cin 1	J. Rudi	3rd	HR	Driving in 1 Run
404	1972	3	Cin 1 Oak 0	C. Geronimo	7th	1B	Driving in only Run
405	1972	4	Oak 3 Cin 2	A. Mangual	9th	1B	Driving in Winning Run

Overall W.S. Game	Year	Game	Score	Player	Inn	Type of Hit	Remarks
406	1972	5	Cin 5 Oak 4	P. Rose	9th	1B	Driving in Winning Run
407	1972	6	Cin 8 Oak 1	D. Concepcion	5th	SF	Driving in 1 Run
408	1972	7	Oak 3 Cin 2	S. Bando	6th	2B	Driving in 1 Run
409	1973	1	Oak 2 NYM 1	J. Rudi	3rd	1B	Driving in 1 Run
410	1973	2	NYM10 Oak 7	Error	12th	ER	Error by 2nd Baseman Allows 3 Runs to Score
411	1973	3	Oak 3 NYM 2	B. Campaneris	11th	1B	Driving in 1 Run
412	1973	4	NYM 6 Oak 1	R. Staub	1st	HR	Driving in 1st 3 Runs of Game
413	1973	5	NYM 2 Oak 0	J. Milner	2nd	1B	Driving in 1st Run of Shutout
414	1973	6	Oak 3 NYM 1	R. Jackson	3rd	2B	Driving in 1 Run
415	1973	7	Oak 5 NYM 2	R. Jackson	3rd	HR	Driving in 2 Runs

World Series Players Driving in Winning or Decisive Runs: Times and Various Types of Hits

	1B	2B	3B	HR	BB	SF	GO	FC	SH	SB	Totals
M. Mantle	0	0	0	6	0	0	1	0	0	0	7
J. DiMaggio	2	0	0	4	0	0	0	0	0	0	6
L. Gehrig	1	0	1	2	0	1	0	0	0	0	5
T. Henrich	2	0	0	3	0	0	0	0	0	0	5
G. Hodges	2	1	0	2	0	0	0	0	0	0	5
T. Lazzeri	1	1	0	0	0	3	0	0	0	0	5
R. Meusel	1	1	2	1	0	0	0	0	0	0	5
H. Bauer	2	0	1	1	0	0	0	0	0	0	4
G. Coleman	2	0	0	0	0	1	1	0	0	0	4
F. Crosetti	1	0	0	1	0	1	1	0	0	0	4
B. Dickey	2	0	1	1	0	0	0	0	0	0	4
J. Gordon	4	0	0	0	0	0	0	0	0	0	4
G. Goslin	3	0	0	1	0	0	0	0	0	0	4
H. Greenberg	0	1	0	3	0	0	0	0	0	0	4
E. Howard	3	0	0	1	0	0	0	0	0	0	4
R. Maris	0	2	0	1	0	0	1	0	0	0	4
D. Snider	0	1	0	3	0	0	0	0	0	0	4
J. F. Baker	0	0	0	2	0	0	0	1	0	0	3
Joe Collins	0	0	0	3	0	0	0	0	0	0	3
K. Cuyler	1	1	0	1	0	0	0	0	0	0	3
J. Foxx	1	1	0	1	0	0	0	0	0	0	3

	1B	2B	3B	HR	BB	SF	GO	FC	SH	SB	Totals
C. Gandil	3	0	0	0	0	0	0	0	0	0	3
L. Gardner	0	0	0	1	0	2	0	0	0	0	3
G. Kelly	2	0	0	0	0	1	0	0	0	0	3
B. Martin	2	0	0	1	0	0	0	0	0	0	3
B. Mazeroski	0	1	0	2	0	0	0	0	0	0	3
T. McCarver	0	0	0	2	0	1	0	0	0	0	3
G. McDougald	0	0	0	2	0	1	0	0	0	0	3
B. Miller	2	1	0	0	0	0	0	0	0	0	3
S. Musial	1	1	0	1	0	0	0	0	0	0	3
B. Robinson	0	0	0	2	0	1	0	0	0	0	3
M. Shannon	2	0	0	1	0	0	0	0	0	0	3
D. Bartell	2	0	0	0	0	0	0	0	0	0	2
P. Blair	1	0	0	1	0	0	0	0	0	0	2
Y. Berra	0	0	0	2	0	0	0	0	0	0	2
C. Boyer	0	0	0	1	0	0	0	1	0	0	2
F. Clarke	0	0	0	1	0	1	0	0	0	0	2
H. Davis	2	0	0	0	0	0	0	0	0	0	2
W. Davis	0	1	0	0	0	1	0	0	0	0	2
L. Doby	1	0	0	1	0	0	0	0	0	0	2
P. Dean	1	0	0	0	0	1	0	0	0	0	2
J. Dykes	0	2	0	0	0	0	0	0	0	0	2
J. Evers	2	0	0	0	0	0	0	0	0	0	2
A. Fletcher	1	1	0	0	0	0	0	0	0	0	2
F. Frisch	0	1	0	0	0	1	0	0	0	0	2
J. Gilliam	1	1	0	0	0	0	0	0	0	0	2
M. Haas	0	0	0	0	1	0	0	1	0	0	2
M. Higgins	0	1	0	1	0	0	0	0	0	0	2
R. Jackson	0	1	0	1	0	0	0	0	0	0	2
C. Keller	1	1	0	0	0	0	0	0	0	0	2
G. Kurowski	1	0	0	1	0	0	0	0	0	0	2
D. Lewis	1	1	0	0	0	0	0	0	0	0	2
B. Lord	1	1	0	0	0	0	0	0	0	0	2
L. Mann	1	1	0	0	0	0	0	0	0	0	2
P. Martin	0	1	0	1	0	0	0	0	0	0	2
E. Mathews	0	1	0	1	0	0	0	0	0	0	2
M. Ott	1	0	0	1	0	0	0	0	0	0	2
J. Pagan	1	1	0	0	0	0	0	0	0	0	2
P. Reese	1	0	0	0	1	0	0	0	0	0	2
D. Rhodes	1	0	0	1	0	0	0	0	0	0	2
J. Ripple	0	1	0	1	0	0	0	0	0	0	2
J. Roseboro	1	0	0	1	0	0	0	0	0	0	2
R. Sanders	0	0	0	2	0	0	0	0	0	0	2
E. Scott	2	0	0	0	0	0	0	0	0	0	2
J. Sebring	1	0	0	0	0	0	0	1	0	0	2
B. Skowron	2	0	0	0	0	0	0	0	0	0	2
J. Slagle	2	0	0	0	0	0	0	0	0	0	2
H. Steinfeldt	1	0	1	0	0	0	0	0	0	0	2
C. Stengel	0	0	0	2	0	0	0	0	0	0	2
R. York	0	0	0	2	0	0	0	0	0	0	2
R. Youngs	1	0	0	0	0	1	0	0	0	0	2
J. Rudi	1	0	0	1	0	0	0	0	0	0	2

	1B	2B	3B	HR	BB	SF	GO	FC	SH	SB	Totals
J. Adcock	1	0	0	0	0	0	0	0	0	0	1
T. Agee	0	0	0	1	0	0	0	0	0	0	1
B. Allison	0	0	0	1	0	0	0	0	0	0	1
M. Alou	0	0	0	0	0	0	1	0	0	0	1
J. Antonelli	0	0	0	0	0	0	0	1	0	0	1
S. Bando	0	1	0	0	0	0	0	0	0	0	1
C. Barnhart	1	0	0	0	0	0	0	0	0	0	1
M. Belanger	1	0	0	0	0	0	0	0	0	0	1
L. Bell	1	0	0	0	0	0	0	0	0	0	1
C. Bender	1	0	0	0	0	0	0	0	0	0	1
J. Bentley	0	0	0	1	0	0	0	0	0	0	1
K. Boyer	0	0	0	1	0	0	0	0	0	0	1
H. Brecheen	1	0	0	0	0	0	0	0	0	0	1
B. Brown	0	0	1	0	0	0	0	0	0	0	1
J. Brown	0	0	0	0	0	0	1	0	0	0	1
B. Bruton	1	0	0	0	0	0	0	0	0	0	1
D. Buford	0	0	0	1	0	0	0	0	0	0	1
L. Burdette	0	0	0	1	0	0	0	0	0	0	1
G. H. Burns	0	1	0	0	0	0	0	0	0	0	1
G. J. Burns	0	1	0	0	0	0	0	0	0	0	1
T. Byrne	1	0	0	0	0	0	0	0	0	0	1
F. Cady	1	0	0	0	0	0	0	0	0	0	1
D. Camilli	1	0	0	0	0	0	0	0	0	0	1
B. Campaneris	1	0	0	0	0	0	0	0	0	0	1
R. Campanella	0	0	0	1	0	0	0	0	0	0	1
A. Carey	1	0	0	0	0	0	0	0	0	0	1
F. Chance	1	0	0	0	0	0	0	0	0	0	1
B. Chapman	1	0	0	0	0	0	0	0	0	0	1
M. Christman	1	0	0	0	0	0	0	0	0	0	1
T. Cobb	0	1	0	0	0	0	0	0	0	0	1
E. Collins	1	0	0	0	0	0	0	0	0	0	1
E. Combs	1	0	0	0	0	0	0	0	0	0	1
D. Concepcion	0	0	0	0	0	1	0	0	0	0	1
W. Cooper	1	0	0	0	0	0	0	0	0	0	1
W. Covington	1	0	0	0	0	0	0	0	0	0	1
C. Cravath	0	0	0	0	0	0	1	0	0	0	1
J. Cronin	0	0	0	0	0	0	1	0	0	0	1
R. Cullenbine	0	1	0	0	0	0	0	0	0	0	1
J. Davenport	1	0	0	0	0	0	0	0	0	0	1
G. Davis	1	0	0	0	0	0	0	0	0	0	1
T. Davis	1	0	0	0	0	0	0	0	0	0	1
J. Delahanty	1	0	0	0	0	0	0	0	0	0	1
J. Devore	0	1	0	0	0	0	0	0	0	0	1
J. Donahue	0	1	0	0	0	0	0	0	0	0	1
P. Dougherty	0	0	0	1	0	0	0	0	0	0	1
T. Douthit	0	0	0	1	0	0	0	0	0	0	1
C. Durst	1	0	0	0	0	0	0	0	0	0	1
O. Felsch	0	0	0	1	0	0	0	0	0	0	1
H. Ferris	1	0	0	0	0	0	0	0	0	0	1
C. Flood	0	0	1	0	0	0	0	0	0	0	1
W. Ford	1	0	0	0	0	0	0	0	0	0	1

	1B	2B	3B	HR	BB	SF	GO	FC	SH	SB	Totals
G. Foster	1	0	0	0	0	0	0	0	0	0	1
J. Foy	0	1	0	0	0	0	0	0	0	0	1
B. Freehan	1	0	0	0	0	0	0	0	0	0	1
B. Freeman	0	0	0	0	0	1	0	0	0	0	1
C. Furillo	1	0	0	0	0	0	0	0	0	0	1
D. Gainor	1	0	0	0	0	0	0	0	0	0	1
C. Gehringer	0	0	0	1	0	0	0	0	0	0	1
C. Geromino	1	0	0	0	0	0	0	0	0	0	1
B. Gibson	0	0	0	1	0	0	0	0	0	0	1
G. Gibson	0	1	0	0	0	0	0	0	0	0	1
W. Gilbert	1	0	0	0	0	0	0	0	0	0	1
L. Gomez	1	0	0	0	0	0	0	0	0	0	1
I. Goodman	1	0	0	0	0	0	0	0	0	0	1
S. Hack	0	1	0	0	0	0	0	0	0	0	1
J. Harris	1	0	0	0	0	0	0	0	0	0	1
S. Harris	0	1	0	0	0	0	0	0	0	0	1
E. Hendricks	0	1	0	0	0	0	0	0	0	0	1
G. Hermanski	1	0	0	0	0	0	0	0	0	0	1
B. Herzog	0	1	0	0	0	0	0	0	0	0	1
C. Hiller	0	0	0	1	0	0	0	0	0	0	1
S. Hofman	1	0	0	0	0	0	0	0	0	0	1
W. Holke	0	1	0	0	0	0	0	0	0	0	1
T. Holmes	1	0	0	0	0	0	0	0	0	0	1
H. Hooper	0	0	0	1	0	0	0	0	0	0	1
W. Hoyt	0	0	0	0	0	0	1	0	0	0	1
R. Hyatt	0	0	0	0	0	1	0	0	0	0	1
M. Irvin	0	0	0	0	0	0	0	0	0	1	1
F. Isbell	0	1	0	0	0	0	0	0	0	0	1
J. Jackson	1	0	0	0	0	0	0	0	0	0	1
B. Johnson	0	0	1	0	0	0	0	0	0	0	1
L. Johnson	0	0	0	1	0	0	0	0	0	0	1
A. Kaline	1	0	0	0	0	0	0	0	0	0	1
B. Kauff	0	0	0	1	0	0	0	0	0	0	1
H. Killebrew	1	0	0	0	0	0	0	0	0	0	1
C. Klein	0	0	0	1	0	0	0	0	0	0	1
T. Kluszewski	1	0	0	0	0	0	0	0	0	0	1
W. Kopf	0	0	1	0	0	0	0	0	0	0	1
H. Lavagetto	0	1	0	0	0	0	0	0	0	0	1
H. Leibold	1	0	0	0	0	0	0	0	0	0	1
F. Lindstrom	0	1	0	0	0	0	0	0	0	0	1
M. Lolich	0	0	0	1	0	0	0	0	0	0	1
J. Lumpe	1	0	0	0	0	0	0	0	0	0	1
G. Mancuso	1	0	0	0	0	0	0	0	0	0	1
A. Mangual	1	0	0	0	0	0	0	0	0	0	1
R. Maranville	1	0	0	0	0	0	0	0	0	0	1
C. Mathewson	1	0	0	0	0	0	0	0	0	0	1
L. May	0	0	0	1	0	0	0	0	0	0	1
M. May	1	0	0	0	0	0	0	0	0	0	1
D. McGann	1	0	0	0	0	0	0	0	0	0	1
S. McInnis	1	0	0	0	0	0	0	0	0	0	1

	1B	2B	3B	HR	BB	SF	GO	FC	SH	SB	Totals
E. McNeeley	1	0	0	0	0	0	0	0	0	0	1
G. McQuinn	0	0	0	1	0	0	0	0	0	0	1
J. Medwick	0	0	0	1	0	0	0	0	0	0	1
F. Merkle	0	0	0	0	0	1	0	0	0	0	1
E. Meusel	0	1	0	0	0	0	0	0	0	0	1
J. Milner	1	0	0	0	0	0	0	0	0	0	1
J. Mize	0	0	0	1	0	0	0	0	0	0	1
Grant Moore	0	0	0	1	0	0	0	0	0	0	1
D. Murphy	0	0	0	1	0	0	0	0	0	0	1
B. Myers	0	0	0	0	0	1	0	0	0	0	1
H. Myers	1	0	0	0	0	0	0	0	0	0	1
C. Neal	0	0	0	1	0	0	0	0	0	0	1
G. Neale	1	0	0	0	0	0	0	0	0	0	1
B. Nicholson	1	0	0	0	0	0	0	0	0	0	1
J. Northrup	0	0	1	0	0	0	0	0	0	0	1
K. O'Dea	1	0	0	0	0	0	0	0	0	0	1
F. O'Doul	1	0	0	0	0	0	0	0	0	0	1
I. Olson	0	0	1	0	0	0	0	0	0	0	1
S. O'Neill	0	1	0	0	0	0	0	0	0	0	1
J. Palmer	0	0	0	0	1	0	0	0	0	0	1
F. Parent	1	0	0	0	0	0	0	0	0	0	1
W. Parker	0	0	0	1	0	0	0	0	0	0	1
R. Peckinpaugh	1	0	0	0	0	0	0	0	0	0	1
J. Podres	0	1	0	0	0	0	0	0	0	0	1
M. Rath	1	0	0	0	0	0	0	0	0	0	1
M. Rettenmund	0	0	0	1	0	0	0	0	0	0	1
E. Reulbach	0	0	0	0	0	0	0	0	1	0	1
S. Rice	1	0	0	0	0	0	0	0	0	0	1
P. Richards	0	1	0	0	0	0	0	0	0	0	1
B. Robertson	0	0	0	1	0	0	0	0	0	0	1
E. Robinson	1	0	0	0	0	0	0	0	0	0	1
F. Robinson	0	0	0	1	0	0	0	0	0	0	1
J. Robinson	1	0	0	0	0	0	0	0	0	0	1
G. Rohe	0	0	1	0	0	0	0	0	0	0	1
P. Rose	1	0	0	0	0	0	0	0	0	0	1
C. Rossman	1	0	0	0	0	0	0	0	0	0	1
C. Ruffing	1	0	0	0	0	0	0	0	0	0	1
B. Ruth	1	0	0	0	0	0	0	0	0	0	1
B. Ryan	1	0	0	0	0	0	0	0	0	0	1
W. Schang	1	0	0	0	0	0	0	0	0	0	1
F. Schulte	1	0	0	0	0	0	0	0	0	0	1
J. Sewell	1	0	0	0	0	0	0	0	0	0	1
J. Sheckard	1	0	0	0	0	0	0	0	0	0	1
A. Simmons	0	1	0	0	0	0	0	0	0	0	1
E. Slaughter	0	0	0	1	0	0	0	0	0	0	1
E. Smith	0	0	0	1	0	0	0	0	0	0	1
F. Snyder	0	1	0	0	0	0	0	0	0	0	1
B. Southworth	0	0	0	1	0	0	0	0	0	0	1
T. Speaker	1	0	0	0	0	0	0	0	0	0	1
O. Stanage	1	0	0	0	0	0	0	0	0	0	1

	1B	2B	3B	HR	BB	SF	GO	FC	SH	SB	Totals
R. Staub	0	0	0	1	0	0	0	0	0	0	1
R. Swoboda	0	1	0	0	0	0	0	0	0	0	1
G. Tenace	0	0	0	1	0	0	0	0	0	0	1
B. Terry	0	0	0	0	0	1	0	0	0	0	1
T. Thevenow	1	0	0	0	0	0	0	0	0	0	1
I. Thomas	0	0	0	0	0	1	0	0	0	0	1
H. Thompson	0	0	0	0	1	0	0	0	0	0	1
J. Tinker	0	0	0	1	0	0	0	0	0	0	1
E. Torgeson	1	0	0	0	0	0	0	0	0	0	1
T. Tresh	0	0	0	1	0	0	0	0	0	0	1
G. Tyler	1	0	0	0	0	0	0	0	0	0	1
E. Verban	1	0	0	0	0	0	0	0	0	0	1
Z. Versalles	0	0	0	1	0	0	0	0	0	0	1
B. Virdon	1	0	0	0	0	0	0	0	0	0	1
H. Wagner	1	0	0	0	0	0	0	0	0	0	1
H. Walker	0	1	0	0	0	0	0	0	0	0	1
G. Watkins	0	0	0	1	0	0	0	0	0	0	1
J. Webb	0	0	0	0	0	0	0	1	0	0	1
A. Weis	1	0	0	0	0	0	0	0	0	0	1
Z. Wheat	0	1	0	0	0	0	0	0	0	0	1
J. White	1	0	0	0	0	0	0	0	0	0	1
J. Wilson	0	0	0	0	0	1	0	0	0	0	1
I. Wingo	1	0	0	0	0	0	0	0	0	0	1
C. Yastrzemski	0	0	0	1	0	0	0	0	0	0	1
S. Yerkes	1	0	0	0	0	0	0	0	0	0	1

3
Types of Hits Involving Decisive or Winning Runs, and Inning in Which Accomplished

Type of Hit		Decisive Inning	
Singles	156	4th	65
Doubles	54	5th	51
Triples	13	6th	46
Home Runs	110	3rd	43
Bases on Balls	4	7th	41
Sacrifice Flies	25	1st	41
Groundouts	9	8th	33
Fielder's Choice	6	2nd	31
Sacrifice Hits	1	9th	29
Stolen Bases	1	10th	19
		11th	6
TOTAL	379	12th	6
		14th	1
Errors	25	13th	0
Tied Games	3	Tied Games	3
Double Plays	3		
Passed Balls	3	GRAND TOTAL	415
Wild Pitches	2		
GRAND TOTAL	415		

4
Decisive Hits in Extra-Inning Games

No.	Year	Game	Player	Inn	Type of Hit
1	1910	4	J. Sheckard	10th	SF
2	1911	3	H. Davis	11th	1B
3	1911	5	F. Merkle	10th	SF
4	1912	8	L. Gardner	10th	SF
5	1913	2	C. Mathewson	10th	1B
6	1914	3	Error	12th	ER
7	1916	2	D. Gainor	14th	1B
8	1919	6	C. Gandil	10th	1B
9	1924	1	G. Kelly	12th	SF
10	1924	7	E. McNeeley	12th	1B
11	1926	5	T. Lazzeri	10th	SF
12	1933	4	B. Ryan	11th	1B
13	1933	5	M. Ott	10th	HR
14	1934	2	G. Goslin	12th	1B
15	1935	3	J. White	11th	1B
16	1936	5	B. Terry	10th	SF
17	1939	4	**J. DiMaggio**	10th	1B

No.	Year	Game	Player	Inn	Type of Hit
18	1944	2	K. Odea	11th	1B
19	1945	6	S. Hack	12th	2B
20	1946	1	R. York	10th	HR
21	1950	2	J. DiMaggio	10th	HR
22	1952	5	D. Snider	11th	2B
23	1954	1	J. Rhodes	10th	HR
24	1956	6	J. Robinson	10th	1B
25	1957	4	E. Mathews	10th	HR
26	1958	1	B. Bruton	10th	1B
27	1958	6	B. Skowron	10th	1B
28	1964	5	T. McCarver	10th	HR
29	1969	4	Error	10th	ER
30	1971	6	B. Robinson	10th	SF
31	1973	2	Error	12th	ER
32	1973	3	B. Campaneris	11th	1B

BY GAME		TYPE OF HIT	
4	1	1B	14
6	2	2B	2
4	3	3B	0
5	4	HR	6
6	5	SF	7
5	6	ER	3
1	7		
1	8	TOTAL	32

TOTAL 32

BY INNING

19	10th
6	11th
6	12th
0	13th
1	14th

TOTAL 32

5
Players Getting Winning or Decisive Runs in Last Game of World Series

Year	Player	Game	Club	Type of Hit
1903	H. Ferris	8	BRS	1B
1905	B. Gilbert	5	NYG	1B
1906	G. S. Davis	6	ChW	1B
1907	H. Steinfeldt	5	ChC	3B
1908	F. Chance	5	ChC	1B
1909	R. Hyatt	7	PP	SF
1910	B. Lord	5	PhA	2B
1911	Error	6	PhA	Error
1912	L. Gardner	8	BRS	SF
1913	J. F. Baker	5	PhA	FC
1914	J. Evers	4	BB	1B
1915	H. Hooper	5	BRS	HR
1916	Error	6	BRS	Error
1917	C. Gandil	6	ChW	1B
1918	Error	6	BRS	Error
1919	G. Neale	8	Cin	1B
1920	Error	7	CL	Error
1921	Error	8	NYG	Error
1922	G. Kelly	5	NYG	1B
1923	B. Meusel	6	NYY	1B
1924	E. McNeeley	7	W	1B

Year	Player	Game	Club	Type of Hit
1925	K. Cuyler	7	PP	2B
1926	T. Thevenow	7	StLC	1B
1927	Wild Pitch	4	NYY	Wild Pitch
1928	T. Lazzeri	4	NYY	2B
1929	Bing Miller	5	PhA	1B
1930	Bing Miller	6	PhA	2B
1931	G. Watkins	7	StLC	HR
1932	J. Sewell	4	NYY	1B
1933	M. Ott	5	NYG	HR
1934	F. Frisch	7	StLC	2B
1935	G. Goslin	6	D	1B
1936	T. Lazzeri	6	NYY	1B
1937	L. Gomez	5	NYY	1B
1938	T. Henrich	4	NYY	HR
1939	J. DiMaggio	4	NYY	1B
1940	B. Myers	7	Cin	SF
1941	J. Gordon	5	NYY	1B
1942	G. Kurowski	5	StLC	HR
1943	B. Dickey	5	NYY	HR
1944	E. Verban	6	StLC	1B
1945	P. Richards	7	D	2B
1946	H. Walker	7	StLC	2B
1947	T. Henrich	7	NYY	1B
1948	E. Robinson	6	CL	1B
1949	G. Coleman	5	NYY	GO
1950	Y. Berra	4	NYY	HR
1951	H. Bauer	6	NYY	3B
1952	M. Mantle	7	NYY	HR
1953	B. Martin	6	NYY	1B
1954	H. Thompson	4	NYG	BB
1955	G. Hodges	7	BR	1B
1956	Y. Berra	7	NYY	HR
1957	E. Mathews	7	Mil	2B
1958	E. Howard	7	NYY	1B
1959	J. Podres	6	LAD	2B
1960	B. Mazeroski	7	PP	HR
1961	R. Maris	5	NYY	2B
1962	DP	7	NYY	DP
1963	W. Davis	4	LAD	SF
1964	T. McCarver	7	StLC	SF
1965	L. Johnson	7	LAD	HR
1966	F. Robinson	4	Balt	HR
1967	B. Gibson	7	StLC	HR
1968	J. Northup	7	D	3B
1969	R. Swoboda	5	NYM	2B
1970	P. Blair	5	Balt	1B
1971	J. Pagan	7	PP	2B
1972	S. Bando	7	Oak	2B
1973	R. Jackson	7	Oak	HR

Number of Times for Players Driving in Winning or Decisive Runs in Last Game of Each World Series

Y. Berra	2	G. Kurowski	1
T. Henrich	2	B. Lord	1
T. Lazzeri	2	M. Mantle	1
Bing Miller	2	R. Maris	1
J. F. Baker	1	B. Martin	1
S. Bando	1	E. Mathews	1
H. Bauer	1	B. Mazeroski	1
P. Blair	1	T. McCarver	1
C. Gandil	1	E. McNeeley	1
F. Chance	1	B. Meusel	1
G. Coleman	1	B. Myers	1
K. Cuyler	1	G. Neale	1
G. S. Davis	1	J. Northup	1
W. Davis	1	M. Ott	1
B. Dickey	1	J. Pagan	1
J. DiMaggio	1	J. Podres	1
J. Evers	1	P. Richards	1
H. Ferriss	1	E. Robinson	1
F. Frisch	1	F. Robinson	1
L. Gardner	1	J. Sewell	1
B. Gibson	1	H. Steinfeldt	1
B. Gilbert	1	R. Swoboda	1
L. Gomez	1	T. Thevenow	1
J. Gordon	1	H. Thompson	1
G. Goslin	1	E. Verban	1
G. Hodges	1	H. Walker	1
H. Hooper	1	G. Watkins	1
E. Howard	1	Errors	5
R. Hyatt	1	Wild Pitch	1
R. Jackson	1	Double Play	1
L. Johnson	1		
G. Kelly	1	TOTAL	70

Type of Hit	No. of Times
1B	25
HR	14
2B	13
SF	5
Errors	5
3B	3
BB	1
FC	1
GO	1
DP	1
WP	1
TOTAL	70

6

Players Driving in Winning or Decisive Runs for Three or More Games, by Series

Player	Total	Series	Games	Series	Games	Series	Games	Series	Games	Series	Games
M. Mantle	7	1952	2	1953	1	1956	1	1960	1	1964	2
J. DiMaggio	6	1937	1	1939	2	1947	1	1950	1	1951	1
L. Gehrig	5	1926	1	1927	2	1932	1	1936	1		
T. Henrich	5	1938	1	1947	3	1949	1				
G. Hodges	5	1949	1	1955	1	1956	2	1959	1		
T. Lazzeri	5	1926	2	1927	1	1928	1	1936	1		
R. Meusel	5	1921	1	1923	3	1928	1				
H. Bauer	4	1951	1	1955	1	1957	1	1958	1		
G. Coleman	4	1949	2	1950	2						
F. Crosetti	4	1936	1	1938	1	1939	1	1943	1		
B. Dickey	4	1936	1	1937	1	1939	1	1943	1		
J. Gordon	4	1938	2	1941	2						
G. Goslin	4	1924	1	1925	1	1934	1	1935	1		
H. Greenberg	4	1934	1	1935	1	1940	1	1945	1		
E. Howard	4	1958	1	1961	1	1964	1	1967	1		
R. Maris	4	1961	2	1967	2						
D. Snider	4	1952	2	1955	2						
J. F. Baker	3	1911	1	1913	2						
Joe Collins	3	1951	1	1953	1	1955	1				
K. Cuyler	3	1925	2	1929	1						
J. Foxx	3	1930	2	1931	1						
C. Gandil	3	1917	1	1919	2						
L. Gardner	3	1912	1	1916	1	1920	1				
G. Kelly	3	1921	1	1922	1	1924	1				
B. Martin	3	1952	1	1953	2						
B. Mazeroski	3	1960	3								
T. McCarver	3	1964	2	1968	1						

Player	Total	Series	Games	Series	Games	Series	Games	Series	Games	Series	Games
G. McDougald	3	1951	1	1956	1	1958	1				
Bing Miller	3	1929	2	1930	1						
S. Musial	3	1942	1	1944	1	1946	1				
M. Shannon	3	1967	1	1968	2						
B. Robinson	3	1966	1	1970	1	1971	1				

7
Players Driving in Winning or Decisive Runs for Two or More Games, by Series

Player	Games Won	Year	1	2	3	4	5	6	7	8	Total Series Games	Comment
R. Meusel	3	1923	0	0	0	W	W	W	X	X	6	Won Last 3 Games of the Series
T. Henrich	3	1947	W	W	0	0	0	0	W	X	7	Won 1st and Last Game of the Series
B. Mazeroski	3	1960	W	0	0	0	W	0	W	X	7	Won 1st and Last Game of the Series
J. Sebring	2	1903	W	0	W	0	0	0	0	0	8	
J. Slagle	2	1907	0	W	0	W	0	X	X	X	5	
F. Clarke	2	1909	0	0	W	0	W	0	0	X	7	
A. Fletcher	2	1912	0	0	W	0	0	0	W	0	8	
J. F. Baker	2	1913	W	0	0	0	W	X	X	X	5	Won 1st and Last Game of the Series
D. Lewis	2	1915	0	0	W	W	0	X	X	X	5	
C. Gandil	2	1919	0	0	W	0	0	W	0	0	8	
R. Youngs	2	1922	W	0	0	W	0	X	X	X	5	
C. Stengel	2	1923	W	0	W	0	0	0	X	X	6	
K. Cuyler	2	1925	0	W	0	0	0	0	W	X	7	
T. Lazzeri	2	1926	0	0	0	W	W	0	0	X	7	
L. Gehrig	2	1927	W	0	W	0	X	X	X	X	4	
B. Miller	2	1929	W	0	0	0	W	X	X	X	5	Won 1st and Last Game of the Series

Player	Games Won	Year	1	2	3	4	5	6	7	8	Total Series Games	Comment
J. Foxx	2	1930	0	W	0	0	W	0	X	X	6	
P. Martin	2	1931	0	0	W	0	W	0	0	X	7	
M. Ott	2	1933	W	0	0	0	W	X	X	X	5	Won 1st and Last Game of the Series
P. Dean	2	1934	0	0	W	0	0	0	W	0	7	
J. Gordon	2	1938	W	0	W	0	X	X	X	X	4	
J. DiMaggio	2	1939	0	0	W	W	X	X	X	X	4	Won Last 2 Games of the Series
J. Ripple	2	1940	0	W	0	W	0	0	0	X	7	
C. Keller	2	1941	0	0	W	W	W	0	X	X	5	
J. Gordon	2	1941	W	0	0	0	W	X	X	X	5	Won 1st and Last Game of the Series
R. York	2	1946	W	0	W	0	0	0	0	X	7	
L. Doby	2	1948	0	W	0	W	0	0	X	X	6	
G. Coleman	2	1949	0	0	W	0	W	X	X	X	5	
G. Coleman	2	1950	W	0	W	0	X	X	X	X	4	
D. Snider	2	1952	W	0	0	0	W	0	0	X	7	
M. Mantle	2	1952	0	0	0	0	0	W	W	X	7	Won Last 2 Games of the Series
B. Martin	2	1953	0	0	0	0	W	W	X	X	6	Won Last 2 Games of the Series
J. Rhodes	2	1954	W	0	W	0	X	X	X	X	4	
D. Snider	2	1955	0	0	0	W	W	0	0	X	7	
G. Hodges	2	1956	W	W	0	0	0	0	0	X	7	
E. Mathews	2	1957	0	0	0	W	0	0	W	X	7	
R. Maris	2	1961	0	0	W	0	W	X	X	X	5	
C. Boyer	2	1962	W	0	W	0	0	0	0	X	7	
W. Davis	2	1963	0	W	0	W	X	X	X	X	4	
M. Mantle	2	1964	0	W	W	0	0	0	0	X	7	
T. McCarver	2	1964	0	0	0	0	W	0	W	X	7	
R. Maris	2	1967	W	0	0	W	0	0	0	X	7	
M. Shannon	2	1968	W	0	0	W	0	0	0	X	7	
J. Pagan	2	1971	0	0	W	0	0	0	W	X	7	
R. Jackson	2	1973	0	0	0	0	0	W	W	X	7	Won Last 2 Games of the Series
Totals	45											

Players Driving in Winning or Decisive Runs for Two or more Games Number of Times

	Times Two or More Games		
G. Coleman	2	T. Lazzeri	1
J. Gordon	2	D. Lewis	1
M. Mantle	2	B. Martin	1

R. Maris	2		P. Martin	1
D. Snider	2		E. Mathews	1
J. F. Baker	1		B. Mazeroski	1
C. Boyer	1		T. McCarver	1
F. Clarke	1		R. Meusel	1
K. Cuyler	1		B. Miller	1
W. Davis	1		M. Ott	1
P. Dean	1		J. Pagan	1
J. DiMaggio	1		J. Rhodes	1
L. Doby	1		J. Ripple	1
A. Fletcher	1		J. Sebring	1
J. Foxx	1		M. Shannon	1
C. Gandil	1		J. Slagle	1
L. Gehrig	1		C. Stengel	1
T. Henrich	1		R. York	1
G. Hodges	1		R. Youngs	1
R. Jackson	1			
C. Keller	1		Total	45

8

Players Driving in Winning or Decisive Runs for Three or More Games, By Game

Player	Game	2	3	4	5	6	7	8	Total
M. Mantle	0	3	1	0	1	1	1	0	7
J. DiMaggio	1	1	1	2	1	0	0	0	6
L. Gehrig	2	0	2	1	0	0	0	0	5
T. Henrich	2	1	0	1	0	0	1	0	5
G. Hodges	1	2	0	1	0	0	1	0	5
T. Lazzeri	0	1	0	2	1	1	0	0	5
R. Meusel	0	0	0	2	2	1	0	0	5
H. Bauer	0	0	1	0	0	3	0	0	4
G. Coleman	1	0	2	0	1	0	0	0	4
F. Crosetti	0	2	1	1	0	0	0	0	4
B. Dickey	1	1	1	0	1	0	0	0	4
J. Gordon	2	0	1	0	1	0	0	0	4
G. Goslin	0	1	0	2	0	1	0	0	4
H. Greenberg	0	2	0	1	1	0	0	0	4
E. Howard	1	0	0	0	1	1	1	0	4
R. Maris	1	0	1	1	1	0	0	0	4
D. Snider	1	0	0	1	2	0	0	0	4
J. F. Baker	1	1	0	0	1	0	0	0	3
Joe Collins	2	1	0	0	0	0	0	0	3

56

Player	Game	2	3	4	5	6	7	8	Total
K. Cuyler	0	1	1	0	0	0	1	0	3
J. Foxx	1	1	0	0	1	0	0	0	3
C. Gandil	0	0	1	0	0	2	0	0	3
L. Gardner	0	0	0	2	0	0	0	1	3
G. Kelly	1	0	0	0	1	1	0	0	3
B. Martin	0	1	0	0	1	1	0	0	3
B. Mazeroski	1	0	0	0	1	0	1	0	3
T. McCarver	0	0	1	0	1	0	1	0	3
G. McDougald	0	0	0	1	2	0	0	0	3
Bing Miller	1	0	0	0	1	1	0	0	3
S. Musial	0	1	0	2	0	0	0	0	3
M. Shannon	1	0	1	1	0	0	0	0	3
B. Robinson	2	0	0	0	0	1	0	0	3

9
Players Driving in Winning or Decisive Runs, by Innings

Inn -	1	2	3	4	5	6	7	8	9	10	11	12	13	14	Totals
M. Mantle	0	0	0	1	1	1	1	2	1	0	0	0	0	0	7
J. DiMaggio	0	0	1	0	2	1	0	0	0	2	0	0	0	0	6
L. Gehrig	1	0	1	0	2	1	0	0	0	0	0	0	0	0	5
T. Henrich	0	0	0	1	2	1	0	0	1	0	0	0	0	0	5
G. Hodges	0	1	1	2	0	0	0	1	0	0	0	0	0	0	5
T. Lazzeri	0	0	1	0	1	0	1	1	0	1	0	0	0	0	5
R. Meusel	1	1	0	2	0	0	0	1	0	0	0	0	0	0	5
H. Bauer	1	0	0	0	1	1	1	0	0	0	0	0	0	0	4
G. Coleman	0	0	0	1	1	0	0	0	2	0	0	0	0	0	4
F. Crosetti	0	0	1	0	0	0	0	3	0	0	0	0	0	0	4
B. Dickey	0	0	2	0	0	1	0	0	1	0	0	0	0	0	4
J. Gordon	0	2	0	0	0	2	0	0	0	0	0	0	0	0	4
G. Goslin	0	0	1	0	1	0	0	0	1	0	0	1	0	0	4
H. Greenberg	1	0	1	0	1	0	1	0	0	0	0	0	0	0	4
E. Howard	0	0	0	1	0	0	0	2	1	0	0	0	0	0	4
R. Maris	1	1	0	0	0	0	1	0	1	0	0	0	0	0	4
D. Snider	0	0	0	0	2	1	0	0	0	0	1	0	0	0	4
J. F. Baker	0	0	1	0	1	0	1	0	0	0	0	0	0	0	3
Joe Collins	0	1	0	0	0	1	1	0	0	0	0	0	0	0	3

	Inn-1	2	3	4	5	6	7	8	9	10	11	12	13	14	Totals
K. Cuyler	0	0	0	0	0	1	0	2	0	0	0	0	0	0	3
J. Foxx	1	0	1	0	0	0	0	0	1	0	0	0	0	0	3
C. Gandil	0	1	0	1	0	0	0	0	0	1	0	0	0	0	3
L. Gardner	1	1	0	0	0	0	0	0	0	1	0	0	0	0	3
G. Kelly	0	0	0	1	0	0	0	1	0	0	0	1	0	0	3
B. Martin	0	0	0	0	1	0	1	0	1	0	0	0	0	0	3
B. Mazeroski	0	1	0	1	0	0	0	0	1	0	0	0	0	0	3
T. McCarver	0	0	0	0	1	0	1	0	0	1	0	0	0	0	3
G. McDougald	0	0	2	1	0	0	0	0	0	0	0	0	0	0	3
B. Miller	1	0	0	0	0	0	0	0	2	0	0	0	0	0	3
S. Musial	1	0	1	0	0	0	0	1	0	0	0	0	0	0	3
B. Robinson	1	0	0	0	0	0	1	0	0	1	0	0	0	0	3
M. Shannon	1	1	0	1	0	0	0	0	0	0	0	0	0	0	3
D. Bartell	0	2	0	0	0	0	0	0	0	0	0	0	0	0	2
P. Blair	0	1	0	0	1	0	0	0	0	0	0	0	0	0	2
Y. Berra	1	0	0	0	0	1	0	0	0	0	0	0	0	0	2
C. Boyer	0	0	0	0	0	0	2	0	0	0	0	0	0	0	2
F. Clarke	0	0	0	0	0	0	1	0	1	0	0	0	0	0	2
H. Davis	0	0	0	0	0	0	1	0	0	0	1	0	0	0	2
W. Davis	1	0	0	0	0	0	1	0	0	0	0	0	0	0	2
P. Dean	0	1	0	0	0	0	1	0	0	0	0	0	0	0	2
L. Doby	0	0	1	1	0	0	0	0	0	0	0	0	0	0	2
J. Dykes	0	0	0	0	0	1	1	0	0	0	0	0	0	0	2
J. Evers	0	0	0	0	1	0	1	0	0	0	0	0	0	0	2
A. Fletcher	1	0	0	0	1	0	0	0	0	0	0	0	0	0	2
F. Frisch	0	0	2	0	0	0	0	0	0	0	0	0	0	0	2
J. Gilliam	1	0	0	1	0	0	0	0	0	0	0	0	0	0	2
M. Haas	0	0	0	1	1	0	0	0	0	0	0	0	0	0	2
M. Higgins	0	0	0	0	0	0	2	0	0	0	0	0	0	0	2
R. Jackson	0	0	2	0	0	0	0	0	0	0	0	0	0	0	2
C. Keller	0	0	0	0	0	0	0	1	1	0	0	0	0	0	2
G. Kurowski	0	0	1	0	0	0	0	0	1	0	0	0	0	0	2
D. Lewis	0	0	0	0	0	1	0	0	1	0	0	0	0	0	2
B. Lord	0	0	1	0	0	0	0	1	0	0	0	0	0	0	2
L. Mann	0	0	1	0	0	0	0	0	1	0	0	0	0	0	2
P. Martin	0	0	0	1	0	1	0	0	0	0	0	0	0	0	2
E. Mathews	0	0	1	0	0	0	0	0	0	1	0	0	0	0	2
M. Ott	0	0	1	0	0	0	0	0	0	1	0	0	0	0	2
J. Pagan	0	0	0	0	0	1	0	1	0	0	0	0	0	0	2
P. Reese	0	1	0	0	0	1	0	0	0	0	0	0	0	0	2
D. Rhodes	0	0	0	1	0	0	0	0	0	1	0	0	0	0	2
J. Ripple	0	0	2	0	0	0	0	0	0	0	0	0	0	0	2
J. Roseboro	0	1	0	1	0	0	0	0	0	0	0	0	0	0	2
J. Rudi	0	0	2	0	0	0	0	0	0	0	0	0	0	0	2
R. Sanders	0	0	0	1	0	1	0	0	0	0	0	0	0	0	2
E. Scott	0	0	0	2	0	0	0	0	0	0	0	0	0	0	2

	Inn - 1	2	3	4	5	6	7	8	9	10	11	12	13	14	Totals
J. Sebring	1	0	1	0	0	0	0	0	0	0	0	0	0	0	2
B. Skowron	0	0	0	1	0	0	0	0	0	1	0	0	0	0	2
J. Slagle	0	0	0	1	1	0	0	0	0	0	0	0	0	0	2
H. Steinfeldt	1	0	1	0	0	0	0	0	0	0	0	0	0	0	2
C. Stengel	0	0	0	0	0	0	1	0	1	0	0	0	0	0	2
R. York	1	0	0	0	0	0	0	0	0	1	0	0	0	0	2
R. Youngs	0	0	0	0	1	0	0	1	0	0	0	0	0	0	2
J. Adcock	0	0	0	0	0	1	0	0	0	0	0	0	0	0	1
T. Agee	1	0	0	0	0	0	0	0	0	0	0	0	0	0	1
B. Allison	0	0	0	1	0	0	0	0	0	0	0	0	0	0	1
M. Alou	0	1	0	0	0	0	0	0	0	0	0	0	0	0	1
J. Antonelli	0	0	0	0	1	0	0	0	0	0	0	0	0	0	1
S. Bando	0	0	0	0	0	1	0	0	0	0	0	0	0	0	1
C. Barnhart	0	0	0	0	0	0	1	0	0	0	0	0	0	0	1
M. Belanger	0	0	0	1	0	0	0	0	0	0	0	0	0	0	1
L. Bell	1	0	0	0	0	0	0	0	0	0	0	0	0	0	1
C. Bender	0	1	0	0	0	0	0	0	0	0	0	0	0	0	1
J. Bentley	0	0	0	0	1	0	0	0	0	0	0	0	0	0	1
K. Boyer	0	0	0	0	0	1	0	0	0	0	0	0	0	0	1
H. Brecheen	0	0	1	0	0	0	0	0	0	0	0	0	0	0	1
B. Brown	0	0	0	0	1	0	0	0	0	0	0	0	0	0	1
J. Brown	0	0	1	0	0	0	0	0	0	0	0	0	0	0	1
B. Bruton	0	0	0	0	0	0	0	0	0	1	0	0	0	0	1
D. Buford	0	0	0	0	1	0	0	0	0	0	0	0	0	0	1
L. Burdette	1	0	0	0	0	0	0	0	0	0	0	0	0	0	1
G. H. Burns	0	0	0	0	0	1	0	0	0	0	0	0	0	0	1
G. J. Burns	0	0	0	0	0	0	0	1	0	0	0	0	0	0	1
T. Byrne	0	0	0	1	0	0	0	0	0	0	0	0	0	0	1
F. Cady	0	0	0	1	0	0	0	0	0	0	0	0	0	0	1
D. Camilli	0	0	0	0	0	1	0	0	0	0	0	0	0	0	1
R. Campanella	0	0	0	0	0	0	0	1	0	0	0	0	0	0	1
B. Campaneris	0	0	0	0	0	0	0	0	0	0	1	0	0	0	1
A. Carey	0	0	0	0	0	1	0	0	0	0	0	0	0	0	1
F. Chance	1	0	0	0	0	0	0	0	0	0	0	0	0	0	1
B. Chapman	0	0	1	0	0	0	0	0	0	0	0	0	0	0	1
M. Christman	0	0	1	0	0	0	0	0	0	0	0	0	0	0	1
T. Cobb	0	0	0	0	0	1	0	0	0	0	0	0	0	0	1
E. Collins	0	0	0	0	0	0	0	1	0	0	0	0	0	0	1
E. Combs	0	0	0	0	0	1	0	0	0	0	0	0	0	0	1
D. Concepcion	0	0	0	0	1	0	0	0	0	0	0	0	0	0	1
W. Cooper	0	0	0	0	0	0	1	0	0	0	0	0	0	0	1
W. Covington	0	0	0	1	0	0	0	0	0	0	0	0	0	0	1
C. Cravath	0	0	0	0	0	0	0	1	0	0	0	0	0	0	1
J. Cronin	1	0	0	0	0	0	0	0	0	0	0	0	0	0	1

Inn	1	2	3	4	5	6	7	8	9	10	11	12	13	14	Totals
R. Cullenbine	0	0	0	1	0	0	0	0	0	0	0	0	0	0	1
J. Davenport	0	0	0	1	0	0	0	0	0	0	0	0	0	0	1
G. Davis	0	1	0	0	0	0	0	0	0	0	0	0	0	0	1
T. Davis	1	0	0	0	0	0	0	0	0	0	0	0	0	0	1
J. Delahanty	0	0	1	0	0	0	0	0	0	0	0	0	0	0	1
J. Devore	0	0	0	0	0	0	1	0	0	0	0	0	0	0	1
J. Donahue	0	0	0	1	0	0	0	0	0	0	0	0	0	0	1
P. Dougherty	1	0	0	0	0	0	0	0	0	0	0	0	0	0	1
T. Douthit	0	0	0	1	0	0	0	0	0	0	0	0	0	0	1
C. Durst	0	1	0	0	0	0	0	0	0	0	0	0	0	0	1
O. Felsch	0	0	0	1	0	0	0	0	0	0	0	0	0	0	1
H. Ferris	0	0	0	1	0	0	0	0	0	0	0	0	0	0	1
C. Flood	0	0	0	0	0	1	0	0	0	0	0	0	0	0	1
W. Ford	0	1	0	0	0	0	0	0	0	0	0	0	0	0	1
G. Foster	0	0	0	0	0	0	0	0	1	0	0	0	0	0	1
J. Foy	0	0	0	0	0	0	1	0	0	0	0	0	0	0	1
B. Freehan	0	1	0	0	0	0	0	0	0	0	0	0	0	0	1
B. Freeman	0	0	0	0	1	0	0	0	0	0	0	0	0	0	1
C. Furillo	0	0	0	0	0	0	1	0	0	0	0	0	0	0	1
D. Gainor	0	0	0	0	0	0	0	0	0	0	0	0	0	1	1
C. Gehringer	0	0	0	0	0	1	0	0	0	0	0	0	0	0	1
C. Geromino	0	0	0	0	0	0	1	0	0	0	0	0	0	0	1
B. Gibson	0	0	0	0	1	0	0	0	0	0	0	0	0	0	1
G. Gibson	0	0	0	0	1	0	0	0	0	0	0	0	0	0	1
W. Gilbert	0	0	0	0	1	0	0	0	0	0	0	0	0	0	1
L. Gomez	0	0	0	0	1	0	0	0	0	0	0	0	0	0	1
I. Goodman	1	0	0	0	0	0	0	0	0	0	0	0	0	0	1
S. Hack	0	0	0	0	0	0	0	0	0	0	0	1	0	0	1
J. Harris	0	0	0	0	0	0	1	0	0	0	0	0	0	0	1
S. Harris	0	0	0	0	1	0	0	0	0	0	0	0	0	0	1
E. Hendricks	0	0	0	0	1	0	0	0	0	0	0	0	0	0	1
G. Hermanski	0	0	0	1	0	0	0	0	0	0	0	0	0	0	1
B. Herzog	1	0	0	0	0	0	0	0	0	0	0	0	0	0	1
C. Hiller	0	0	0	0	0	0	1	0	0	0	0	0	0	0	1
S. Hofman	0	0	0	0	0	0	0	0	1	0	0	0	0	0	1
W. Holke	0	0	0	1	0	0	0	0	0	0	0	0	0	0	1
T. Holmes	0	0	0	0	0	0	0	1	0	0	0	0	0	0	1
H. Hooper	0	0	0	0	0	0	0	0	1	0	0	0	0	0	1
W. Hoyt	0	0	0	1	0	0	0	0	0	0	0	0	0	0	1
R. Hyatt	0	1	0	0	0	0	0	0	0	0	0	0	0	0	1
M. Irvin	1	0	0	0	0	0	0	0	0	0	0	0	0	0	1
F. Isbell	0	0	0	0	0	1	0	0	0	0	0	0	0	0	1
J. Jackson	0	0	1	0	0	0	0	0	0	0	0	0	0	0	1
B. Johnson	0	0	0	0	0	0	0	1	0	0	0	0	0	0	1
L. Johnson	0	0	0	1	0	0	0	0	0	0	0	0	0	0	1

Inn -	1	2	3	4	5	6	7	8	9	10	11	12	13	14	Totals
A. Kaline	0	0	0	0	0	0	1	0	0	0	0	0	0	0	1
B. Kauff	0	0	0	1	0	0	0	0	0	0	0	0	0	0	1
H. Killebrew	0	0	0	0	0	1	0	0	0	0	0	0	0	0	1
C. Klein	0	0	1	0	0	0	0	0	0	0	0	0	0	0	1
T. Kluszewski	1	0	0	0	0	0	0	0	0	0	0	0	0	0	1
W. Kopf	0	0	0	1	0	0	0	0	0	0	0	0	0	0	1
H. Lavagetto	0	0	0	0	0	0	0	0	1	0	0	0	0	0	1
H. Leibold	0	0	0	1	0	0	0	0	0	0	0	0	0	0	1
F. Lindstrom	0	0	0	0	0	1	0	0	0	0	0	0	0	0	1
M. Lolich	0	0	1	0	0	0	0	0	0	0	0	0	0	0	1
J. Lumpe	0	0	1	0	0	0	0	0	0	0	0	0	0	0	1
G. Mancuso	0	0	0	0	0	1	0	0	0	0	0	0	0	0	1
A. Mangual	0	0	0	0	0	0	0	0	1	0	0	0	0	0	1
R. Maranville	0	1	0	0	0	0	0	0	0	0	0	0	0	0	1
C. Mathewson	0	0	0	0	0	0	0	0	0	1	0	0	0	0	1
L. May	0	0	0	0	0	0	0	1	0	0	0	0	0	0	1
M. May	0	0	0	0	0	0	1	0	0	0	0	0	0	0	1
D. McGann	1	0	0	0	0	0	0	0	0	0	0	0	0	0	1
S. McInnis	0	0	0	1	0	0	0	0	0	0	0	0	0	0	1
E. McNeeley	0	0	0	0	0	0	0	0	0	0	0	1	0	0	1
G. McQuinn	0	0	0	1	0	0	0	0	0	0	0	0	0	0	1
J. Medwick	0	0	0	0	1	0	0	0	0	0	0	0	0	0	1
F. Merkle	0	0	0	0	0	0	0	0	0	1	0	0	0	0	1
E. Meusel	0	0	0	0	0	0	1	0	0	0	0	0	0	0	1
J. Milner	0	1	0	0	0	0	0	0	0	0	0	0	0	0	1
J. Mize	0	0	0	1	0	0	0	0	0	0	0	0	0	0	1
Grant Moore	0	0	0	0	1	0	0	0	0	0	0	0	0	0	1
D. Murphy	0	0	1	0	0	0	0	0	0	0	0	0	0	0	1
B. Myers	0	0	0	0	0	0	1	0	0	0	0	0	0	0	1
H. Myers	1	0	0	0	0	0	0	0	0	0	0	0	0	0	1
C. Neal	0	0	0	0	0	0	1	0	0	0	0	0	0	0	1
G. Neale	0	0	0	0	1	0	0	0	0	0	0	0	0	0	1
B. Nicholson	0	0	0	1	0	0	0	0	0	0	0	0	0	0	1
J. Northrup	0	0	0	0	0	0	1	0	0	0	0	0	0	0	1
K. O'Dea	0	0	0	0	0	0	0	0	0	0	1	0	0	0	1
F. O'Doul	0	0	0	0	0	1	0	0	0	0	0	0	0	0	1
I. Olson	0	0	0	0	1	0	0	0	0	0	0	0	0	0	1
S. O'Neill	0	1	0	0	0	0	0	0	0	0	0	0	0	0	1
J. Palmer	0	0	0	1	0	0	0	0	0	0	0	0	0	0	1
F. Parent	0	0	0	1	0	0	0	0	0	0	0	0	0	0	1
W. Parker	0	0	0	1	0	0	0	0	0	0	0	0	0	0	1
R. Peckinpaugh	0	0	0	0	0	0	0	0	1	0	0	0	0	0	1
J. Podres	0	0	0	1	0	0	0	0	0	0	0	0	0	0	1
M. Rath	0	0	0	0	0	1	0	0	0	0	0	0	0	0	1

Inn -	1	2	3	4	5	6	7	8	9	10	11	12	13	14	Totals
M. Rettenmund	0	0	1	0	0	0	0	0	0	0	0	0	0	0	1
E. Reulbach	0	1	0	0	0	0	0	0	0	0	0	0	0	0	1
S. Rice	0	0	0	0	1	0	0	0	0	0	0	0	0	0	1
P. Richards	1	0	0	0	0	0	0	0	0	0	0	0	0	0	1
B. Robertson	0	1	0	0	0	0	0	0	0	0	0	0	0	0	1
E. Robinson	0	0	0	0	0	0	0	1	0	0	0	0	0	0	1
F. Robinson	0	0	0	1	0	0	0	0	0	0	0	0	0	0	1
J. Robinson	0	0	0	0	0	0	0	0	0	1	0	0	0	0	1
G. Rohe	0	0	0	0	0	1	0	0	0	0	0	0	0	0	1
P. Rose	0	0	0	0	0	0	0	0	1	0	0	0	0	0	1
C. Rossman	0	0	0	0	0	1	0	0	0	0	0	0	0	0	1
C. Ruffing	0	0	0	0	1	0	0	0	0	0	0	0	0	0	1
B. Ruth	1	0	0	0	0	0	0	0	0	0	0	0	0	0	1
B. Ryan	0	0	0	0	0	0	0	0	0	0	1	0	0	0	1
W. Schang	0	0	0	0	1	0	0	0	0	0	0	0	0	0	1
F. Schulte	0	0	0	1	0	0	0	0	0	0	0	0	0	0	1
J. Sewell	0	0	0	0	0	0	1	0	0	0	0	0	0	0	1
J. Sheckard	0	0	0	0	0	0	0	0	0	1	0	0	0	0	1
A. Simmons	1	0	0	0	0	0	0	0	0	0	0	0	0	0	1
E. Slaughter	0	0	0	0	0	1	0	0	0	0	0	0	0	0	1
E. Smith	1	0	0	0	0	0	0	0	0	0	0	0	0	0	1
F. Snyder	0	0	0	0	0	0	1	0	0	0	0	0	0	0	1
B. Southworth	0	0	0	0	0	0	1	0	0	0	0	0	0	0	1
T. Speaker	0	0	1	0	0	0	0	0	0	0	0	0	0	0	1
O. Stanage	0	1	0	0	0	0	0	0	0	0	0	0	0	0	1
R. Staub	1	0	0	0	0	0	0	0	0	0	0	0	0	0	1
R. Swoboda	0	0	0	0	0	0	0	1	0	0	0	0	0	0	1
G. Tenace	0	0	0	0	1	0	0	0	0	0	0	0	0	0	1
B. Terry	0	0	0	0	0	0	0	0	0	1	0	0	0	0	1
T. Thevenow	0	0	0	1	0	0	0	0	0	0	0	0	0	0	1
I. Thomas	0	0	0	1	0	0	0	0	0	0	0	0	0	0	1
H. Thompson	0	0	0	0	1	0	0	0	0	0	0	0	0	0	1
J. Tinker	0	0	0	0	0	0	0	1	0	0	0	0	0	0	1
E. Torgeson	0	0	0	0	0	0	1	0	0	0	0	0	0	0	1
T. Tresh	0	0	0	0	0	0	0	1	0	0	0	0	0	0	1
G. Tyler	0	1	0	0	0	0	0	0	0	0	0	0	0	0	1
E. Verban	0	0	0	1	0	0	0	0	0	0	0	0	0	0	1
Z. Versalles	0	0	1	0	0	0	0	0	0	0	0	0	0	0	1
B. Virdon	0	0	0	0	1	0	0	0	0	0	0	0	0	0	1
H. Wagner	0	0	0	0	0	0	1	0	0	0	0	0	0	0	1
H. Walker	0	0	0	0	0	0	0	1	0	0	0	0	0	0	1
G. Watkins	0	0	0	1	0	0	0	0	0	0	0	0	0	0	1
J. Webb	0	0	0	0	0	1	0	0	0	0	0	0	0	0	1
A. Weis	0	0	0	0	0	0	0	0	1	0	0	0	0	0	1

Inn -	1	2	3	4	5	6	7	8	9	10	11	12	13	14	Totals
Z. Wheat	1	0	0	0	0	0	0	0	0	0	0	0	0	0	1
J. White	0	0	0	0	0	0	0	0	0	0	1	0	0	0	1
J. Wilson	0	1	0	0	0	0	0	0	0	0	0	0	0	0	1
I. Wingo	0	0	0	1	0	0	0	0	0	0	0	0	0	0	1
C. Yastrzemski	0	0	0	1	0	0	0	0	0	0	0	0	0	0	1
S. Yerkes	0	0	0	0	0	0	1	0	0	0	0	0	0	0	1
	36	30	40	58	45	38	41	30	27	18	5	4	0	1	
Errors	3	0	3	5	4	4	0	3	0	1	0	2	0	0	25
Double Plays	0	0	0	2	1	0	0	0	0	0	0	0	0	0	3
Passed Balls	1	0	0	0	1	0	0	0	1	0	0	0	0	0	3
Wild Pitches	0	0	0	0	0	1	0	0	1	0	0	0	0	0	2
Tied Games	X	X	X	X	X	X	X	X	X	X	X	X	X	X	3
Total	41	31	46	65	51	43	41	33	29	19	6	6	0	1	415

10

Players Driving in Winning or Decisive Runs for Three or More Games, by Innings

Players	Early Innings					Total	Late Innings				Total	Extra Innings					Total	Game Total
	1	2	3	4	5		6	7	8	9		10	11	12	13	14		
M. Mantle	0	0	0	1	1	2	1	1	2	1	5	0	0	0	0	0	0	7
J. DiMaggio	0	0	1	0	2	3	1	0	0	0	1	2	0	0	0	0	2	6
T. Henrich	0	0	0	1	2	3	1	0	0	1	2	0	0	0	0	0	0	5
L. Gehrig	1	0	1	0	2	4	1	0	0	0	1	0	0	0	0	0	0	5
R. Meusel	1	1	0	2	0	4	0	0	1	0	1	0	0	0	0	0	0	5
G. Hodges	0	1	1	2	0	4	0	0	1	0	1	0	0	0	0	0	0	5
T. Lazzeri	0	0	1	0	1	2	0	1	1	0	2	1	0	0	0	0	1	5
H. Bauer	1	0	0	0	1	2	1	1	0	0	2	0	0	0	0	0	0	4
G. Coleman	0	0	0	1	1	2	0	0	0	2	2	0	0	0	0	0	0	4
F. Crosetti	0	0	1	0	0	1	0	0	3	0	3	0	0	0	0	0	0	4
B. Dickey	0	0	2	0	0	2	1	0	0	1	2	0	0	0	0	0	0	4
J. Gordon	0	2	0	0	0	2	2	0	0	0	2	0	0	0	0	0	0	4
G. Goslin	0	0	1	0	1	2	0	0	0	1	1	0	0	1	0	0	1	4
H. Greenberg	1	0	1	0	1	3	0	1	0	0	1	0	0	0	0	0	0	4
E. Howard	0	0	0	1	0	1	0	0	2	1	3	0	0	0	0	0	0	4
R. Maris	1	1	0	0	0	2	0	1	0	1	2	0	0	0	0	0	0	4
D. Snider	0	0	0	0	2	2	1	0	0	0	1	0	1	0	0	0	1	4
J. F. Baker	0	0	1	0	1	2	0	1	0	0	1	0	0	0	0	0	0	3
Joe Collins	0	1	0	0	0	1	1	1	0	0	2	0	0	0	0	0	0	3
K. Cuyler	0	0	0	0	0	0	1	0	2	0	3	0	0	0	0	0	0	3

Players	Early Innings						Late Innings					Extra Innings						Game
	1	2	3	4	5	Total	6	7	8	9	Total	10	11	12	13	14	Total	Total
J. Foxx	1	0	1	0	0	2	0	0	0	1	1	0	0	0	0	0	0	3
C. Gandil	0	1	0	1	0	2	0	0	0	0	0	1	0	0	0	0	1	3
L. Gardner	1	1	0	0	0	2	0	0	0	0	0	1	0	0	0	0	1	3
G. Kelly	0	0	0	1	0	1	0	0	1	0	1	0	0	1	0	0	1	3
B. Martin	0	0	0	0	1	1	0	1	0	1	2	0	0	0	0	0	0	3
B. Mazeroski	0	1	0	1	0	2	0	0	0	1	1	0	0	0	0	0	0	3
T. McCarver	0	0	0	0	1	1	0	1	0	0	1	1	0	0	0	0	1	3
G. McDougald	0	0	2	1	0	3	0	0	0	0	0	0	0	0	0	0	0	3
Bing Miller	1	0	0	0	0	1	0	0	0	2	2	0	0	0	0	0	0	3
S. Musial	1	0	1	0	0	2	0	0	1	0	1	0	0	0	0	0	0	3
M. Shannon	1	1	0	1	0	3	0	0	0	0	0	0	0	0	0	0	0	3
B. Robinson	1	0	0	0	0	1	0	1	0	0	1	1	0	0	0	0	1	3

Leaders in the Early Innings

L. Gehrig	4
G. Hodges	4
R. Meusel	4

Leader in the Late Innings

M. Mantle	5

Leader in the Extra Innings

J. DiMaggio	2

Part Two: World Series Individual Offensive Records

11
The Top Ten Players in Each Offensive Department

Series		Games		T. A. B.	
Y. Berra	14	Y. Berra	75	Y. Berra	259
M. Mantle	12	M. Mantle	65	M. Mantle	230
J. DiMaggio	10	E. Howard	54	J. DiMaggio	199
E. Howard	10	H. Bauer	53	F. Frisch	197
B. Ruth	10	G. McDougald	53	G. McDougald	190
H. Bauer	9	P. Rizzuto	52	H. Bauer	188
P. Rizzuto	9	J. DiMaggio	51	P. Rizzuto	183
B. Dickey	8	F. Frisch	50	E. Howard	171
F. Frisch	8	P. Reese	44	P. Reese	169
G. McDougald	8	R. Maris	41	R. Maris	151
B. Skowron	8	B. Ruth	41		

Runs		Hits	
M. Mantle	42	Y. Berra	71
Y. Berra	41	M. Mantle	59
B. Ruth	37	F. Frisch	58
L. Gehrig	30	J. DiMaggio	54
J. DiMaggio	27	H. Bauer	46
E. Howard			

Runs		Hits	
M. Mantle	42	Y. Berra	71
Y. Berra	41	M. Mantle	59
B. Ruth	37	F. Frisch	58
L. Gehrig	30	J. DiMaggio	54
J. DiMaggio	27	H. Bauer	46
R. Maris	26	P. Reese	46
E. Howard	25	G. McDougald	45
G. McDougald	23	P. Rizzuto	45
J. Robinson	22	L. Gehrig	43
H. Bauer	21	E. Collins	42
P. Rizzuto	21	E. Howard	42
D. Snider	21	B. Ruth	42
G. Woodling	21		

Singles		Doubles		Triples	
Y. Berra	49	Y. Berra	10	B. Johnson	4
F. Frisch	45	F. Frisch	10	T. Leach	4
J. DiMaggio	40	J. Barry	9	T. Speaker	4
P. Rizzuto	40	P. Fox	9	H. Bauer	3
P. Reese	39	C. Furillo	9	B. Brown	3
H. Bauer	34	L. Gehrig	8	B. Freeman	3
E. Collins	33	D. Snider	8	F. Frisch	3
M. Mantle	33	J. F. Baker	7	L. Gehrig	3
G. McDougald	33	E. Collins	7	B. Martin	3
B. Richardson	31	C. Hafey	7	T. McCarver	3
		E. Howard	7	R. Meusel	3
		H. Greenberg	7	F. Parent	3
		P. Martin	7	C. Stahl	3
		M. Marion	7		
		R. Meusel	7		
		D. Murphy	7		
		S. Musial	7		
		J. Robinson	7		

Home Runs

M. Mantle	18
B. Ruth	15
Y. Berra	12
D. Snider	11
L. Gehrig	10
J. DiMaggio	8
F. Robinson	8
B. Skowron	8
H. Bauer	7
G. Goslin	7
G. McDougald	7

R. B. I.

M. Mantle	40
Y. Berra	39
L. Gehrig	35
B. Ruth	32
J. DiMaggio	30
B. Skowron	29
D. Snider	26
H. Bauer	24
B. Dickey	24
G. McDougald	24

TB

M. Mantle	123
Y. Berra	117
B. Ruth	96
L. Gehrig	90
J. DiMaggio	84
D. Snider	79
H. Bauer	75
F. Frisch	74
G. McDougald	72
B. Skowron	69

LH

M. Mantle	26
Y. Berra	22
B. Ruth	22
L. Gehrig	21
D. Snider	19
J. DiMaggio	14
H. Greenberg	14
E. Howard	13
F. Frisch	13
B. Skowron	13

EB   LH

M. Mantle	64
B. Ruth	54
Y. Berra	46
L. Gehrig	44
D. Snider	41
J. DiMaggio	30
B. Skowron	30
H. Bauer	29
F. Robinson	28
G. McDougald	27

SB

L. Brock	14
E. Collins	14
F. Chance	10
P. Rizzuto	10
F. Frisch	9
H. Wagner	9
J. Evers	8

SH

E. Collins	8
L. Gardner	7
E. Scott	7
H. Steinfeldt	7
F. Frisch	6
W. Schang	6
J. Barry	5

SB		SH	
P. Martin	7	F. Clarke	5
J. Robinson	6	J. Daubert	5
J. Slagle	6	W. Davis	5
M. Wills	6	T. Lazzeri	5
		D. Lewis	5
		M. Marion	5
		T. Moore	5
		P. Rizzuto	5
		J. Sheckard	5
		J. Tinker	5

BB		BA Based upon 20 or more Games	
M. Mantle	43	L. Brock	.391
B. Ruth	33	J. Baker	.363
Y. Berra	32	L. Gehrig	.361
P. Rizzuto	30	B. Martin	.333
L. Gehrig	26	E. Collins	.328
M. Cochrane	25	B. Ruth	.326
J. Gilliam	21	G. Gehringer	.321
J. Robinson	21	H. Greenberg	.318
G. McDougald	20	G. Woodling	.318
J. DiMaggio	19	J. Evers	.316
G. Woodling	19		

Players Leading in Offensive Departments 10 or More Times

		Runs	Hits	1B	2B	3B	HR	RBI	TB	LH	EB LH	SP	SH	SB	BB	BA	Total
B. Ruth	1	3	1	1	2	1	4	2	4	3	3	3	0	2	3	1	33
L. Gehrig	2	2	1	0	1	2	4	3	2	3	4	2	1	0	4	1	30
M. Mantle	3	4	1	0	1	2	5	1	2	1	2	2	0	2	3	1	27
C. Keller	4	2	2	0	1	2	2	3	2	2	2	1	0	1	0	1	21
J. Gordon	5	0	1	0	1	1	3	2	2	1	1	2	0	2	2	1	19
H. Greenberg	6	2	1	0	1	2	3	2	3	1	2	2	0	0	0	0	19
J. F. Baker	7	2	3	3	0	0	2	2	2	1	1	1	0	0	0	1	18
Y. Berra	8	2	2	2	2	0	2	1	1	1	1	1	0	0	1	2	18
L. Brock	9	2	2	1	2	1	1	0	1	1	1	1	0	2	0	2	17
H. Bauer	10	2	2	1	0	2	1	1	1	2	1	1	1	1	0	0	16
E. Collins	11	2	1	1	1	1	0	0	2	1	0	1	0	4	1	1	16
P. Rizzutto	12	1	1	2	0	0	1	0	0	0	0	0	2	6	1	1	15

		Runs	Hits	1B	2B	3B	HR	RBI	TB	LH	EB LH	SP	SH	SB	BB	BA	Total
D. Snider	13	1	1	0	2	0	2	2	2	2	2	1	0	0	0	0	15
M. Marion	14	0	0	0	2	1	1	0	1	2	1	1	2	1	1	1	14
P. Martin	15	2	2	1	1	1	0	0	2	1	0	1	0	2	0	1	14
F. Frisch	16	1	1	2	2	2	0	0	0	1	0	0	1	4	0	0	14
B. Robinson	17	1	2	2	1	1	0	1	1	1	0	0	1	2	0	1	14
J. DiMaggio	18	2	0	1	1	0	6	0	0	0	2	0	0	0	1	0	13
A. Simmons	19	1	1	0	0	0	3	1	1	1	3	1	0	0	0	1	13
G. Woodling	20	1	1	1	1	2	1	0	0	1	1	0	0	0	2	2	13
F. Crosetti	21	1	0	1	1	1	1	1	1	1	1	0	1	1	1	0	12
B. Martin	22	0	1	1	0	2	1	1	1	1	1	1	0	1	0	1	12
S. Musial	23	0	1	1	1	1	1	0	1	2	1	0	1	1	1	0	12
R. Rolfe	24	1	1	2	2	1	0	0	0	2	0	0	2	1	0	0	12
F. Robinson	25	2	0	0	0	1	3	1	1	1	1	1	0	0	1	0	12
H. Aaron	26	1	1	2	0	1	1	1	1	0	1	1	0	0	0	1	11
R. Fairly	27	1	1	0	1	0	1	1	1	1	1	1	0	0	1	1	11
G. Goslin	28	0	1	0	1	0	2	2	1	1	1	1	0	0	1	0	11
H. Gowdy	29	1	0	0	1	1	1	1	1	1	1	1	0	0	1	1	11
H. Hooper	30	2	1	1	0	1	1	0	2	0	1	0	1	1	0	0	11
G. McQuinn	31	0	1	0	0	0	1	1	1	1	1	1	2	0	1	1	11
M. Ott	32	1	1	0	0	0	2	1	1	1	1	1	0	0	1	1	11
T. Tresh	33	1	1	1	1	0	2	0	1	0	0	0	2	1	1	0	11
T. Henrich	34	1	1	2	0	0	3	0	1	0	0	0	1	0	0	1	10
B. Herzog	35	1	1	0	1	1	0	0	1	1	0	1	0	1	1	1	10
D. Lewis	36	0	1	1	0	1	0	0	1	1	0	2	1	0	0	2	10
G. Selkirk	37	1	0	0	0	1	1	1	1	0	1	1	0	0	3	0	10

12
Leaders in Runs Scored—Both Clubs

1903			1909			1914	
F. Parent	8		T. Leach	8		C. Deal	2
						J. Evers	2
1905			1910			H. Gowdy	2
M. Donlin	4		J. F. Baker	6		S. McInnis	2
			D. Murphy	6		P. Moran	2
1906						E. Murphy	2
E. Hahn	4		1911			G. J. Schmidt	2
F. Isbell	4		J. F. Baker	7		G. Whitted	2
F. Jones	4						
J. Tinker	4		1912			1915	
			B. Herzog	6		H. Hooper	4
1907							
J. Tinker	4		1913				
			E. Collins	5		1916	
1908			R. Oldring	5		H. Hooper	6
J. Evers	5						

1917
E. Collins   4
O. Felsch   4
J. Jackson   4

1918
M. Flack   2
C. Hollocher   2
B. Killifer   2
S. McInnis   2
C. Pick   2
D. Shean   2
G. Whiteman   2

1919
H. Groh   6
E. Roush   6

1920
T. Speaker   6

1921
F. Frisch   5

1922
D. Bancroft   4
J. Dugan   4
H. Groh   4

1923
B. Ruth   8

1924
G. Kelly   7

1925
Grant Moore   7

1926
B. Ruth   6
B. Southworth   6

1927
E. Combs   6

1928
B. Ruth   9

1929
A. Simmons   6

1930
M. Bishop   5
M. Cochrane   5

1931
P. Martin   5

1932
L. Gehrig   9

1933
T. Jackson   3
M. Ott   3
B. Terry   3

1934
P. Martin   8

1935
C. Gehringer   4

1936
J. Powell   8

1937
G. Selkirk   5

1938
J. DiMaggio   4
L. Gehrig   4

1939
C. Keller   8

1940
I. Goodman   5
H. Greenberg   5
B. McCosky   5
B. Werber   5

1941
C. Keller   5

1942
R. Rolfe   5

1943
F. Crosetti   4

1944
R. Sanders   5

1945
P. Cavaretta   7
R. Cramer   7
H. Greenberg   7

1946
R. York   6

1947
B. Johnson   8

1948
B. Elliott   4
L. Mitchell   4

1949		1956		1965	
T. Henrich	4	M. Mantle	6	R. Fairly	7
		E. Slaughter	6		
1950				**1966**	
Y. Berra	2	**1957**		F. Robinson	4
B. Brown	2	H. Aaron	5		
G. Coleman	2	Y. Berra	5	**1967**	
J. DiMaggio	2	J. Logan	5	L. Brock	8
G. Woodling	2				
		1958		**1968**	
1951		H. Bauer	6	A. Kaline	6
A. Dark	5			L. Brock	6
P. Rizzuto	5	**1959**		W. Horton	6
		J. Landis	6		
				1969	
1952		**1960**		D. Clendenon	4
M. Mantle	5	M. Mantle	8		
G. McDougald	5	B. Richardson	8	**1970**	
D. Snider	5			B. Powell	6
		1961		L. May	6
1953		E. Howard	5		
H. Bauer	6				
R. Campanella	6	**1962**		**1971**	
		T. Tresh	5	F. Robinson	5
1954					
H. Thompson	6	**1963**		**1972**	
		J. Gilliam	3	G. Tenace	5
1955		**1964**		**1973**	
Joe Collins	6	M. Mantle	8	B. Campaneris	6

Times Leading in Runs Scored - Both Clubs

M. Mantle	4	D. Clendenon	1	E. Howard	1	P. Rizzutto	1
B. Ruth	3	M. Cochrane	1	F. Isbell	1	R. Rolfe	1
J. F. Baker	2	G. Coleman	1	J. Jackson	1	E. Roush	1
H. Bauer	2	Joe Collins	1	T. Jackson	1	R. Sanders	1
Y. Berra	2	E. Combs	1	B. Johnson	1	G. J. Schmidt	1
L. Brock	2	R. Cramer	1	F. Jones	1	G. Selkirk	1

E. Collins	2	P. Cavarretta	1	W. Horton	1	B. Richardson	1
J. DiMaggio	2	F. Crosetti	1	A. Kaline	1	D. Shean	1
J. Evers	2	A. Dark	1	G. Kelly	1	A. Simmons	1
L. Gehrig	2	C. Deal	1	B. Killifer	1	D. Snider	1
H. Greenberg	2	M. Donlin	1	J. Landis	1	B. Southworth	1
H. Groh	2	J. Dugan	1	T. Leach	1	T. Speaker	1
H. Hooper	2	B. Elliott	1	J. Logan	1	E. Slaughter	1
C. Keller	2	R. Fairly	1	L. May	1	G. Tenace	1
P. Martin	2	O. Felsch	1	B. McCosky	1	B. Terry	1
S. McInnis	2	M. Flack	1	G. McDougald	1	H. Thompson	1
J. Powell	2	F. Frisch	1	L. Mitchell	1	T. Tresh	1
F. Robinson	2	C. Gehringer	1	Grant Moore	1	B. Werber	1
J. Tinker	2	J. Gilliam	1	P. Moran	1	G. Whiteman	1
H. Aaron	1	I. Goodman	1	D. Murphy	1	G. Whitted	1
D. Bancroft	1	H. Gowdy	1	E. Murphy	1	G. Woodling	1
M. Bishop	1	E. Hahn	1	R. Oldring	1	R. York	1
B. Brown	1	T. Henrich	1	M. Ott	1		
R. Campanella	1	B. Herzog	1	F. Parent	1	Total	119
B. Campaneris	1	C. Hollocher	1	C. Pick	1		

8 or More Runs Scored - Per Series

B. Ruth	9	1928	*
L. Gehrig	9	1932	*
L. Brock	8	1967	*
E. Combs	8	1932	
B. Johnson	8	1947	*
C. Keller	8	1939	*
T. Leach	8	1909	*
M. Mantle	8	1960	*
M. Mantle	8	1964	*
P. Martin	8	1934	*
F. Parent	8	1903	*
J. Powell	8	1936	*
B. Richardson	8	1960	*
B. Ruth	8	1923	*

Times 8 or More Runs Scored - Per Series

M. Mantle	2
B. Ruth	2
L. Brock	1
E. Combs	1
L. Gehrig	1
B. Johnson	1
C. Keller	1
T. Leach	1
P. Martin	1
F. Parent	1
J. Powell	1
B. Richardson	1
TOTAL	14

* Denotes Series Leader

13
Leaders in Total Hits—Both Clubs

1903			1910			1916	
J. Sebring	11		J. F. Baker	9		H. Hooper	7
			E. Collins	9			
1905						1917	
M. Donlin	6		1911			D. Robertson	11
			J. F. Baker	9			
1906						1918	
F. Isbell	8		1912			C. Pick	7
			B. Herzog	12			
1907						1919	
C. Rossman	8		1913			J. Jackson	12
H. Steinfeldt	8		J. F. Baker	9			
1908			1914			1920	
F. Chance	8		J. Evers	7		Z. Wheat	9
1909			1915			1921	
J. Delehanty	9		D. Lewis	8		G. J. Burns	11

1922
H. Groh 9

1923
F. Frisch 10
A. Ward 10

1924
G. Goslin 11
S. Harris 11

1925
S. Rice 12

1926
J. Bottomley 10
E. Combs 10
B. Southworth 10
T. Thevenow 10

1927
M. Koenig 9

1928
B. Ruth 10

1929
J. Dykes 8
H. Wilson 8

1930
A. Simmons 8

1931
P. Martin 12

1932
L. Gehrig 9

1933
J. Cronin 7
G. Davis 7
M. Ott 7
F. Schulte 7

1934
Rip Collins 11
C. Gehringer 11
P. Martin 11
J. Medwick 11

1935
P. Fox 10

1936
R. Rolfe 10
J. Powell 10

1937
JoJo Moore 9

1938
S. Hack 8

1939
C. Keller 7

1940
H. Greenberg 10
B. Werber 10

1941
J. Gordon 7
C. Keller 7

1942
P. Rizzuto 8

1943
B. Johnson 6

1944
W. Cooper 7
G. McQuinn 7
S. Musial 7
E. Verban 7

1945
P. Cavarretta 11
R. Cramer 11
S. Hack 11

1946
B. Doerr 9

1947
T. Henrich 10

1948
L. Doby 7
B. Elliott 7
E. Torgeson 7

1949
B. Brown 6
P. Reese 6

1950
G. Hamner 6
G. Woodling 6

1951
M. Irvin 11

1952
M. Mantle 10
P. Reese 10
D. Snider 10

1953		1960		1967	
B. Martin	12	B. Skowron	12	L. Brock	12

1954		1961		1968	
V. Wertz	8	B. Richardson	9	L. Brock	13

1955		1962		1969	
Y. Berra	10	T. Tresh	9	R. Swoboda	6

1956		1963		1970	
Y. Berra	9	T. Davis	6	P. Blair	9
H. Bauer	9			B. Robinson	9

1957		1964		
H. Aaron	11	B. Richardson	13	

		1965		1971	
		R. Fairly	11	R. Clemente	12

1958		1965		
H. Bauer	10	M. Wills	11	

			1972	
		T. Perez	10	

1959		1966		1973	
C. Neal	10	B. Powell	5	R. Staub	11

Times Leading in Total Hits - Both Clubs

J. F. Baker	3	G. Davis	1	M. Irvin	1	R. Rolfe	1
H. Bauer	2	T. Davis	1	F. Isbell	1	C. Rossman	1
Y. Berra	2	J. Delahanty	1	J. Jackson	1	B. Ruth	1
L. Brock	2	L. Doby	1	B. Johnson	1	Fred Schulte	1
S. Hack	2	B. Doerr	1	M. Koenig	1	J. Sebring	1
C. Keller	2	M. Donlin	1	D. Lewis	1	A. Simmons	1
P. Martin	2	J. Dykes	1	M. Mantle	1	B. Skowron	1
P. Reese	2	B. Elliott	1	B. Martin	1	D. Snider	1
B. Richardson	2	J. Evers	1	G. McQuinn	1	B. Southworth	1
H. Aaron	1	R. Fairly	1	J. Medwick	1	R. Staub	1
P. Blair	1	P. Fox	1	JoJo Moore	1	H. Steinfeldt	1
J. Bottomley	1	F. Frisch	1	S. Musial	1	R. Swoboda	1
B. Brown	1	L. Gehrig	1	C. Neal	1	T. Thevenow	1
G. J. Burns	1	C. Gehringer	1	M. Ott	1	E. Torgeson	1

P. Cavarretta	1	J. Gordon	1	C. Pick		T. Tresh	1
F. Chance	1	G. Goslin	1	T. Perez	1	E. Verban	1
R. Clemente	1	H. Greenberg	1	B. Powell	1	A. Ward	1
E. Collins	1	H. Groh	1	J. Powell	1	B. Werber	1
Rip Collins	1	G. Hamner	1	S. Rice	1	V. Wertz	1
E. Combs	1	S. Harris	1	P. Rizzutto	1	Z. Wheat	1
W. Cooper	1	T. Henrich	1	D. Robertson	1	M. Wills	1
R. Cramer	1	B. Herzog	1	B. Robinson	1	H. Wilson	1
J. Cronin	1	H. Hooper	1			G. Woodling	1

TOTAL 101

10 or More Total Hits - Per Series

L. Brock	13	1968	*	B. Richardson	11	1960	
B. Richardson	13	1964	*	D. Robertson	11	1917	*
L. Brock	12	1967	*	J. Sebring	11	1903	*
R. Clemente	12	1971	*	R. Staub	11	1973	*
B. Herzog	12	1912	*	B. Weaver	11	1919	
J. Jackson	12	1919	*	M. Wills	11	1965	*
B. Martin	12	1953	*	H. Bauer	10	1958	*
P. Martin	12	1931	*	Y. Berra	10	1955	*
S. Rice	12	1925	*	J. Bottomley	10	1926	*
B. Skowron	12	1960	*	E. Combs	10	1926	*
H. Aaron	11	1957	*	A. Dark	10	1951	
G. J. Burns	11	1921	*	P. Fox	10	1935	*
M. Carey	11	1925		F. Frisch	10	1923	*
P. Cavarretta	11	1945	*	F. Frisch	10	1924	
Rip Collins	11	1934	*	H. Greenberg	10	1940	*
R. Cramer	11	1945	*	T. Henrich	10	1947	*
R. Fairly	11	1965	*	J. Judge	10	1924	
C. Gehringer	11	1934	*	T. Kubek	10	1960	
G. Goslin	11	1924	*	F. Lindstrom	10	1924	
S. Hack	11	1945	*	M. Mantle	10	1952	*
J. Harris	11	1925		M. Mantle	10	1960	
S. Harris	11	1924	*	R. Maris	10	1967	
M. Irvin	11	1951	*	E. Meusel	10	1921	
P. Martin	11	1934	*	C. Meyers	10	1912	
T. McCarver	11	1964		R. Murray	10	1912	
J. Medwick	11	1934	*	C. Neal	10	1959	*

G. Neale	10	1919		D. Snider	10	1952	*
T. Perez	10	1972	*	B. Southworth	10	1926	*
J. Powell	10	1936	*	C. Stahl	10	1903	
J. Rawlings	10	1921		T. Thevenow	10	1926	*
P. Reese	10	1952	*	A. Ward	10	1923	*
R. Rolfe	10	1936	*	B. Werber	10	1940	*
B. Ruth	10	1928	*	C. Yastrzemski	10	1967	
M. Sanguillen	10	1971					

Times 10 or More Total Hits - Per Series

L. Brock	2	S. Hack	1	P. Reese	1
F. Frisch	2	J. Harris	1	S. Rice	1
M. Mantle	2	S. Harris	1	D. Robertson	1
P. Martin	2	T. Henrich	1	R. Rolfe	1
B. Richardson	2	B. Herzog	1	B. Ruth	1
H. Aaron	1	M. Irvin	1	M. Sanguillen	1
H. Bauer	1	J. Jackson	1	J. Sebring	1
Y. Berra	1	J. Judge	1	B. Skowron	1
J. Bottomley	1	T. Kubek	1	D. Snider	1
G. J. Burns	1	F. Lindstrom	1	B. Southworth	1
M. Carey	1	R. Maris	1	C. Stahl	1
P. Cavarretta	1	B. Martin	1	R. Staub	1
R. Clemente	1	T. McCarver	1	T. Thevenow	1
Rip Collins	1	J. Medwick	1	A. Ward	1
E. Combs	1	E. Meusel	1	B. Weaver	1
R. Cramer	1	C. Meyers	1	B. Werber	1
A. Dark	1	R. Murray	1	M. Wills	1
R. Fairly	1	C. Neal	1	C. Yastrzemski	1
P. Fox	1	G. Neale	1		
C. Gehringer	1	T. Perez	1	TOTAL	67
G. Goslin	1	J. Powell	1		
H. Greenberg	1	J. Rawlings	1		

Players Having Four Hits in a World Series Game

	Series	Series Game	TAB	HITS	LH	1B	2B	3B	HR
T. Leach	1903	1	5	4	2	2	0	2	0
G. Beaumont	1903	6	5	4	0	4	0	0	0
F. Isbell	1906	5	5	4	4	0	4	0	0
E. Hahn	1906	6	5	4	0	4	0	0	0
T. Cobb	1908	3	5	4	1	3	1	0	0
L. Doyle	1911	5	5	4	2	2	2	0	0
D. Murphy	1911	6	4	4	1	3	1	0	0
F. Frisch	1921	1	4	4	1	3	0	1	0
G. J. Burns	1921	3	6	4	2	2	1	1	0
F. Snyder	1921	3	5	4	0	4	0	0	0
R. Youngs	1923	4	5	4	1	3	0	0	1
J. Dugan	1923	5	5	4	1	3	0	0	1
G. Goslin	1924	4	4	4	1	3	0	0	1
F. Lindstrom	1924	5	5	4	0	4	0	0	0
M. Carey	1925	7	5	4	3	1	3	0	0
M. Ott	1933	1	4	4	1	3	0	0	1
J. Medwick	1934	1	5	4	1	3	0	0	1
H. Greenberg	1934	4	5	4	2	2	2	0	0
Rip Collins	1934	7	5	4	0	4	0	0	0
B. Dickey	1938	1	4	4	0	4	0	0	0
C. Keller	1941	4	5	4	2	2	2	0	0
S. Hack	1945	6	5	4	1	3	1	0	0
W. Moses	1946	4	5	4	0	4	0	0	0
E. Slaughter	1946	4	6	4	2	2	1	0	1
G. Kurowski	1946	4	5	4	2	2	2	0	0
J. Garagiola	1946	4	5	4	1	3	1	0	0
M. Irvin	1951	1	5	4	1	3	0	1	0
V. Wertz	1954	1	5	4	2	2	1	1	0
J. Giliam	1959	5	5	4	0	4	0	0	0
M. Mantle	1960	3	5	4	2	2	1	0	1
M. Wills	1965	5	5	4	2	2	2	0	0
L. Brock	1967	1	4	4	0	4	0	0	0
B. Robinson	1970	4	4	4	1	3	0	0	1
R. Jackson	1973	2	6	4	2	2	1	1	0
R. Staub	1973	4	4	4	1	3	0	0	1

14
Leaders in Singles—Both Clubs

1903			1910			1916	
J. Sebring	9		J. F. Baker	6		H. Hooper	5
1905			**1911**			**1917**	
M. Donlin	5		J. F. Baker	5		D. Robertson	9
			E. Collins	5			
1906						**1918**	
E. Hahn	6		**1912**			C. Pick	6
S. Hofman	6		C. Meyers	9			
						1919	
1907						G. Neale	8
C. Rossman	7		**1913**			J. Jackson	8
			J. F. Baker	8			
1908						**1920**	
F. Chance	8		**1914**			I. Olson	7
			J. Evers	7		Z. Wheat	7
1909						**1921**	
J. Miller	6		**1915**			F. Frisch	8
D. Jones	6		D. Lewis	6			

1922
H. Groh 8

1923
F. Frisch 9
A. Ward 9

1924
S. Harris 9
J. Judge 9

1925
S. Rice 12

1926
T. Thevenow 8
E. Combs 8

1927
M. Koenig 7

1928
B. Ruth 4

1929
J. Dykes 7

1930
C. Gelbert 5

1931
P. Martin 7
J. Foxx 7
D. Williams 7

1932
B. Dickey 7
R. Stephenson 7

1933
J. Cronin 7

1934
Rip Collins 10

1935
M. Cochrane 6
P. Fox 6
C. Gehringer 6
G. Hartnett 6

1936
R. Rolfe 10

1937
JoJo Moore 8

1938
S. Hack 7

1939
F. McCormick 5

1940
B. Campbell 7

1941
R. Rolfe 6
J. Sturm 6

1942
J. DiMaggio 7
P. Rizzuto 7

1943
W. Cooper 5
F. Crosetti 5
S. Musial 5

1944
E. Verban 7

1945
R. Cramer 11

1946
B. Doerr 7
J. Pesky 7

1947
T. Henrich 7
P. Rizzuto 7

1948
M. McCormick 6
E. Robinson 6

1949
P. Reese 4
T. Henrich 4

1950
G. Woodling 6

1951
M. Irvin 10

1952
P. Reese 9

1953
Y. Berra 7
G. Hodges 7
B. Martin 7

1954
A. Dark 7
D. Mueller 7

1955
Y. Berra 8

1956
H. Bauer 8

1957		1962		1968	
H. Aaron	7	T. Kubek	7	N. Cash	9
		T. Tresh	7		
1958				1969	
H. Aaron	7	1963		B. Powell	5
W. Covington	7	E. Howard	5	R. Swoboda	5
				1970	
1959		1964		P. Blair	8
L. Aparicio	7	B. Richardson	11		
G. Hodges	7			1971	
J. Landis	7	1965		M. Sanguillen	10
		M. Wills	8		
1960		1966		1972	
R. Clemente	9	B. Powell	4	T. Perez	8
T. Kubek	9				
		1967		1973	
1961		L. Brock	8	J. Grote	8
B. Richardson	8	R. Maris	8	J. Milner	8
				R. Staub	8

Times Leading in Singles - Both Clubs

J. F. Baker	3	B. Campbell	1	B. Doerr	1	E. Howard	1
H. Aaron	2	N. Cash	1	M. Donlin	1	M. Irvin	1
Y. Berra	2	F. Chance	1	J. Dykes	1	J. Jackson	1
F. Frisch	2	R. Clemente	1	J. Evers	1	D. Jones	1
T. Henrich	2	M. Cochrane	1	P. Fox	1	J. Judge	1
G. Hodges	2	E. Collins	1	J. Foxx	1	M. Koenig	1
T. Kubek	2	Rip Collins	1	C. Gelbert	1	J. Landis	1
B. Powell	2	E. Combs	1	C. Gehringer	1	D. Lewis	1
P. Reese	2	W. Cooper	1	J. Grote	1	R. Maris	1
B. Richardson	2	W. Covington	1	H. Groh	1	B. Martin	1
P. Rizzutto	2	R. Cramer	1	S. Hack	1	P. Martin	1
R. Rolfe	2	J. Cronin	1	E. Hahn	1	F. McCormick	1
L. Aparicio	1	F. Crosetti	1	S. Harris	1	M. McCormick	1
H. Bauer	1	A. Dark	1	G. Hartnett	1	C. Meyers	1
P. Blair	1	B. Dickey	1	S. Hofman	1	J. Miller	1
L. Brock	1	J. DiMaggio	1	H. Hooper	1	J. Milner	1

JoJo Moore	1	S. Rice	1	R. Stephenson	1	M. Wills	1
D. Mueller	1	D. Robertson	1	J. Sturm	1	D. Williams	1
S. Musial	1	E. Robinson	1	R. Swoboda	1	G. Woodling	1
G. Neale	1	C. Rossman	1	T. Thevenow	1		
I. Olson	1	B. Ruth	1	T. Tresh	1	TOTAL	104
T. Perez	1	M. Sanguillen	1	E. Verban	1		
J. Pesky	1	J. Sebring	1	A. Ward	1		
C. Pick	1	R. Staub	1	Z. Wheat	1		

8 or More Singles - Per Series

S. Rice	12	1925 *	Y. Berra	8	1955 *
R. Cramer	11	1945 *	G. Beaumont	8	1903
B. Richardson	11	1964 *	P. Blair	8	1970 *
Rip Collins	10	1934 *	L. Brock	8	1967 *
M. Irvin	10	1951 *	P. Cavarretta	8	1945
T. Perez	10	1972 *	F. Chance	8	1908 *
R. Rolfe	10	1936 *	E. Collins	8	1917
M. Sanguillen	10	1971 *	E. Combs	8	1926 *
N. Cash	9	1968 *	H. Ferris	8	1903
R. Clemente	9	1960 *	F. Frisch	8	1921 *
F. Frisch	9	1923 *	J. Grote	8	1973 *
C. Gehringer	9	1934	H. Groh	8	1922 *
S. Harris	9	1924 *	S. Hack	8	1945
J. Judge	9	1924 *	J. Jackson	8	1919 *
T. Kubek	9	1960 *	H. Lowrey	8	1945
J. Medwick	9	1934	R. Maris	8	1967 *
C. Meyers	9	1912 *	J. Milner	8	1973 *
P. Reese	9	1952 *	T. McCarver	8	1964
D. Robertson	9	1917 *	JoJo Moore	8	1937 *
J. Sebring	9	1903 *	G. Neale	8	1919 *
A. Ward	9	1923 *	J. Powell	8	1936
J. F. Baker	8	1913 *	B. Richardson	8	1961 *
H. Bauer	8	1956 *	R. Staub	8	1973 *
			T. Thevenow	8	1926 *
			M. Wills	8	1965 *

* Denotes Series Leader

F. Frisch	2		J. Jackson	1
B. Richardson	2		J. Judge	1
J. F. Baker	1		T. Kubek	1
H. Bauer	1		H. Lowery	1
Y. Berra	1		R. Maris	1
G. Beaumont	1		T. McCarver	1
P. Blair	1		J. Medwick	1
L. Brock	1		C. Meyers	1
N. Cash	1		J. Milner	1
P. Cavarretta	1		Jo Jo Moore	1
F. Chance	1		G. Neale	1
R. Clemente	1		T. Perez	1
E. Collins	1		J. Powell	1
Rip Collins	1		P. Reese	1
E. Combs	1		S. Rice	1
R. Cramer	1		D. Robertson	1
H. Ferris	1		R. Rolfe	1
C. Gehringer	1		M. Sanguillen	1
H. Groh	1		J. Sebring	1
J. Grote	1		R. Staub	1
S. Hack	1		T. Thevenow	1
S. Harris	1		A. Ward	1
M. Irvin	1		M. Wills	1
			TOTAL	**48**

15
Leaders in Doubles—Both Clubs

1903			1909			1915	
F. Clarke	2		**J. Delahanty**	**4**		F. Luderus	2
G. LaChance	2		**T. Leach**	**4**			
E. Phelps	2					1916	
			1910			H. Lanvrin	3
1905			E. Collins	4			
R. Bresnahan	2					1917	
D. McGann	2		1911			W. Holke	2
			J. Barry	4			
1906						1918	
F. Isbell	4		1912			L. Mann	2
			B. Herzog	4			
			R. Murray	4			
1907						1919	
J. Evers	2		1913			B. Weaver	4
J. Sheckard	2		J. Barry	3			
						1920	
1908			1914			S. O'Neill	3
J. Sheckard	2		H. Gowdy	3			

1921
G. J. Burns   4

1922
J. Dugan   1
F. Frisch   1
H. McQuillan   1
R. Meusel   1
W. Pipp   1
B. Ruth   1
W. Schang   1
W. Witt   1

1923
J. Dugan   2
W. Witt   2

1924
F. Frisch   4

1925
M. Carey   4

1926
J. Bottomley   3

1927
L. Gehrig   2
M. Koenig   2

1928
B. Ruth   3

1929
W. English   2

1930
C. Hafey   5

1931
P. Martin   4

1932
B. Chapman   2
C. Grimm   2
G. Hartnett   2

1933
O. Bluege   1
G. Davis   1
G. Goslin   1
T. Jackson   1
JoJo Moore   1
G. Mancuso   1
B. Myer   1
Fred Schulte   1
B. Terry   1

1934
P. Fox   6

1935
P. Fox   3
C. Gehringer   3

1936
D. Bartell   3
J. DiMaggio   3

1937
R. Rolfe   2
B. Whitehead   2

1938
F. Crosetti   2
J. Gordon   2

1939
B. Dahlgren   2

1940
B. Werber   4

1941
C. Keller   2
D. Walker   2

1942
R. Rolfe   2

1943
M. Marion   2
M. Russo   2

1944
M. Marion   3
M. Kreevich   3

1945
H. Greenberg   3
S. Hack   3
M. Livington   3

1946
S. Musial   4

1947
J. Lindell   3

1948
L. Boudreau   4

1949
G. Coleman   3
G. Woodling   3

1950
G. Hamner   2

1951
A. Dark   3

1952		
B. Cox	2	
C. Furillo	2	
D. Snider	2	

1953		
B. Cox	3	
J. Gilliam	3	
D. Snider	3	

1954		
V. Wertz	2	

1955		
R. Campanella	3	

1956		
Y. Berra	2	
J. Collins	2	
C. Furillo	2	
G. Hodges	2	

1957		
E. Mathews	3	

1958		
Y. Berra	3	
R. Schoendienst	3	

1959		
N. Fox	3	
Al Smith	3	

1960		
B. Virdon	3	

1961		
E. Howard	3	

1962		
C. Hiller	3	

1963		
W. Davis	2	
H. Lopez	2	

1964		
L. Brock	2	
M. Mantle	2	
B. Richardson	2	
T. Tresh	2	

1965		
R. Fairly	3	
M. Wills	3	

1966		
W. Parker	2	

1967		
J. Javier	3	

1968		
L. Brock	3	

1969		
J. Grote	2	

1970		
D. Johnson	2	
L. May	2	
H. McRae	2	
B. Robinson	2	

1971		
R. Clemente	2	
A. Oliver	2	
J. Pagan	2	

1972		
D. Green	2	
J. Morgan	2	
T. Perez	2	

1973		
R. Jackson	3	

Times Leading in Doubles - Both Clubs

J. Barry	2	F. Crosetti	1	W. Holke	1	J. Morgan	1
Y. Berra	2	A. Dark	1	E. Howard	1	R. Murray	1
L. Brock	2	B. Dahlgren	1	F. Isbell	1	S. Musial	1
B. Cox	2	G. Davis	1	R. Jackson	1	B. Myer	1
J. Dugan	2	W. Davis	1	T. Jackson	1	A. Oliver	1
P. Fox	2	J. Delahanty	1	H. Janvrin	1	S. O'Neill	1
F. Frisch	2	J. DiMaggio	1	J. Javier	1	J. Pagan	1
C. Furillo	2	W. English	1	D. Johnson	1	W. Parker	1
M. Marion	2	J. Evers	1	C. Keller	1	T. Perez	1
R. Rolfe	2	R. Fairly	1	M. Koenig	1	E. Phelps	1
B. Ruth	2	N. Fox	1	M. Kreevich	1	W. Pipp	1
J. Sheckard	2	L. Gehrig	1	G. LaChance	1	B. Robinson	1
D. Snider	2	C. Gehringer	1	T. Leach	1	B. Richardson	1
W. Witt	2	J. Gilliam	1	J. Lindell	1	M. Russo	1
D. Bartell	1	J. Gordon	1	M. Livingston	1	W. Schang	1
O. Bluege	1	G. Goslin	1	H. Lopez	1	R. Schoendienst	1
L. Boudreau	1	H. Gowdy	1	F. Luderus	1	Fred Schulte	1
J. Bottomley	1	D. Green	1	L. Mann	1	Al Smith	1
R. Bresnahan	1	H. Greenberg	1	M. Mantle	1	B. Terry	1
G. J. Burns	1	C. Grimm	1	G. Mancuso	1	T. Tresh	1
R. Campanella	1	J. Grote	1	P. Martin	1	B. Virdon	1
M. Carey	1	S. Hack	1	E. Mathews	1	D. Walker	1
B. Chapman	1	C. Hafey	1	L. May	1	B. Weaver	1
F. Clarke	1	G. Hammer	1	D. McGann	1	B. Werber	1
R. Clemente	1	G. Hartnett	1	H. McQuillan	1	V. Wertz	1
G. Coleman	1	B. Herzog	1	H. McRae	1	B. Whitehead	1
E. Collins	1	C. Hiller	1	R. Meusel	1	M. Wills	1
Joe Collins	1	G. Hodges	1	JoJo Moore	1	G. Woodling	1

TOTAL   126

4 or More Doubles - Per Series

P. Fox	6	1934 *		B. Herzog	4	1912 *	
C. Hafey	5	1930 *		F. Isbell	4	1906 *	
J. Barry	4	1911 *		T. Leach	4	1909 *	
L. Boudreau	4	1948 *		P. Martin	4	1931 *	
G. J. Burns	4	1921 *		R. Murray	4	1912 *	
M. Carey	4	1925 *		S. Musial	4	1946 *	
E. Collins	4	1910 *		B. Weaver	4	1919 *	
J. Delahanty	4	1909 *		B. Werber	4	1940 *	
F. Frisch	4	1924 *					

* Denotes Series Leaders

92

16

Leaders in Triples—Both Clubs

1903			1909			1914	
T. Leach	4		H. Wagner	1		H. Gowdy	1
						G. Whitted	1
1905			**1910**				
None	0		F. Chance	1		**1915**	
			A. Strunk	1		C. Cravath	1
1906						L. Gardner	1
G. Rohe	2					T. Speaker	1
			1911				
			L. Doyle	1		**1916**	
1907						J. Daubert	1
T. Cobb						D. Hoblitzel	1
C. Rossman	1		**1912**			H. Hooper	1
H. Steinfeldt	1		T. Speaker	2		J. Johnston	1
			S. Yerkes	2		D. Lewis	1
						C. Meyers	1
1908						I. Olson	1
S. Hofman	1		**1913**			E. Scott	1
Frank Schulte	1		E. Collins	2		I. Thomas	1

| C. Walker | 1 |
| Z. Wheat | 1 |

1917

B. Herzog	1
G. McCarty	1
D. Robertson	1
H. Zimmermann	1

1918

C. Hollocher	1
B. Ruth	1
A. Strunk	1
G. Whiteman	1

1919

| H. Kopf | 2 |
| W. Ruether | 2 |

1920

E. Konetchy	1
E. Smith	1
T. Speaker	1

1921

G. J. Burns	1
F. Frisch	1
E. Meusel	1
W. Schang	1
R. Youngs	1

1922

| H. Groh | 1 |
| W. Witt | 1 |

1923

| R. Meusel | 2 |

1924

| F. Frisch | 1 |
| B. Terry | 1 |

1925

| H. Traynor | 2 |

1926

| R. Meusel | 1 |
| B. Southworth | 1 |

1927

| L. Gehrig | 2 |

1928

| J. Bottomley | 1 |

1929

| R. Hornsby | 1 |
| H. Wilson | 1 |

1930

J. Foxx	1
C. Gelbert	1
M. Haas	1

1931

| None | 0 |

1932

| K. Cuyler | 1 |
| M. Koenig | 1 |

1933

| None | 0 |

1934

L. Durocher	1
H. Greenberg	1
P. Martin	1
J. Medwick	1
E. Orsatti	1
J. Rothrock	1

1935

P. Fox	1
S. Hack	1
B. Herman	1

1936

| G. Selkirk | 1 |

1937

B. Dickey	1
L. Gehrig	1
T. Lazzeri	1
R. Rolfe	1

1938

| F. Crosetti | 1 |
| G. Hartnett | 1 |

1939

| C. Keller | 1 |
| B. Myers | 1 |

1940

H. Greenberg	1
M. Higgins	1
R. York	1

1941

J. Gordon	1
M. Owen	1
P. Reiser	1

1942

| G. Kurowski | 1 |
| M. Marion | 1 |

1943

| B. Johnson | 1 |
| C. Keller | 1 |

1944	
W. Cooper	1
C. Laabs	1

1945	
R. Johnson	1
B. Nicholson	1
A. Pafko	1

1946	
S. Musial	1
E. Slaughter	1
R. York	1

1947	
B. Johnson	3

1948	
None	0

1949	
B. Brown	2

1950	
B. Brown	1
G. Hamner	1

1951	
H. Bauer	1
M. Irvin	1
G. Woodling	1

1952	
M. Mantle	1
G. Woodling	1

1953	
B. Martin	2

1954	
V. Wertz	1

1955	
A. Carey	1
B. Martin	1
J. Robinson	1

1956	
P. Reese	1

1957	
H. Aaron	1
H. Bauer	1

1958	
M. Mantle	1
R. Schoendienst	1

1959	
G. Hodges	1

1960	
B. Richardson	2

1961	
H. Lopez	1

1962	
F. Alou	1
W. McCovey	1
B. Skowron	1

1963	
T. Davis	2

1964	
C. Flood	1
D. Groat	1
T. McCarver	1

1965	
E. Battey	1
W. Parker	1
Z. Versalles	1

1966	
F. Robinson	1

1967	
L. Brock	1
D. Maxvill	1
G. Scott	1

1968	
T. McCarver	2

1969	
None	0

1970	
D. Concepcion	1

1971	
M. Belanger	1
G. Clines	1
R. Clemente	1

1972	
D. Concepcion	1

1973	
S. Bando	1
B. Campaneris	1
R. Hahn	1
R. Jackson	1
F. Millan	1

T. Speaker	3	L. Doyle	1	M. Marion	1
H. Bauer	2	L. Durocher	1	P. Martin	1
B. Brown	2	C. Flood	1	D. Maxvill	1
D. Concepcion	2	P. Fox	1	G. McCarty	1
F. Frisch	2	J. Foxx	1	W. McCovey	1
L. Gehrig	2	L. Gardner	1	J. Medwick	1
H. Greenberg	2	C. Gelbert	1	E. Meusel	1
B. Johnson	2	J. Gordon	1	C. Meyers	1
C. Keller	2	H. Gowdy	1	F. Millan	1
M. Mantle	2	D. Groat	1	S. Musial	1
B. Martin	2	H. Groh	1	B. Myers	1
T. McCarver	2	M. Haas	1	B. Nicholson	1
R. Meusel	2	S. Hack	1	I Olson	1
A. Strunk	2	R. Hahn	1	E. Orsatti	1
G. Woodling	2	G. Hamner	1	M. Owen	1
R. York	2	G. Hartnett	1	A. Pafko	1
H. Aaron	1	B. Herzog	1	W. Parker	1
F. Alou	1	B. Herman	1	P. Reese	1
S. Bando	1	M. Higgins	1	P. Reiser	1
E. Battey	1	D. Hoblitzel	1	B. Richardson	1
M. Belanger	1	S. Hofman	1	D. Robertson	1
J. Bottomley	1	G. Hodges	1	F. Robinson	1
L. Brock	1	C. Hollocher	1	J. Robinson	1
G. J. Burns	1	H. Hooper	1	G. Rohe	1
B. Campaneris	1	R. Hornsby	1	R. Rolfe	1
A. Carey	1	M. Irvin	1	J. Rothrock	1
F. Chance	1	R. Jackson	1	C. Rossman	1
R. Clemente	1	R. Johnson	1	W. Ruether	1
G. Clines	1	J. Johnston	1	B. Ruth	1
T. Cobb	1	M Koenig	1	W. Schang	1
E. Collins	1	E. Konetchy	1	R. Schoendienst	1
W. Cooper	1	H. Kopf	1	Frank Schulte	1
C. Cravath	1	G. Kurowski	1	E. Scott	1
F. Crosetti	1	C. Laabs	1	G. Scott	1
K. Cuyler	1	T. Lazzeri	1	G. Selkirk	1
J. Daubert	1	T. Leach	1	B. Skowron	1
T. Davis	1	D. Lewis	1	E. Slaughter	1
B. Dickey	1	H. Lopez	1	E. Smith	1

H. Steinfeldt	1	C. Walker	1	H. Wilson	1
B. Southworth	1	H. Wagner	1	W. Witt	1
B. Terry	1	V. Wertz	1	S. Yerkes	1
I. Thomas	1	G. Whiteman	1	R. Youngs	1
H. Traynor	1	Z. Wheat	1	H. Zimmerman	1
Z. Versalles	1	G. Whitted	1	TOTAL	148

2 or More Triples - Per Series

T. Leach	4	1903	*
B. Freeman	3	1903	
F. Parent	3	1903	
C. Stahl	3	1903	
B. Johnson	3	1947	*
B. Brown	2	1949	*
E. Collins	2	1913	*
T. Davis	2	1963	*
L. Gehrig	2	1927	*
H. Kopf	2	1919	*
B. Martin	2	1953	*
R. Meusel	2	1923	*
B. Richardson	2	1960	*
G. Rohe	2	1906	*
W. Ruether	2	1919	*
T. Speaker	2	1912	*
H. Traynor	2	1925	*
S. Yerkes	2	1912	*
T. McCarver	2	1968	*

* Denotes Series Leader

17
Leaders in Home Runs—Both Clubs

1903			**1910**			**1915**		
P. Dougherty	2		D. Murphy	1		H. Hooper	2	
1905			**1911**			**1916**		
None	0		J. F. Baker	2		L. Gardner	2	
1906			**1912**			**1917**		
None	0		L. Doyle	1		B. Kauff	2	
			L. Gardner	1				
1907						**1918**		
None	0		**1913**			None	0	
			F. Merkle	1				
			J. F. Baker	1		**1919**		
1908			W. Schang	1		J. Jackson	1	
J. Tinker	1							
						1920		
1909			**1914**			E. Smith	1	
F. Clarke	2		H. Gowdy	1		J. Bagby Sr.	1	

1921
B. Ruth   1
W. Fewster   1
F. Snyder   1
E. Meusel   1

1922
A. Ward   2

1923
B. Ruth   3

1924
G. Goslin   3

1925
G. Goslin   3
J. Harris   3

1926
B. Ruth   4

1927
B. Ruth   2

1928
L. Gehrig   4

1929
J. Foxx   2
M. Haas   2
A. Simmons   2

1930
M. Cochrane   2
A. Simmons   2

1931
A. Simmons   2

1932
L. Gehrig   3

1933
M. Ott   2

1934
H. Greenberg   1
C. Gehringer   1
J. Medwick   1
B. Delancey   1

1935
F. Demaree   2

1936
L. Gehrig   2
G. Selkirk   2

1937
L. Gehrig   1
J. DiMaggio   1
T. Lazzeri   1
M. Hoag   1
M. Ott   1

1938
J. DiMaggio   1
J. Gordon   1
B. Dickey   1
T. Henrich   1
F. Crosetti   1
J. Marty   1
K. O'Dea   1

1939
C. Keller   3

1940
H. Greenberg   1
R. York   1
M. Higgins   1
B. Campbell   1
J. Ripple   1
B. Walters   1

1941
J. Gordon   1
T. Henrich   1
P. Reiser   1

1942
C. Keller   2

1943
J. Gordon   1
B. Dickey   1
R. Sanders   1
M. Marion   1

1944
S. Musial   1
D. Litwhiler   1
R. Sanders   1
G. McQuinn   1

1945
H. Greenberg   2

1946
R. York   2

1947
J. DiMaggio   2

1948
B. Elliott   2

1949
J. DiMaggio   1
T. Henrich   1
P. Reese   1
L. Olmo   1
G. Hodges   1
R. Campanella   1

1950
J. DiMaggio   1
Y. Berra   1

1951			1959			1966	
J. DiMaggio	1		T. Kluszewski	3		F. Robinson	2
J. Collins	1						
G. Woodling	1		**1960**			**1967**	
G. McDougald	1		M. Mantle	3		C. Yastrzemski	3
P. Rizzuto	1						
A. Dark	1		**1961**			**1968**	
W. Lockman	1		J. Blanchard	2		L. Brock	2
						O. Cepeda	2
1952			**1962**			A. Kaline	2
D. Snider	4		T. Tresh	1		J. Northrup	2
			C. Boyer	1			
1953			R. Maris	1		**1969**	
M. Mantle	2		J. Pagan	1		D. Clendenon	3
G. McDougald	2		W. McCovey	1			
B. Martin	2		T. Haller	1		**1970**	
J. Gilliam	2		C. Hiller	1		L. May	2
			E. Bailey	1		B. Powell	2
1954						B. Robinson	2
D. Rhodes	2					F. Robinson	2
			1963				
1955			M. Mantle	1		**1971**	
D. Snider	4		T. Tresh	1		D. Buford	2
			F. Howard	1		R. Clemente	2
1956			J. Roseboro	1		B. Robertson	2
M. Mantle	3		B. Skowron	1		F. Robinson	2
Y. Berra	3						
			1964			**1972**	
1957			M. Mantle	3		G. Tenace	4
H. Aaron	3						
			1965			**1973**	
1958			R. Fairly	2		W. Garrett	2
H. Bauer	4		L. Johnson	2			

J. DiMaggio 6
M. Mantle 5
L. Gehrig 4
B. Ruth 4
J. Gordon 3
H. Greenberg 3
T. Henrich 3
F. Robinson 3
A. Simmons 3
J. F. Baker 2
Y. Berra 2
B. Dickey 2
L. Gardner 2
G. Goslin 2
C. Keller 2
G. McDougald 2
M. Ott 2
R. Sanders 2
D. Snider 2
T. Tresh 2
R. York 2
H. Aaron 1
J. Bagby Sr. 1
E. Bailey 1
H. Bauer 1
J. Blanchard 1
C. Boyer 1
L. Brock 1
D. Buford 1
R. Campanella 1
B. Campbell 1
O. Cepeda 1
F. Clarke 1
R. Clemente 1
D. Clendenon 1

M. Cochrane
J. Collins 1
F. Crosetti 1
A. Dark 1
B. Delancey 1
F. Demaree 1
P. Dougherty 1
L. Doyle 1
B. Elliott 1
R. Fairly 1
W. Fewster 1
J. Foxx 1
W. Garrett 1
C. Gehringer 1
J. Gilliam 1
H. Gowdy 1
M. Haas 1
T. Haller 1
J. Harris 1
M. Higgins 1
C. Hiller 1
M. Hoag 1
G. Hodges 1
H. Hooper 1
F. Howard 1
J. Jackson 1
L. Johnson 1
A. Kaline 1
B. Kauff 1
T. Kluszewaki 1
T. Lazzeri 1
D. Litwhiler 1
W. Lockman 1
M. Marion 1
R. Maris 1

B. Martin 1
J. Marty 1
L. May 1
W. McCovey 1
G. McQuinn 1
J. Medwick 1
F. Merkle 1
E. Meusel 1
D. Murphy 1
S. Musial 1
J. Northrup 1
K. O'Dea 1
L. Olmo 1
J. Pagan 1
B. Powell 1
P. Reese 1
P. Reiser 1
D. Rhodes 1
J. Ripple 1
P. Rizzutto 1
B. Robertson 1
B. Robinson 1
J. Roseboro 1
W. Schang 1
G. Selkirk 1
B. Skowron 1
E. Smith 1
F. Snyder 1
G. Tenace 1
J. Tinker 1
A. Ward 1
B. Walters 1
G. Woodling 1
C. Yastrzemski 1

TOTAL 141

H. Bauer	4	1958	*
L. Gehrig	4	1928	*
B. Ruth	4	1926	*
D. Snider	4	1952	*
D. Snider	4	1955	*
G. Tenace	4	1972	*
H. Aaron	3	1957	*
Y. Berra	3	1956	*
L. Gehrig	3	1932	*
G. Goslin	3	1924	*
G. Goslin	3	1925	*
J. Harris	3	1925	*
C. Keller	3	1939	*
T. Kluszewski	3	1959	*
M. Mantle	3	1956	*
M. Mantle	3	1960	*
M. Mantle	3	1964	*
J. Mize	3	1952	
B. Ruth	3	1923	*
B. Ruth	3	1928	
C. Yastrzemski	3	1967	*
D. Clendenon	3	1969	*

M. Mantle	3
B. Ruth	3
L. Gehrig	2
G. Goslin	2
D. Snider	2
H. Aaron	1
H. Bauer	1
Y. Berra	1
D. Clendenon	1
J. Harris	1
C. Keller	1
T. Klusezewski	1
J. Mize	1
C. Yastrzemski	1
G. Tenace	1
TOTAL	22

18
Leaders in R.B.I.'s—Both Clubs

1903		
T. Leach	8	

1905		
D. McGann	4	

1906		
G. S. Davis	6	

1907		
J. Slagle	4	

1908		
J. Tinker	5	

1909		
F. Clarke	7	
H. Wagner	7	

1910		
D. Murphy	8	

1911		
J. F. Baker	5	
H. Davis	5	

1912		
R. Murray	5	

1913		
J. F. Baker	7	

1914		
H. Gowdy	3	
R. Maranville	3	
G. Whitted	3	

1915		
F. Luderus	6	

1916		
L. Gardner	6	

1917		
C. Gandil	5	
B. Kauff	5	

1918		
B. Killifer	2	
L. Mann	2	
G. Paskert	2	
B. Ruth	2	
G. Tyler	2	

1919		
L. Duncan	8	

1920		
E. Smith	5	

1921		
E. Meusel	7	

1922		
E. Meusel	7	

1923		
R. Meusel	8	

1924		
G. Goslin	7	
S. Harris	7	

1925		
K. Cuyler	6	
G. Goslin	6	
J. Harris	6	

1926		
L. Bell	6	

1927		
B. Ruth	7	

1928		
L. Gehrig	9	

1929		
M. Haas	6	

1930		
J. Dykes	5	

1931		
A. Simmons	8	

1932		
L. Gehrig	8	

1933		
M. Ott	4	
Fred Schulte	4	

1934		
H. Greenberg	7	

1935		
B. Herman	6	

1936		
L. Gehrig	7	
T. Lazzeri	7	

1937		
G. Selkirk	6	

1938		
J. Gordon	6	
F. Crosetti	6	

1939		
C. Keller	6	

1940		
H. Greenberg	6	
M. Higgins	6	
J. Ripple	6	

1941		
J. Gordon	5	
C. Keller	5	

1942		
C. Keller	5	
G. Kurowski	5	

1943		
B. Dickey	4	

1944		
G. McQuinn	5	

1945		
B. Nicholson	8	

1946		
H. Walker	6	

1947		
J. Lindell	7	

1948		
B. Elliott	5	
J. Hegan	5	

1949		
B. Brown	5	

1950		
G. Coleman	3	

1951		
G. McDougald	7	

1952		
D. Snider	8	

1953		
B. Martin	8	

1954		
D. Rhodes	7	

1955		
D. Snider	7	

1956		
Y. Berra	10	

1957
H. Aaron   7

1958
H. Bauer   8

1959
T. Kluszewski   10

1960
B. Richardson   12

1961
H. Lopez   7

1962
C. Hiller   5
R. Maris   5

1963
W. Davis   3
J. Roseboro   3
B. Skowron   3

1964
M. Mantle   8

1965
R. Fairly   6

1966
F. Robinson   3

1967
R. Maris   7

1968
A. Kaline   8
J. Northrup   8

1969
D. Clendenon   4

1970
L. May   8

1971
B. Robertson   5
B. Robinson   5

1972
G. Tenace   9

1973
R. Jackson   6
R. Staub   6

Times Leading in R. B. I.'s - Both Clubs

L. Gehrig	3		C. Gandil	1		G. McQuinn	1
C. Keller	3		L. Gardner	1		R. Meusel	1
J. F. Baker	2		H. Gowdy	1		D. Murphy	1
J. Gordon	2		M. Haas	1		R. Murray	1
G. Goslin	2		J. Harris	1		B. Nicholson	1
H. Greenberg	2		S. Harris	1		J. Northrup	1
R. Maris	2		J. Hegan	1		M. Ott	1
E. Meusel	2		B. Herman	1		G. Paskert	1
B. Ruth	2		M. Higgins	1		B. Richardson	1
D. Snider	2		C. Hiller	1		D. Rhodes	1
H. Aaron	1		R. Jackson	1		J. Ripple	1
H. Bauer	1		A. Kaline	1		B. Robertson	1
L. Bell	1		B. Kauff	1		B. Robinson	1
Y. Berra	1		B. Killifer	1		F. Robinson	1
B. Brown	1					J. Roseboro	1
F. Clarke	1		T. Kluszewski	1		Fred Schulte	1
D. Clendenon	1		G. Kurowski	1		G. Selkirk	1
G. Coleman	1		T. Lazzeri	1		A. Simmons	1
F. Crosetti	1		T. Leach	1		J. Slagle	1
K. Cuyler	1		J. Lindell	1		B. Skowron	1
G. S. Davis	1		H. Lopez	1		E. Smith	1
H. Davis	1		F. Luderus	1		R. Staub	1
W. Davis	1		L. Mann	1		G. Tenace	1
B. Dickey	1		M. Mantle	1		J. Tinker	1
L. Duncan	1		R. Maranville	1		G. Tyler	1
J. Dykes	1		B. Martin	1		H. Wagner	1
B. Elliott	1		L. May	1		H. Walker	1
R. Fairly	1		G. McDougald	1		G. Whitted	1
			D. McGann	1		TOTAL	96

8 or More R. B. I. ' s - Per Series

B. Richardson	12	1960	*
M. Mantle	11	1960	
Y. Berra	10	1956	*
T. Kluszewski	10	1959	*
L. Gehrig	9	1928	*
G. Tenace	9	1972	*
H. Bauer	8	1958	*
Y. Berra	8	1960	
L. Duncan	8	1919	*
L. Gehrig	8	1932	*
G. Hodges	8	1956	
A. Kaline	8	1968	*
T. Leach	8	1903	*
M. Mantle	8	1964	*
B. Martin	8	1953	*
L. May	8	1970	*
R. Meusel	8	1923	*
D. Murphy	8	1910	*
B. Nicholson	8	1945	*
J. Northrup	8	1968	*
A. Simmons	8	1931	*
D. Snider	8	1952	*

Times 8 or More R. B. I. ' s - Per Series

Y. Berra	2
L. Gehrig	2
M. Mantle	2
H. Bauer	1
L. Duncan	1
G. Hodges	1
A. Kaline	1
T. Kluszewski	1
T. Leach	1
B. Martin	1
L. May	1
R. Meusel	1
D. Murphy	1
B. Nicholson	1
J. Northup	1
B. Richardson	1
A. Simmons	1
D. Snider	1
G. Tenace	1
TOTAL	22

* Denotes Series Leader

4 or More R. B. I. ' s in One Game

B. Richardson	6	1960	*		G. McDougald	4	1951	*
T. Lazzeri	5	1936	*		B. Martin	4	1952	
B. Dickey	5	1936			D. Snider	4	1952	
T. Kluszewski	5	1959			M. Mantle	4	1953	*
M. Mantle	5	1960			D. Snider	4	1953	
H. Lopez	5	1961			Y. Berra	4	1956	*
R. Staub	5	1973			Y. Berra	4	1956	
J. Sebring	4	1903			G. Hodges	4	1956	
D. McGann	4	1905			B. Skowron	4	1956	*
C. Schmidt	4	1909			T. Kubek	4	1957	
E. Roush	4	1919			H. Bauer	4	1958	
E. Smith	4	1920	*		B. Skowron	4	1958	
G. Goslin	4	1924			Y. Berra	4	1960	
B. Ruth	4	1926			C. Hiller	4	1962	*
L. Bell	4	1926			K. Boyer	4	1964	*
B. Rogell	4	1934			J. Pepitone	4	1964	*
A. Simmons	4	1929			Z. Versalles	4	1965	
J. Powell	4	1936			C. Yastrzemski	4	1967	
P. Martin	4	1931			J. Northrup	4	1968	*
F. Crosetti	4	1938			A. Kaline	4	1968	
C. Keller	4	1939			L. Brock	4	1968	
H. Greenberg	4	1940			D. McNally	4	1970	*
B. Ruth	4	1932			L. May	4	1970	
P. Richards	4	1945						
B. Elliott	4	1948						

* Denotes Grand Slam Homeruns

Times 4 or More R. B. I. ' s in One Game

Y. Berra	3		H. Lopez	1
M. Mantle	2		B. Martin	1
B. Ruth	2		P. Martin	1
B. Skowron	2		L. May	1
D. Snider	2		G. McDougald	1
H. Bauer	1		D. McGann	1
L. Bell	1		D. McNally	1
K. Boyer	1		J. Northrup	1
L. Brock	1		J. Pepitone	1
F. Crosetti	1		J. Powell	1
B. Dickey	1		P. Richards	1
B. Elliott	1		B. Richardson	1
G. Goslin	1		B. Rogell	1
H. Greenberg	1		E. Roush	1
C. Hiller	1		C. Schmidt	1
G. Hodges	1		J. Sebring	1
A. Kaline	1		A. Simmons	1
C. Keller	1		E. Smith	1
T. Kluszewski	1		R. Staub	1
T. Kubek	1		Z. Versalles	1
T. Lazzeri	1		C. Yastrzemski	1
			TOTAL	48

Leaders in Total Bases—Both Clubs

1903			**1910**			**1916**		
	P. Dougherty	18		E. Collins	13		H. Hooper	10
				D. Murphy	13		D. Lewis	10
1905								
	R. Bresnahan	7	**1911**			**1917**		
	M. Donlin	7		J. F. Baker	17		D. Robertson	14
1906			**1912**			**1918**		
	G. Rohe	12		B. Herzog	18		C. Pick	8
	F. Isbell	12						
			1913			**1919**		
1907				J. F. Baker	12		J. Jackson	18
	H. Steinfeldt	11		E. Collins	12			
						1920		
1908							T. Speaker	12
	F. Schulte	9	**1914**					
				H. Gowdy	14			
1909						**1921**		
	J. Delehanty	13	**1915**				G. J. Burns	17
	S. Crawford	13		H. Hooper	13		E. Meusel	17

1922
H. Groh   11

1923
B. Ruth   19

1924
G. Goslin   21

1925
J. Harris   22

1926
B. Ruth   1 8

1927
B. Ruth   12

1928
B. Ruth   22

1929
J. Foxx   14

1930
A. Simmons   16

1931
P. Martin   19

1932
L. Gehrig   19

1933
M. Ott   13

1934
P. Martin   16
J. Medwick   16
H. Greenberg   16

1935
P. Fox   15
B. Herman   15

1936
G. Selkirk   16

1937
L. Gehrig   11
T. Lazzeri   11

1938
F. Crosetti   11
J. Gordon   11

1939
C. Keller   19

1940
H. Greenberg   17
M. Higgins   17

1941
J. Gordon   13

1942
C. Keller   10

1943
M. Marion   10

1944
G. McQuinn   12
S. Musial   12

1945
H. Greenberg   16
P. Cavarretta   16

1946
R. York   15

1947
T. Henrich   15

1948
B. Elliott   13

1949
B. Brown   11

1950
G. Hamner   10

1951
A. Dark   16

1952
D. Snider   24

1953
B. Martin   23

1954
V. Wertz   15

1955
D. Snider   21

1956
Y. Berra   20

1957
H. Aaron   22

1958
H. Bauer   22

1959
T. Kluszewski   19

1960			1965			1970	
M. Mantle	20		R. Fairly	20		B. Robinson	17
B. Skowron	20						
B. Richardson	20						
						1971	
1961			**1966**			R. Clemente	22
J. Blanchard	11		F. Robinson	12			
E. Howard	11						
						1972	
1962			**1967**			G. Tenace	21
C. Hiller	13		C. Yastrzemski	21			
T. Tresh	13						
			1968			**1973**	
1963			L. Brock	24		R. Jackson	17
T. Davis	10						
1964			**1969**				
M. Mantle	19		D. Clendenon	15			

Times Leading in Total Bases - Both Clubs

B. Ruth	4	J. Delahanty	1	G. McQuinn	1
H. Greenberg	3	P. Dougherty	1	J. Medwick	1
J. F. Baker	2	B. Elliott	1	E. Meusel	1
E. Collins	2	R. Fairly	1	D. Murphy	1
L. Gehrig	2	P. Fox	1	S. Musial	1
J. Gordon	2	J. Foxx	1	M. Ott	1
H. Hooper	2	G. Goslin	1	C. Pick	1
C. Keller	2	H. Gowdy	1	B. Richardson	1
M. Mantle	2	H. Groh	1	D. Robertson	1
P. Martin	2	G. Hamner	1	B. Robinson	1
D. Snider	2	J. Harris	1	F. Robinson	1
H. Aaron	1	T. Henrich	1	G. Rohe	1
H. Bauer	1	B. Herman	1	Frank Schulte	1
J. Blanchard	1	B. Herzog	1	G. Selkirk	1
R. Bresnahan	1	M. Higgins	1	A. Simmons	1
Y. Berra	1	C. Hiller	1	T. Speaker	1
L. Brock	1	E. Howard	1	H. Steinfeldt	1
B. Brown	1	F. Isbell	1	B. Skowron	1
G. J. Burns	1	J. Jackson	1	G. Tenace	1
P. Cavarretta	1	R. Jackson	1	T. Tresh	1
R. Clemente	1	T. Kluszewski	1	V. Wertz	1
D. Clendenon	1	T. Lazzeri	1	C. Yastrzemski	1
S. Crawford	1	D. Lewis	1	R. York	1
F. Crosetti	1	M. Marion	1		
A. Dark	1	B. Martin	1		
T. Davis	1	D. McGann	1	TOTAL	89

L. Brock	24	1968	*	M. Higgins	17	1940	*
D. Snider	24	1952	*	R. Jackson	17	1973	*
B. Martin	23	1953	*	T. Leach	17	1903	
H. Aaron	22	1957	*	T. McCarver	17	1964	
H. Bauer	22	1958	*	G. McDougald	17	1958	
R. Clemente	22	1971	*	E. Meusel	17	1921	*
J. Harris	22	1925	*	B. Robinson	17	1970	*
B. Ruth	22	1928	*	A. Simmons	17	1931	
G. Goslin	21	1924	*	C. Stahl	17	1903	
D. Snider	21	1955	*	R. Campanella	16	1955	*
G. Tenace	21	1972	*	P. Cavarretta	16	1945	*
C. Yastrzemski	21	1967	*	A. Dark	16	1951	*
Y. Berra	20	1956	*	F. Frisch	16	1924	
M. Mantle	20	1960	*	H. Greenberg	16	1934	*
B. Richardson	20	1960	*	H. Greenberg	16	1945	*
B. Skowron	20	1960	*	L. Johnson	16	1965	
R. Fairly	20	1965	*	M. Mantle	16	1956	
L. Brock	19	1967		P. Martin	16	1934	*
L. Gehrig	19	1928		B. Mazeroski	16	1960	
L. Gehrig	19	1932	*	J. Medwick	16	1934	*
C. Keller	19	1939	*	J. Mize	16	1952	
T. Kluszewski	19	1959	*	J. Sebring	16	1903	
M. Mantle	19	1952		G. Selkirk	16	1936	*
M. Mantle	19	1964	*	A. Simmons	16	1930	*
P. Martin	19	1931	*	B. Southworth	16	1926	
B. Ruth	19	1923	*	R. Staub	16	1973	
H. Bauer	18	1957		M. Carey	15	1925	
P. Dougherty	18	1903	*	D. Clendenon	15	1969	*
G. Goslin	18	1925		P. Fox	15	1935	*
B. Herzog	18	1912	*	B. Freeman	15	1903	
J. Jackson	18	1919	*	C. Gehringer	15	1934	
C. Neal	18	1959		T. Henrich	15	1947	*
B. Ruth	18	1926	*	B. Herman	15	1935	*
J. F. Baker	17	1911	*	J. Javier	15	1967	
G. J. Burns	17	1921	*	R. Maris	15	1960	
J. Gilliam	17	1953		L. May	15	1970	
H. Greenberg	17	1940	*	F. Parent	15	1903	
S. Harris	17	1924		B. Richardson	15	1964	
				V. Wertz	15	1954	*
				R. York	15	1946	*
				TOTAL	78		

M. Mantle	4	P. Dougherty	1	B. Martin	1
H. Greenberg	3	R. Fairly	1	L. May	1
B. Ruth	3	B. Freeman	1	B. Mazeroski	1
H. Bauer	2	F. Frisch	1	T. McCarver	1
L. Brock	2	P. Fox	1	G. McDougald	1
L. Gehrig	2	C. Gehringer	1	J. Medwick	1
G. Goslin	2	J. Gilliam	1	E. Meusel	1
P. Martin	2	J. Harris	1	J. Mize	1
B. Richardson	2	S. Harris	1	C. Neal	1
A. Simmons	2	T. Henrich	1	F. Parent	1
D. Snider	2	W. Herman	1	B. Robinson	1
H. Aaron	1	B. Herzog	1	J. Sebring	1
J. F. Baker	1	M. Higgins	1	G. Selkirk	1
Y. Berra	1	J. Jackson	1	B. Skowron	1
G. J. Burns	1	R. Jackson	1	B. Southworth	1
M. Carey	1	J. Javier	1	C. Stahl	1
R. Campanella	1	L. Johnson	1	R. Staub	1
P. Cavarretta	1	C. Keller	1	G. Tenace	1
R. Clemente	1	T. Kluszewski	1	V. Wertz	1
D. Clendenon	1	T. Leach	1	C. Yastrzemski	1
A. Dark	1	R. Maris	1	R. York	1
				TOTAL	**78**

20

Leaders in Long Hits—Both Clubs

1903		1909		1913	
P. Dougherty	4	S. Crawford	4	J. Barry	3
T. Leach	4	J. Delahanty	4		
C. Stahl	4	T. Leach	4	**1914**	
				H. Gowdy	5
1905					
R. Bresnahan	2	**1910**		**1915**	
D. McGann	2	E. Collins	4	F. Luderus	3
		D. Murphy	4		
1906				**1916**	
F. Isbell	4			H. Janvrin	3
		1911		D. Lewis	3
1907		J. F. Baker	4		
J. Evers	2	J. Barry	4	**1917**	
J. Sheckard	2	L. Doyle	4	B. Kauff	3
H. Steinfeldt	2				
		1912		**1918**	
1908		B. Herzog	5	L. Mann	2
J. Sheckard	2	R. Murray	5	A. Strunk	2

1919
B. Weaver — 5

1920
S. O'Neill — 3
T. Speaker — 3

1921
G. J. Burns — 5

1922
W. Witt — 2
A. Ward — 2

1923
B. Ruth — 5

1924
F. Frisch — 5

1925
J. Harris — 5

1926
B. Ruth — 4

1927
L. Gehrig — 4

1928
B. Ruth — 6

1929
J. Foxx — 3
A. Simmons — 3

1930
C. Hafey — 5

1931
P. Martin — 5

1932
L. Gehrig — 4

1933
G. Goslin — 2
M. Ott — 2
Fred Schulte — 2
B. Terry — 2

1934
P. Fox — 6

1935
P. Fox — 4
B. Herman — 4

1936
D. Bartell — 4

1937
L. Gehrig — 3
R. Rolfe — 3

1938
F. Crosetti — 4

1939
C. Keller — 5

1940
M. Higgins — 5

1941
J. Gordon — 3
P. Reiser — 3

1942
E. Slaughter — 2
G. Kurowski — 2
C. Keller — 2
R. Rolfe — 2

1943
M. Marion — 3

1944
S. Musial — 3
W. Cooper — 3
M Marion — 3
M. Kreevich — 3
G. McQuinn — 3

1945
H. Greenberg — 5

1946
S. Musial — 5

1947
J. Lindell — 4

1948
L. Boudreau — 4

1949
G. Woodling — 3
B. Brown — 3
G. Coleman — 3

1950
G. Hamner — 3

1951
A. Dark — 4

1952
D. Snider — 6

1953
B. Martin — 5
J. Gilliam — 5

1954			1960			1967	
V. Wertz	4		B. Richardson	5		C. Yastrzemski	5
1955			1961			1968	
R. Campanella	5		E. Howard	4		L. Brock	6
D. Snider	5						
			1962				
1956			C. Hiller	4		1969	
Y. Berra	5					D. Clendenon	4
			1963				
1957			H. Lopez	2		1970	
H. Bauer	5		W. Davis	2		B. Robinson	4
			T. Davis	2		L. May	4
			F. Howard	2			
1958			1964				
H. Bauer	4		M. Mantle	5		1971	
G. McDougald	4					R. Clemente	5
R. Schoendienst	4		1965				
			R. Fairly	5		1972	
1959						G. Tenace	5
T. Kluszewski	4		1966			1973	
C. Neal	4		F. Robinson	3		R. Jackson	5

L. Gehrig	3	P. Dougherty	1	M. Mantle	1
B. Ruth	3	L. Doyle	1	B. Martin	1
J. Barry	2	J. Evers	1	P. Martin	1
H. Bauer	2	R. Fairly	1	L. May	1
P. Fox	2	J. Foxx	1	G. McDougald	1
C. Keller	2	F. Frisch	1	D. McGann	1
T. Leach	2	J. Gilliam	1	G. McQuinn	1
M. Marion	2	J. Gordon	1	D. Murphy	1
S. Musial	2	G. Goslin	1	R. Murray	1
R. Rolfe	2	H. Gowdy	1	C. Neal	1
J. Sheckard	2	H. Greenberg	1	S. O'Neill	1
D. Snider	2	C. Hafey	1	M. Ott	1
J. F. Baker	1	G. Hamner	1	P. Reiser	1
D. Bartell	1	J. Harris	1	B. Richardson	1
Y. Berra	1	B. Herman	1	B. Robinson	1
L. Boudreau	1	B. Herzog	1	F. Robinson	1
R. Bresnahan	1	M. Higgins	1	R. Schoendienst	1
L. Brock	1	C. Hiller	1	Fred Schulte	1
B. Brown	1	E. Howard	1	A. Simmons	1
G. J. Burns	1	F. Howard	1	E. Slaughter	1
R. Campanella	1	F. Isbell	1	T. Speaker	1
R. Clemente	1	R. Jackson	1	C. Stahl	1
D. Clendenon	1	H. Janvrin	1	H. Steinfeldt	1
G. Coleman	1	B. Kauff	1	A. Strunk	1
E. Collins	1	T. Kluszewski	1	G. Tenace	1
W. Cooper	1	M. Kreevich	1	B. Terry	1
S. Crawford	1	G. Kurowski	1	A. Ward	1
F. Crosetti	1	D. Lewis	1	B. Weaver	1
A. Dark	1	J. Lindell	1	V. Wertz	1
T. Davis	1	H. Lopez	1	W. Witt	1
W. Davis	1	F. Luderus	1	G. Woodling	1
J. Delahanty	1	L. Mann	1	C. Yastrzemski	1

TOTAL 110

5 or More Long Hits - Per Series

L. Brock	6	1968	*	J. Harris	5	1925	*
P. Fox	6	1934	*	B. Herzog	5	1912	*
B. Ruth	6	1928	*	M. Higgins	5	1940	*
D. Snider	6	1952	*	R. Jackson	5	1973	*
H. Bauer	5	1957	*	C. Keller	5	1939	*
Y. Berra	5	1956	*	M. Mantle	5	1964	*
G. J. Burns	5	1921	*	B. Martin	5	1953	*
R. Campanella	5	1955	*	P. Martin	5	1931	*
R. Clemente	5	1971	*	S. Musial	5	1946	*
R. Fairly	5	1965	*	R. Murray	5	1912	*
F. Frisch	5	1924	*	B. Richardson	5	1960	*
L. Gehrig	5	1928		B. Ruth	5	1923	*
H. Gowdy	5	1914	*	D. Snider	5	1955	*
H. Greenberg	5	1945	*	G. Tenace	5	1972	*
J. Gilliam	5	1953	*	B. Weaver	5	1919	*
C. Hafey	5	1930	*	C. Yastrzemski	5	1967	*
				TOTAL	32		

* Denotes Series Leader

Times 5 or More Long Hits - Per Series

B. Ruth	2	F. Frisch	1	M. Mantle	1
D. Snider	2	L. Gehrig	1	B. Martin	1
H. Bauer	1	J. Gilliam	1	P. Martin	1
Y. Berra	1	H. Greenberg	1	R. Murray	1
L. Brock	1	H. Gowdy	1	S. Musial	1
G. J. Burns	1	C. Hafey	1	B. Richardson	1
R. Campanella	1	J. Harris	1	G. Tenace	1
R. Clemente	1	B. Herzog	1	B. Weaver	1
R. Fairly	1	M. Higgins	1	C. Yastrzemski	1
P. Fox	1	C. Keller	1		
		R. Jackson	1	TOTAL	32

119

Leaders in Extra Bases on Long Hits - Both Clubs

1903			**1916**			**1928**	
P. Dougherty	10		L. Gardner	6		L. Gehrig	13
1905			**1917**			**1929**	
R. Bresnahan	2		B. Kauff	7		J. Foxx	7
D. McGann	2					A. Simmons	7
			1918				
1906			A. Strunk	3		**1930**	
G. Rohe	5					A. Simmons	8
			1919				
1907			J. Jackson	6		**1931**	
H. Steinfeldt	3		B. Weaver	6		A. Simmons	8
1908			**1920**			**1932**	
J. Tinker	3		E. Smith	5		L. Gehrig	10
1909			**1921**			**1933**	
F. Clarke	6		E. Meusel	7		M. Ott	6
S. Crawford	6						
			1922			**1934**	
1910			A. Ward	6		H. Greenberg	7
D. Murphy	6						
			1923			**1935**	
1911			B. Ruth	12		F. Demaree	7
J. F. Baker	8					B. Herman	7
			1924				
1912			G. Goslin	10		**1936**	
L. Gardner	7					G. Selkirk	8
			1925				
1913			J. Harris	11		**1937**	
W. Schang	5					L. Gehrig	6
			1926				
1914			B. Ruth	12		**1938**	
H. Gowdy	8					F. Crosetti	7
			1927				
1915			B. Ruth	6		**1939**	
H. Hooper	6		L. Gehrig	6		C. Keller	12

1940
M. Higgins   8

1941
J. Gordon   6
P. Reiser   6

1942
C. Keller   6

1943
M. Marion   5

1944
S. Musial   5
G. McQuinn   5

1945
H. Greenberg   9

1946
R. York   9

1947
B. Johnson   6
J. DiMaggio   6

1948
B. Elliott   6

1949
B. Brown   5

1950
J. DiMaggio   4
G. Hamner   4

1951
A. Dark   6
G. Woodling   6

1952
D. Snider   14

1953
B. Martin   11

1954
V. Wertz   7

1955
D. Snider   13

1956
Y. Berra   11

1957
H. Aaron   11

1958
H. Bauer   12

1959
T. Kluszewski   10

1960
M. Mantle   10

1961
J. Blanchard   7

1962
C. Hiller   6

1963
T. Davis   4
F. Howard   4

1964
M. Mantle   11

1965
R. Fairly   9

1966
F. Robinson   8

1967
C. Yastrzemski   11

1968
L. Brock   11

1969
D. Clendenon   10

1970
B. Robinson   8
L. May   8

1971
R. Clemente   10

1972
G. Tenace   13

1973
R. Jackson   8

L. Gehrig	4	T. Davis	1	D. McGann	1
B. Ruth	3	F. Demaree	1	G. McQuinn	1
A. Simmons	3	P. Dougherty	1	E. Meusel	1
J. DiMaggio	2	B. Elliott	1	D. Murphy	1
L. Gardner	2	R. Fairly	1	S. Musial	1
H. Greenberg	2	J. Foxx	1	M. Ott	1
C. Keller	2	J. Gordon	1	P. Reiser	1
M. Mantle	2	G. Goslin	1	B. Robinson	1
D. Snider	2	H. Gowdy	1	F. Robinson	1
H. Aaron	1	G. Hamner	1	G. Rohe	1
J. F. Baker	1	J. Harris	1	W. Schang	1
H. Bauer	1	B. Herman	1	G. Selkirk	1
Y. Berra	1	M. Higgins	1	E. Smith	1
J. Blanchard	1	C. Hiller	1	H. Steinfeldt	1
R. Bresnahan	1	H. Hooper	1	A. Strunk	1
L. Brock	1	F. Howard	1	G. Tenace	1
B. Brown	1	B. Johnson	1	J. Tinker	1
F. Clarke	1	J. Jackson	1	A. Ward	1
S. Crawford	1	R. Jackson	1	B. Weaver	1
R. Clemente	1	B. Kauff	1	V. Wertz	1
D. Clendenon	1	T. Kluszewski	1	G. Woodling	1
F. Crosetti	1	M. Marion	1	C. Yastrzemski	1
A. Dark	1	B. Martin	1	R. York	1
		L. May	1		
				TOTAL	83

Times 10 or More Extra Bases on Long Hits - Per Series

D. Snider	14	1952	*		M. Mantle	3
L. Gehrig	13	1928	*		B. Ruth	3
D. Snider	13	1955	*		H. Bauer	2
G. Tenace	13	1972	*		L. Gehrig	2
H. Bauer	12	1958	*		G. Goslin	2
C. Keller	12	1939	*		D. Snider	2
B. Ruth	12	1923	*		H. Aaron	1
B. Ruth	12	1926	*		L. Brock	1
B. Ruth	12	1928			Y. Berra	1
H. Aaron	11	1957	*		R. Clemente	1
Y. Berra	11	1956	*		D. Clendenon	1
L. Brock	11	1968	*		P. Dougherty	1
J. Harris	11	1925	*		J. Harris	1
M. Mantle	11	1964	*		C. Keller	1
B. Martin	11	1953	*		T. Kluszewski	1
C. Yastrzemski	11	1967	*		B. Martin	1
H. Bauer	10	1957			J. Mize	1
R. Clemente	10	1971	*		G. Tenace	1
D. Clendenon	10	1969	*		C. Yastrzemski	1
P. Dougherty	10	1903	*			
L. Gehrig	10	1932	*		TOTAL	27
G. Goslin	10	1924	*			
G. Goslin	10	1925				
T. Kluszewski	10	1959	*			
M. Mantle	10	1956				
M. Mantle	10	1960	*			
J. Mize	10	1952				

21
Slugging Percentage Leaders—Both Clubs

Based Upon 10 or More Times at Bat

1903		1909		1914	
J. Sebring	.533	F. Clarke	.526	H. Gowdy	1.273
1905		**1910**		**1915**	
R. Bresnahan	.437	D. Murphy	.650	D. Lewis	.667
1906		**1911**		**1916**	
G. Rohe	.571	J. F. Baker	.708	D. Lewis	.588
1907		**1912**		**1917**	
H. Steinfeldt	.647	B. Herzog	.600	D. Robertson	.636
1908		**1913**		**1918**	
Frank Schulte	.500	E. Collins	.632	C. Pick	.444

	1919			1932			1945	
J. Jackson		.563	L. Gehrig		1.118	H. Greenberg		.696
	1920			1933			1946	
T. Speaker		.480	M. Ott		.722	R. York		.652
	1921			1934			1947	
E. Meusel		.586	H. Greenberg		.571	J. Lindell		.778
	1922			1935			1948	
H. Groh		.579	B. Herman		.625	B. Elliott		619
	1923			1936			1949	
B. Ruth		1.000	D. Bartell		.667	B. Brown		.917
			G. Selkirk		.667			
	1924			1937			1950	
G. Goslin		.656	T. Lazzeri		.733	G. Hamner		.714
	1925			1938			1951	
J. Harris		.880	J. Gordon		.733	A. Dark		.667
	1926			1939			1952	
B. Ruth		.900	C. Keller		1.188	J. Mize		1.067
	1927			1940			1953	
B. Ruth		.800	M. Higgins		.708	B. Martin		.958
	1928			1941			1954	
L. Gehrig		1.727	J. Gordon		.928	V. Wertz		.938
	1929			1942			1955	
J. Foxx		.700	G. Kurowski		.600	D. Snider		.840
	1930			1943			1956	
A. Simmons		.727	M. Marion		.714	Y. Berra		.880
	1931			1944			1957	
P. Martin		.792	G. McQuinn		.750	H. Aaron		.786

1958		1963		1968	
H. Bauer	.710	F. Howard	.700	L. Brock	.857
1959		**1964**		**1969**	
T. Kluszewski	.826	M. Mantle	.792	D. Clendenon	1.071
1960		**1965**		**1970**	
M. Mantle	.800	R. Fairly	.690	L. May	.833
1961		**1966**		**1971**	
J. Blanchard	1.100	F. Robinson	.858	R. Clemente	.758
1962		**1967**		**1972**	
T. Haller	.571	C. Yastrzemski	.840	G. Tenace	.913
				1973	
				R. Staub	.615

Times Leading in Slugging Percentage - Both Clubs

B. Ruth	3	R. Fairly	1	L. May	1
L. Gehrig	2	J. Foxx	1	G. McQuinn	1
J. Gordon	2	G. Goslin	1	E. Meusel	1
H. Greenberg	2	H. Gowdy	1	J. Mize	1
D. Lewis	2	H. Groh	1	D. Murphy	1
M. Mantle	2	T. Haller	1	M. Ott	1
H. Aaron	1	G. Hamner		C. Pick	1
J. F. Baker	1	J. Harris	1	D. Robertson	1
D. Bartell	1	B. Herman	1	F. Robinson	1
H. Bauer	1	B. Herzog	1	G. Rohe	1
Y. Berra	1	M. Higgins	1	Frank Schulte	1
J. Blanchard	1	F. Howard	1	J. Sebring	1
R. Bresnahan	1	J. Jackson	1	G. Selkirk	1
B. Brown	1	C. Keller	1	A. Simmons	1
L. Brock	1	T. Kluszewski	1	D. Snider	1
F. Clarke	1	G. Kurowski	1	T. Speaker	1
R. Clemente	1	T. Lazzeri	1	R. Staub	1
D. Clendenon	1	J. Lindell	1	H. Steinfeldt	1
E. Collins	1	M. Marion	1	G. Tenace	1
A. Dark	1	B. Martin	1	V. Wertz	1
B. Elliott	1	P. Martin	1	C. Yastrzemski	1
				R. York	1

TOTAL   71

.700 or More Slugging Percentages - Per Series
Based Upon 15 or More Total Bases

		TAB	TB	S. P.	
L. Gehrig	1928	11	19	1.727	*
B. Ruth	1928	16	22	1.375	
C. Keller	1939	16	19	1.188	*
L. Gehrig	1932	17	19	1.118	*
D. Clendenon	1969	14	15	1.071	*
J. Mize	1952	15	16	1.067	*
B. Ruth	1923	19	19	1.000	*
B. Martin	1953	24	23	.958	*
V. Wertz	1954	16	15	.938	*
G. Tenace	1972	23	21	.913	*
B. Ruth	1923	20	18	.900	*
J. Harris	1925	25	22	.880	*
L. Brock	1968	28	24	.857	*
D. Snider	1955	25	21	.840	*
C. Yastrzemski	1967	25	21	.840	*
L. May	1970	18	15	.833	*
D. Snider	1952	29	24	x.828	
T. Kluszewski	1959	23	19	.826	*
B. Robinson	1970	21	17	.810	
Y. Berra	1956	25	20	.800	*
M. Mantle	1960	25	20	.800	*
P. Martin	1931	24	19	.792	*
M. Mantle	1964	24	19	.792	*
H. Aaron	1957	28	22	.786	*
R. Clemente	1971	29	22	.758	*
T. McCarver	1964	23	17	.739	
A. Simmons	1930	22	16	.727	*
H. Bauer	1958	31	22	.710	*
J. F. Baker	1911	24	17	.708	*
M. Higgins	1940	24	17	.708	*

* Led Both Clubs

Times 700 or More Slugging Percentage - Per Series - Based Upon 15 or More Total Bases.

B. Ruth	3
L. Gehrig	2
M. Mantle	2
D. Snider	2
H. Aaron	1
J. F. Baker	1
H. Bauer	1
Y. Berra	1
L. Brock	1
R. Clemente	1
D. Clendenon	1
J. Harris	1
M. Higgins	1
C. Keller	1
T. Kluszewski	1
B. Martin	1
P. Martin	1
L. May	1
T. McCarver	1
J. Mize	1
B. Robinson	1
A. Simmons	1
G. Tenace	1
V. Wertz	1
C. Yastrzemski	1
TOTAL	30

22
Leaders in Sacrifice Hits—Both Clubs

1903		1909		1914	
G. LaChance	2	F. Clarke	5	R. Oldring	2
				1915	
1905		1910		E. Scott	2
C. Mathewson	2	J. Barry	2		
		H. Davis	2	1916	
1906		S. Hofman	2	D. Lewis	4
J. Sheckard	3	Frank Schulte	2		
H. Steinfeldt	3	H. Zimmerman	2	1917	
J. Tinker	3			F. McMullin	2
		1911			
1907		J. Barry	3	1918	
O. Overall	2	1912		C. Hollocher	2
J. Tinker	2	L. Gardner	3	H. Hooper	2
1908		1913		1919	
H. Steinfeldt	3	S. McInnis	3	J. Daubert	5

1920
J. Johnston	2

1921
W. Pipp	3
A. Ward	3

1922
W. Schang	3

1923
W. Schang	2

1924
O. Bluege	2
T. Jackson	2
M. Ruel	2

1925
S. Harris	4

1926
R. Meusel	3

1927
J. Dugan	2
L. Gehrig	2
P. Waner	2
G. Wright	2

1928
F. Frisch	2

1929
J. Boley	3

1930
J. Dykes	2
B. Miller	2

1931
M. Haas	2

1932
F. Crosetti	1
B. Jurges	1

1933
O. Bluege	2
T. Jackson	2

1934
J. Rothrock	2
S. Rowe	2

1935
B. Lee	3

1936
D. Bartell	2
J. Ripple	2

1937
M. Hoag	1
R. Rolfe	1

1938
F. Demaree	1
R. Ruffing	1

1939
F. McCormick	1
M. Pearson	1
R. Rolfe	1
G. Thompson	1

1940
B. Newsom	2

1941
None	0

1942
T. Moore	3

1943
T. Stainback	2

1944
M. Cooper	1
W. Cooper	1
G. Kurowski	1
M. Lanier	1
M. Marion	1
G. McQuinn	1
S. Musial	1
T. Wilks	1

1945
R. Johnson	4

1946
M. Marion	3

1947
F. Bevens	1
C. Furillo	1
T. Henrich	1
G. McQuinn	1
J. Robinson	1
E. Stanky	1

1948
V. Bickford	1
A. Clark	1
A. Dark	1
B. Feller	1
J. Hegan	1
M. McCormick	1
J. Sain	1
B. Salkeld	1
E. Stanky	1
B. Voiselle	1

1949
P. Rizzuto	2

1950			1960			1966	
A. Seminick	2		W. Ford	1		D. McNally	1
			V. Law	1		B. Powell	1
1951			B. Mazeroski	1		M. Wills	1
D. Koslo	2		B. Skinner	1			
			B. Skowron	1			
1952			B. Turley	1		**1967**	
P. Roe	2					M. Andrews	2
			1961				
1953			B. Daley	2		**1968**	
H. Bauer	1					B. Gibson	1
B. Cox	1					R. Oyler	1
B. Loes	1		**1962**			D. McLain	1
J. McDonald	1		F. Alou	1			
V. Raschi	1		C. Boyer	1			
P. Rizzuto	1		B. O'Dell	1		**1969**	
			J. Pagan	1		W. Garrett	1
1954			J. Sanford	1		J. C. Martin	1
W. Westrum	3		T. Tresh	1			
						1970	
1955			**1963**			P. Blair	1
G. Hodges	2		W. Davis	3		A. Bravo	1
						M. Cuellar	1
1956						G. Nolan	1
R. Campanella	2		**1964**				
G. McDougald	2		C. Boyer	1		**1971**	
			K. Boyer	1		N. Briles	2
1957			B. Gibson	1			
L. Burdette	2		D. Maxvill	1		**1972**	
W. Covington	2		T. McCarver	1		R. Fingers	2
G. McDougald	2		B. Richardson	1			
			M. Shannon	1		**1973**	
1958			C. Simmons	1		S. Bando	1
J. Logan	2		T. Tresh	1		J. Grote	1
						J. Matlack	1
1959			**1965**			T. McGraw	1
J. Roseboro	2		W. Davis	2		F. Millan	1
B. Shaw	2		W. Parker	2		J. Rudi	1

Times Leading in Sacrifice Hits - Both Clubs

J. Barry	2	R. Fingers	1	B. Newsom	1
O. Bluege	2	W. Ford	1	G. Nolan	1
C. Boyer	2	F. Frisch	1	B. O'Dell	1
W. Davis	2	C. Furillo	1	R. Oldring	1
B. Gibson	2	L. Gardner	1	O. Overall	1
T. Jackson	2	W. Garrett	1	R. Oyler	1
M. Marion	2	L. Gehrig	1	J. Pagan	1
G. McDougald	2	J. Grote	1	W. Parker	1
G. McQuinn	2	M. Haas	1	M. Pearson	1
P. Rizzutto	2	S. Harris	1	W. Pipp	1
R. Rolfe	2	J. Hegan	1	B. Powell	1
W. Schang	2	T. Henrich	1	V. Raschi	1
E. Stanky	2	M. Hoag	1	B. Richardson	1
H. Steinfeldt	2	G. Hodges	1	J. Ripple	1
J. Tinker	2	S. Hofman	1	J. Robinson	1
T. Tresh	2	C. Hollocher	1	P. Roe	1
F. Alou	1	H. Hooper	1	J. Roseboro	1
M. Andrews	1	R. Johnson	1	J. Rothrock	1
S. Bando	1	J. Johnston	1	S. Rowe	1
D. Bartell	1	B. Jurges	1	J. Rudi	1
H. Bauer	1	D. Koslo	1	M. Ruel	1
F. Bevens	1	G. Kurowski	1	R. Ruffing	1
V. Bickford	1	G. LaChance	1	J. Sain	1
P. Blair	1	M. Lanier	1	B. Salkeld	1
J. Boley	1	V. Law	1	J. Sanford	1
K. Boyer	1	B. Lee	1	Frank Schulte	1
A. Bravo	1	D. Lewis	1	E. Scott	1
N. Briles	1	B. Loes	1	A. Seminick	1
L. Burdette	1	J. Logan	1	M. Shannon	1
R. Campanella	1	J. C. Martin	1	B. Shaw	1
A. Clark	1	C. Mathewson	1	J. Sheckard	1
F. Clarke	1	D. Maxvill	1	C. Simmons	1
M. Cooper	1	J. Matlack	1	B. Skinner	1
W. Cooper	1	B. Mazeroski	1	B. Skowron	1
W. Covington	1	T. McCarver	1	T. Stainback	1
B. Cox	1	F. McCormick	1	G. Thompson	1
F. Crosetti	1	M. McCormick	1	B. Turley	1
M. Cuellar	1	J. McDonald	1	B. Voiselle	1
B. Daley	1	T. McGraw	1	P. Waner	1
A. Dark	1	S. McInnis	1	A. Ward	1
J. Daubert	1	D. McLain	1	W. Westrum	1
H. Davis	1	F. McMullen	1	T. Wilks	1
F. Demaree	1	D. McNally	1	M. Wills	1
J. Dugan	1	R. Meusel	1	G. Wright	1
J. Dykes	1	F. Millan	1	H. Zimmermann	1
B. Feller	1	B. Miller	1		
		T. Moore	1		
		S. Musial	1	TOTAL	155

F. Clarke	5	1909	*
J. Daubert	5	1919	*
O. Felsch	4	1919	
S. Harris	4	1925	*
R. Johnson	4	1945	*
D. Lewis	4	1916	*
J. Barry	3	1911	*
J. Boley	3	1929	*
K. Cuyler	3	1925	
W. Davis	3	1963	*
L. Duncan	3	1919	
L. Gardner	3	1912	*
B. Lee	3	1935	*
M. Marion	3	1946	*
S. McInnis	3	1913	*
R. Meusel	3	1926	*
T. Moore	3	1942	*
W. Pipp	3	1921	*
W. Schang	3	1922	*
J. Sheckard	3	1906	*
H. Steinfeldt	3	1906	*
H. Steinfeldt	3	1908	*
J. Tinker	3	1906	*
A. Ward	3	1921	*
W. Westrum	3	1954	*

TOTAL   25

* Denotes Series Leader

Leaders in Stolen Bases—Both Clubs

1903		1909		1914	
Jim Collins	3	H. Wagner	6	C. Deal	2
H. Wagner	3			R. Maranville	2

1905		1910		1915	
A. Devlin	3	E. Collins	4	J. Dugey	1
				D. Hoblitzel	1
				G. Whitted	1

1906		1911	
F. Chance	2	J. Barry	2
P. Dougherty	2	E. Collins	2
J. Evers	2	L. Doyle	2
G. Rohe	2	B. Herzog	2
J. Tinker	2		

1916	
H. Hooper	1
Z. Wheat	1

1907		1912	
J. Slagle	6	J. Devore	4

1908		1913		1917	
F. Chance	5	E. Collins	3	E. Collins	3

1918			1927			1938	
M. Flack	1		R. Meusel	1		B. Dickey	1
C. Hollocher	1		B. Ruth	1		J. Gordon	1
C. Pick	1					R. Rolfe	1
W. Schang	1		1928				
D. Shean	1		F. Frisch	2		1939	
G. Whiteman	1		T. Lazzeri	2		I. Goodman	1
			R. Meusel	2			
1919						1940	
M. Rath	2		1929			J. Wilson	1
E. Roush	2		N. McMillan	1			
						1941	
1920			1930			P. Rizzutto	1
C. Jamieson	1		F. Frisch	1		J. Sturm	1
J. Johnston	1						
W. Johnston	1		1931			1942	
			P. Martin	5		P. Rizzutto	2
1921							
F. Frisch	3		1932			1943	
			K. Cuyler	1		F. Crosetti	1
1922			B. Jurges	1		M. Marion	1
F. Frisch	1					C. Keller	1
R. Meusel	1		1933				
W. Pipp	1		L. Sewell	1		1944	
						None	0
1923			1934				
D. Bancroft	1		P. Martin	2		1945	
A. Ward	1					R. Cullenbine	1
			1935			R. Cramer	1
1924			S. Hack	1		R. Johnson	1
S. Rice	2		C. Gehringer	1		J. Outlaw	1
						A. Pafko	1
1925			1936				
M. Carey	3		J. Powell	1		1946	
						L. Culbertson	1
1926						S. Musial	1
R. Hornsby	1					J. Pesky	1
B. Ruth	1		1937			R. Schoendienst	1
B. Southworth	1		B. Whitehead	1		E. Slaughter	1

1947
P. Reese 3

1948
J. Gordon 1
J. Hegan 1
E. Torgeson 1

1949
B. Johnson 1
P. Reese 1
P. Rizzuto 1

1950
G. Hamner 1
P. Rizzuto 1

1951
M. Irvin 2

1952
J. Robinson 2

1953
G. Hodges 1
B. Martin 1
P. Rizzuto 1
J. Robinson 1

1954
W. Mays 1

1955
P. Rizzuto 2

1956
H. Bauer 1
J. Gilliam 1
M. Mantle 1

1957
W. Covington 1
G. McDougald 1

1958
E. Howard 1
E. Mathews 1

1959
J. Gilliam 2

1960
B. Skinner 1
B. Virdon 1

1961
B. Richardson 1

1962
M. Mantle 2
T. Tresh 2

1963
T. Davis 1
M. Wills 1

1964
C. Boyer 1
T. McCarver 1
B. Richardson 1
M. Shannon 1
B. White 1

1965
M. Wills 3
W. Davis 3

1966
M. Wills 1

1967
L. Brock 7

1968
L. Brock 7

1969
P. Blair 1
T. Agee 1

1970
B. Tolan 1

1971
M. Sanguillen 2

1972
B. Tolan 5

1973
B. Campaneris 3

P. Rizzuto	6	J. Devore	1	N. McMillan	1
E. Collins	4	B. Dickey	1	S. Musial	1
F. Frisch	4	P. Dougherty	1	J. Outlaw	1
R. Meusel	3	L. Doyle	1	A. Pafko	1
M. Wills	3	J. Dugey	1	J. Pesky	1
L. Brock	2	J. Evers	1	C. Pick	1
F. Chance	2	M. Flack	1	W. Pipp	1
J. Gilliam	2	C. Gehringer	1	J. Powell	1
J. Gordon	2	I. Goodman	1	M. Rath	1
M. Mantle	2	S. Hack	1	S. Rice	1
P. Martin	2	G. Hamner	1	G. Rohe	1
P. Reese	2	J. Hegan	1	R. Rolfe	1
B. Richardson	2	B. Herzog	1	E. Roush	1
J. Robinson	2	D. Hoblitzel	1	M. Sanguillen	1
B. Ruth	2	G. Hodges	1	W. Schang	1
B. Tolan	2	C. Hollocher	1	R. Schoendienst	1
H. Wagner	2	H. Hooper	1	L. Sewell	1
T. Agee	1	E. Howard	1	M. Shannon	1
D. Bancroft	1	R. Hornsby	1	D. Shean	1
J. Barry	1	M. Irvin	1	B. Skinner	1
H. Bauer	1	C. Jamieson	1	J. Slagle	1
P. Blair	1	B. Johnson	1	E. Slaughter	1
C. Boyer	1	R. Johnson	1	B. Southworth	1
B. Campaneris	1	J. Johnston	1	J. Sturm	1
M. Carey	1	W. Johnston	1	J. Tinker	1
Jim Collins	1	B. Jurges	1	E. Torgeson	1
W. Covington	1	C. Keller	1	T. Tresh	1
R. Cramer	1	T. Lazzeri	1	B. Virdon	1
F. Crosetti	1	R. Maranville	1	A. Ward	1
L. Culbertson	1	M. Marion	1	Z. Wheat	1
R. Cullenbine	1	B. Martin	1	B. White	1
K. Cuyler	1	E. Mathews	1	B. Whitehead	1
T. Davis	1	W. Mays	1	G. Whiteman	1
W. Davis	1	T. McCarver	1	G. Whitted	1
C. Deal	1	G. McDougald	1	J. Wilson	1
A. Devlin	1				

TOTAL   133

3 or More Stolen Bases - Per Series				Times 3 or More Stolen Bases - Per Series	
L. Brock	7	1968	*	E. Collins	3
L. Brock	7	1967	*	L. Brock	2
J. Slagle	6	1907	*	F. Chance	2
H. Wagner	6	1909	*	H. Wagner	2
F. Chance	5	1908	*	B. Campaneris	1
P. Martin	5	1931	*	M. Carey	1
B. Tolan	5	1972	*	F. Clarke	1
E. Collins	4	1910	*	Jim Collins	1
J. Devore	4	1912	*	W. Davis	1
B. Campaneris	3	1973	*	A. Devlin	1
M. Carey	3	1925	*	J. Devore	1
F. Chance	3	1907		J. Evers	1
F. Clarke	3	1909		F. Frisch	1
E. Collins	3	1913	*	T. Jones	1
E. Collins	3	1917	*	P. Martin	1
Jim Collins	3	1903	*	J. Miller	1
W. Davis	3	1965	*	P. Reese	1
A. Devlin	3	1905	*	J. Slagle	1
J. Evers	3	1907		B. Tolan	1
F. Frisch	3	1921	*	M. Wills	1
T. Jones	3	1907			
J. Miller	3	1909		TOTAL	25
P. Reese	3	1947	*		
H. Wagner	3	1903	*		
M. Wills	3	1965	*		

* Denotes Series Leaders

24
Leaders in Bases on Balls—Both Clubs

1903			1910			1914	
C. Ritchey	4		J. Sheckard	7		H. Gowdy	5
			1911				
1905			E. Collins	2		**1915**	
R. Bresnahan	4		O. Crandall	2		T. Speaker	4
			L. Doyle	2			
1906			B. Herzog	2		**1916**	
G. Rohe	4		F. Merkle	2		D. Hoblitzel	6
J. Kling	4		R. Murray	2			
			F. Snodgrass	2			
1907						**1917**	
D. Jones	4		**1912**			G. J. Burns	3
			J. Devore	7			
1908						**1918**	
F. Chance	3		**1913**			M. Flack	4
M. McIntyre	3		D. Murphy	2		F. Merkle	4
			R. Murray	2		D. Shean	4
1909			W. Schang	2			
O. Bush	5		H. Shafer	2		**1919**	
F. Clarke	5		A. Strunk	2		H. Groh	8

1920
S. O'Neill 4

1921
R. Youngs 7

1922
R. Youngs 3
A. Ward 3

1923
B. Ruth 8

1924
J. Judge 6
M. Ruel 6

1925
Grant Moore 5

1926
B. Ruth 11

1927
L. Gehrig 3
P. Collins 3

1928
L. Gehrig 6

1929
M. Cochrane 7

1930
M. Bishop 7

1931
J. Foxx 6

1932
B. Ruth 4
E. Combs 4
J. Sewell 4

1933
M. Ott 4

1934
Jo Jo White 8

1935
Jo Jo White 5
G. Goslin 5

1936
T. Lazzeri 4
J. Powell 4
G. Selkirk 4
D. Bartell 4

1937
L. Gehrig 5

1938
L. Gehrig 2
F. Crosetti 2
G. Selkirk 2

1939
G. Selkirk 3

1940
B. McCosky 7

1941
J. Gordon 7

1942
S. Musial 4

1943
J. Gordon 3
M. Marion 3
R. Sanders 3

1944
G. McQuinn 7

1945
R. Cullenbine 8

1946
R. York 6

1947
G. Stirnweiss 8

1948
E. Stanky 7

1949
J. Robinson 4

1950
J. DiMaggio 3
P. Rizzutto 3

1951
G. Woodling 5
H. Thompson 5
B. Thomson 5
W. Westrum 5

1952
J. Robinson 7

1953
G. Woodling 6

1954
H. Thompson 7

1955
J. Gilliam 8

1956
J. Gilliam 7

1957
E. Mathews 8

1958
M. Mantle 7

1959
N. Fox 4
A. Smith 4

1960
M. Mantle 8

1961			1966			1970	
Y. Berra	5		J. Lefebvre	3		D. Johnson	5
1962			M. Wills	3		B. Powell	5
R. Maris	5						
			1967			1971	
1963			D. Maxvill	4		W. Stargell	7
J. Gilliam	3		C. Yastrzemski	4			
R. Fairly	3					1972	
			1968			J. Bench	5
1964			D. Wert	6		M. Epstein	5
M. Mantle	6						
T. Tresh	6						
			1969			1973	
1965			F. Robinson	4		G. Tenace	11
H. Killebrew	6		A. Weis	4			

Times Leading Bases on Balls - Both Clubs

L. Gehrig	4	J. DiMaggio	1	M. Ott	1
J. Gilliam	3	L. Doyle	1	B. Powell	1
M. Mantle	3	M. Epstein	1	J. Powell	1
B. Ruth	3	R. Fairly	1	C. Ritchey	1
G. Selkirk	3	M. Flack	1	F. Robinson	1
J. Gordon	2	N. Fox	1	P. Rizzuto	1
F. Merkle	2	J. Foxx	1	G. Rohe	1
R. Murray	2	G. Goslin	1	M. Ruel	1
J. Robinson	2	H. Gowdy	1	R. Sanders	1
H. Thompson	2	H. Groh	1	W. Schang	1
Jo Jo White	2	B. Herzog	1	J. Sewell	1
G. Woodling	2	D. Hoblitzel	1	H. Shafer	1
R. Youngs	2	D. Johnson	1	D. Shean	1
D. Bartell	1	D. Jones	1	J. Sheckard	1
J. Bench	1	J. Judge	1	Al Smith	1
Y. Berra	1	H. Killebrew	1	F. Snodgrass	1
M. Bishop	1	J. Kling	1	T. Speaker	1
R. Bresnahan	1	T. Lazzeri	1	E. Stanky	1
G. J. Burns	1	J. Lefebvre	1	W. Stargell	1
O. Bush	1	M. Marion	1	G. Stirnweiss	1
F. Chance	1	R. Maris	1	A. Strunk	1
F. Clarke	1	E. Mathews	1	G. Tenace	1
M. Cochrane	1	D. Maxvill	1	B. Thomson	1
E. Collins	1	B. McCosky	1	T. Tresh	1
P. Collins	1	G. McQuinn	1	A. Ward	1
E. Combs	1	M. McIntyre	1	A. Weis	1
O. Crandall	1	Grant Moore	1	D. Wert	1
F. Crosetti	1	D. Murphy	1	W. Westrum	1
R. Cullenbine	1	S. Musial	1	M. Wills	1
J. Devore	1	S. O'Neill	1	C. Yastrzemski	1
				R. York	1

TOTAL   110

6 or More Bases on Balls - Per Series

B. Ruth	11	1926	*	H. Thompson	7	1954	*
G. Tenace	11	1973	*	R. Youngs	7	1921	*
R. Cullenbine	8	1945	*	Joe Collins	6	1955	
J. Gilliam	8	1955	*	J. DiMaggio	6	1947	
H. Groh	8	1919	*	J. Foxx	6	1931	*
M. Mantle	8	1960	*	L. Gehrig	6	1928	*
E. Mathews	8	1957	*	H. Greenberg	6	1945	
B. Ruth	8	1923	*	D. Hoblitzel	6	1916	*
G. Stirnweiss	8	1947	*	J. Judge	6	1924	*
Jo Jo White	8	1934	*	H. Killebrew	6	1965	
M. Bishop	7	1930	*	M. Mantle	6	1956	
M. Cochrane	7	1929	*	M. Mantle	6	1964	*
J. Devore	7	1912	*	E. Mathews	6	1958	
J. Gilliam	7	1956	*	R. Meusel	6	1926	
J. Gordon	7	1941	*	P. Reese	6	1947	
M. Mantle	7	1958	*	M. Ruel	6	1924	*
B. McCosky	7	1940	*	D. Snider	6	1956	
G. McQuinn	7	1944	*	T. Tresh	6	1964	*
J. Robinson	7	1952	*	R. York	6	1946	*
J. Sheckard	7	1910	*	D. Wert	6	1968	*
E. Stanky	7	1948	*	G. Woodling	6	1953	*
W. Stargell	7	1971	*				

* Denotes Series Leader

Times 6 or More Bases on Balls - Per Series

M. Mantle	4	G. McQuinn	1
J. Gilliam	2	R. Meusel	1
E. Mathews	2	P. Reese	1
B. Ruth	2	J. Robinson	1
M. Bishop	1	M. Ruel	1
M. Cochrane	1	J. Sheckard	1
Joe Collins	1	D. Snider	1
R. Cullenbine	1	E. Stanky	1
J. DiMaggio	1	W. Stargell	1
J. Devore	1	G. Stirnweiss	1
J. Foxx	1	H. Thompson	1
L. Gehrig	1	G. Tenace	1
J. Gordon	1	T. Tresh	1
H. Greenberg	1	Jo Jo White	1
H. Groh	1	G. Woodling	1
D. Hoblitzel	1	R. York	1
J. Judge	1	R. Youngs	1
H. Killebrew	1	D. Wert	1
B. McCosky	1		
		TOTAL	43

25
Leaders in Batting Average—Both Clubs

1903
J. Sebring .367

1905
M. Donlin .316

1906
G. Rohe .333
J. Donahue .333

1907
H. Steinfeldt .471

1908
F. Chance .421

1909
J. Delahanty .346

1910
E. Collins .429

1911
J. F. Baker .375

1912
B. Herzog .400

1913
J. McLean .500

1914
H. Gowdy .545

1915
D. Lewis .444

1916
D. Lewis .353

1917
D. Robertson .500

1918
C. Pick .389

1919
J. Jackson .375

1920
Z. Wheat .333
S. O'Neill .333

1921
E. Meusel .345

1922
H. Groh .474

1923
C. Stengel .417
A. Ward .417

1924
J. Judge .385

1925
M. Carey .458

1926
T. Thevenow .417

1927
M. Koenig .500

1928
B. Ruth .625

1929
H. Wilson .471

1930
A. Simmons .364

1931
P. Martin .500

1932
L. Gehrig .529

1933
M. Ott .389

1934
J. Medwick .379
C. Gehringer .379

1935
P. Fox .385

1936
J. Powell .455

1937
T. Lazzeri .400

1938
S. Hack .471

1939
C. Keller .438

1940
M. Higgins .375

1941
J. Gordon .500

1942
P. Rizzuto .381

1943
M. Marion .357

1944
G. McQuinn .438

1945
P. Cavarretta .423

1946
H. Walker .412

1947
T. Henrich .323

1948
B. Elliott .333

1949
P. Reese .316

1950
G. Hamner .429
G. Woodling .429

1951
M. Irvin .458

1952
G. Woodling .348

1953
B. Martin .500

1954
V. Wertz .500

1955
Y. Berra .417

1956
Y. Berra .360

1957
H. Aaron .393

1958
B. Bruton .412

1959
G. Hodges .391
T. Kluszewski .391

1960
M. Mantle .400

1961
B. Richardson .391

1962
J. Pagan .368

1963
T. Davis .400

1964
T. McCarver .478

1965
R. Fairly .379

1966
B. Powell .357

1967
L. Brock .414

1968
L. Brock .464

	1969			1971			1973	
A. Weis		.454	R. Clemente		.414	R. Staub		.423
	1970			1972				
P. Blair		.474	T. Perez		.435			

Times Leading in Batting Average - Both Clubs

Y. Berra	2	H. Groh	1	M. Ott	1
L. Brock	2	S. Hack	1	J. Pagan	1
D. Lewis	2	G. Hamner	1	T. Perez	1
G. Woodling	2	T. Henrich	1	C. Pick	1
H. Aaron	1	B. Herzog	1	B. Powell	1
J. F. Baker	1	M. Higgins	1	J. Powell	1
P. Blair	1	G. Hodges	1	P. Reese	1
B. Bruton	1	M. Irvin	1	B. Richardson	1
M. Carey	1	J. Jackson	1	P. Rizzuto	1
P. Cavaretta	1	J. Judge	1	D. Robertson	1
F. Chance	1	C. Keller	1	G. Rohe	1
R. Clemente	1	T. Kluszewski	1	B. Ruth	1
E. Collins	1	M. Koenig	1	J. Sebring	1
T. Davis	1	T. Lazzeri	1	A. Simmons	1
J. Delahanty	1	M. Mantle	1	R. Staub	1
J. Donahue	1	M. Marion	1	H. Steinfeldt	1
M. Donlin	1	B. Martin	1	C. Stengel	1
B. Elliott	1	P. Martin	1	T. Thevenow	1
R. Fairly	1	T. McCarver	1	H. Walker	1
P. Fox	1	J. McLean	1	A. Ward	1
L. Gehrig	1	G. McQuinn	1	V. Wertz	1
C. Gehringer	1	J. Medwick	1	Z. Wheat	1
J. Gordon	1	E. Meusel	1	H. Wilson	1
H. Gowdy	1	S. O'Neill	1	A. Weis	1

TOTAL   76

B. Ruth	.625	1928	*	G. Hamner	.429	1950	*
H. Gowdy	.545	1914	*	B. Robinson	.429	1970	
L. Gehrig	.545	1928		G. Woodling	.429	1950	*
L. Gehrig	.529	1932	*	P. Cavarretta	.423	1945	*
J. McLean	.500	1913	*	R. Staub	.423	1973	*
D. Robertson	.500	1917	*	F. Chance	.421	1908	*
M. Koenig	.500	1927	*	E. Collins	.421	1913	
P. Martin	.500	1931	*	J. Dykes	.421	1929	
J. Gordon	.500	1941	*	A. Ward	.417	1923	*
B. Martin	.500	1953	*	C. Stengel	.417	1923	*
V. Wertz	.500	1954	*	T. Thevenow	.417	1926	*
T. McCarver	.478	1964	*	A. Dark	.417	1951	
P. Blair	.474	1970	*	Y. Berra	.417	1955	*
H. Groh	.474	1922	*	L. Brock	.414	1967	*
H. Steinfeldt	.471	1907	*	R. Clemente	.414	1971	*
F. Frisch	.471	1922		E. Verban	.412	1944	
H. Wilson	.471	1929	*	H. Walker	.412	1946	*
S. Hack	.471	1938	*	A. Dark	.412	1954	
L. Brock	.464	1968	*	B. Bruton	.412	1958	*
P. Cavarretta	.462	1938		J. F. Baker	.409	1910	
M. Carey	.458	1925	*	E. Collins	.409	1917	
M. Irvin	.458	1951	*	B. Richardson	.406	1964	
J. Powell	.455	1936	*	L. Waner	.400	1927	
A. Weis	.454	1969	*	M. Cochrane	.400	1929	
J. F. Baker	.450	1913		R. Rolfe	.400	1936	
D. Lewis	.444	1915	*	T. Lazzeri	.400	1937	*
R. Stephenson	.444	1932		B. Dickey	.400	1938	
J. Harris	.440	1925		J. Gordon	.400	1938	
J. Evers	.438	1914		F. McCormick	.400	1939	
F. Luderus	.438	1915		M. Mantle	.400	1960	*
B. Dickey	.438	1932		T. Davis	.400	1963	*
C. Keller	.438	1939	*	C. Rossman	.400	1907	
G. McQuinn	.438	1944	*	B. Herzog	.400	1912	*
T. Perez	.435	1972	*	F. Frisch	.400	1923	
Y. Berra	.429	1953		B. Ruth	.400	1927	
E. Collins	.429	1910	*	R. Swoboda	.400	1969	

TOTAL 72

E. Collins	3	H. Gowdy	1	J. Powell	1
J. F. Baker	2	H. Groh	1	B. Richardson	1
Y. Berra	2	S. Hack	1	D. Robertson	1
L. Brock	2	G. Hamner	1	B. Robinson	1
P. Cavarretta	2	J. Harris	1	R. Rolfe	1
A. Dark	2	B. Herzog	1	C. Rossman	1
B. Dickey	2	M. Irvin	1	R. Staub	1
F. Frisch	2	C. Keller	1	H. Steinfeldt	1
L. Gehrig	2	M. Koenig	1	C. Stengel	1
J. Gordon	2	T. Lazzeri	1	R. Stephenson	1
B. Ruth	2	D. Lewis	1	R. Swoboda	1
P. Blair	1	F. Luderus	1	T. Thevenow	1
B. Bruton	1	M. Mantle	1	E. Verban	1
M. Carey	1	B. Martin	1	H. Walker	1
F. Chance	1	P. Martin	1	L. Waner	1
R. Clemente	1	T. McCarver	1	A. Ward	1
M. Cochrane	1	F. McCormick	1	A. Weis	1
T. Davis	1	J. McLean	1	V. Wertz	1
J. Dykes	1	G. McQuinn	1	H. Wilson	1
J. Evers	1	T. Perez	1	G. Woodling	1

TOTAL   72

26
Players Leading in Offensive Departments—Per Series

1903		1911		1917	
P. Dougherty	4	J. F. Baker	10	D. Robertson	6
J. Sebring	4				
		1912		**1918**	
1905		B. Herzog	7	C. Pick	6
R. Bresnahan	6				
		1913		**1919**	
1906		J. F. Baker	5	J. Jackson	7
G. Rohe	7	E. Collins	5		
				1920	
1907		**1914**		T. Speaker	5
H. Steinfeldt	6	H. Gowdy	11		
				1921	
1908		**1915**		E. Meusel	7
F. Chance	5	H. Hooper	4		
		D. Lewis	4	**1922**	
1909				H. Groh	7
F. Clarke	6	**1916**			
		H. Hooper	6	**1923**	
1910		D. Lewis	6	B. Ruth	7
D. Murphy	7				

1924
G. Goslin 6

1925
J. Harris 6

1926
B. Ruth 8

1927
L. Gehrig 6
B. Ruth 6

1928
B. Ruth 7

1929
J. Foxx 5

1930
A. Simmons 6

1931
P. Martin 9

1932
L. Gehrig 9

1933

M. Ott 10

1934
H. Greenberg 6

1935
P. Fox 7

1936
G. Selkirk 6

1937
L. Gehrig 6

1938
F. Crosetti 8

1939
C. Keller 10

1940
M. Higgins 8

1941
J. Gordon 10

1942
C. Keller 5

1943
M. Marion 8

1944
G. McQuinn 9

1945
H. Greenberg 7

1946
R. York 7

1947
T. Henrich 5

1948
B. Elliott 8

1949
B. Brown 7

1950
G. Hamner 9

1951
A. Dark 7

1952
D. Snider 7

1953
B. Martin 11

1954
V. Wertz 8

1955
D. Snider 6

1956
Y. Berra 9

1957
H. Aaron 10

1958
H. Bauer 8

1959
T. Kluszewski 7

1960
M. Mantle 7

1961
E. Howard 4
J. Blanchard 4
B. Richardson 4

1962
T. Tresh 7

1963
T. Davis 7

1964
M. Mantle 9

1965
R. Fairly 10

1966
F. Robinson 8

1967
L. Brock 6
C. Yastrzemski 6

<table>
<tr><td colspan="2">1968</td><td colspan="2">1970</td><td colspan="2">1972</td></tr>
<tr><td>L. Brock</td><td>10</td><td>L. May</td><td>7</td><td>G. Tenace</td><td>7</td></tr>
<tr><td colspan="2">1969</td><td colspan="2">1971</td><td colspan="2">1973</td></tr>
<tr><td>D. Clendenon</td><td>7</td><td>R. Clemente</td><td>9</td><td>R. Jackson</td><td>6</td></tr>
</table>

Times Players Leading in Offensive Departments - Per Series

B. Ruth	4	A. Dark	1	P. Martin	1
L. Gehrig	3	T. Davis	1	L. May	1
J. F. Baker	2	P. Dougherty	1	E. Meusel	1
L. Brock	2	B. Elliot	1	G. McQuinn	1
H. Greenberg	2	R. Fairly	1	D. Murphy	1
H. Hooper	2	P. Fox	1	M. Ott	1
C. Keller	2	J. Foxx	1	C. Pick	1
D. Lewis	2	J. Gordon	1	B. Richardson	1
M. Mantle	2	G. Goslin	1	D. Robertson	1
D. Snider	2	H. Gowdy	1	F. Robinson	1
H. Aaron	1	H. Groh	1	G. Rohe	1
H. Bauer	1	G. Hamner	1	J. Sebring	1
Y. Berra	1	J. Harris	1	G. Selkirk	1
J. Blanchard	1	T. Henrich	1	A. Simmons	1
R. Bresnahan	1	B. Herzog	1	T. Speaker	1
B. Brown	1	M. Higgins	1	H. Steinfeldt	1
F. Chance	1	E. Howard	1	G. Tenace	1
F. Clarke	1	J. Jackson	1	T. Tresh	1
R. Clemente	1	R. Jackson	1	V. Wertz	1
D. Clendenon	1	T. Kluszewski	1	C. Yastrzemski	1
XXXXX		M. Marion	1	R. York	1
E. Collins	1	B. Martin	1		
F. Crosetti	1			TOTAL	78

1	H. Gowdy	11	1914	Braves
2	B. Martin	11	1953	Yanks
3	J. F. Baker	10	1911	A's
4	M. Ott	10	1933	Giants
5	C. Keller	10	1939	Yanks
6	J. Gordon	10	1941	Yanks
7	H. Aaron	10	1957	Braves
8	R. Fairly	10	1965	Dodgers
9	L. Brock	10	1968	Cards
10	P. Martin	9	1931	Cards
11	L. Gehrig	9	1932	Yanks
12	G. McQuinn	9	1944	Browns
13	G. Hamner	9	1950	Phillies
14	Y. Berra	9	1956	Yanks
15	M. Mantle	9	1964	Yanks
16	R. Clemente	9	1971	Pirates
17	B. Ruth	8	1926	Yanks
18	F. Crosetti	8	1938	Yanks
19	M. Higgins	8	1940	Tigers
20	M. Marion	8	1943	Cards
21	B. Elliott	8	1948	Braves
22	V. Wertz	8	1954	Indians
23	H. Bauer	8	1958	Yanks
24	F. Robinson	8	1966	Orioles

TOTAL   24

By Clubs

Yanks	9
Cards	3
Braves	3
A's	1
Browns	1
Dodgers	1
Giants	1
Indians	1
Orioles	1
Phillies	1
Pirates	1
Tigers	1
TOTAL	24

27
Triple Crown Leaders

	Home Runs		R. B. I.		Batting Average	
1911	J. F. Baker	2	J. F. Baker	5	J. F. Baker	.375
1914	H. Gowdy	1	H. Gowdy	3	H. Gowdy	.545
1921	E. Meusel	1	E. Meusel	7	E. Meusel	.345
1932	L. Gehrig	3	L. Gehrig	8	L. Gehrig	.529
1933	M. Ott	2	M. Ott	4	M. Ott	.389
1939	C. Keller	3	C. Keller	6	C. Keller	.438
1940	M. Higgins	1	M. Higgins	6	M. Higgins	.375
1941	J. Gordon	1	J. Gordon	5	J. Gordon	.500
1944	G. McQuinn	1	G. McQuinn	5	G. McQuinn	.438
1948	B. Elliott	2	B. Elliott	5	B. Elliott	.333
1953	B. Martin	2	B. Martin	8	B. Martin	.500
1956	Y. Berra	3	Y. Berra	10	Y. Berra	.360
1957	H. Aaron	3	H. Aaron	7	H. Aaron	.393
1959	T. Kluszewski	3	T. Kluszewski	10	T. Kluszewski	.391
1965	R. Fairly	2	R. Fairly	6	R. Fairly	.379

Part Three: World Series Individual Home Run Records

28

World Series Total Home Run Records

* Winning Game or Deciding outcome of Game with Home Run

Player	HR No.	Year	Game	Inn.	Batt. Style	Pitcher	Pitch Style	COMMENTS
J. Sebring	1	1903	1	7th	L	C. Young	R	
P. Dougherty*	2	1903	2	1st	L	S. Leever	R	(First Player to hit two HR's)
P. Dougherty	3	1903	2	6th	L	F. Veil	R	(In a Game — 1st HR won Ball) (Game.)
J. Tinker*	4	1908	2	8th	R	W. Donovan	R	Won Ball Game with HR
F. Clarke	5	1909	1	4th	L	G. Mullin	R	
D. Jones	6	1909	5	1st	L	B. Adams	R	
F. Clarke*	7	1909	5	7th	L	O. Summers	R	Won Ball Game with HR
S. Crawford	8	1909	5	8th	L	B. Adams	R	
D. Murphy*	9	1910	3	3rd	R	H. McIntire	R	Won Ball Game with HR
J. F. Baker*	10	1911	2	7th	L	R. Marquard	L	Won Ball Game with HR
J. F. Baker	11	1911	3	9th	L	C. Mathewson	R	
R. Oldring	12	1911	5	3rd	R	R. Marquard	L	
L. Gardner	13	1912	7	2nd	L	J. Tesreau	R	
L. Doyle	14	1912	7	6th	L	C. Hall	R	
J. F. Baker *	15	1913	1	5th	L	R. Marquard	L	Won Ball Game with HR
W. Schang	16	1913	3	8th	L	J. Crandall	R	
F. Merkle	17	1913	4	7th	R	C. Bender	R	
H. Gowdy	18	1914	3	10th	R	L. Bush	R	
H. Hooper	19	1915	5	3rd	L	J. Mayer	R	
F. Luderus	20	1915	5	4th	L	G. Foster	R	
D. Lewis	21	1915	5	8th	L	E. Rixey	L	
H. Hooper*	22	1915	5	9th	L	E. Rixey	L	Won Ball Game with 2nd HR of the Game
H. Myers	23	1916	2	1st	R	B. Ruth	L	
L. Gardner	24	1916	3	7th	L	J. Coombs	R	
L. Gardner*	25	1916	4	2nd	L	R. Marquard	L	Won Ball Game with HR
O. Felsch*	26	1917	1	4th	R	H. Sallee	L	Won Ball Game with HR
B. Kauff*	27	1917	4	4th	L	U. Faber	R	Won Ball Game with HR
B. Kauff	28	1917	4	8th	L	D. Danforth	L	Hit his 2nd HR of the Game
J. Jackson	29	1919	8	3rd	L	H. Eller	R	

Player	HR No.	Year	Game	Inn	Batt. Style	Pitcher	Pitch Style	COMMENTS
E. Smith*	30	1920	5	1st	L	B. Grimes	R	Hit 1st Grand Slam HR in World Series history to win Ball Game
J. Bagby, Sr.	31	1920	5	4th	L	B. Grimes	R	
B. Ruth	32	1921	4	9th	L	P. Douglas	R	
E. Meusel	33	1921	6	2nd	R	H. Harper	L	
F. Snyder	34	1921	6	2nd	R	H. Harper	L	
W. Fewster	35	1921	6	2nd	R	J. Barnes	R	
E. Meusel	36	1922	2	1st	R	B. Shawkey	R	
A. Ward	37	1922	2	4th	R	J. Barnes	R	
A. Ward	38	1922	4	7th	R	H. McQuillan	R	
C. Stengel*	39	1923	1	9th	L	L. Bush	R	Won Ball Game with HR-Score-1-0
A. Ward	40	1923	2	2nd	R	H. McQuillan	R	
E. Meusel	41	1923	2	2nd	R	H. Pennock	L	
B. Ruth	42	1923	2	4th	L	H. McQuillan	R	
B. Ruth	43	1923	2	5th	L	J. Bentley	L	Hit his 2nd HR of the Game
C. Stengel*	44	1923	3	7th	L	S. Jones	R	Won Ball Game with HR
R. Youngs	45	1923	4	9th	R	H. Pennock	L	
J. Dugan	46	1923	5	2nd	R	J. Bentley	L	
B. Ruth	47	1923	6	1st	L	A. Nehf	L	
F. Snyder	48	1923	6	5th	R	H. Pennock	L	
G. Kelly	49	1924	1	2nd	R	W. Johnson	R	
B. Terry	50	1924	1	4th	L	W. Johnson	R	
G. Goslin	51	1924	2	1st	L	J. Bentley	L	
S. Harris	52	1924	2	5th	R	J. Bentley	L	
J. Ryan	53	1924	3	4th	L	A. Russell	R	
G. Goslin	54	1924	4	3rd	L	J. Barnes	R	
J. Bentley*	55	1924	5	5th	L	W. Johnson	R	Won Ball Game with HR
G. Goslin	56	1924	5	8th	L	J. Bentley	L	
S. Harris	57	1924	7	4th	R	J. Barnes	R	
J. Harris	58	1925	1	2nd	R	H. Meadows	R	
H. Traynor	59	1925	1	5th	R	W. Johnson	R	
J. Judge	60	1925	2	2nd	L	V. Aldridge	R	
G. Wright	61	1925	2	4th	R	S. Coveleskie	R	
K. Cuyler*	62	1925	2	8th	R	S. Coveleskie	R	Won Ball Game with HR
G. Goslin	63	1925	3	6th	L	R. Kremer	R	
G. Goslin*	64	1925	4	3rd	L	E. Yde	L	Won Ball Game with HR
J. Harris	65	1925	4	3rd	R	E. Yde	L	
J. Harris	66	1925	5	4th	R	V. Aldridge	R	
G. Goslin	67	1925	6	1st	L	R. Kremer	R	
Grant Moore*	68	1925	6	5th	R	J. Ferguson	R	Won Ball Game with HR
R. Peckinpaugh	69	1925	7	8th	R	R. Kremer	R	
B. Southworth*	70	1926	2	7th	L	U. Shocker	R	Won Ball Game with HR
T. Thevenow	71	1926	2	9th	R	S. Jones	R	
J. Haines	72	1926	3	4th	R	W. Ruether	L	
B. Ruth	73	1926	4	1st	L	F. Rhem	R	
B. Ruth	74	1926	4	3rd	L	F. Rhem	R	Hit his 2nd HR of the Game
B. Ruth	75	1926	4	6th	L	H. Bell	R	500 ft. HR–3rd HR of the Gm
L. Bell	76	1926	6	7th	R	U. Shocker	R	
B. Ruth	77	1926	7	3rd	L	J. Haines	R	
B. Ruth	78	1927	3	7th	L	M. Cvengros	L	
B. Ruth	79	1927	4	5th	L	C. Hill	R	
R. Meusel*	80	1928	1	4th	R	W. Sherdel	L	Won Ball Game with HR
J. Bottomley	81	1928	1	7th	L	W. Hoyt	R	
L. Gehrig	82	1928	2	1st	L	G. Alexander	R	
L. Gehrig	83	1928	3	2nd	L	J. Haines	R	
L. Gehrig	84	1928	3	4th	L	J. Haines	R	Hit his 2nd HR of the Game
B. Ruth	85	1928	4	4th	L	W. Sherdel	L	
B. Ruth	86	1928	4	7th	L	W. Sherdel	L	Hit his 2nd HR of the Game
L. Gehrig	87	1928	4	7th	L	W. Sherdel	L	
C. Durst	88	1928	4	8th	L	G. Alexander	R	
B. Ruth	89	1928	4	8th	L	G. Alexander	R	Hit his 3rd HR of the Game

Player	HR No.	Year	Game	Inn.	Batt. Style	Pitcher	Pitch Style	COMMENTS
J. Foxx	90	1929	1	7th	R	C. Root	R	
J. Foxx	91	1929	2	3rd	R	P. Malone	R	
A. Simmons	92	1929	2	8th	R	H. Carlson	R	
C. Grimm	93	1929	4	4th	L	J. Quinn	R	
A. Simmons	94	1929	4	7th	R	C. Root	R	
M. Haas	95	1929	4	7th	L	A. Nehf	L	
M. Haas	96	1929	5	9th	L	P. Malone	R	
A. Simmons	97	1930	1	4th	R	B. Grimes	R	
M. Cochrane	98	1930	1	8th	L	B. Grimes	R	
M. Cochrane	99	1930	2	1st	L	F. Rhem	R	
G. Watkins	100	1930	2	2nd	L	G. Earnshaw	R	
T. Douthit*	101	1930	3	4th	R	R. Walberg	L	Won Ball Game with HR
J. Foxx*	102	1930	5	9th	R	B. Grimes	R	Won Ball Game with HR
A. Simmons	103	1930	6	3rd	R	S. Johnson	R	
J. Dykes	104	1930	6	4th	R	S. Johnson	R	
A. Simmons	105	1931	1	7th	R	P. Derringer	R	
A. Simmons	106	1931	3	9th	R	B. Grimes	R	
J. Foxx	107	1931	4	6th	R	S. Johnson	R	
P. Martin*	108	1931	5	6th	R	W. Hoyt	R	Won Ball Game with HR
G. Watkins*	109	1931	7	3rd	L	G. Earnshaw	R	Won Ball Game with HR
L. Gehrig	110	1932	1	4th	L	G. Bush	R	
B. Ruth	111	1932	3	1st	L	C. Root	R	
L. Gehrig	112	1932	3	3rd	L	C. Root	R	
K. Cuyler	113	1932	3	3rd	R	G. Pipgras	R	
B. Ruth	114	1932	3	5th	L	C. Root	R	Hit his 2nd HR of the Game
L. Gehrig *	115	1932	3	5th	L	C. Root	R	Won Ball Game with 2nd HR
G. Hartnett	116	1932	3	9th	R	G. Pipgras	R	
F. Demaree	117	1932	4	1st	R	J. Allen	R	
T. Lazzeri	118	1932	4	3rd	R	L. Warneke	R	
E. Combs	119	1932	4	9th	L	B. Grimes	R	
T. Lazzeri	120	1932	4	9th	R	B. Grimes	R	Hit his 2nd HR of the Game
M. Ott	121	1933	1	1st	L	W. Stewart	L	
G. Goslin	122	1933	2	3rd	L	H. Schumacher	R	Hit 500 ft. HR
B. Terry	123	1933	4	4th	L	M. Weaver	R	
Fred Schulte	124	1933	5	6th	R	H. Schumacher	R	
M. Ott*	125	1933	5	10th	L	J. Russell	R	Won Ball Game with HR
J. Medwick*	126	1934	1	5th	R	A. Crowder	R	Won Ball Game with HR
H. Greenberg	127	1934	1	8th	R	J. Dean	R	
C. Gehringer*	128	1934	5	6th	L	J. Dean	R	Won Ball Game with HR
B. Delancey	129	1934	5	7th	L	T. Bridges	R	
F. Demaree	130	1935	1	9th	R	S. Rowe	R	
H. Greenberg*	131	1935	2	1st	R	C. Root	R	Won Ball Game with HR
F. Demaree	132	1935	3	2nd	R	E. Auker	R	
G. Hartnett	133	1935	4	2nd	R	A. Crowder	R	
C. Klein*	134	1935	5	3rd	L	S. Rowe	R	Won Ball Game with HR
B. Herman	135	1935	6	5th	R	T. Bridges	R	
G. Selkirk	136	1936	1	3rd	L	C. Hubbell	L	
D. Bartell	137	1936	1	5th	R	C. Ruffing	R	
T. Lazzeri	138	1936	2	3rd	R	D. Coffman	R	Hit 2nd Grand Slam HR in W. S. History
B. Dickey	139	1936	2	9th	L	H. Gumbert	R	
L. Gehrig*	140	1936	3	2nd	L	F. Fitzsimmons	R	Won Ball Game with HR
J. Ripple	141	1936	3	5th	L	B. Hadley	R	
L. Gehrig	142	1936	4	3rd	L	C. Hubbell	L	
G. Selkirk	143	1936	5	2nd	L	H. Schumacher	R	
J. Powell	144	1936	6	2nd	R	F. Fitzsimmons	R	
M. Ott	145	1936	6	5th	L	L. Gomez	L	
J. Moore	146	1936	6	8th	L	J. Murphy	R	
T. Lazzeri	147	1937	1	8th	R	Al Smith	L	
L. Gehrig	148	1937	4	9th	L	C. Hubbell	L	
M. Hoag	149	1937	5	2nd	R	C. Melton	L	
J. DiMaggio	150	1937	5	3rd	R	C. Melton	L	

Player	HR No.	Year	Game	Inn.	Batt. Style	Pitcher	Pitch Style	COMMENTS
M. Ott	151	1937	5	3rd	L	L. Gomez	L	
F. Crosetti*	152	1938	2	8th	R	J. Dean	R	Won Ball Game with HR
J. DiMaggio	153	1938	2	9th	R	J. Dean	R	
J. Gordon	154	1938	3	5th	R	C. Bryant	R	
J. Marty	155	1938	3	8th	R	M. Pearson	R	
B. Dickey	156	1938	3	8th	L	L. French	L	
T. Henrich*	157	1938	4	6th	L	C. Root	R	Won Ball Game with HR
K. O'Dea	158	1938	4	8th	L	C. Ruffing	R	
B. Dahlgren	159	1939	2	4th	L	B. Walters	R	
C. Keller	160	1939	3	1st	L	G. Thompson	R	
J. DiMaggio*	161	1939	3	3rd	R	G. Thompson	R	Won Ball Game with HR
C. Keller	162	1939	3	5th	L	G. Thompson	R	Hit his 2nd HR of the Game
B. Dickey	163	1939	3	5th	L	G. Thompson	R	
C. Keller	164	1939	4	7th	L	P. Derringer	R	
B. Dickey	165	1939	4	7th	L	P. Derringer	R	
B. Campbell	166	1940	1	5th	L	L. Moore	R	
J. Ripple*	167	1940	2	3rd	L	S. Rowe	R	Won Ball Game with HR
R. York	168	1940	3	7th	R	J. Turner	R	
M. Higgins*	169	1940	3	7th	R	J. Turner	R	Won Ball Game with HR
H. Greenberg*	170	1940	5	3rd	R	G. Thompson	R	Won Ball Game with HR
B. Walters	171	1940	6	8th	R	F. Hutchinson	R	
J. Gordon	172	1941	1	2nd	R	C. Davis	R	
P. Reiser	173	1941	4	5th	L	A. Donald	R	
T. Henrich	174	1941	5	5th	L	W. Wyatt	R	
C. Keller	175	1942	2	8th	L	J. Beazley	R	
C. Keller	176	1942	4	6th	L	M. Cooper	R	
P. Rizzuto	177	1942	5	1st	R	J. Beazley	R	
E. Slaughter	178	1942	5	4th	L	C. Ruffing	R	
G. Kurowski*	179	1942	5	9th	R	C. Ruffing	R	Won Ball Game with HR
J. Gordon	180	1943	1	4th	R	M. Lanier	L	
M. Marion	181	1943	2	3rd	R	E. Bonham	R	
R. Sanders*	182	1943	2	4th	L	E. Bonham	R	Won Ball Game with HR
B. Dickey*	183	1943	5	6th	L	M. Cooper	R	Won Ball Game with HR
G. McQuinn*	184	1944	1	4th	L	M. Cooper	R	Won Ball Game with HR
S. Musial*	185	1944	4	1st	L	S. Jakucki	R	Won Ball Game with HR
R. Sanders*	186	1944	5	6th	L	D. Galehouse	R	Won Ball Game with HR
D. Litwhiler	187	1944	5	8th	R	D. Galehouse	R	
P. Cavaretta	188	1945	1	7th	L	J. Tobin	R	
H. Greenberg*	189	1945	2	5th	R	H. Wyse	R	Won Ball Game with HR
H. Greenberg	190	1945	6	8th	R	R. Prim	L	
R. York*	191	1946	1	10th	R	H. Pollett	L	Won Ball Game with HR
R. York*	192	1946	3	1st	R	M. Dickson	R	Won Ball Game with HR
E. Slaughter	193	1946	4	2nd	L	T. Hughson	R	
B. Doerr	194	1946	4	8th	R	G. Munger	R	
L. Culbertson	195	1946	5	6th	R	A. Brazle	L	
D. Walker	196	1947	2	4th	L	A. Reynolds	R	
T. Henrich*	197	1947	2	5th	L	V. Lombardi	L	Won Ball Game with HR
J. DiMaggio	198	1947	3	5th	R	J. Hatten	L	
Y. Berra	199	1947	3	7th	L	R. Branca	R	Hit 1st Pinch Hit HR in W. S. History
J. DiMaggio *	200	1947	5	5th	R	R. Barney	R	Won Ball Game with HR
L. Doby*	201	1948	4	3rd	L	J. Sain	R	Won Ball Game with HR
M. Rickert	202	1948	4	7th	L	S. Gromek	R	
R. Elliott	203	1948	5	1st	R	B. Feller	R	
D. Mitchell	204	1948	5	1st	L	N. Potter	R	
R. Elliott	205	1948	5	3rd	R	B. Feller	R	Hit his 2nd HR of the Game
J. Hegan	206	1948	5	4th	R	N. Potter	R	
B. Salkeld	207	1948	5	6th	L	B. Feller	R	
J. Gordon	208	1948	6	6th	R	B. Voiselle	R	
T. Henrich*	209	1949	1	9th	L	D. Newcombe	R	Won Ball Game with HR

Player	HR No.	Year	Game	Inn.	Batt. Style	Pitcher	Pitch Style	COMMENTS
P. Reese	210	1949	3	4th	R	T. Byrne	L	
L. Olmo	211	1949	3	9th	R	J. Page	L	
R. Campanella	212	1949	3	9th	R	J. Page	L	
J. DiMaggio	213	1949	5	4th	R	J. Banta	R	
G. Hodges	214	1949	5	7th	R	V. Raschi	R	
J. DiMaggio*	215	1950	2	10th	R	R. Roberts	R	Won Ball Game with HR
Y. Berra*	216	1950	4	6th	L	J. Konstanty	R	Won Ball Game with HR
A. Dark	217	1951	1	6th	R	A. Reynolds	R	
J. Collins*	218	1951	2	2nd	L	L. Jansen	R	Won Ball Game with HR
W. Lockman	219	1951	3	5th	L	V. Raschi	R	
G. Woodling	220	1951	3	9th	L	S. Jones	R	
J. DiMaggio*	221	1951	4	5th	R	S. Maglie	R	Won Ball Game with HR
G. McDougald*	222	1951	5	3rd	R	L. Jansen	R	Hit 3rd Grand Slam HR in W.S. History, winning Ball Game
P. Rizzuto	223	1951	5	4th	R	M. Kennedy	L	
J. Robinson	224	1952	1	2nd	R	A. Reynolds	R	
G. McDougald	225	1952	1	3rd	R	J. Black	R	
D. Snider*	226	1952	1	6th	L	A. Reynolds	R	Won Ball Game with HR
P. Reese	227	1952	1	8th	R	R. Scarborough	R	
B. Martin	228	1952	2	6th	R	B. Loes	R	
Y. Berra	229	1952	3	8th	L	P. Roe	L	
J. Mize	230	1952	3	9th	L	P. Roe	L	Hit 2nd Pinch Hit HR in W.S. History
J. Mize*	231	1952	4	4th	L	J. Black	R	Won Ball Game with HR
D. Snider	232	1952	5	5th	L	E. Blackwell	R	
J. Mize	233	1952	5	5th	L	C. Erskine	R	
D. Snider	234	1952	6	6th	L	V. Raschi	R	
Y. Berra	235	1952	6	7th	L	B. Loes	R	
M. Mantle*	236	1952	6	8th	L	B. Loes	R	Won Ball Game with HR
D. Snider	237	1952	6	8th	L	V. Raschi	R	Hit his 2nd HR of Game
G. Woodling	238	1952	7	5th	L	J. Black	R	
M. Mantle*	239	1952	7	6th	L	J. Black	R	Won Ball Game with HR
J. Gilliam	240	1953	1	5th	L	A. Reynolds	R	
Y. Berra	241	1953	1	5th	L	J. Hughes	R	
G. Hodges	242	1953	1	6th	R	A. Reynolds	R	
G. Shuba	243	1953	1	6th	L	A. Reynolds	R	Hit 3rd Pinch Hit HR in W.S. History
J. Collins*	244	1953	1	7th	L	C. Labine	R	Won Ball Game with HR
B. Martin	245	1953	2	7th	R	P. Roe	L	
M. Mantle*	246	1953	2	8th	R	P. Roe	L	Won Ball Game with HR
R. Campanella*	247	1953	3	8th	R	V. Raschi	R	Won Ball Game with HR
G. McDougald	248	1953	4	5th	R	B. Loes	R	
D. Snider	249	1953	4	6th	L	J. Sain	R	
G. Woodling	250	1953	5	1st	L	J. Podres	L	
M. Mantle	251	1953	5	3rd	L	R. Meyer	R	Hit 4th Grand Slam HR in W.S. History
B. Martin*	252	1953	5	7th	R	R. Meyer	R	Won Ball Game with HR
B. Cox	253	1953	5	8th	R	J. McDonald	R	
G. McDougald	254	1953	5	9th	R	J. Black	R	
J. Gilliam	255	1953	5	9th	R	B. Kuzava	L	
C. Furillo	256	1953	6	9th	R	A. Reynolds	R	
D. Rhodes*	257	1954	1	10th	L	B. Lemon	R	Won Ball Game with 4th Pinch Hit HR in W. S. History
A. Smith	258	1954	2	1st	R	J. Antonelli	L	
D. Rhodes	259	1954	2	7th	L	E. Wynn	R	
V. Wertz	260	1954	3	7th	L	R. Gomez	R	
H. Majeski	261	1954	4	5th	R	D. Liddle	L	Hit 5th Pinch Hit HR in W.S. History
C. Furillo	262	1955	1	2nd	R	W. Ford	L	
E. Howard	263	1955	1	2nd	R	D. Newcombe	R	
D. Snider	264	1955	1	3rd	L	W. Ford	L	

Player	HR No.	Year	Game	Inn.	Batt. Style	Pitcher	Pitch Style	COMMENTS
J. Collins	265	1955	1	4th	L	D. Newcombe	R	
J. Collins*	266	1955	1	6th	L	D. Newcombe	R	Won Ball Game with 2nd HR of the Game
R. Campanella	267	1955	3	1st	R	B. Turley	R	
M. Mantle	268	1955	3	2nd	R	J. Podres	L	
G. McDougald	269	1955	4	1st	R	C. Erskine	R	
R. Campanella	270	1955	4	4th	R	D. Larsen	R	
G. Hodges	271	1955	4	4th	R	D. Larsen	R	
D. Snider*	272	1955	4	5th	L	J. Kucks	R	Won Ball Game with HR
S. Amoros	273	1955	5	2nd	L	B. Grim	R	
D. Snider	274	1955	5	3rd	L	B. Grim	R	
D. Snider*	275	1955	5	5th	L	B. Grim	R	Won Ball Game with 2nd HR of the Game
B. Cerv	276	1955	5	7th	R	R. Craig	R	Hit 6th Pinch Hit HR in W. S. History
Y. Berra	277	1955	5	8th	L	C. Labine	R	
B. Skowron	278	1955	6	1st	L	K. Spooner	L	
M. Mantle	279	1956	1	1st	L	S. Maglie	R	
J. Robinson	280	1956	1	2nd	R	W. Ford	L	
G. Hodges*	281	1956	1	3rd	R	W. Ford	L	Won Ball Game with HR
B. Martin	282	1956	1	4th	R	S. Maglie	R	
Y. Berra	283	1956	2	2nd	L	D. Newcombe	R	Hit 5th Grand Slam HR in W. S. History
D. Snider	284	1956	2	2nd	L	T. Byrne	L	
B. Martin	285	1956	3	2nd	R	R. Craig	R	
E. Slaughter*	286	1956	3	6th	L	R. Craig	R	Won Ball Game with HR
M. Mantle	287	1956	4	6th	L	E. Roebuck	R	
H. Bauer	288	1956	4	7th	R	D. Drysdale	R	
M. Mantle*	289	1956	5	4th	L	S. Maglie	R	HR Driving in 1st Run of Don Larsen's perfect game - Won Game with HR
Y. Berra*	290	1956	7	1st	L	D. Newcombe	R	Won Ball Game with HR
Y. Berra	291	1956	7	3rd	L	D. Newcombe	R	Hit his 2nd HR of the Game
E. Howard	292	1956	7	4th	R	D. Newcombe	R	
B. Skowron	293	1956	7	7th	R	R. Craig	R	Hit 6th Grand Slam HR in W. S. History
J. Logan	294	1957	2	3rd	R	B. Shantz	L	
H. Bauer	295	1957	2	3rd	R	L. Burdette	R	
T. Kubek	296	1957	3	1st	L	B. Buhl	R	
M. Mantle	297	1957	3	4th	L	G. Conley	R	
H. Aaron	298	1957	3	5th	R	D. Larsen	R	
T. Kubek	299	1957	3	7th	L	B. Trowbridge	R	Hit his 2nd HR of the Game
H. Aaron	300	1957	4	4th	R	T. Sturdivant	R	
F. Torre	301	1957	4	4th	L	T. Sturdivant	R	
E. Howard	302	1957	4	9th	R	W. Spahn	L	
E. Mathews*	303	1957	4	10th	L	B. Grim	R	Won Ball Game with HR
Y. Berra	304	1957	6	3rd	L	B. Buhl	R	
F. Torre	305	1957	6	5th	L	B. Turley	R	
H. Aaron	306	1957	6	7th	R	B. Turley	R	
H. Bauer*	307	1957	6	7th	R	E. Johnson	R	Won Ball Game with HR
D. Crandall	308	1957	7	8th	R	T. Byrne	L	
B. Skowron	309	1958	1	4th	R	W. Spahn	L	
H. Bauer	310	1958	1	5th	R	W. Spahn	L	
B. Bruton	311	1958	2	1st	L	B. Turley	R	
L. Burdette*	312	1958	2	1st	R	D. Maas	R	Won Ball Game with HR
M. Mantle	313	1958	2	4th	L	L. Burdette	R	
H. Bauer	314	1958	2	9th	R	L. Burdette	R	
M. Mantle	315	1958	2	9th	L	L. Burdette	R	Hit his 2nd HR of the Game
H. Bauer	316	1958	3	7th	R	D. McMahon	R	
G. McDougald *	317	1958	5	3rd	R	L. Burdette	R	Won Ball Game with HR

Player	HR No.	Year	Game	Inn.	Batt. Style	Pitcher	Pitch Style	COMMENTS
H. Bauer	318	1958	6	1st	R	W. Spahn	L	
G. McDougald	319	1958	6	10th	R	W. Spahn	L	
D. Crandall	320	1958	7	6th	R	B. Turley	R	
B. Skowron	321	1958	7	8th	R	L. Burdette	R	
T. Kluszewski	322	1959	1	3rd	L	R. Craig	R	
T. Kluszewski	323	1959	1	4th	L	C. Churn	R	Hit his 2nd HR of the Game
C. Neal	324	1959	2	5th	R	B. Shaw	R	
C. Essegian	325	1959	2	7th	R	B. Shaw	R	Hit 7th Pinch Hit HR in W.S. History
C. Neal *	326	1959	2	7th	R	B. Shaw	R	Won Ball Game with 2nd HR of the Game
S. Lollar	327	1959	4	7th	R	R. Craig	R	
G. Hodges *	328	1959	4	8th	R	G. Staley	R	Won Ball Game with HR
D. Snider	329	1959	6	3rd	L	E. Wynn	R	
W. Moon	330	1959	6	4th	L	D. Donovan	R	
T. Kluszewski	331	1959	6	4th	L	J. Podres	L	
C. Essegian	332	1959	6	9th	R	R. Moore	R	Hit 8th Pinch Hit HR in W. S. History
R. Maris	333	1960	1	1st	L	V. Law	R	
B. Mazeroski *	334	1960	1	4th	R	J. Coates	R	Won Ball Game with HR
E. Howard	335	1960	1	9th	R	E. Face	R	Hit 9th Pinch Hit HR in W.S. History
M. Mantle *	336	1960	2	5th	R	F. Green	L	Won Ball Game with HR
M. Mantle	337	1960	2	7th	R	J. Gibbon	L	Hit his 2nd HR of the Game
B. Richardson	338	1960	3	1st	R	C. Labine	R	Hit 7th Grand Slam HR in W.S. History
M. Mantle	339	1960	3	4th	R	F. Green	L	
B. Skowron	340	1960	4	4th	R	V. Law	R	
R. Maris	341	1960	5	3rd	L	H. Haddix	L	
R. Nelson	342	1960	7	1st	L	B. Turley	R	
B. Skowron	343	1960	7	5th	R	V. Law	R	
Y. Berra	344	1960	7	6th	L	E. Face	R	
H. Smith	345	1960	7	8th	R	J. Coates	R	
B. Mazeroski *	346	1960	7	9th	R	R. Terry	R	Won Ball Game with HR
E. Howard *	347	1961	1	4th	R	J. O'Toole	L	Won Ball Game with HR
B. Skowron	348	1961	1	6th	R	J. O'Toole	L	
Gord. Coleman	349	1961	2	4th	R	R. Terry	R	
Y. Berra	350	1961	2	4th	L	J. Jay	R	
J. Blanchard	351	1961	3	8th	L	B. Purkey	R	Hit 10th Pinch Hit HR in W.S. History
R. Maris *	352	1961	3	9th	L	B. Purkey	R	Won Ball Game with HR
J. Blanchard	353	1961	5	1st	L	J. Jay	R	
F. Robinson	354	1961	5	3rd	R	R. Terry	R	
H. Lopez	355	1961	5	4th	R	B. Henry	L	
W. Post	356	1961	5	5th	R	B. Daley	L	
C. Boyer *	357	1962	1	7th	R	B. O'Dell	L	Won Ball Game with HR
W. McCovey	358	1962	2	7th	L	R. Terry	R	
E. Bailey	359	1962	3	9th	L	B. Stafford	R	
T. Haller	360	1962	4	2nd	L	W. Ford	L	
C. Hiller *	361	1962	4	7th	R	M. Bridges	L	Hit 8th Grand Slam HR in W.S. History to win Ball Game
J. Pagan	362	1962	5	5th	R	R. Terry	R	
T. Tresh *	363	1962	5	8th	L	J. Sanford	R	Won Ball Game with HR
R. Maris	364	1962	6	5th	L	B. Pierce	L	
J. Roseboro *	365	1963	1	2nd	L	W. Ford	L	Won Ball Game with HR
T. Tresh	366	1963	1	8th	R	S. Koufax	L	
B. Skowron	367	1963	2	4th	R	A. Downing	L	
F. Howard	368	1963	4	5th	R	W. Ford	L	
M. Mantle	369	1963	4	7th	R	S. Koufax	L	

Player	HR No.	Year	Game	Inn.	Batt. Style	Pitcher	Pitch Style	COMMENTS
T. Tresh	370	1964	1	2nd	R	R. Sadecki	L	
M. Shannon	371	1964	1	6th	R	W. Ford	L	
P. Linz	372	1964	2	9th	R	B. Schultz	R	
M. Mantle*	373	1964	3	9th	L	B. Schultz	R	Won Ball Game with HR
K. Boyer*	374	1964	4	6th	R	A. Downing	L	Hit 9th Grand Slam HR in W. S. History to win Ball Game
T. Tresh	375	1964	5	9th	L	B. Gibson	R	
T. McCarver*	376	1964	5	10th	L	P. Mikkelson	R	Won Ball Game with HR
R. Maris	377	1964	6	6th	L	C. Simmons	L	
M. Mantle	378	1964	6	6th	R	C. Simmons	L	
J. Pepitone	379	1964	6	8th	L	G. Richardson	L	Hit 10th Grand Slam HR in W.S. History
L. Brock	380	1964	7	5th	L	A. Downing	L	
M. Mantle	381	1964	7	6th	L	B. Gibson	R	
K. Boyer	382	1964	7	7th	R	S. Hamilton	L	
C. Boyer	383	1964	7	9th	R	B. Gibson	R	
P. Linz	384	1964	7	9th	R	B. Gibson	R	
R. Fairly	385	1965	1	2nd	L	J. Grant	R	
D. Mincher	386	1965	1	2nd	L	D. Drysdale	R	
Z. Versalles*	387	1965	1	3rd	R	D. Drysdale	R	Won Ball Game with HR
H. Killebrew	388	1965	4	4th	R	D. Drysdale	R	
W. Parker*	389	1965	4	4th	L	J. Grant	R	Won Ball Game with HR
T. Oliva	390	1965	4	6th	L	D. Drysdale	R	
L. Johnson	391	1965	4	8th	R	B. Pleis	L	
B. Allison*	392	1965	6	4th	R	C. Osteen	L	Won Ball Game with HR
J. Grant	393	1965	6	6th	R	H. Reed	R	
R. Fairly	394	1965	6	7th	L	J. Grant	R	
L. Johnson*	395	1965	7	4th	R	J. Kaat	L	Won Ball Game with HR
F. Robinson	396	1966	1	1st	R	D. Drysdale	R	
B. Robinson*	397	1966	1	1st	R	D. Drysdale	R	Won Ball Game with HR
J. Lefebvre	398	1966	1	2nd	R	D. McNally	L	
P. Blair*	399	1966	3	5th	R	C. Osteen	L	Won Ball Game with HR
F. Robinson*	400	1966	4	4th	R	D. Drysdale	R	Won Ball Game with HR
J. Santiago	401	1967	1	3rd	R	B. Gibson	R	
C. Yastrzemski*	402	1967	2	4th	L	D. Hughes	R	Won Ball Game driving in first run of the shut out.
C. Yastrzemski	403	1967	2	7th	L	J. Hoerner	L	Hit his 2nd HR of the Game
M. Shannon*	404	1967	3	2nd	R	G. Bell	R	Won Game with 2 Run HR
R. Smith	405	1967	3	7th	L	N. Briles	R	
R. Maris	406	1967	5	9th	L	J. Lonborg	R	Driving in the only run in the 1st two games - Lonborg pitched.
R. Petrocelli	407	1967	6	2nd	R	D. Hughes	R	
C. Yastrzemski	408	1967	6	4th	L	D. Hughes	R	
R. Smith	409	1967	6	4th	L	D. Hughes	R	
R. Petrocelli	410	1967	6	4th	R	D. Hughes	R	Driving in his second HR of the game - which was a back to back HR.
L. Brock	411	1967	6	7th	L	J. Wyatt	R	
B. Gibson*	412	1967	7	5th	R	J. Lonborg	R	Won Game with HR
J. Javier	413	1967	7	6th	R	J. Lonborg	R	
L. Brock	414	1968	1	7th	L	P. Dobson	R	
W. Horton	415	1968	2	2nd	R	N. Briles	R	
M. Lolich*	416	1968	2	3rd	R	N. Briles	R	Won Game with HR
N. Cash	417	1968	2	6th	L	N. Briles	R	
A. Kaline	418	1968	3	3rd	R	R. Washburn	R	
T. McCarver*	419	1968	3	5th	L	P. Dobson	R	Won Game with 3 run HR
D. McAuliffe	420	1968	3	5th	L	R. Washburn	R	
O. Cepeda	421	1968	3	7th	R	D. McMahon	R	
L. Brock	422	1968	4	1st	L	D. McLain	R	
B. Gibson	423	1968	4	4th	R	J. Sparma	R	
J. Northrup	424	1968	4	4th	L	B. Gibson	R	
O. Cepeda	425	1968	5	1st	R	M. Lolich	L	

Player	HR No.	Year	Game	Inn.	Batt Style	Pitcher	Pitch Style	COMMENTS
J. Northrup	426	1968	6	3rd	L	L. Jaster	L	Hit 11th Grand Slam HR in W. S. History
A. Kaline	427	1968	6	5th	R	S. Carlton	L	
M. Shannon	428	1968	7	9th	R	M. Lolich	L	
D. Buford	429	1969	1	1st	L	T. Seaver	R	Led off HR, 1st Lead Off HR in 1st Game of any W. S.
D. Clendenon	430	1969	2	4th	R	D. McNally	L	
T. Agee*	431	1969	3	1st	R	J. Palmer	R	Won B. G. with Lead Off HR in shutout.
E. Kranepool	432	1969	3	8th	L	D. Leonhard	R	
D. Clendenon	433	1969	4	2nd	R	M. Cuellar	L	
D. McNally	434	1969	5	3rd	R	J. Koosman	L	
F. Robinson	435	1969	5	3rd	R	J. Koosman	L	
D. Clendenon	436	1969	5	6th	R	D. McNally	L	
A. Weis	437	1969	5	7th	R	D. McNally	L	
L. May	438	1970	1	3rd	R	J. Palmer	R	Driving in 2 Runs
B. Powell	439	1970	1	4th	L	G. Nolan	R	Driving in 2 Runs
E. Hendricks	440	1970	1	5th	L	G. Nolan	R	Tied Ball Game
B. Robinson*	441	1970	1	7th	R	G. Nolan	R	Won Ball Game with HR
B. Tolan	442	1970	2	3rd	L	M. Cuellar	L	
B. Powell	443	1970	2	4th	L	J. McGlothlin	R	
J. Bench	444	1970	2	6th	R	M. Drabowsky	R	
F. Robinson	445	1970	3	3rd	R	T. Cloninger	R	
D. Buford*	446	1970	3	5th	L	T. Cloninger	R	Won B. G. with HR
D. McNally	447	1970	3	6th	R	W. Granger	R	12th Grand Slam HR - 1st by Pitcher
B. Robinson	448	1970	4	2nd	R	G. Nolan	R	
P. Rose	449	1970	4	5th	L	J. Palmer	R	
L. May	450	1970	4	8th	R	E. Watt	R	
F. Robinson	451	1970	5	1st	R	J. Merritt	L	
M. Rettenmund	452	1970	5	5th	R	T. Cloninger	R	
F. Robinson	453	1971	1	2nd	R	D. Ellis	R	
M. Rettenmund*	454	1971	1	3rd	R	D. Ellis	R	Won B. G. with 3 run HR
D. Buford	455	1971	1	5th	L	B. Moose	R	
R. Hebner	456	1971	2	8th	L	J. Palmer	R	
F. Robinson	457	1971	3	7th	R	S. Blass	R	
B. Robertson	458	1971	3	7th	R	M. Cuellar	L	
B. Robertson*	459	1971	5	2nd	R	D. McNally	L	Won B. G. driving in 1st Run
R. Clemente	460	1971	6	3rd	R	J. Palmer	R	
D. Buford	461	1971	6	6th	L	B. Moose	R	
R. Clemente	462	1971	7	4th	R	M. Cuellar	L	
G. Tenace	463	1972	1	2nd	R	G. Nolan	R	
G. Tenace *	464	1972	1	5th	R	G. Nolan	R	1st Player to hit HR's his 1st-two times at bat & Won B. G.
J. Rudi*	465	1972	2	3rd	R	R. Grimsley	L	Won B. G. with HR
G. Tenace	466	1972	4	5th	R	D. Gullett	L	
P. Rose	467	1972	5	1st	L	J. Hunter	R	Leading off game with HR
G. Tenace	468	1972	5	2nd	R	J. McGlothlin	R	
D. Menke	469	1972	5	4th	R	J. Hunter	R	
J. Bench	470	1972	6	4th	R	V. Blue	L	
C. Jones	471	1973	2	2nd	R	V. Blue	L	
W. Garrett	472	1973	2	3rd	L	V. Blue	L	
W. Garrett	473	1973	3	1st	L	J. Hunter	R	Led off with HR in last of the 1st Inn.
R. Staub *	474	1973	4	1st	L	K. Holtzman	L	Drove in 1st three runs of the game
D. Campaneris	475	1973	7	3rd	R	J. Matlack	L	Drove in two runs
R. Jackson *	476	1973	7	3rd	L	J. Matlack	L	Driving in 3rd & 4th runs for Oak.

Players Having 1 or More Total Home Runs

Player	HR	Player	HR	Player	HR
M. Mantle	18	T. McCarver	2	J. Judge	1
B. Ruth	15	D. McNally	2	G. Kelly	1
Y. Berra	12	C. Neal	2	E. Kranepool	1
D. Snider	11	J. Northrup	2	H. Killebrew	1
L. Gehrig	10	R. Petrocelli	2	C. Klein	1
J. DiMaggio	8	B. Powell	2	G. Kurowski	1
F. Robinson	8	P. Reese	2	J. Lefebvre	1
B. Skowron	8	M. Rettenmund	2	D. Lewis	1
H. Bauer	7	D. Rhodes	2	D. Litwhiler	1
G. Goslin	7	J. Ripple	2	W. Lockman	1
G. McDougald	7	P. Rizzutto	2	J. Logan	1
R. Maris	6	B. Robertson	2	S. Lollar	1
A. Simmons	6	J. Robinson	2	M. Lolich	1
B. Dickey	5	P. Rose	2	H. Lopez	1
H. Greenberg	5	R. Sanders	2	F. Luderus	1
G. Hodges	5	G. Selkirk	2	H. Majeski	1
E. Howard	5	R. Smith	2	M. Marion	1
C. Keller	5	F. Snider	2	P. Martin	1
B. Martin	5	C. Stengel	2	J. Marty	1
L. Brock	4	B. Terry	2	E. Mathews	1
D. Buford	4	F. Torre	2	D. McAuliffe	1
R. Campanella	4	G. Watkins	2	W. McCovey	1
Joe Collins	4	T. Agee	1	G. McQuinn	1
J. Foxx	4	B. Allison	1	J. Medwick	1
J. Gordon	4	S. Amoros	1	D. Menke	1
T. Henrich	4	J. Bagby, Sr.	1	F. Merkle	1
T. Lazzeri	4	E. Bailey	1	R. Meusel	1
M. Ott	4	D. Bartell	1	D. Mincher	1
G. Tenace	4	L. Bell	1	D. Mitchell	1
T. Tresh	4	J. Bentley	1	W. Moon	1
H. Aaron	3	P. Blair	1	Grant Moore	1
J. F. Baker	3	J. Bottomley	1	Jo Jo Moore	1
D. Clendenon	3	B. Bruton	1	D. Murphy	1
F. Demaree	3	L. Burdette	1	S. Musial	1
L. Gardner	3	B. Campbell	1	H. Myers	1
J. Harris	3	N. Cash	1	R. Nelson	1
T. Kluszewski	3	P. Cavarretta	1	K. O'Dea	1
E. Meusel	3	B. Cerv	1	R. Oldring	1
J. Mize	3	Gord. Coleman	1	T. Oliva	1

B. Robinson	3	E. Combs	1	L. Olmo	1
M. Shannon	3	B. Cox	1	J. Pagan	1
E. Slaughter	3	S. Crawford	1	W. Parker	1
A. Ward	3	F. Crosetti	1	R. Peckinpaugh	1
G. Woodling	3	L. Culbertson	1	J. Pepitone	1
C. Yastrzemski	3	B. Dahlgren	1	W. Post	1
R. York	3	A. Dark	1	J. Powell	1
J. Bench	2	B. Delancey	1	P. Reiser	1
J. Blanchard	2	L. Doby	1	B. Richardson	1
C. Boyer	2	B. Doerr	1	M. Rickert	1
K. Boyer	2	T. Douthit	1	J. Roseboro	1
B. Campaneris	1	L. Doyle	1	J. Rudi	1
O. Cepeda	2	J. Dugan	1	J. Ryan	1
F. Clarke	2	C. Durst	1	B. Salkeld	1
R. Clemente	2	J. Dykes	1	J. Santiago	1
M. Cochrane	2	O. Felsch	1	W. Schang	1
D. Crandall	2	W. Fewster	1	Fred Schulte	1
K. Cuyler	2	C. Gehringer	1	J. Sebring	1
P. Dougherty	2	H. Gowdy	1	G. Shuba	1
B. Elliott	2	J. Grant	1	A. Smith	1
C. Essegian	2	C. Grimm	1	E. Smith	1
R. Fairly	2	J. Haines	1	H. Smith	1
C. Furillo	2	T. Haller	1	B. Southworth	1
W. Garrett	2	R. Hebner	1	R. Staub	1
B. Gibson	2	J. Hegan	1	T. Thevenow	1
J. Gilliam	2	E. Hendricks	1	J. Tinker	1
M. Haas	2	B. Herman	1	B. Tolan	1
S. Harris	2	M. Higgins	1	H. Traynor	1
G. Hartnett	2	C. Hiller	1	Z. Versalles	1
H. Hooper	2	M. Hoag	1	D. Walker	1
L. Johnson	2	W. Horton	1	B. Walters	1
A. Kaline	2	F. Howard	1	A. Weis	1
B. Kauff	2	J. Jackson	1	V. Wertz	1
T. Kubek	2	R. Jackson	1	G. Wright	1
P. Linz	2	J. Javier	1	R. Youngs	1
B. Mazeroski	2	C. Jones	1		
L. May	2	D. Jones	1	TOTAL	476

D. Drysdale	8		J. Jay	2		B. Henry	1
W. Ford	8		S. Jones	2		C. Hill	1
B. Grimes	8		J. Koosman	2		J. Hoerner	1
D. Newcombe	8		S. Koufax	2		K. Holtzman	1
A. Reynolds	8		M. Lolich	2		J. Hughes	1
C. Root	8		P. Malone	2		T. Hughson	1
L. Burdette	6		J. Matlack	2		F. Hutchinson	1
R. Craig	6		J. McGlothlin	2		S. Jakucki	1
B. Gibson	6		D. McMahon	2		L. Jaster	1
G. Nolan	6		C. Melton	2		E. Johnson	1
B. Turley	6		R. Meyer	2		Sheldon Jones	1
J. Bentley	5		B. Moose	2		J. Kaat	1
J. Black	5		A. Nehf	2		M. Kennedy	1
D. Hughes	5		C. Osteen	2		J. Konstanty	1
D. McNally	5		J. O'Toole	2		J. Kucks	1
J. Palmer	5		J. Page	2		B. Kuzava	1
V. Raschi	5		G. Pipgras	2		M. Lanier	1
W. Spahn	5		N. Potter	2		S. Leever	1
R. Terry	5		B. Purkey	2		B. Lemon	1
G. Thompson	5		E. Rixey	2		D. Leonhard	1
J. Barnes	4		J. Sain	2		D. Liddle	1
N. Briles	4		B. Schultz	2		V. Lombardi	1
M. Cuellar	4		C. Simmons	2		D. Maas	1
J. Dean	4		U. Shocker	2		C. Mathewson	1
B. Grim	4		T. Sturdivant	2		J. Mayer	1
W. Johnson	4		J. Turner	2		J. McDonald	1
B. Loes	4		R. Washburn	2		H. McIntyre	1
S. Maglie	4		E. Wynn	2		D. McLain	1
R. Marquard	4		E. Yde	2		H. Meadow	1
P. Roe	4		J. Allen	1		J. Merritt	1
C. Ruffing	4		J. Antonelli	1		P. Mikkelson	1
W. Sherdell	4		E. Auker	1		L. Moore	1
G. Alexander	3		J. Banta	1		R. Moore	1
V. Blue	3		R. Barney	1		G. Mullin	1
T. Byrne	3		G. Bell	1		G. Munger	1
T. Cloninger	3		H. Bell	1		J. Murphy	1
M. Cooper	3		C. Bender	1		B. O'Dell	1
P. Derringer	3		E. Blackwell	1		M. Pearson	1

A. Downing	3	S. Blass	1	B. Pleis	1
B. Feller	3	R. Branca	1	H. Pollet	1
J. Grant	3	A. Brazle	1	R. Prim	1
J. Haines	3	M. Bridges	1	J. Quinn	1
C. Hubbell	3	C. Bryant	1	H. Reed	1
J. Hunter	3	G. Bush	1	G. Richardson	1
S. Johnson	3	S. Carlton	1	R. Roberts	1
R. Kremer	3	H. Carlson	1	E. Roebuck	1
C. Labine	3	C. Churn	1	W. Ruether	1
D. Larsen	3	D. Coffman	1	A. Russell	1
V. Law	3	G. Conley	1	J. Russell	1
J. Lonborg	3	J. Coombs	1	B. Ruth	1
H. McQuillan	3	J. Crandall	1	R. Sadecki	1
H. Pennock	3	M. Cvengros	1	J. Sanford	1
J. Podres	3	B. Daley	1	H. Sallee	1
F. Rhem	3	D. Danforth	1	R. Scarborough	1
S. Rowe	3	C. Davis	1	B. Shantz	1
B. Shaw	3	M. Dickson	1	T. Seaver	1
H. Schumacher	3	A. Donald	1	B. Shawkey	1
B. Adams	2	D. Donovan	1	A. Smith	1
V. Aldridge	2	B. Donovan	1	J. Sparma	1
J. Beazley	2	P. Douglas	1	K. Spooner	1
E. Bonham	2	M. Drabowski	1	B. Stafford	1
T. Bridges	2	H. Eller	1	G. Staley	1
B. Buhl	2	U. Faber	1	W. Stewart	1
L. Bush	2	J. Ferguson	1	W. Summers	1
J. Coates	2	G. Foster	1	J. Tesreau	1
S. Coveleskie	2	L. French	1	J. Tobin	1
A. Crowder	2	J. Gibbon	1	B. Trowbridge	1
P. Dobson	2	R. Gomez	1	F. Veil	1
G. Earnshaw	2	W. Granger	1	B. Voiselle	1
D. Ellis	2	R. Grimsley	1	R. Walberg	1
C. Erskine	2	S. Gromek	1	B. Walters	1
E. Face	2	D. Gullett	1	L. Warneke	1
F. Fitzsimmons	2	H. Gumbert	1	E. Watt	1
D. Galehouse	2	H. Haddix	1	M. Weaver	1
L. Gomez	2	B. Hadley	1	J. Wyatt	1
F. Green	2	C. Hall	1	W. Wyatt	1
H. Harper	2	S. Hamilton	1	H. Wyse	1
W. Hoyt	2	J. Hatten	1	C. Young	1
L. Jansen	2	B. Pierce	1		

TOTAL 476

29

Total Home Run Records by Team

NEW YORK YANKEES

	BB-Mil	BR-LAD	ChC	Cin	NyM	NY SFG	PhP	PP	St. LC	Total
M. Mantle	3	9	0	0	0	0	0	3	3	18
B. Ruth	0	0	2	0	0	4	0	2	7	15
Y. Berra	1	8	0	1	0	0	1	1	0	12
L. Gehrig	0	0	3	0	0	3	0	0	4	10
J. DiMaggio	0	3	1	1	0	2	1	0	0	8
H. Bauer	6	1	0	0	0	0	0	0	0	7
G. McDougald	2	4	0	0	0	1	0	0	0	7
B. Skowron	2	2	0	1	0	0	0	2	0	7
C. Keller	0	0	0	3	0	0	0	0	2	5
B. Martin	0	5	0	0	0	0	0	0	0	5
B. Dickey	0	0	1	2	0	1	0	0	1	5
E. Howard	1	2	0	1	0	0	0	1	0	5
R. Maris	0	0	0	1	0	1	0	2	1	5
T. Lazzeri	0	0	2	0	0	2	0	0	0	4
T. Henrich	0	3	1	0	0	0	0	0	0	4
Joe Collins	0	3	0	0	0	1	0	0	0	4
T. Tresh	0	1	0	0	0	1	0	0	2	4

	BB-Mil	BR-LAD	ChC	Cin	NyM	NY SFG	PhP	PP	St.LC	Total
J. Gordon	0	1	1	0	0	0	0	0	1	3
J. Mize	0	3	0	0	0	0	0	0	0	3
G. Woodling	0	2	0	0	0	1	0	0	0	3
A. Ward	0	0	0	0	0	3	0	0	0	3
C. Boyer	0	0	0	0	0	1	0	0	1	2
J. Blanchard	0	0	0	2	0	0	0	0	0	2
T. Kubek	2	0	0	0	0	0	0	0	0	2
P. Rizzuto	0	0	0	0	0	1	0	0	1	2
P. Linz	0	0	0	0	0	0	0	0	2	2
G. Selkirk	0	0	0	0	0	2	0	0	0	2
B. Cerv	0	1	0	0	0	0	0	0	0	1
E. Slaughter	0	1	0	0	0	0	0	0	0	1
E. Combs	0	0	1	0	0	0	0	0	0	1
F. Crosetti	0	0	1	0	0	0	0	0	0	1
H. Lopez	0	0	0	1	0	0	0	0	0	1
B. Dahlgren	0	0	0	1	0	0	0	0	0	1
J. Dugan	0	0	0	0	0	1	0	0	0	1
M. Hoag	0	0	0	0	0	1	0	0	0	1
W. Fewster	0	0	0	0	0	1	0	0	0	1
J. Powell	0	0	0	0	0	1	0	0	0	1
B. Richardson	0	0	0	0	0	0	0	1	0	1
C. Durst	0	0	0	0	0	0	0	0	1	1
R. Meusel	0	0	0	0	0	0	0	0	1	1
J. Pepitone	0	0	0	0	0	0	0	0	1	1
TOTAL	17	49	13	14	0	28	2	12	28	163

BOSTON RED SOX

	BB-Mil	BR-LAD	ChC	Cin	NyM	NY SFG	PhP	PP	St. LC	Total
C. Yastrzemski	0	0	0	0	0	0	0	0	3	3
L. Gardner	0	2	0	0	0	1	0	0	0	3
P. Dougherty	0	0	0	0	0	0	0	2	0	2
H. Hooper	0	0	0	0	0	0	2	0	0	2
R. Petrocelli	0	0	0	0	0	0	0	0	2	2
R. Smith	0	0	0	0	0	0	0	0	2	2
R. York	0	0	0	0	0	0	0	0	2	2
L. Culbertson	0	0	0	0	0	0	0	0	1	1
B. Doerr	0	0	0	0	0	0	0	0	1	1
D. Lewis	0	0	0	0	0	0	1	0	0	1
J. Santiago	0	0	0	0	0	0	0	0	1	1
TOTAL	0	2	0	0	0	1	3	2	12	20

PHILADELPHIA – OAKLAND ATHLETICS

	BB-Mil	BR-LAD	ChC	Cin	NyM	NY-SFG	PhP	PP	St. LC	Total
A. Simmons	0	0	2	0	0	0	0	0	4	6
J. Foxx	0	0	2	0	0	0	0	0	2	4
G. Tenace	0	0	0	4	0	0	0	0	0	4
J. F. Baker	0	0	0	0	0	3	0	0	0	3
M. Cochrane	0	0	0	0	0	0	0	0	2	2
M. Haas	0	0	2	0	0	0	0	0	0	2
J. Dykes	0	0	0	0	0	0	0	0	1	1
D. Murphy	0	0	1	0	0	0	0	0	0	1
R. Oldring	0	0	0	0	0	1	0	0	0	1
J. Rudi	0	0	0	1	0	0	0	0	0	1
W. Schang	0	0	0	0	0	1	0	0	0	1
B. Campaneris	0	0	0	0	1	0	0	0	0	1
R. Jackson	0	0	0	0	1	0	0	0	0	1
TOTAL	0	0	7	5	2	5	0	0	9	28

DETROIT TIGERS

	BB-Mil	BR-LAD	ChC	Cin	NyM	NY-SFG	PhP	PP	St. LC	Total
H. Greenberg	0	0	3	1	0	0	0	0	1	5
A. Kaline	0	0	0	0	0	0	0	0	2	2
J. Northrup	0	0	0	0	0	0	0	0	2	2
B. Campbell	0	0	0	1	0	0	0	0	0	1
N. Cash	0	0	0	0	0	0	0	0	1	1
S. Crawford	0	0	1	0	0	0	0	0	0	1
C. Gehringer	0	0	0	0	0	0	0	0	1	1
M. Higgins	0	0	0	1	0	0	0	0	0	1
W. Horton	0	0	0	0	0	0	0	0	1	1
D. Jones	0	0	1	0	0	0	0	0	0	1
M. Lolich	0	0	0	0	0	0	0	0	1	1
D. Mc Auliffe	0	0	0	0	0	0	0	0	1	1
R. York	0	0	0	1	0	0	0	0	0	1
TOTAL	0	0	5	4	0	0	0	0	10	19

BALTIMORE ORIOLES

	BB-Mil	BR-LAD	ChC	Cin	NyM	NY-SFG	PhP	PP	St. LC	Total
F. Robinson	0	2	0	2	1	0	0	2	0	7
D. Buford	0	0	0	1	1	0	0	2	0	4
B. Robinson	0	1	0	2	0	0	0	0	0	3
D. Mc Nally	0	0	0	1	1	0	0	0	0	2
B. Powell	0	0	0	2	0	0	0	0	0	2
M. Rettenmund	0	0	0	1	0	0	0	1	0	2
P. Blair	0	1	0	0	0	0	0	0	0	1
E. Hendricks	0	0	0	1	0	0	0	0	0	1
TOTAL	0	4	0	10	3	0	0	5	0	22

WASHINGTON SENATORS

	BB-Mil	BR-LAD	ChC	Cin	NyM	NY-SFG	PhP	PP	St. LC	Total
G. Goslin	0	0	0	0	0	4	0	3	0	7
J. Harris	0	0	0	0	0	0	0	3	0	3
S. Harris	0	0	0	0	0	2	0	0	0	2
J. Judge	0	0	0	0	0	0	0	1	0	1
R. Peckinpaugh	0	0	0	0	0	0	0	1	0	1
Fred Schulte	0	0	0	0	0	1	0	0	0	1
TOTAL	0	0	0	0	0	7	0	8	0	15

CHICAGO WHITE SOX

	BB-Mil	BR-LAD	ChC	Cin	NyM	NY-SFG	PhP	PP	St. LC	Total
T. Kluszewski	0	3	0	0	0	0	0	0	0	3
S. Lollar	0	1	0	0	0	0	0	0	0	1
J. Jackson	0	0	0	1	0	0	0	0	0	1
O. Felsch	0	0	0	0	0	1	0	0	0	1
TOTAL	0	4	0	1	0	1	0	0	0	6

CLEVELAND INDIANS

	BB-Mil	BR-LAD	ChC	Cin	NyM	NY-SFG	PhP	PP	St. LC	Total
E. Smith	0	1	0	0	0	0	0	0	0	1
J. Bagby, Sr.	0	1	0	0	0	0	0	0	0	1
L. Doby	1	0	0	0	0	0	0	0	0	1
J. Gordon	1	0	0	0	0	0	0	0	0	1
J. Hegan	1	0	0	0	0	0	0	0	0	1
D. Mitchell	1	0	0	0	0	0	0	0	0	1
A. Smith	0	0	0	0	0	1	0	0	0	1
H. Majeski	0	0	0	0	0	1	0	0	0	1
V. Wertz	0	0	0	0	0	1	0	0	0	1
TOTAL	4	2	0	0	0	3	0	0	0	9

MINNESOTA TWINS

	BB-Mil	BR-LAD	ChC	Cin	NyM	NY-SFG	PhP	PP	St. LC	Total
B. Allison	0	1	0	0	0	0	0	0	0	1
J. Grant	0	1	0	0	0	0	0	0	0	1
H. Killebrew	0	1	0	0	0	0	0	0	0	1
D. Mincher	0	1	0	0	0	0	0	0	0	1
T. Oliva	0	1	0	0	0	0	0	0	0	1
Z. Versalles	0	1	0	0	0	0	0	0	0	1
TOTAL	0	6	0	0	0	0	0	0	0	6

ST. LOUIS BROWNS

	BB-Mil	BR-LAD	ChC	Cin	NyM	NY SFG	PhP	PP	St. LC	Total
G. McQuinn	0	0	0	0	0	0	0	0	1	1
TOTAL	0	0	0	0	0	0	0	0	1	1

BROOKLYN – LOS ANGELES DODGERS

	BRS	Balt	ChW	CL	D	Minn	NYY	Ph-Oak	St. LB	W	Total
D. Snider	0	0	1	0	0	0	10	0	0	0	11
G. Hodges	0	0	1	0	0	0	4	0	0	0	5
R. Campanella	0	0	0	0	0	0	4	0	0	0	4
J. Robinson	0	0	0	0	0	0	2	0	0	0	2
P. Reese	0	0	0	0	0	0	2	0	0	0	2
J. Gilliam	0	0	0	0	0	0	2	0	0	0	2
C. Furillo	0	0	0	0	0	0	2	0	0	0	2
C. Neal	0	0	2	0	0	0	0	0	0	0	2
C. Essegian	0	0	2	0	0	0	0	0	0	0	2
R. Fairly	0	0	0	0	0	2	0	0	0	0	2
L. Johnson	0	0	0	0	0	2	0	0	0	0	2
P. Reiser	0	0	0	0	0	0	1	0	0	0	1
D. Walker	0	0	0	0	0	0	1	0	0	0	1
L. Olmo	0	0	0	0	0	0	1	0	0	0	1
B. Cox	0	0	0	0	0	0	1	0	0	0	1
G. Shuba	0	0	0	0	0	0	1	0	0	0	1
S. Amoros	0	0	0	0	0	0	1	0	0	0	1
J. Roseboro	0	0	0	0	0	0	1	0	0	0	1
B. Skowron	0	0	0	0	0	0	1	0	0	0	1
F. Howard	0	0	0	0	0	0	1	0	0	0	1
H. Myers	1	0	0	0	0	0	0	0	0	0	1
W. Moon	0	0	1	0	0	0	0	0	0	0	1
W. Parker	0	0	0	0	0	1	0	0	0	0	1
J. Lefebvre	0	1	0	0	0	0	0	0	0	0	1
TOTAL	1	1	7	0	0	5	35	0	0	0	49

NEW YORK – SAN FRANCISCO GIANTS

	BRS	Balt	ChW	CL	D	Minn	NYY	Ph-Oak	St. LB	W	Total
M. Ott	0	0	0	0	0	0	2	0	0	2	4
E. Meusel	0	0	0	0	0	0	3	0	0	0	3
B. Kauff	0	0	2	0	0	0	0	0	0	0	2
C. Stengel	0	0	0	0	0	0	2	0	0	0	2
B. Terry	0	0	0	0	0	0	0	0	0	2	2
F. Snyder	0	0	0	0	0	0	2	0	0	0	2
J. Rhodes	0	0	0	2	0	0	0	0	0	0	2
J. Ripple	0	0	0	0	0	0	1	0	0	0	1
Jo Jo Moore	0	0	0	0	0	0	1	0	0	0	1
A. Dark	0	0	0	0	0	0	1	0	0	0	1
D. Bartell	0	0	0	0	0	0	1	0	0	0	1
W. Lockman	0	0	0	0	0	0	1	0	0	0	1
C. Hiller	0	0	0	0	0	0	1	0	0	0	1
T. Haller	0	0	0	0	0	0	1	0	0	0	1
E. Bailey	0	0	0	0	0	0	1	0	0	0	1
J. Pagan	0	0	0	0	0	0	1	0	0	0	1
W. McCovey	0	0	0	0	0	0	1	0	0	0	1
R. Youngs	0	0	0	0	0	0	1	0	0	0	1
L. Doyle	1	0	0	0	0	0	0	0	0	0	1
F. Merkle	0	0	0	0	0	0	0	1	0	0	1
J. Bentley	0	0	0	0	0	0	0	0	0	1	1
W. Ryan	0	0	0	0	0	0	0	0	0	1	1
G. Kelly	0	0	0	0	0	0	0	0	0	1	1
TOTAL	1	0	2	2	0	0	20	1	0	7	33

ST. LOUIS CARDINALS

	BRS	Balt	ChW	CL	D	Minn	NYY	Ph-Oak	St. LB	W	Total
L. Brock	1	0	0	0	2	0	1	0	0	0	4
M. Shannon	1	0	0	0	1	0	1	0	0	0	3
K. Boyer	0	0	0	0	0	0	2	0	0	0	2
O. Cepeda	0	0	0	0	2	0	0	0	0	0	2
B. Gibson	1	0	0	0	1	0	0	0	0	0	2
T. McCarver	0	0	0	0	1	0	1	0	0	0	2
R. Sanders	0	0	0	0	0	0	1	0	1	0	2
E. Slaughter	1	0	0	0	0	0	1	0	0	0	2
G. Watkins	0	0	0	0	0	0	0	2	0	0	2
L. Bell	0	0	0	0	0	0	1	0	0	0	1
J. Bottomley	0	0	0	0	0	0	1	0	0	0	1
B. Delancey	0	0	0	0	1	0	0	0	0	0	1
T. Douthit	0	0	0	0	0	0	0	1	0	0	1
J. Haines	0	0	0	0	0	0	1	0	0	0	1
J. Javier	1	0	0	0	0	0	0	0	0	0	1
G. Kurowski	0	0	0	0	0	0	1	0	0	0	1
D. Litwhiler	0	0	0	0	0	0	0	0	1	0	1
M. Marion	0	0	0	0	0	0	1	0	0	0	1
R. Maris	1	0	0	0	0	0	0	0	0	0	1
P. Martin	0	0	0	0	0	0	0	1	0	0	1
J. Medwick	0	0	0	0	1	0	0	0	0	0	1
S. Musial	0	0	0	0	0	0	0	0	1	0	1
B. Southworth	0	0	0	0	0	0	1	0	0	0	1
T. Thevenow	0	0	0	0	0	0	1	0	0	0	1
TOTAL	6	0	0	0	9	0	14	4	3	0	36

BOSTON – MILWAUKEE BRAVES

	BRS	Balt	ChW	CL	D	Minn	NYY	Ph-Oak	St. LB	W	Total
H. Aaron	0	0	0	0	0	0	3	0	0	0	3
F. Torre	0	0	0	0	0	0	2	0	0	0	2
D. Crandall	0	0	0	0	0	0	2	0	0	0	2
B. Elliott	0	0	0	2	0	0	0	0	0	0	2
H. Gowdy	0	0	0	0	0	0	0	1	0	0	1
M. Rickert	0	0	0	1	0	0	0	0	0	0	1
B. Salkeld	0	0	0	1	0	0	0	0	0	0	1
L. Burdette	0	0	0	0	0	0	1	0	0	0	1
B. Bruton	0	0	0	0	0	0	1	0	0	0	1
J. Logan	0	0	0	0	0	0	1	0	0	0	1
E. Mathews	0	0	0	0	0	0	1	0	0	0	1
TOTAL	0	0	0	4	0	0	11	1	0	0	16

CHICAGO CUBS

	BRS	Balt	ChW	CL	D	Minn	NYY	Ph-Oak	St. LB	W	Total
F. Demaree	0	0	0	0	2	0	1	0	0	0	3
G. Hartnett	0	0	0	0	1	0	1	0	0	0	2
J. Tinker	0	0	0	0	1	0	0	0	0	0	1
C. Grimm	0	0	0	0	0	0	0	1	0	0	1
K. Cuyler	0	0	0	0	0	0	1	0	0	0	1
C. Klein	0	0	0	0	1	0	0	0	0	0	1
B. Herman	0	0	0	0	1	0	0	0	0	0	1
J. Marty	0	0	0	0	0	0	1	0	0	0	1
K. O'Dea	0	0	0	0	0	0	1	0	0	0	1
P. Cavarretta	0	0	0	0	1	0	0	0	0	0	1
TOTAL	0	0	0	0	7	0	5	1	0	0	13

PITTSBURGH PIRATES

	BRS	Balt	ChW	CL	D	Minn	NYY	Ph-Oak	St. LB	W	Total
F. Clarke	0	0	0	0	2	0	0	0	0	0	2
R. Clemente	0	2	0	0	0	0	0	0	0	0	2
B. Mazeroski	0	0	0	0	0	0	2	0	0	0	2
D. Robertson	0	2	0	0	0	0	0	0	0	0	2
K. Cuyler	0	0	0	0	0	0	0	0	0	1	1
R. Hebner	0	1	0	0	0	0	0	0	0	0	1
Grant Moore	0	0	0	0	0	0	0	0	0	1	1
R. Nelson	0	0	0	0	0	0	1	0	0	0	1
J. Sebring	1	0	0	0	0	0	0	0	0	0	1
H. Smith	0	0	0	0	0	0	1	0	0	0	1
H. Traynor	0	0	0	0	0	0	0	0	0	1	1
G. Wright	0	0	0	0	0	0	0	0	0	1	1
TOTAL	1	5	0	0	2	0	4	0	0	4	16

NEW YORK METS

	BRS	Balt	ChW	CL	D	Minn	NYY	Ph-Oak	St. LB	W	Total
D. Clendenon	0	3	0	0	0	0	0	0	0	0	3
W. Garrett	0	0	0	0	0	0	0	2	0	0	2
C. Jones	0	0	0	0	0	0	0	1	0	0	1
T. Agee	0	1	0	0	0	0	0	0	0	0	1
E. Kranepool	0	1	0	0	0	0	0	0	0	0	1
R. Staub	0	0	0	0	0	0	0	1	0	0	1
A. Weis	0	1	0	0	0	0	0	0	0	0	1
TOTAL	0	6	0	0	0	0	0	4	0	0	10

PHILADELPHIA PHILLIES

	BRS	Balt	ChW	CL	D	Minn	NYY	Ph-Oak	St. LB	W	Total
F. Luderus	1	0	0	0	0	0	0	0	0	0	1
TOTAL	1	0	0	0	0	0	0	0	0	0	1

CINCINNATI REDS

	BRS	Balt	ChW	CL	D	Minn	NYY	Ph-Oak	St. LB	W	Total
J. Bench	0	1	0	0	0	0	0	1	0	0	2
L. May	0	2	0	0	0	0	0	0	0	0	2
P. Rose	0	1	0	0	0	0	0	1	0	0	2
Gord Coleman	0	0	0	0	0	0	1	0	0	0	1
D. Menke	0	0	0	0	0	0	0	1	0	0	1
W. Post	0	0	0	0	0	0	1	0	0	0	1
J. Ripple	0	0	0	0	1	0	0	0	0	0	1
F. Robinson	0	0	0	0	0	0	1	0	0	0	1
B. Tolan	0	1	0	0	0	0	0	0	0	0	1
B. Walters	0	0	0	0	1	0	0	0	0	0	1
TOTAL	0	5	0	0	2	0	3	3	0	0	13

30
Home Run Comparison—American League versus National League

AMERICAN LEAGUE

YANKEES	FOR	AGAINST	MARGIN
Dodgers	49	35	+14
Cardinals	28	14	+14
Giants	28	20	+ 8
Braves	17	11	+ 6
Reds	14	3	+11
Cubs	13	5	+ 8
Pirates	12	4	+ 8
Phillies	2	0	+ 2
TOTALS	163	92	+71

ATHLETICS	FOR	AGAINST	MARGIN
Cardinals	9	4	+ 5
Cubs	7	1	+ 6
Giants	5	1	+ 4
Reds	5	3	+ 2
Braves	0	1	- 1
Mets	2	4	- 2
TOTALS	28	14	- 14

RIOLES	FOR	AGAINST	MARGIN
eds	10	5	+ 5
rates	5	5	Even
odgers	4	1	+ 3
ets	3	6	- 3
OTALS	22	17	+ 5

ED SOX	FOR	AGAINST	MARGIN
rdinals	12	6	+6
illies	3	1	+ 2
odgers	2	1	+ 1
ates	2	1	+ 1
ants	1	1	Even
TALS	20	10	+10

GERS	FOR	AGAINST	MARGIN
dinals	10	9	+ 1
ls	4	2	+ 2
tes	2	2	Even
s	3	7	- 4
TALS	19	20	- 1

ATORS	FOR	AGAINST	MARGIN
tes	8	4	+ 4
ts	7	7	Even
ALS	15	11	+ 4

INDIANS	FOR	AGAINST	MARGIN
Dodgers	2	0	+ 2
Braves	4	4	Even
Giants	3	2	† 1
TOTALS	9	6	+ 3

TWINS	FOR	AGAINST	MARGIN
Dodgers	6	5	+ 1
TOTAL	6	5	+ 1

WHITE SOX	FOR	AGAINST	MARGIN
Dodgers	4	7	- 3
Giants	1	2	- 1
Reds	1	0	+ 1
TOTALS	6	9	- 3

BROWNS	FOR	AGAINST	MARGIN
Cardinals	1	3	- 2
TOTAL	1	3	- 2

A. L.	289
N. L.	187
TOTAL	476

DODGERS	FOR	AGAINST	MARGIN
Yankees	35	49	- 14
White Sox	7	4	+ 3
Twins	5	6	- 1
Red Sox	1	2	- 1
Orioles	1	4	- 3
Indians	0	2	- 2
TOTALS	49	67	- 18

BRAVES	FOR	AGAINST	MARGIN
Yankees	11	17	- 6
Indians	4	4	Even
Athletics	1	0	+ 1
TOTALS	16	21	- 5

CARDINALS	FOR	AGAINST	MARGIN
Yankees	14	28	- 14
Tigers	9	10	- 1
Red Sox	6	12	- 6
Athletics	4	9	- 5
Browns	3	1	+ 2
TOTALS	36	60	- 24

PIRATES	FOR	AGAINST	MARGIN
Orioles	5	5	Even
Senators	4	8	- 4
Yankees	4	12	- 8
Tigers	2	2	Even
Red Sox	1	2	- 1
TOTALS	16	29	- 13

GIANTS	FOR	AGAINST	MARGIN
Yankees	20	28	- 8
Senators	7	7	Even
White Sox	2	1	+ 1
Indians	2	3	- 1
Red Sox	1	1	Even
Athletics	1	5	- 4
TOTALS	33	45	- 12

CUBS	FOR	AGAINST	MARGIN
Tigers	7	3	+ 4
Yankees	5	13	- 8
Athletics	1	7	- 6
White Sox	0	0	Even
TOTALS	13	23	- 10

EDS	FOR	AGAINST	MARGIN
ioles	5	10	- 5
hletics	3	5	- 2
nkees	3	14	- 11
ers	2	4	- 2
ite Sox	0	1	- 1
TALS	13	34	- 21

TS	FOR	AGAINST	MARGIN
oles	6	3	+ 3
hletics	4	2	+ 2
TAL	10	5	+ 5

PHILLIES	FOR	AGAINST	MARGIN
Red Sox	1	3	- 2
Yankees	0	2	- 2
TOTALS	1	5	- 4

	FOR	AGAINST
N.L.	183	289
A.L.	289	187
TOTALS	476	476

31
Total Home Run Record

<table>
<tr><td colspan="2">BY GAME</td><td colspan="2">BY INNINGS</td></tr>
<tr><td>1st Game</td><td>82</td><td>4th Inn.</td><td>72</td></tr>
<tr><td>5th Game</td><td>81</td><td>5th Inn.</td><td>59</td></tr>
<tr><td>4th Game</td><td>80</td><td>7th Inn.</td><td>58</td></tr>
<tr><td>2nd Game</td><td>76</td><td>3rd Inn.</td><td>59</td></tr>
<tr><td>3rd Game</td><td>74</td><td>2nd Inn.</td><td>47</td></tr>
<tr><td>6th Game</td><td>50</td><td>1st Inn.</td><td>46</td></tr>
<tr><td>7th Game</td><td>32</td><td>8th Inn.</td><td>44</td></tr>
<tr><td>8th Game</td><td>1</td><td>6th Inn.</td><td>43</td></tr>
<tr><td></td><td>476</td><td>9th Inn.</td><td>40</td></tr>
<tr><td></td><td></td><td>10th Inn.</td><td>8</td></tr>
<tr><td></td><td></td><td></td><td>476</td></tr>
</table>

32

Individual Home Run Records—Most Home Runs Against Opponents

American League

	Team	Total HR	National League Opponent
M. Mantle	NYY	9	BR-LAD
B. Ruth	NYY	7	St. LC
H. Bauer	NYY	6	BB-Mil
B. Ruth	NYY	4	NY-SFG
G. Goslin	W	4	NY-SFG
G. Tenace	Ph-Oak	4	Cin
L. Gehrig	NYY	3	ChC
H. Greenberg	D	3	ChC
M. Mantle	NYY	3	PP
G. Goslin	W	3	PP
J. Harris	W	3	PP
H. Hooper	BRS	2	PhP
D. Buford	Balt	1	NYM
D. McNally	Balt	1	NYM
F. Robinson	Balt	1	NYM
B. Campaneris	Ph-Oak	1	NYM
R. Jackson	Ph-Oak	1	NYM

National League

	Team	Total HR	American League Opponent
D. Snider	BR-LAD	10	NYY
D. Clendenon	NYM	3	Balt
C. Essegian	BR-LAD	2	ChW
B. Kauff	NY-SFG	2	ChW
C. Neal	BR-LAD	2	ChW
B. Elliott	BB-Mil	2	CL
D. Rhodes	NY-SFG	2	CL
L. Brock	St. LC	2	D
O. Cepeda	St. LC	2	D
F. Demaree	ChC	2	D
R. Fairly	BR-LAD	2	Minn
L. Johnson	BR-LAD	2	Minn
W. Garrett	NYM	2	Ph-Oak
G. Watkins	St. LC	2	Ph. Oak
M. Ott	NY-SFG	2	W
B. Terry	NY-SFG	2	W
L. Brock	St. LC	1	BRS
L. Doyle	NY-SFG	1	BRS
B. Gibson	St. LC	1	BRS
J. Javier	St. LC	1	BRS
F. Luderus	PhP	1	BRS
R. Maris	St. LC	1	BRS
H. Myers	BR-LAD	1	BRS
M. Shannon	St. LC	1	BRS
E. Slaughter	St. LC	1	BRS
J. Sebring	PP	1	BRS
D. Litwhiler	St. LC	1	St. LB
S. Musial	St. LC	1	St. LB
R. Sanders	St. LC	1	St. LB

33

Outstanding Home Run Feats

Players Hitting World Series Grand Slam Home Runs

Year	Player	Club	Game	Inn.	Batting Style	Pitcher	Pitch Style
1920	E. Smith	CL	5	1st	L	B. Grimes	R
1936	T. Lazzeri	NYY	2	3rd	R	D. Coffman	R
1951	G. McDougald	NYY	5	3rd	R	L. Jansen	R
1953	M. Mantle	NYY	5	3rd	L	R. Meyer	R
1956	Y. Berra	NYY	2	2nd	L	D. Newcombe	R
1956	B. Skowron	NYY	7	7th	R	R. Craig	R
1960	B. Richardson	NYY	3	1st	R	C. Labine	R
1962	C. Hiller	NY-SFG	4	7th	R	M. Bridges	L
1964	K. Boyer	St. LC	4	6th	R	A. Downing	L
1964	J. Pepitone	NYY	6	8th	L	G. Richardson	L
1968	J. Northrup	D	6	3rd	L	L. Jaster	L
1970	D. McNally	Balt	3	6th	R	W. Granger	R

Players Hitting World Series Pinch Hit Home Runs

Year	Player	Club	Game	Inn.	Batting Style	Pitcher	Pitch Style
1947	Y. Berra	NYY	3	7th	L	R. Branca	R
1952	J. Mize	NYY	3	9th	L	P. Roe	L
1953	G. Shuba	BR-LAD	1	6th	L	A. Reynolds	R
1954	D. Rhodes	NY-SFG	1	10th	L	B. Lemon	R
1954	H. Majeski	CL	4	5th	R	D. Liddle	L
1955	B. Cerv	NYY	5	7th	R	R. Craig	R
1959	C. Essegian	BR-LAD	2	7th	R	B. Shaw	R
1959	C. Essegian	BR-LAD	6	9th	R	R. Moore	R
1960	E. Howard	NYY	1	9th	R	E. Face	R
1961	J. Blanchard	NYY	3	8th	L	B. Purkey	R

Players Hitting Home Run First Time at Bat in World Series

G. Tenace	Ph-Oak	1972	*
D. Rhodes	NY-SFG	1954	
E. Howard	NYY	1955	
R. Maris	NYY	1960	
D. Mincher	Minn	1965	
B. Robinson	Balt	1966	
J. Santiago	Bos	1967	
M. Lolich	Det	1968	
D. Buford	Balt	1969	

* Hitting home runs for first 2 times at bat

Year	Player	Club	Game	Inn.	Batting Style	Pitcher	Pitch Style
1903	P. Dougherty	BRS	2	1st	L	S. Leever	R
1909	D. Jones	D	5	1st	L	B. Adams	R
1942	P. Rizzutto	NYY	5	1st	R	J. Beazley	R
1948	D. Mitchell	CL	5	1st	L	N. Potter	R
1953	G. Woodling	NYY	5	1st	L	J. Podres	L
1954	A. Smith	CL	2	1st	R	J. Antonelli	L
1958	B. Bruton	BB-Mil	2	1st	L	B. Turley	R
1968	L. Brock	St. LC	4	1st	L	D. McLain	R
1969	D. Buford	Balt	1	1st	L	T. Seaver	R
1969	T. Agee	NYM	3	1st	R	J. Palmer	R
1972	P. Rose	Cin	5	1st	L	J. Hunter	R
1973	W. Garrett	NYM	3	1st	L	J. Hunter	R

34

Home Runs, Per Inning, Per Game—Consecutive Series

Players with 7 or More World Series Home Runs

BY INNING	1	2	3	4	5	6	7	8	9	10	Total
M. Mantle*	1	1	1	4	1	4	2	2	2	0	18
B. Ruth	3	0	2	2	3	1	2	1	1	0	15
Y. Berra	1	1	2	1	1	2	2	2	0	0	12
D. Snider	0	1	3	0	3	3	0	1	0	0	11
L. Gehrig	1	2	2	2	1	0	1	0	1	0	10
J. DiMaggio	0	0	2	1	3	0	0	0	1	1	8
F. Robinson	2	1	3	1	0	0	1	0	0	0	8
B. Skowron	1	0	0	3	1	1	1	1	0	0	8
H. Bauer	1	0	1	0	1	0	3	0	1	0	7
G. Goslin	2	0	3	0	0	1	0	1	0	0	7
G. McDougald	1	0	3	0	1	0	0	0	1	1	7

BY GAME	1	2	3	4	5	6	7	Total
M. Mantle**	1	5	4	2	2	2	2	18
B. Ruth	0	2	3	8	0	1	1	15
Y. Berra**	1	2	2	1	1	2	3	12
D. Snider	2	1	0	2	3	3	0	11
L. Gehrig	1	1	5	3	0	0	0	10
J. DiMaggio	0	2	2	1	3	0	0	8
F. Robinson	2	0	2	1	3	0	0	8
B. Skowron	2	1	0	1	0	1	3	8
H. Bauer	1	2	1	1	0	2	0	7
G. Goslin	0	2	1	2	1	1	0	7
G. McDougald	1	0	0	2	3	1	0	7

RECORD FOR 7 CONSECUTIVE SERIES WITH 1 or MORE HOME RUNS

	1951	1952	1953	1955	1956	1957	1958	1960	1961	1962	1963	1964	Total
Mantle	0	2	2	1	3	1	2	3	0	0	1	3	18

* Only player in World Series history to hit at least one Home Run in each Inning in a Regular Nine Inning Game.

** Only players in World Series History to hit at least one Home Run in each Game.

35
Top Ten Home Run Hitters

	Tot HR	Players on Bases				Total RBI By HRs	Total W. S. RBI
		0	1	2	3		
M. Mantle	18	9	6	2	1	31	40
B. Ruth	15	11	2	2	0	21	32
Y. Berra	12	6	4	1	1	21	39
D. Snider	11	6	3	2	0	18	26
L. Gehrig	10	6	3	1	0	15	35
F. Robinson	8	5	2	1	0	12	14
B. Skowron	8	5	0	2	1	15	29
J. DiMaggio	8	4	3	1	0	13	30
H. Bauer	7	2	3	2	0	14	24
G. McDougald	7	3	3	0	1	13	24
G. Goslin	7	4	1	2	0	12	19

36
Consecutive Back-to-Back Home Runs

Year	Club	Game	Inn	1st Player		2nd Player	Pitcher	Club
1925	W	4	3rd	G. Goslin	+	J. Harris	E. Yde	PP
1928	NYY	4	7th	B. Ruth	+	L. Gehrig	W. Sherdel	St. LC
1932	NYY	3	5th	B. Ruth	+	L. Gehrig	C. Root	ChC
1964	NYY	6	6th	R. Maris	+	M. Mantle	C. Simmons	St. LC
1966	Balt	1	1st	F. Robinson	+	B. Robinson	D. Drysdale	BR-LAD
1967	BRS	6	4th	R. Smith	+	R. Petrocelli	D. Hughes	St. LC

37
Two or More Home Runs, One Series—Switch Hitters

	HRS	Game	Inn	Pitcher	Pitch Style	Batt. Style	
M. Mantle 1953	2	2	8	P. Roe	L	R	Won Ball Game with 2 Run Home Run
		5	3	R. Meyer	R	L	Hit Grand Slam HR
J. Gilliam 1953	2	1	5	A. Reynolds	R	L	Driving in 1 Run
		5	9	B. Kuzava	L	R	Driving in 1 Run

38
Comparison between the New York Yankees and the Other American and National League Clubs

Yankees

Mantle	18	More than	Browns - 1 Phillies - Mets - 10 - Reds - 13 - Twins - 6 White Sox - 6 - Indians - 9 - Pirates - 16 - Cubs - 13 - Senators - 15 - Braves - 16
Ruth	15		
	33	More than	Tigers - 19 - Orioles - 22 Red Sox - 20 - Athletics - 28 - Tied with Giants - 33
Berra	12		
	45	More than	Giants - 33 - Cardinals - 36
Gehrig	10	More than	Dodgers - 49
	55		

39

Players Hitting Two or More Home Runs—Per Series

B. Ruth	4	1926	B. Ruth	2	1927	F. Torre	2	1957
L. Gehrig	4	1928	J. Foxx	2	1929	M. Mantle	2	1958
D. Snider	4	1952	M. Haas	2	1929	G. McDougald	2	1958
D. Snider	4	1955	A. Simmons	2	1929	B. Skowron	2	1958
H Bauer	4	1958	M. Cochrane	2	1930	C. Essegian	2	1959
G. Tenace	4	1972	A. Simmons	2	1930	C. Neal	2	1959
B. Ruth	3	1923	A. Simmons	2	1931	R. Maris	2	1960
G. Goslin	3	1924	T. Lazzeri	2	1932	B. Mazeroski	2	1960
G. Goslin	3	1925	B. Ruth	2	1932	B. Skowron	2	1960
J. Harris	3	1925	M. Ott	2	1933	J. Blanchard	2	1961
B. Ruth	3	1928	F. Demaree	2	1935	K. Boyer	2	1964
L. Gehrig	3	1932	L. Gehrig	2	1936	F. Linz	2	1964
C. Keller	3	1939	G. Selkirk	2	1936	T. Tresh	2	1964
J. Mize	3	1952	B. Dickey	2	1939	R. Fairly	2	1965
Y. Berra	3	1956	C. Keller	2	1942	L. Johnson	2	1965
M. Mantle	3	1956	H. Greenberg	2	1945	F. Robinson	2	1966
H. Aaron	3	1957	R. York	2	1946	R. Petrocelli	2	1967
T. Kluszewski	3	1959	J. DiMaggio	2	1947	R. Smith	2	1967

M. Mantle	3	1960	B. Elliott	2	1948	L. Brock	2	1968
M. Mantle	3	1964	Y. Berra	2	1952	O. Cepeda	2	1968
C. Yastrzemski	3	1967	M. Mantle	2	1952	A. Kaline	2	1968
D. Clendenon	3	1969	J. Gilliam	2	1953	J. Northrup	2	1968
P. Dougherty	2	1903	M. Mantle	2	1953	L. May	2	1970
F. Clarke	2	1909	B. Martin	2	1953	B. Powell	2	1970
J. F. Baker	2	1911	G. McDougald	2	1953	B. Robinson	2	1970
H. Hooper	2	1915	D. Rhodes	2	1954	F. Robinson	2	1970
L. Gardner	2	1916	R. Campanella	2	1955	D. Buford	2	1971
B. Kauff	2	1917	Joe Collins	2	1955	R. Clemente	2	1971
A. Ward	2	1922	B. Martin	2	1956	B. Robertson	2	1971
C. Stengel	2	1923	H. Bauer	2	1957	F. Robinson	2	1971
S. Harris	2	1924	T. Kubek	2	1957	W. Garrett	2	1973
						TOTAL	93	

Times 2 or More Home Runs - Per Series

M. Mantle	6	D. Clendenon	1	T. Lazzeri	1
B. Ruth	5	M. Cochrane	1	P. Linz	1
L. Gehrig	3	Joe Collins	1	R. Maris	1
F. Robinson	3	F. Demaree	1	L. May	1
A. Simmons	3	B. Dickey	1	B. Mazeroski	1
H. Bauer	2	J. DiMaggio	1	J. Mize	1
Y. Berra	2	P. Dougherty	1	C. Neal	1
G. Goslin	2	B. Elliott	1	J. Northrup	1
C. Keller	2	C. Essegian	1	M. Ott	1
B. Martin	2	R. Fairly	1	R. Petrocelli	1
G. McDougald	2	J. Foxx	1	B. Powell	1
B. Skowron	2	L. Gardner	1	D. Rhodes	1
D. Snider	2	W. Garrett	1	B. Robertson	1
H. Aaron	1	J. Gilliam	1	B. Robinson	1
J. F. Baker	1	H. Greenberg	1	G. Selkirk	1
J. Blanchard	1	M. Haas	1	R. Smith	1
K. Boyer	1	J. Harris	1	C. Stengel	1
L. Brock	1	S. Harris	1	G. Tenace*	1
D. Buford	1	H. Hooper	1	F. Torre	1
R. Campanella	1	L. Johnson	1	T. Tresh	1

O. Cepeda	1	A. Kaline	1	A. Ward	1
F. Clarke	1	B. Kauff	1	C. Yastrzemski	1
R. Clemente	1	T. Kluszewski	1	R. York	1
		T. Kubek	1		
				TOTAL	93

* First Ball Player in History to hit Home Runs his first two appearances at bat in a World Series.

2 or More Home Runs in a Single Series Game

B. Ruth	3	1926
B. Ruth	3	1928
P. Dougherty	2	1903
H. Hooper	2	1915
B. Kauff	2	1917
B. Ruth	2	1923
L. Gehrig	2	1928
B. Ruth	2	1932
L. Gehrig	2	1932
T. Lazzeri	2	1932
C. Keller	2	1939
B. Elliott	2	1948
D. Snider	2	1952
Joe Collins	2	1955
D. Snider	2	1955
Y. Berra	2	1956
T. Kubek	2	1957
M. Mantle	2	1958
T. Kluszewski	2	1959
C. Neal	2	1959
M. Mantle	2	1960
C. Yastrzemski	2	1967
R. Petrocelli	2	1967
G. Tenace	2	1972

Times 2 or More Home Runs in a World Series Game

1	B. Ruth	4
2	L. Gehrig	2
3	M. Mantle	2
4	D. Snider	2
5	P. Dougherty	1
6	H. Hooper	1
7	B. Kauff	1
8	T. Lazzeri	1
9	C. Keller	1
10	B. Elliott	1
11	Joe Collins	1
12	Y. Berra	1
13	T. Kubek	1
14	T. Kluszewski	1
15	C. Neal	1
16	C. Yastrzemski	1
17	R. Petrocelli	1
18	G. Tenace	1

TOTAL 24

Two or More Consecutive Home Runs in a Game

Year	Player	Game	Inn.	Inn.	Inn.
1926	B. Ruth	4	1st	3rd	6th
1928	B. Ruth	4	4th	7th	8th
1923	B. Ruth	2	4th	5th	
1928	L. Gehrig	3	2nd	4th	
1932	L. Gehrig	3	3rd	5th	
1939	C. Keller	3	1st	5th	
1948	B. Elliott	5	1st	3rd	
1952	D. Snider	6	6th	8th	
1955	Joe Collins	1	4th	6th	
1955	D. Snider	5	3rd	5th	
1956	Y. Berra	7	1st	3rd	
1959	T. Kluszewski	1	3rd	4th	
1959	C. Neal	2	5th	7th	
1967	R. Petrocelli	2	2nd	4th	
1972	G. Tenace	2	2nd	5th	

Times Hitting Two or More Consecutive Home Runs in a Game

B. Ruth	3
L. Gehrig	2
D. Snider	2
Y. Berra	1
Joe Collins	1
B. Elliott	1
C. Keller	1
T. Kluszewski	1
C. Neal	1
R. Petrocelli	1
G. Tenace	1
TOTAL	15

Total HRs	Year	Club	Game	Inn	Opp	Player	Player	Player
3	1967	BRS	6	4	St. LC	C. Yastrzemski	*R. Smith	*R. Petrocelli
2	1921	NYG	6	2	NYY	E. Meusel	F. Snyder	
2	1925	W	4	3	PP	*G. Goslin	*J. Harris	
2	1928	NYY	4	7	St. LC	*B. Ruth	*L. Gehrig	
2	1928	NYY	4	8	St. LC	C. Durst	B. Ruth	
2	1929	PhA	4	7	ChC	A. Simmons	M. Haas	
2	1932	NYY	3	5	ChC	*B. Ruth	*L. Gehrig	
2	1932	NYY	4	9	ChC	E. Combs	T. Lazzeri	
2	1939	NYY	3	5	Cin	C. Keller	B. Dickey	
2	1939	NYY	4	7	Cin	C. Keller	B. Dickey	
2	1940	D	3	7	Cin	R. York	M. Higgins	
2	1949	Br LAD	3	9	NYY	L. Olmo	R. Campanella	
2	1953	Br LAD	1	6	NYY	G. Hodges	G. Shuba	
2	1955	Br LAD	4	4	NYY	R. Campanella	G. Hodges	
2	1957	BB-Mil	4	4	NYY	H. Aaron	F. Torre	
2	1958	BB-Mil	2	1	NYY	B. Bruton	L. Burdette	
2	1958	NYY	2	9	BB-Mil	H. Bauer	M. Mantle	
2	1959	BB-LAD	2	7	ChW	C. Essegain	C. Neal	
2	1964	NYY	6	6	St. LC	*R. Maris	*M. Mantle	
2	1964	NYY	7	9	St. LC	C. Boyer	P. Linz	
2	1966	Balt	1	1	BR-LAD	*F. Robinson	*B. Robinson	
2	1969	Balt	5	3	NYM	D. McNally	F. Robinson	
2	1973	Ph-Oak	7	3	NYM	B. Campaneris	R. Jackson	

* Consecutive Home Runs

40
Players Hitting Home Runs to Win World Series Game

M. Mantle	6	F. Clarke	1	G. McQuinn	1
J. DiMaggio	4	F. Crosetti	1	J. Medwick	1
Joe Collins	3	K. Cuyler	1	J. Mize	1
H. Greenberg	3	B. Dickey	1	R. Meusel	1
T. Henrich	3	L. Doby	1	D. Murphy	1
D. Snider	3	P. Dougherty	1	S. Musial	1
J. F. Baker	2	T. Douthit	1	G. Moore	1
Y. Berra	2	O. Felsch	1	C. Neal	1
L. Gehrig	2	J. Foxx	1	M. Ott	1
G. Hodges	2	L. Gardner	1	W. Parker	1
B. Mazeroski	2	C. Gehringer	1	M. Rettenmund	1
T. McCarver	2	B. Gibson	1	D. Rhodes	1
G. McDougald	2	G. Goslin	1	J. Ripple	1
B. Robinson	2	M. Higgins	1	B. Robertson	1
R. Sanders	2	C. Hiller	1	F. Robinson	1
C. Stengel	2	H. Hooper	1	J. Roseboro	1
R. York	2	E. Howard	1	J. Rudi	1
T. Agee	1	R. Jackson	1	M. Shannon	1
B. Allison	1	L. Johnson	1	E. Slaughter	1

H. Bauer	1	B. Kauff	1	E. Smith	1
J. Bentley	1	C. Klein	1	B. Southworth	1
P. Blair	1	G. Kurowski	1	R. Staub	1
C. Boyer	1	M. Lolich	1	Gene Tenace	1
K. Boyer	1	R. Maris	1	J. Tinker	1
D. Buford	1	B. Martin	1	T. Tresh	1
L. Burdette	1	P. Martin	1	Z. Versalles	1
R. Campanella	1	E. Mathews	1	G. Watkins	1
		L. May	1	C. Yastrzemski	1

TOTAL	110

41
Pitchers Allowing Deciding Home Runs

D. Drysdale	3	M. Bridges	1	J. Grant	1	J. Matlack	1
R. Marquard	3	N. Briles	1	F. Green	1	D. Maas	1
D. Newcombe	3	L. Burdette	1	R. Grimsley	1	H. McIntyre	1
C. Root	3	L. Bush	1	K. Holtzman	1	P. Mikkelson	1
J. Black	2	T. Cloninger	1	W. Hoyt	1	R. Meyer	1
M. Cooper	2	J. Coates	1	D. Hughes	1	D. McNally	1
J. Dean	2	R. Craig	1	J. Kaat	1	B. O'Dell	1
W. Ford	2	S. Coveleskie	1	J. Konstanty	1	J. O'Toole	1
B. Grim	2	A. Crowder	1	J. Kucks	1	J. Palmer	1
B. Grimes	2	M. Dickson	1	S. Jakucki	1	H. Pollet	1
L. Jansen	2	P. Dobson	1	E. Johnson	1	B. Purkey	1
S. Maglie	2	B. Donovan	1	W. Johnson	1	V. Raschi	1
G. Nolan	2	A. Downing	1	S. Jones	1	A. Reynolds	1
C. Osteen	2	G. Earnshaw	1	C. Labine	1	E. Rixey	1
S. Rowe	2	D. Ellis	1	S. Leever	1	R. Roberts	1
G. Thompson	2	U. Faber	1	B. Lemon	1	P. Roe	1
R. Barney	1	J. Ferguson	1	B. Loes	1	C. Ruffing	1
G. Bell	1	F. Fitzsimmons	1	V. Lombardi	1	J. Russell	1
E. Bonham	1	D. Galehouse	1	J. Lonborg	1	J. Sain	1

H. Sallee	1	W. Sherdel	1	R. Terry	1	H. Wyse	1
J. Sanford	1	U. Shocker	1	J. Turner	1	E. Yde	1
B. Schultz	1	G. Staley	1	R. Walberg	1		
B. Shaw	1	O. Summers	1	E. Watt	1	TOTAL	110

42
Home Runs Winning Ball Games

Grand Slam Home Runs

1920	Elmer Smith	Cleveland	AL
1951	Gilbert McDougald	New York	AL
1962	Charles Hiller	San Francisco	NL
1964	Kenton Boyer	St. Louis	NL

Pinch Hit - Home Runs

1954	James Rhodes	New York	NL

Extra Inning - Home Runs

1933	Mel Ott	New York	NL
1946	Rudy York	Boston	AL
1950	Joe DiMaggio	New York	AL
1954	James Rhodes	New York	NL
1957	Eddie Mathews	Milwaukee	NL
1964	Tim McCarver	St. Louis	NL

43
Players Hitting Game-Winning Home Runs by Positions

1B		2B		3B		SS		C	
Joe Collins	3	B. Mazeroski	2	J. F. Baker	2	F. Crosetti	1	Y. Berra	2
L. Gehrig	2	G. McDougald	2	B. Robinson	2	J. Tinker	1	T. McCarver	2
H. Greenberg*	2	C. Gehringer	1	C. Boyer	1	Z. Versalles	1	R. Campanella	1
G. Hodges	2	C. Hiller	1	K. Boyer	1			B. Dickey	1
R. Sanders	2	B. Martin	1	M. Higgins	1			E. Howard	1
R. York	2	Grant Moore	1	G. Kurowski	1			J. Roseboro	1
J. Foxx	1	C. Neal	1	E. Mathews	1			G. Tenace	1
T. Henrich*	1			M. Shannon	1				
L. May	1			L. Gardner	1				
G. McQuinn	1								
J. Mize	1								
W. Parker	1								
B. Robertson	1								
TOTAL	20	TOTAL	9	TOTAL	11	TOTAL	3	TOTAL	9

*Playing more than one position

OUT		OUT		OUT		OUT		P	
M. Mantle	6	F. Clarke	1	B. Kauff	1	D. Rhodes	1	J. Bentley	1
J. DiMaggio	4	K. Cuyler	1	C. Klein	1	J. Ripple	1	L. Burdette	1
D. Snider	3	L. Doby	1	R. Maris	1	F. Robinson	1	B. Gibson	1
T. Henrich*	2	P. Dougherty	1	P. Martin	1	J. Rudi	1	M. Lolich	1
C. Stengel	2	T. Douthit	1	J. Medwick	1	E. Slaughter	1		
T. Agee	1	O. Felsch	1	R. Meusel	1	E. Smith	1		
B. Allison	1	G. Goslin	1	D. Murphy	1	B. Southworth	1		
H. Bauer	1	H. Greenberg*		S. Musial	1	R. Staub	1		
P. Blair	1	H. Hooper	1	M. Ott	1	T. Tresh	1	TOTAL	4
D. Buford	1	R. Jackson	1	M. Rettenmund	1	C. Watkins	1		
		L. Johnson	1			C. Yastrzemski	1		

Out	54
1B	20
2B	11
3B	9
C	9
P	4
SS	3
TOTAL	110

TOTAL   54

44
Mickey Mantle's Home Run Record

Year	Game	Inn	Score		Ball Park	Pitcher	Pitch Style	Hitting Style	COMMENTS
1952	6	8	NYY 3	BR 2	Ebbets Field	B. Loes	R	L	Driving in the winning run with an opposite field Home run into the left center field stands.
1952	7	6	NYY 4	BR 2	Ebbets Field	J. Black	R	L	Driving in decisive run with HR over right field scoreboard - also drove in insurance run in the 7th inning.
1953	2	8	NYY 4	BR 2	Yankee Stadium	P. Roe	L	R	Drove in winning run and also an insurance run with HR into the lower left field stands
1953	5	3	NYY 11	BR 7	Ebbets Field	R. Meyer	R	L	Hit grand slam Home Run to opposite field, into upper left field on the first pitch.
1955	3	2	BR 8	NYY 3	Ebbets Field	J. Podres	L	R	Driving in the first run of the game with HR - into lower center field stands at the 393 ft. mark.
1956	1	1	BR 6	NYY 3	Ebbets Field	S. Maglie	R	L	Drove in the 1st two runs of the series with a HR over right field screen.
1956	4	6	NYY 6	BR 2	Yankee Stadium	E. Roebuck	R	L	Homered into right-center field bleachers.
1956	5	4	NYY 2	BR 0	Yankee Stadium	S. Maglie	R	L	Drove in 1st run of Don Larsen's perfect no hit-no run game with HR

Year	Game	Inn	Score	Ball Park	Pitcher	Pitch Style	Hitting Style	COMMENTS
1957	3	4	NYY 12 MIL 8	County Stadium	G. Conley	R	L	Hit HR into right center field bullpen driving in 2 runs
1958	2	4	MIL 13 NYY 5	County Stadium	L. Burdette	R	L	Hit a 400 ft. HR - over center field fence leading off the 4th inning.
1958	2	9	MIL 13 NYY 5	County Stadium	L. Burdette	R	L	Hit 2nd HR of game - into left center field bleachers--driving in 2 runs.
1960	2	5	NYY 16 PP 3	Forbes Field	F. Green	L	R	Drove over a 400 ft. opposite field HR - driving in 2 runs.
1960	2	7	NYY 16 PP 3	Forbes Field	J. Gibbon	L	R	Drove 475 ft. opposite field HR over right center field wall driving in 3 runs - was second home run of the game for Mantle total R.B.I.S. Game - 5
1960	3	4	NYY 10 PP 0	Yankee Stadium	F. Green	L	R	Hit a 430 foot HR into left field bullpen--driving in 2 runs.
1963	4	7	LAD 2 NYY 1	Chavez Ravine	S. Koufax	L	R	Tied up game with a long 380 ft. Home run - drove in only run for the Yankees.
1964	3	9	NYY 2 St. LC 1	Yankee Stadium	B. Schultz	R	L	Hit the first pitch deep into the right field stand for game-winning HR.
1964	6	6	NYY 8 St. LC 3	Busch Stadium	C. Simmons	L	R	Drove in 2nd consecutive HR of the Inning - against the screen to the rear of right field pavilion roof.
1964	7	6	St. LC 7 NYY 5	Busch Stadium	B. Gibson	R	L	Driving in the 1st 3 Yankee runs with an opposite field Home run into the left field bleachers.

Home Run	RBI	Home Runs off Right Hand Pitchers		Home Runs off Left Hand Pitchers		Home Runs by Opponents		Home Runs by Ball Parks	
1	1	S. Maglie	2	F. Green	2	Dodgers	9	Yankee Stadium	5
2	1	L. Burdette	2	J. Gibbon	1	Cardinals	3	Ebbets Field	5
3	2	J. Black	1	S. Koufax	1	Braves	3	County Stadium	3
4	4	G. Conley	1	J. Podres	1	Pirates	3	Busch Stadium	2
5	1	B. Gibson	1	P. Roe	1			Forbes Field	2
6	2	B. Loes	1	C. Simmons	1			Chavez Ravine	1
7	1	R. Meyer	1						
8	1	E. Roebuck	1						
9	2	B. Schultz	1					HOME	5
10	1							AWAY	13
11	2	TOTAL	11	TOTAL	7	TOTAL	18	TOTAL	18
12	2								
13	3								
14	2								
15	1								
16	1								
17	1								
18	3								
TOTAL	31								

45

Home Run Hitters by Positions

Outfielders				1B		C	
M. Mantle	18	B. Campbell	1	L. Gehrig	10	Y. Berra	9
B. Ruth	15	E. Combs	1	B. Skowron	8	B. Dickey	5
D. Snider	11	S. Crawford	1	G. Hodges	5	R. Campanella	4
J. DiMaggio	8	L. Culbertson	1	Joe Collins	4	G. Tenace	4
F. Robinson	8	L. Doby	1	J. Foxx	4	J. Bench	2
H. Bauer	7	T. Douthit	1	D. Clendenon	3	M. Cochrane	2
G. Goslin	7	C. Durst	1	T. Kluszewski	3	D. Crandall	2
R. Maris	6	O. Felsch	1	R. York	3	G. Hartnett	2
A. Simmons	6	W. Fewster	1	O. Cepeda	2	T. McCarver	2
C. Keller	5	M. Hoag	1	H. Greenberg*	2	F. Snyder	2
L. Brock	4	W. Horton	1	L. May	2	E. Bailey	1
D. Buford	4	F. Howard	1	J. Mize*	2	B. Delancey	1
T. Tresh	4	J. Jackson	1	B. Powell	2	H. Gowdy	1
H. Aaron	3	R. Jackson	1	B. Robertson	2	T. Haller	1
F. Demaree	3	C. Jones	1	R. Sanders	2	J. Hegan	1
H. Greenberg*	3	D. Jones	1	B. Terry	2	E. Hendricks	1
J. Harris	3	G. Kelly	1	F. Torre	2	E. Howard*	1

Outfielders				1B		C	
T. Henrich*	3	C. Klein	1	G. Watkins	2	S. Lollar	1
E. Meusel	3	D. Lewis	1	J. Bottomley	1	K. O'Dea	1
M. Ott*	3	D. Litwhiler	1	N. Cash	1	J. Roseboro	1
E. Slaughter	3	H. Lopez	1	P. Cavarretta	1	B. Salkeld	1
G. Woodling	3	P. Martin	1	Gord Coleman	1	W. Schang	1
C. Yastrzemski	3	J. Marty	1	B. Dahlgren	1	H. Smith	1
Y. Berra*	2	J. Medwick	1	C. Grimm	1		
F. Clarke	2	B. Meusel	1	T. Henrich*	1	TOTAL	47
R. Clemente	2	D. Mitchell	1	E. Howard*	1		
K. Cuyler	2	W. Moon	1	J. Judge	1		
P. Dougherty	2	Jo Jo Moore	1	E. Kranepool	1		
R. Fairly	2	D. Murphy	1	W. Lockman	1		
C. Furillo	2	S. Musial	1	F. Luderus	1		
M. Haas	2	H. Myers	1	F. Merkle	1		
H. Hooper	2	R. Oldring	1	W. McCovey	1		
E. Howard*	2	T. Oliva	1	G. McQuinn	1		
L. Johnson	2	L. Olmo	1	D. Mincher	1		
A. Kaline	2	W. Post	1	R. Nelson	1		
B. Kauff	2	J. Powell	1	W. Parker	1		
T. Kubek	2	P. Reiser	1	J. Pepitone	1		
J. Northrup	2	D. Rhodes	1	V. Wertz	1		
M. Rettenmund	2	M. Rickert	1				
J. Ripple	2	J. Rudi	1	TOTAL	80		
P. Rose	2	J. Sebring	1				
G. Selkirk	2	Frank Schulte	1				
R. Smith	2	M. Shannon	1				
C. Stengel	2	A. Smith	1				
T. Agee	1	E. Smith	1				
B. Allison	1	B. Southworth	1				
S. Amoros	1	R. Staub	1				
P. Blair	1	B. Tolan	1				
J. Blanchard*	1	D. Walker	1				
B. Bruton	1	R. Youngs	1				

TOTAL   231

<table>
<tr><td align="center">2B</td><td align="center">3B</td><td align="center">SS</td><td align="center">Pitchers</td></tr>
</table>

2B		3B		SS		Pitchers	
B. Martin	5	G. McDougald*	4	P. Linz	2	B. Gibson	2
J. Gordon	4	J. F. Baker	3	R. Petrocelli	2	D. McNally	2
T. Lazzeri	4	L. Gardner	3	P. Reese	2	J. Bagby Sr.	1
G. McDougald*	3	B. Robinson	3	P. Rizzuto	2	J. Bentley	1
A. Ward	3	C. Boyer	2	D. Bartell	1	L. Burdette	1
J. Gilliam	2	K. Boyer	2	B. Campaneris	1	J. Grant	1
S. Harris	2	B. Elliott	2	F. Crosetti	1	J. Haines	1
B. Mazeroski	2	W. Garrett	2	A. Dark	1	M. Lolich	1
C. Neal	2	M. Shannon	2	J. Logan	1	W. Ryan	1
B. Doerr	1	L. Bell	1	M. Marion	1	J. Santiago	1
L. Doyle	1	B. Cox	1	J. Pagan	1	B. Walters	1
C. Gehringer	1	J. Dugan	1	R. Peckinpaugh	1		
B. Herman	1	J. Dykes	1	T. Thevenow	1		
C. Hiller	1	R. Hebner	1	J. Tinker	1		
J. Javier	1	M. Higgins	1	Z. Versalles	1		
J. Lefebvre	1	H. Killebrew	1	G. Wright	1		
D. McAuliffe	1	G. Kurowski	1				
Grant Moore	1	E. Mathews	1				
B. Richardson	1	D. Menke	1				
J. Robinson*	1	M. Ott*	1				
A. Weis	1	J. Robinson	1				
		H. Traynor	1				
TOTAL	**39**	**TOTAL**	**36**	**TOTAL**	**20**	**TOTAL**	**13**

Pinch Hitters		Recapitulation	
C. Essegian	2	Outfielders	231
Y. Berra*	1	First Baseman	80
J. Blanchard*	1	Catcher	47
B. Cerv	1	Second Baseman	39
E. Howard*	1	Third Baseman	36
H. Majeski	1	Shortstops	20
J. Mize*	1	Pitchers	13
D. Rhodes*	1	Pinch Hitters	10
G. Shuba	1		
		TOTAL	**476**
TOTAL	**10**		

* Indicates players in more than one position

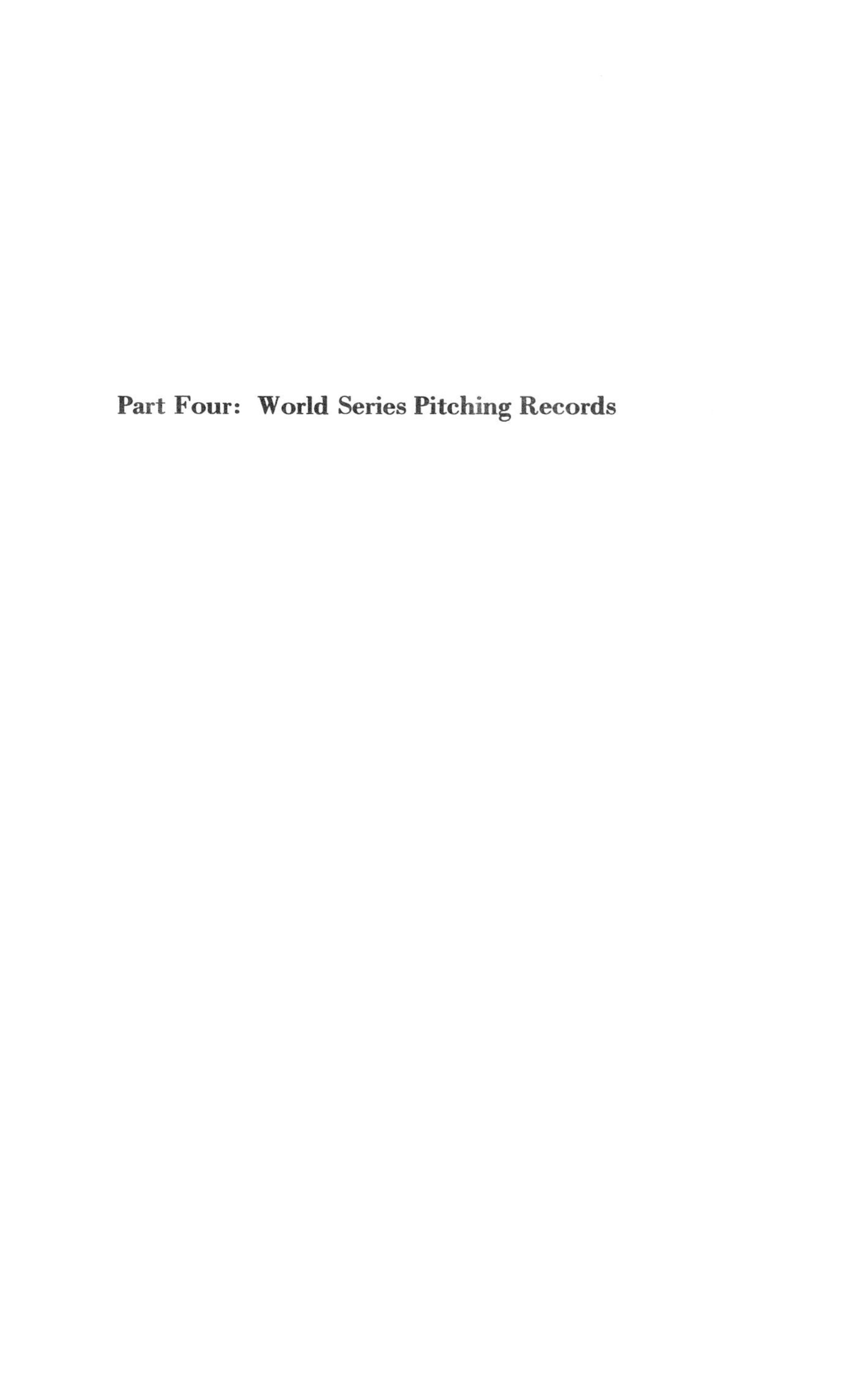

Part Four: World Series Pitching Records

46
Winning and Losing Pitchers

Overall WS Game	Year	Game No.		Score			Winning Pitcher	Pitch Style	Losing Pitcher	Pitch Style
1	1903	1	PP	7	BRS	3	D. Phillippe	R	C. Young	R
2	1903	2	BRS	3	PP	0	B. Dinneen	R	S. Leever	R
3	1903	3	PP	4	BRS	2	D. Phillippe	R	T. Hughes	R
4	1903	4	PP	5	BRS	4	D. Phillippe	R	B. Dinneen	R
5	1903	5	BRS	11	PP	2	C. Young	R	W. Kennedy	R
6	1903	6	BRS	6	PP	3	B. Dinneen	R	S. Leever	R
7	1903	7	BRS	7	PP	3	C. Young	R	D. Phillippe	R
8	1903	8	BRS	3	PP	0	B. Dinneen	R	D. Phillippe	R
9	1905	1	NYG	3	PhA	0	C. Mathewson	R	E. Plank	L
10	1905	2	PhA	3	NYG	0	C. Bender	R	J. McGinnity	R
11	1905	3	NYG	9	PhA	0	C. Mathewson	R	A. Coakley	R
12	1905	4	NYG	1	PhA	0	J. McGinnity	R	E. Plank	L
13	1905	5	NYG	2	PhA	0	C. Mathewson	R	C. Bender	R
14	1906	1	ChW	2	ChC	1	N. Altrock	L	M. Brown	R
15	1906	2	ChC	7	ChW	1	E. Reulbach	R	G. White	L

Overall WS Game	Year	Game No.	Score				Winning Pitcher	Pitch Style	Losing Pitcher	Pitch Style
16	1906	3	ChW	3	ChC	0	E. Walsh	R	J. Pfeister	L
17	1906	4	ChC	1	ChW	0	M. Brown	R	N. Altrock	L
18	1906	5	ChW	8	ChC	6	E. Walsh	R	J. Pfeister	L
19	1906	6	ChW	6	ChC	3	G. White	L	M. Brown	R
20	1907	1	D	3	ChC	3	Tied		Game	
21	1907	2	ChC	3	D	1	J. Pfeister	L	G. Mullin	R
22	1907	3	ChC	5	D	1	E. Reulbach	R	E. Siever	L
23	1907	4	ChC	6	D	1	O. Overall	R	B. Donovan	R
24	1907	5	ChC	2	D	0	M. Brown	R	G. Mullin	R
25	1908	1	ChC	10	D	6	M. Brown	R	E. Summers	R
26	1908	2	ChC	6	D	1	O. Overall	R	B. Donovan	R
27	1908	3	D	8	ChC	3	G. Mullin	R	J. Pfeister	L
28	1908	4	ChC	3	D	0	M. Brown	R	E. Summers	R
29	1908	5	ChC	2	D	0	O. Overall	R	B. Donovan	R
30	1909	1	PP	4	D	1	B. Adams	R	G. Mullin	R
31	1909	2	D	7	PP	2	B. Donovan	R	H. Camnitz	R
32	1909	3	PP	8	D	6	N. Maddox	R	E. Summers	R
33	1909	4	D	5	PP	0	G. Mullin	R	A. Leifield	L
34	1909	5	PP	8	D	4	B. Adams	R	E. Summers	R
35	1909	6	D	5	PP	4	G. Mullin	R	V. Willis	R
36	1909	7	PP	8	D	0	B. Adams	R	B. Donovan	R
37	1910	1	PhA	4	ChC	1	C. Bender	R	O. Overall	R
38	1910	2	PhA	9	ChC	3	J. Coombs	R	M. Brown	R
39	1910	3	PhA	12	ChC	5	J. Coombs	R	H. McIntire	R
40	1910	4	ChC	4	PhA	3	M. Brown	R	C. Bender	R
41	1910	5	PhA	7	ChC	2	J. Coombs	R	M. Brown	R
42	1911	1	NYG	2	PhA	1	C. Mathewson	R	C. Bender	R
43	1911	2	PhA	3	NYG	1	E. Plank	L	R. Marquard	L
44	1911	3	PhA	3	NYG	2	J. Coombs	R	C. Mathewson	R
45	1911	4	PhA	4	NYG	2	C. Bender	R	C. Mathewson	R
46	1911	5	NYG	4	PhA	3	O. Crandall	R	E. Plank	L
47	1911	6	PhA	13	NYG	2	C. Bender	R	L. Ames	R
48	1912	1	BRS	4	NYG	3	J. Wood	R	J. Tesreau	R
49	1912	2	NYG	6	BRS	6	Tied		Game	
50	1912	3	NYG	2	BRS	1	R. Marquard	L	T. O'Brien	R
51	1912	4	BRS	3	NYG	1	J. Wood	R	J. Tesreau	R
52	1912	5	BRS	2	NYG	1	H. Bedient	R	C. Mathewson	R

Overall WS Game	Year	Game No.		Score				Winning Pitcher	Pitch Style	Losing Pitcher	Pitch Style
53	1912	6	NYG	5	BRS	2		R. Marquard	L	T. O'Brien	R
54	1912	7	NYG	11	BRS	4		J. Tesreau	R.	J. Wood	R
55	1912	8	BRS	3	NYG	2		J. Wood	R	C. Mathewson	R
56	1913	1	PhA	6	NYG	4		C. Bender	R	R. Marquard	L
57	1913	2	NYG	3	PhA	0		C. Mathewson	R	E. Plank	L
58	1913	3	PhA	8	NYG	2		L. Bush	R	J. Tesreau	R
59	1913	4	PhA	6	NYG	5		C. Bender	R	A. Demaree	R
60	1913	5	PhA	3	NYG	1		E. Plank	L	C. Mathewson	R
61	1914	1	BBR	7	PhA	1		D. Rudolph	R	C. Bender	R
62	1914	2	BBR	1	PhA	0		B. James	R	E. Plank	L
63	1914	3	BBR	5	PhA	4		B. James	R	L. Bush	R
64	1914	4	BBR	3	PhA	1		D. Rudolph	R	B. Shawkey	R
65	1915	1	PhP	3	BRS	1		G. Alexander	R	E. Shore	R
66	1915	2	BRS	2	PhP	1		G. Foster	R	J. Mayer	R
67	1915	3	BRS	2	PhP	1		H. Leonard	L	G. Alexander	R
68	1915	4	BRS	2	PhP	1		E. Shore	R	G. Chalmers	R
69	1915	5	BRS	5	PhP	4		G. Foster	R	E. Rixey	L
70	1916	1	BRS	6	BR	5		E. Shore	R	R. Marquard	L
71	1916	2	BRS	2	BR	1		B. Ruth	L	S. Smith	L
72	1916	3	BR	4	BRS	3		J. Coombs	R	C. Mays	R
73	1916	4	BRS	6	BR	2		H. Leonard	L	R. Marquard	L
74	1916	5	BRS	4	BR	1		E. Shore	R	E. Pfeffer	R
75	1917	1	ChW	2	NYG	1		E. Cicotte	R	H. Sallee	L
76	1917	2	ChW	7	NYG	2		U. Faber	R	J. Anderson	R
77	1917	3	NYG	2	ChW	0		J. Benton	L	E. Cicotte	R
78	1917	4	NYG	5	ChW	0		F. Schupp	L	U. Faber	R
79	1917	5	ChW	8	NYG	5		U. Faber	R	H. Sallee	L
80	1917	6	ChW	4	NYG	2		U. Faber	R	J. Benton	L
81	1918	1	BRS	1	ChC	0		B. Ruth	L	H. Vaughan	L
82	1918	2	ChC	3	BRS	1		G. Tyler	L	L. Bush	R
83	1918	3	BRS	2	ChC	1		C. Mays	R	H. Vaughan	L
84	1918	4	BRS	3	ChC	2		B. Ruth	L	P. Douglas	R
85	1918	5	ChC	3	BRS	0		H. Vaughan	L	S. Jones	R
86	1918	6	BRS	2	ChC	1		C. Mays	R	G. Tyler	L
87	1919	1	Cin	9	ChW	1		W. Ruether	L	E. Cicotte	R

Overall WS Game	Year	Game No.		Score			Winning Pitcher	Pitch Style	Losing Pitcher	Pitch Style
88	1919	2	Cin	4	ChW	2	H. Sallee	L	C. Williams	L
89	1919	3	ChW	3	Cin	0	D. Kerr	L	R. Fisher	R
90	1919	4	Cin	2	ChW	0	J. Ring	R	E. Cicotte	R
91	1919	5	Cin	5	ChW	0	H. Eller	R	C. Williams	L
92	1919	6	ChW	5	Cin	4	D. Kerr	L	J. Ring	R
93	1919	7	ChW	4	Cin	1	E. Cicotte	R	H. Sallee	L
94	1919	8	Cin	10	ChW	5	H. Eller	R	C. Williams	L
95	1920	1	CL	3	BR	1	S. Coveleskie	R	R. Marquard	L
96	1920	2	BR	3	CL	0	B. Grimes	R	J. Bagby Sr.	R
97	1920	3	BR	2	CL	1	S. Smith	L	R. Caldwell	R
98	1920	4	CL	5	BR	1	S. Coveleskie	R	L. Cadore	R
99	1920	5	CL	8	BR	1	J. Bagby Sr.	R	B. Grimes	R
100	1920	6	CL	1	BR	0	W. Mails	L	S. Smith	L
101	1920	7	CL	2	BR	0	S. Coveleskie	R	B. Grimes	R
102	1921	1	NYY	3	NYG	0	C. Mays	R	P. Douglas	R
103	1921	2	NYY	3	NYG	0	W. Hoyt	R	A. Nehf	L
104	1921	3	NYG	13	NYY	5	J. Barnes	R	J. Quinn	R
105	1921	4	NYG	4	NYY	2	P. Douglas	R	C. Mays	R
106	1921	5	NYY	3	NYG	1	W. Hoyt	R	A. Nehf	L
107	1921	6	NYG	8	NYY	5	J. Barnes	R	B. Shawkey	R
108	1921	7	NYG	2	NYY	1	P. Douglas	R	C. Mays	R
109	1921	8	NYG	1	NYY	0	A. Nehf	L	W. Hoyt	R
110	1922	1	NYG	3	NYY	2	W. Ryan	R	L. Bush	R
111	1922	2	NYG	3	NYY	3	Tied		Game	
112	1922	3	NYG	3	NYY	0	J. Scott	R	W. Hoyt	R
113	1922	4	NYG	4	NYY	3	H. McQuillan	R	C. Mays	R
114	1922	5	NYG	5	NYY	3	A. Nehf	L	L. Bush	R
115	1923	1	NYG	5	NYY	4	W. Ryan	R	L. Bush	R
116	1923	2	NYY	4	NYG	2	H. Pennock	L	H. McQuillan	R
117	1923	3	NYG	1	NYY	0	A. Nehf	L	S. Jones	R
118	1923	4	NYY	8	NYG	4	B. Shawkey	R	J. Scott	R
119	1923	5	NYY	8	NYG	1	L. Bush	R	J. Bentley	L
120	1923	6	NYY	6	NYG	4	H. Pennock	L	A. Nehf	L
121	1924	1	NYG	4	W	3	A. Nehf	L	W. Johnson	R
122	1924	2	W	4	NYG	3	T. Zachary	L	J. Bentley	L
123	1924	3	NYG	6	W	4	H. McQuillan	R	F. Marberry	R
124	1924	4	W	7	NYG	4	G. Mogridge	L	J. Barnes	R
125	1924	5	NYG	6	W	2	J. Bentley	L	W. Johnson	R

Overall WS Game	Year	Game No.		Score				Winning Pitcher	Pitch Style	Losing Pitcher	Pitch Style
126	1924	6	W	2	NYG	1		T. Zachary	L	A. Nehf	L
127	1924	7	W	4	NYG	3		W. Johnson	R	J. Bentley	L
128	1925	1	W	4	PP	1		W. Johnson	R	L. Meadows	R
129	1925	2	PP	3	W	2		V. Aldridge	R	S. Coveleskie	R
130	1925	3	W	4	PP	3		J. Ferguson	R	R. Kremer	R
131	1925	4	W	4	PP	0		W. Johnson	R	E. Yde	L
132	1925	5	PP	6	W	3		V. Aldridge	R	S. Coveleskie	R
133	1925	6	PP	3	W	2		R. Kremer	R	J. Ferguson	R
134	1925	7	PP	9	W	7		R. Kremer	R	W. Johnson	R
135	1926	1	NYY	2	StLC	1		H. Pennock	L	W. Sherdel	L
136	1926	2	StLC	6	NYY	2		G. Alexander	R	U. Shocker	R
137	1926	3	StLC	4	NYY	0		J. Haines	R	W. Ruether	L
138	1926	4	NYY	10	StLC	5		W. Hoyt	R	A. Reinhart	L
139	1926	5	NYY	3	StLC	2		H. Pennock	L	W. Sherdel	L
140	1926	6	StLC	10	NYY	2		G. Alexander	R	B. Shawkey	R
141	1926	7	StLC	3	NYY	2		J. Haines	R	W. Hoyt	R
142	1927	1	NYY	5	PP	4		W. Hoyt	R	R. Kremer	R
143	1927	2	NYY	6	PP	2		G. Pipgras	R	V. Aldridge	R
144	1927	3	NYY	8	PP	1		H. Pennock	L	L. Meadows	R
145	1927	4	NYY	4	PP	3		W. Moore	R	J. Miljus	R
146	1928	1	NYY	4	StLC	1		W. Hoyt	R	W. Sherdel	L
147	1928	2	NYY	9	StLC	3		G. Pipgras	R	G. Alexander	R
148	1928	3	NYY	7	StLC	3		T. Zachary	L	J. Haines	R
149	1928	4	NYY	7	StLC	3		W. Hoyt	R	W. Sherdel	L
150	1929	1	PhA	3	ChC	1		H. Ehmke	R	C. Root	R
151	1929	2	PhA	9	ChC	3		G. Earnshaw	R	P. Malone	R
152	1929	3	ChC	3	PhA	1		G. Bush	R	G. Earnshaw	R
153	1929	4	PhA	10	ChC	8		E. Rommel	R	S. Blake	R
154	1929	5	PhA	3	ChC	2		R. Walberg	L	P. Malone	R
155	1930	1	PhA	5	StLC	2		L. Grove	L	B. Grimes	R
156	1930	2	PhA	6	StLC	1		G. Earnshaw	R	F. Rhem	R
157	1930	3	StLC	5	PhA	0		B. Hallahan	L	R. Walberg	L
158	1930	4	StLC	3	PhA	1		J. Haines	R	L. Grove	L
159	1930	5	PhA	2	StLC	0		L. Grove	L	B. Grimes	R
160	1930	6	PhA	7	StLC	1		G. Earnshaw	R	B. Hallahan	L

Overall WS Game	Year	Game No.	Score				Winning Pitcher	Pitch Style	Losing Pitcher	Pitch Style
161	1931	1	PhA	6	StLC	2	L. Grove	L	P. Derringer	R
162	1931	2	StLC	2	PhA	0	B. Hallahan	L	G. Earnshaw	R
163	1931	3	StLC	5	PhA	2	B. Grimes	R	L. Grove	L
164	1931	4	PhA	3	StLC	0	G. Earnshaw	R	S. Johnson	R
165	1931	5	StLC	5	PhA	1	B. Hallahan	L	W. Hoyt	R
166	1931	6	PhA	8	StLC	1	L. Grove	L	P. Derringer	R
167	1931	7	StLC	4	PhA	2	B. Grimes	R	G. Earnshaw	R
168	1932	1	NYY	12	ChC	6	C. Ruffing	R	G. Bush	R
169	1932	2	NYY	5	ChC	2	L. Gomez	L	L. Warneke	R
170	1932	3	NYY	7	ChC	5	G. Pipgras	R	C. Root	R
171	1932	4	NYY	13	ChC	6	W. Moore	R	F. May	L
172	1933	1	NYG	4	W	2	C. Hubbell	L	W. Stewart	L
173	1933	2	NYG	6	W	1	H. Schumacher	R	A. Crowder	R
174	1933	3	W	4	NYG	0	E. Whitehill	L	F. Fitzsimmons	R
175	1933	4	NYG	2	W	1	C. Hubbell	L	M. Weaver	R
176	1933	5	NYG	4	W	3	A. Luque	R	J. Russell	R
177	1934	1	StLC	8	D	3	J. Dean	R	A. Crowder	R
178	1934	2	D	3	StLC	2	S. Rowe	R	W. Walker	L
179	1934	3	StLC	4	D	1	P. Dean	R	T. Bridges	R
180	1934	4	D	10	StLC	4	E. Auker	R	W. Walker	L
181	1934	5	D	3	StLC	1	T. Bridges	R	J. Dean	R
182	1934	6	StLC	4	D	3	P. Dean	R	S. Rowe	R
183	1934	7	StLC	11	D	0	J. Dean	R	E. Auker	R
184	1935	1	ChC	3	D	0	L. Warneke	R	S. Rowe	R
185	1935	2	D	8	ChC	3	T. Bridges	R	C. Root	R
186	1935	3	D	6	ChC	5	S. Rowe	R	L. French	L
187	1935	4	D	2	ChC	1	A. Crowder	R	T. Carleton	R
188	1935	5	ChC	3	D	1	L. Warneke	R	S. Rowe	R
189	1935	6	D	4	ChC	3	T. Bridges	R	L. French	L
190	1936	1	NYG	6	NYY	1	C. Hubbell	L	C. Ruffing	R
191	1936	2	NYY	18	NYG	4	L. Gomez	L	H. Schumacher	R
192	1936	3	NYY	2	NYG	1	B. Hadley	R	F. Fitzsimmons	R
193	1936	4	NYY	5	NYG	2	M. Pearson	R	C. Hubbell	L
194	1936	5	NYG	5	NYY	4	H. Schumacher	R	P. Malone	R
195	1936	6	NYY	13	NYG	5	L. Gomez	L	F. Fitzsimmons	R
196	1937	1	NYY	8	NYG	1	L. Gomez	L	C. Hubbell	L

Overall WS Game	Year	Game No.		Score				Winning Pitcher	Pitch Style	Losing Pitcher	Pitch Style
197	1937	2	NYY	8	NYG	1		C. Ruffing	R	C. Melton	L
198	1937	3	NYY	5	NYG	1		M. Pearson	R	H. Schumacher	R
199	1937	4	NYG	7	NYY	3		C. Hubbell	L	B. Hadley	R
200	1937	5	NYY	4	NYG	2		L. Gomez	L	C. Melton	L
201	1938	1	NYY	3	ChC	1		C. Ruffing	R	B. Lee	R
202	1938	2	NYY	6	ChC	3		L. Gomez	L	J. Dean	R
203	1938	3	NYY	5	ChC	2		M. Pearson	R	C. Bryant	R
204	1938	4	NYY	8	ChC	3		C. Ruffing	R	B. Lee	R
205	1939	1	NYY	2	Cin	1		C. Ruffing	R	P. Derringer	R
206	1939	2	NYY	4	Cin	0		M. Pearson	R	B. Walters	R
207	1939	3	NYY	7	Cin	3		B. Hadley	R	G. Thompson	R
208	1939	4	NYY	7	Cin	4		J. Murphy	R	B. Walters	R
209	1940	1	D	7	Cin	2		B. Newsom	R	P. Derringer	R
210	1940	2	Cin	5	D	2		B. Walters	R	S. Rowe	R
211	1940	3	D	7	Cin	4		T. Bridges	R	J. Turner	R
212	1940	4	Cin	5	D	2		P. Derringer	R	D. Trout	R
213	1940	5	D	8	Cin	0		B. Newsom	R	G. Thompson	R
214	1940	6	Cin	4	D	0		B. Walters	R	S. Rowe	R
215	1940	7	Cin	2	D	1		P. Derringer	R	B. Newsom	R
216	1941	1	NYY	3	BR	2		C. Ruffing	R	C. Davis	R
217	1941	2	BR	3	NYY	2		W. Wyatt	R	S. Chandler	R
218	1941	3	NYY	2	BR	1		M. Russo	L	H. Casey	R
219	1941	4	NYY	7	BR	4		J. Murphy	R	H. Casey	R
220	1941	5	NYY	3	BR	1		E. Bonham	R	W. Wyatt	R
221	1942	1	NYY	7	StLC	4		C. Ruffing	R	M. Cooper	R
222	1942	2	StLC	4	NYY	3		J. Beazley	R	E. Bonham	R
223	1942	3	StLC	2	NYY	0		E. White	L	S. Chandler	R
224	1942	4	StLC	9	NYY	6		M. Lanier	L	A. Donald	R
225	1942	5	StLC	4	NYY	2		J. Beazley	R	C. Ruffing	R
226	1943	1	NYY	4	StLC	2		S. Chandler	R	M. Lanier	L
227	1943	2	StLC	4	NYY	3		M. Cooper	R	E. Bonham	R
228	1943	3	NYY	6	StLC	2		H. Borowy	R	A. Brazle	L
229	1943	4	NYY	2	StLC	1		M. Russo	L	H. Brecheen	L
230	1943	5	NYY	2	StLC	0		S. Chandler	R	M. Cooper	R
231	1944	1	StLB	2	StLC	1		D. Galehouse	R	M. Cooper	R

Overall WS Game	Year	Game No.	Score				Winning Pitcher	Pitch Style	Losing Pitcher	Pitch Style
232	1944	2	StLC	3	StLB	2	B. Donnelly	R	B. Muncrief	R
233	1944	3	StLB	6	StLC	2	J. Kramer	R	T. Wilks	R
234	1944	4	StLC	5	StLB	1	H. Brecheen	L	S. Jakucki	R
235	1944	5	StLC	2	StLB	0	M. Cooper	R	D. Galehouse	R
236	1944	6	StLC	3	StLB	1	M. Lanier	L	N. Potter	R
237	1945	1	ChC	9	D	0	H. Borowy	R	H. Newhouser	L
238	1945	2	D	4	ChC	1	V. Trucks	R	H. Wyse	R
239	1945	3	ChC	3	D	0	C. Passeau	R	F. Overmire	L
240	1945	4	D	4	ChC	1	D. Trout	R	R. Prim	L
241	1945	5	D	8	ChC	4	H. Newhouser	L	H. Borowy	R
242	1945	6	ChC	8	D	7	H. Borowy	R	D. Trout	R
243	1945	7	D	9	ChC	3	H. Newhouser	L	H. Borowy	R
244	1946	1	BRS	3	StLC	2	E. Johnson	L	H. Pollet	L
245	1946	2	StLC	3	BRS	0	H. Brecheen	L	M. Harris	L
246	1946	3	BRS	4	StLC	0	D. Ferriss	R	M. Dickson	R
247	1946	4	StLC	12	BRS	3	G. Munger	R	T. Hughson	R
248	1946	5	BRS	6	StLC	3	J. Dobson	R	A. Brazle	L
249	1946	6	StLC	4	BRS	1	H. Brecheen	L	M. Harris	L
250	1946	7	StLC	4	BRS	3	H. Brecheen	L	R. Klinger	R
251	1947	1	NYY	5	BR	3	F. Shea	R	R. Branca	R
252	1947	2	NYY	10	BR	3	A. Reynolds	R	V. Lombardi	L
254	1947	3	BR	9	NYY	8	H. Casey	R	B. Newsom	R
254	1947	4	BR	3	NYY	2	H. Casey	R	F. Bevens	R
255	1947	5	NYY	2	BR	1	F. Shea	R	R. Barney	R
256	1947	6	BR	8	NYY	6	R. Branca	R	J. Page	L
257	1947	7	NYY	5	BR	2	J. Page	L	H. Gregg	R
258	1948	1	BBR	1	CL	0	J. Sain	R	B. Feller	R
259	1948	2	CL	4	BBR	1	B. Lemon	R	W. Spahn	L
260	1948	3	CL	2	BBR	0	G. Bearden	L	V. Bickford	R
261	1948	4	CL	2	BBR	1	S. Gromek	R	J. Sain	R
262	1948	5	BBR	11	CL	5	W. Spahn	L	B. Feller	R
263	1948	6	CL	4	BBR	3	B. Lemon	R	B. Voiselle	R
264	1949	1	NYY	1	BR	0	A. Reynolds	R	D. Newcombe	R
265	1949	2	BR	1	NYY	0	P. Roe	L	V. Raschi	R
266	1949	3	NYY	4	BR	3	J. Page	L	R. Branca	R
267	1949	4	NYY	6	BR	4	E. Lopat	L	D. Newcombe	R
268	1949	5	NYY	10	BR	6	V. Raschi	R	R. Barney	R

Overall WS Game	Year	Game No.	Score				Winning Pitcher	Pitch Style	Losing Pitcher	Pitch Style
269	1950	1	NYY	1	PhP	0	V. Raschi	R	J. Konstanty	R
270	1950	2	NYY	2	PhP	1	A. Reynolds	R	R. Roberts	R
271	1950	3	NYY	3	PhP	2	T. Ferrick	R	R. Meyer	R
272	1950	4	NYY	5	PhP	2	W. Ford	L	B. Miller	R
273	1951	1	NYG	5	NYY	1	D. Koslo	L	A. Reynolds	R
274	1951	2	NYY	3	NYG	1	E. Lopat	L	L. Jansen	R
275	1951	3	NYG	6	NYY	2	J. Hearn	R	V. Raschi	R
276	1951	4	NYY	6	NYG	2	A. Reynolds	R	S. Maglie	R
277	1951	5	NYY	13	NYG	1	E. Lopat	L	L. Jansen	R
278	1951	6	NYY	4	NYG	3	V. Raschi	R	D. Koslo	L
279	1952	1	BR	4	NYY	2	J. Black	R	A. Reynolds	R
280	1952	2	NYY	7	BR	1	V. Raschi	R	C. Erskine	R
281	1952	3	BR	5	NYY	3	P. Roe	L	E. Lopat	L
282	1952	4	NYY	2	BR	0	A. Reynolds	R	J. Black	R
283	1952	5	BR	6	NYY	5	C. Erskine	R	J. Sain	R
284	1952	6	NYY	3	BR	2	V. Raschi	R	B. Loes	R
285	1952	7	NYY	4	BR	2	A. Reynolds	R	J. Black	R
286	1953	1	NYY	9	BR	5	J. Sain	R	C. Labine	R
287	1953	2	NYY	4	BR	2	E. Lopat	L	P. Roe	L
288	1953	3	BR	3	NYY	2	C. Erskine	R	V. Raschi	R
289	1953	4	BR	7	NYY	3	B. Loes	R	W. Ford	L
290	1953	5	NYY	11	BR	7	J. McDonald	R	J. Podres	L
291	1953	6	NYY	4	BR	3	A. Reynolds	R	C. Labine	R
292	1954	1	NYG	5	CL	2	M. Grissom	R	B. Lemon	R
293	1954	2	NYG	3	CL	1	J. Antonelli	L	E. Wynn	R
294	1954	3	NYG	6	CL	2	R. Gomez	R	M. Garcia	R
295	1954	4	NYG	7	CL	4	D. Liddle	L	B. Lemon	R
296	1955	1	NYY	6	BR	5	W. Ford	L	D. Newcombe	R
297	1955	2	NYY	4	BR	2	T. Byrne	L	B. Loes	R
298	1955	3	BR	8	NYY	3	J. Podres	L	B. Turley	R
299	1955	4	BR	8	NYY	5	C. Labine	R	D. Larsen	R
300	1955	5	BR	5	NYY	3	R. Craig	R	B. Grim	R
301	1955	6	NYY	5	BR	1	W. Ford	L	K. Spooner	L
302	1955	7	BR	2	NYY	0	J. Podres	L	T. Byrne	L
303	1956	1	BR	6	NYY	3	S. Maglie	R	W. Ford	L
304	1956	2	BR	13	NYY	8	D. Bessent	R	T. Morgan	R
305	1956	3	NYY	5	BR	3	W. Ford	L	R. Craig	R

Overall WS Game	Year	Game No.	Score				Winning Pitcher	Pitch Style	Losing Pitcher	Pitch Style
306	1956	4	NYY	6	BR	2	T. Sturdivant	R	C. Erskine	R
307	1956	5	NYY	2	BR	0	D. Larsen	R	S. Maglie	R
308	1956	6	BR	1	NYY	0	C. Labine	R	B. Turley	R
309	1956	7	NYY	9	BR	0	J. Kucks	R	D. Newcombe	R
310	1957	1	NYY	3	Mil	1	W. Ford	L	W. Spahn	L
311	1957	2	Mil	4	NYY	2	L. Burdette	R	B. Shantz	L
312	1957	3	NYY	12	Mil	3	D. Larsen	R	B. Buhl	R
313	1957	4	Mil	7	NYY	5	W. Spahn	L	B. Grim	R
314	1957	5	Mil	1	NYY	0	L. Burdette	R	W. Ford	L
315	1957	6	NYY	3	Mil	2	B. Turley	R	E. Johnson	R
316	1957	7	Mil	5	NYY	0	L. Burdette	R	D. Larsen	R
317	1958	1	Mil	4	NYY	3	W. Spahn	L	R. Duren	R
318	1958	2	Mil	13	NYY	5	L. Burdette	R	B. Turley	R
319	1958	3	NYY	4	Mil	0	D. Larsen	R	B. Rush	R
320	1958	4	Mil	3	NYY	0	W. Spahn	L	W. Ford	L
321	1958	5	NYY	7	Mil	0	B. Turley	R	L. Burdette	R
322	1958	6	NYY	4	Mil	3	R. Duren	R	W. Spahn	L
323	1958	7	NYY	6	Mil	2	B. Turley	R	L. Burdette	R
324	1959	1	ChW	11	LAD	0	E. Wynn	R	R. Craig	R
325	1959	2	LAD	4	ChW	3	J. Podres	L	B. Shaw	R
326	1959	3	LAD	3	ChW	1	D. Drysdale	R	D. Donovan	R
327	1959	4	LAD	5	ChW	4	L. Sherry	R	G. Staley	R
328	1959	5	ChW	1	LAD	0	B. Shaw	R	S. Koufax	L
329	1959	6	LAD	9	ChW	3	L. Sherry	R	E. Wynn	R
330	1960	1	PP	6	NYY	4	V. Law	R	A. Ditmar	R
331	1960	2	NYY	16	PP	3	B. Turley	R	B. Friend	R
332	1960	3	NYY	10	PP	0	W. Ford	L	W. Mizell	L
333	1960	4	PP	3	NYY	2	V. Law	R	R. Terry	R
334	1960	5	PP	5	NYY	2	H. Haddix	L	A. Ditmar	R
335	1960	6	NYY	12	PP	0	W. Ford	L	B. Friend	R
336	1960	7	PP	10	NYY	9	H. Haddix	L	R. Terry	R
337	1961	1	NYY	2	Cin	0	W. Ford	L	J. O'Toole	L
338	1961	2	Cin	6	NYY	2	J. Jay	R	R. Terry	R
339	1961	3	NYY	3	Cin	2	L. Arroyo	L	B. Purkey	R
340	1961	4	NYY	7	Cin	0	W. Ford	L	J. O'Toole	L
341	1961	*5	NYY	13	Cin	5	B. Daley	L	J. Jay	R
342	1962	1	NYY	6	SF	2	W. Ford	L	B. O'Dell	L

Overall WS Game	Year	Game No.		Score			Winning Pitcher	Pitch Style	Losing Pitcher	Pitch Style
343	1962	2	SF	2	NYY	0	J. Sanford	R	R. Terry	R
344	1962	3	NYY	3	SF	2	B. Stafford	R	B. Pierce	L
345	1962	4	SF	7	NYY	3	D. Larsen	R	J. Coates	R
346	1962	5	NYY	5	SF	3	R. Terry	R	J. Sanford	R
347	1962	6	SF	5	NYY	2	B. Pierce	L	W. Ford	L
348	1962	7	NYY	1	SF	0	R. Terry	R	J. Sanford	R
349	1963	1	LAD	5	NYY	2	S. Koufax	L	W. Ford	L
350	1963	2	LAD	4	NYY	1	J. Podres	L	A. Downing	L
351	1963	3	LAD	1	NYY	0	D. Drysdale	R	J. Bouton	R
352	1963	4	LAD	2	NYY	1	S. Koufax	L	W. Ford	L
353	1964	1	StLC	9	NYY	5	R. Sadecki	L	W. Ford	L
354	1964	2	NYY	8	StLC	3	M. Stottlemyre	R	B. Gibson	R
355	1964	3	NYY	2	StLC	1	J. Bouton	R	B. Schultz	R
356	1964	4	StLC	4	NYY	3	R. Craig	R	A. Downing	L
357	1964	5	StLC	5	NYY	2	B. Gibson	R	P. Mikkelson	R
358	1964	6	NYY	8	StLC	3	J. Bouton	R	C. Simmons	L
359	1964	7	StLC	7	NYY	5	B. Gibson	R	M. Stottlemyre	R
360	1965	1	Minn	8	LAD	2	J. Grant	R	D. Drysdale	R
361	1965	2	Min	5	LAD	1	J. Kaat	L	S. Koufax	L
362	1965	3	LAD	4	Minn	0	C. Osteen	L	C. Pascual	R
363	1965	4	LAD	7	Minn	2	D. Drysdale	R	J. Grant	R
364	1965	5	LAD	7	Minn	0	S. Koufax	L	J. Kaat	L
365	1965	6	Minn	5	LAD	1	J. Grant	R	C. Osteen	L
366	1965	7	LAD	2	Minn	0	S. Koufax	L	J. Kaat	L
367	1966	1	Balt	5	LAD	2	M. Drabowsky	R	D. Drysdale	R
368	1966	2	Balt	6	LAD	0	J. Palmer	R	S. Koufax	L
369	1966	3	Balt	1	LAD	0	W. Bunker	R	C. Osteen	L
370	1966	4	Balt	1	LAD	0	D. McNally	L	D. Drysdale	R
371	1967	1	StLC	2	BRS	1	B. Gibson	R	J. Santiago	R
372	1967	2	BRS	5	StLC	0	J. Lonborg	R	D. Hughes	R
373	1967	3	StLC	5	BRS	2	N. Briles	R	G. Bell	R
374	1967	4	StLC	6	BRS	0	B. Gibson	R	J. Santiago	R
375	1967	5	BRS	3	StLC	1	J. Lonborg	R	S. Carlton	L
376	1967	6	BRS	8	StLC	4	J. Wyatt	R	J. Lamabe	R
377	1967	7	StLC	7	BRS	2	B. Gibson	R	J. Lonborg	R
378	1968	1	StLC	4	D	0	B. Gibson	R	D. McLain	R
379	1968	2	D	8	StLC	1	M. Lolich	L	N. Briles	R

Overall WS Game	Year	Game No.	Score				Winning Pitcher	Pitch Style	Losing Pitcher	Pitch Style
380	1968	3	StLC	7	D	4	R. Washburn	R	E. Wilson	R
381	1968	4	StLC	10	D	1	B. Gibson	R	D. McLain	R
382	1968	5	D	5	StLC	3	M. Lolich	L	J. Hoerner	L
383	1968	6	D	13	StLC	1	D. McLain	R	R. Washburn	R
384	1968	7	D	4	StLC	1	M. Lolich	L	B. Gibson	R
385	1969	1	Balt	4	NYM	1	M. Cuellar	L	T. Seaver	R
386	1969	2	NYM	2	Balt	1	J. Koosman	L	D. McNally	L
387	1969	3	NYM	5	Balt	0	G. Gentry	R	J. Palmer	R
388	1969	4	NYM	2	Balt	1	T. Seaver	R	D. Hall	R
389	1969	5	NYM	5	Balt	3	J. Koosman	L	E. Watt	R
390	1970	1	Balt	4	Cin	3	J. Palmer	R	G. Nolan	R
391	1970	2	Balt	6	Cin	5	T. Phoebus	R	M. Wilcox	R
392	1970	3	Balt	9	Cin	3	D. McNally	L	T. Cloninger	R
393	1970	4	Cin	6	Balt	5	C. Carroll	R	E. Watt	R
394	1970	5	Balt	9	Cin	3	M. Cuellar	L	J. Merritt	L
395	1971	1	Balt	5	PP	3	D. McNally	L	D. Ellis	R
396	1971	2	Balt	11	PP	3	J. Palmer	R	B. Johnson	R
397	1971	3	PP	5	Balt	1	S. Blass	R	M. Cuellar	L
398	1971	4	PP	4	Balt	3	B. Kison	R	E. Watt	R
399	1971	5	PP	4	Balt	0	N. Briles	R	D. McNally	L
400	1971	6	Balt	3	PP	2	D. McNally	L	R. Miller	R
401	1971	7	PP	2	Balt	1	S. Blass	R	M. Cuellar	L
402	1972	1	PhOak	3	Cin.	2	K. Holtzman	L	G. Nolan	R
403	1972	2	PhOak	2	Cin	1	J. Hunter	R	R. Grimsley	L
404	1972	3	Cin	1	PhOak	0	J. Billingham	R	J. Odom	R
405	1972	4	PhOak	3	Cin	2	R. Fingers	R	C. Carroll	R
406	1972	5	Cin	5	PhOak	4	R. Grimsley	L	R. Fingers	R
407	1972	6	Cin	8	PhOak	1	R. Grimsley	L	V. Blue	L
408	1972	7	PhOak	3	Cin	2	J. Hunter	R	P. Borbon	R
409	1973	1	PhOak	2	NYM	1	K. Holtzman	L	J. Matlack	L
410	1973	2	NYM	10	PhOak	7	T. McGraw	L	R. Fingers	R
411	1973	3	PhOak	3	NYM	2	P. Lindblad	L	H. Parker	R
412	1973	4	NYM	6	PhOak	1	J. Matlack	L	K. Holtzman	L
413	1973	5	NYM	2	PhOak	0	J. Koosman	L	V. Blue	L
414	1973	6	PhOak	3	NYM	1	J. Hunter	R	T. Seaver	R
415	1973	7	PhOak	5	NYM	2	K. Hotlzman	L	J. Matlack	L

47
Records for Individual Pitchers

	W	L			W	L			W	L	
W. Ford	10	8	L	D. McNally	4	2	L	J. Wood	3	1	R
B. Gibson	7	2	R	G. Earnshaw	4	3	R	G. Alexander	3	2	R
A. Reynolds	7	2	R	S. Koufax	4	3	L	H. Borowy	3	2	R
C. Ruffing	7	2	R	W. Spahn	4	3	L	S. Coveleskie	3	2	R
L. Gomez	6	0	L	B. Turley	4	3	R	D. Phillippe	3	2	R
C. Bender	6	4	R	A. Nehf	4	4	L	D. Drysdale	3	3	R
W. Hoyt	6	4	R	B. Adams	3	0	R	W. Johnson	3	3	R
J. Coombs	5	0	R	J. Hunter	3	0	R	G. Mullin	3	3	R
H. Pennock	5	0	L	J. Koosman	3	0	L	B. Grimes	3	4	R
V. Raschi	5	3	R	M. Lolich	3	0	L	C. Mays	3	4	R
M. Brown	5	4	R	G. Pipgras	3	0	R	J. Beazley	2	0	R
C. Mathewson	5	5	R	B. Ruth	3	0	L	S. Blass	2	0	R
M. Pearson	4	0	R	T. Zachary	3	0	L	P. Dean	2	0	R
H. Brecheen	4	1	L	B. Dinneen	3	1	R	H. Eller	2	0	R
T. Bridges	4	1	R	U. Faber	3	1	R	G. Foster	2	0	R
E. Lopat	4	1	L	J. Haines	3	1	R	H. Haddix	2	0	L
J. Podres	4	1	L	B. Hallahan	3	1	L	B. James	2	0	R
L. Burdette	4	2	R	K. Holtzman	3	1	L	D. Kerr	2	0	L
L. Grove	4	2	L	O. Overall	3	1	R	V. Law	2	0	R
C. Hubbell	4	2	L	J. Palmer	3	1	R	H. Leonard	2	0	L
D. Larsen	4	2	R	E. Shore	3	1	R	W. Moore	2	0	R

	W	L			W	L			W	L	
J. Murphy	2	0	R	H. Bedient	1	0	R	R. Duren	1	1	R
E. Reulbach	2	0	R	D. Bessent	1	0	R	J. Ferguson	1	1	R
D. Rudolph	2	0	R	J. Billingham	1	0	R	D. Galehouse	1	1	R
M. Russo	2	0	L	W. Bunker	1	0	R	J. Jay	1	1	R
W. Ryan	2	0	R	O. Crandall	1	0	R	D. Koslo	1	1	L
F. Shea	2	0	R	B. Daley	1	0	L	J. McGinnity	1	1	R
L. Sherry	2	0	R	J. Dobson	1	0	R	B. Pierce	1	1	L
E. Walsh	2	0	R	B. Donnelly	1	0	R	J. Ring	1	1	R
V. Aldridge	2	1	R	M. Drabowsky	1	0	R	W. Ruether	1	1	L
J. Barnes	2	1	R	H. Ehmke	1	0	R	J. Scott	1	1	R
J. Bouton	2	1	R	T. Ferrick	1	0	R	B. Shaw	1	1	R
N. Briles	2	1	R	D. Ferriss	1	0	R	M. Stottlemyre	1	1	R
J. Grant	2	1	R	G. Gentry	1	0	R	G. Tyler	1	1	L
R. Grimsley	2	1	L	R. Gomez	1	0	R	R. Walberg	1	1	L
B. Hadley	2	1	R	M. Grissom	1	0	R	R. Washburn	1	1	R
M. Lanier	2	1	L	S. Gromek	1	0	R	G. White	1	1	L
J. Lonborg	2	1	R	J. Hearn	1	0	R	W. Wyatt	1	1	R
H. McQuillan	2	1	R	Earl Johnson	1	0	L	J. Black	1	2	R
H. Newhouser	2	1	L	J. Kramer	1	0	R	E. Bonham	1	2	R
J. Page	2	1	L	B. Kison	1	0	R	R. Branca	1	2	R
P. Roe	2	1	L	J. Kucks	1	0	R	A. Crowder	1	2	R
L. Warneke	2	1	R	D. Liddle	1	0	L	R. Fingers	1	2	R
C. Young	2	1	R	P. Lindblad	1	0	L	J. Kaat	1	2	L
H. Casey	2	2	R	A. Luque	1	0	R	B. Loes	1	2	R
S. Chandler	2	2	R	N. Maddox	1	0	R	S. Maglie	1	2	R
R. Craig	2	2	R	W. Mails	1	0	L	J. Matlack	1	2	L
M. Cuellar	2	2	L	J. McDonald	1	0	R	D. McLain	1	2	R
J. Dean	2	2	R	T. McGraw	1	0	L	C. Osteen	1	2	L
P. Douglas	2	2	R	G. Mogridge	1	0	L	J. Sanford	1	2	R
C. Erskine	2	2	R	G. Munger	1	0	R	T. Seaver	1	2	R
R. Kremer	2	2	R	C. Passeau	1	0	R	S. Smith	1	2	L
C. Labine	2	2	R	T. Phoebus	1	0	R	D. Trout	1	2	R
B. Lemon	2	2	R	E. Rommel	1	0	R	H. Vaughan	1	2	L
B. Newsom	2	2	R	R. Sadecki	1	0	L	E. Wynn	1	2	R
J. Sain	2	2	R	F. Schupp	1	0	L	J. Bentley	1	3	L
H. Schumacher	2	2	R	B. Stafford	1	0	R	J. Pfeister	1	3	L
B. Walters	2	2	R	T. Sturdivant	1	0	R	H. Sallee	1	3	L
E. Cicotte	2	3	R	V. Trucks	1	0	R	B. Shawkey	1	3	R
M. Cooper	2	3	R	E. White	1	0	L	J. Tesreau	1	3	R
P. Derringer	2	4	R	E. Whitehill	1	0	L	B. Donovan	1	4	R
R. Terry	2	4	R	J. Wyatt	1	0	R	L. Ames	0	1	R
L. Bush	2	5	R	N. Altrock	1	1	L	J. Anderson	0	1	R
R. Marquard	2	5	L	E. Auker	1	1	R	G. Bell	0	1	R
E. Plank	2	5	L	J. Bagby Sr.	1	1	R	F. Bevens	0	1	R
S. Rowe	2	5	R	J. Benton	1	1	L	V. Bickford	0	1	R
J. Antonelli	1	0	L	G. Bush	1	1	R	S. Blake	0	1	R
L. Arroyo	1	0	L	T. Byrne	1	1	L	P. Borbon	0	1	R
G. Bearden	1	0	L	C. Carroll	1	1	R	C. Bryant	0	1	R

Name	W	L		Name	W	L		Name	W	L	
B. Buhl	0	1	R	H. McIntire	0	1	R	M. Weaver	0	1	R
L. Cadore	0	1	R	J. Merritt	0	1	L	M. Wilcox	0	1	R
R. Caldwell	0	1	R	R. Meyer	0	1	R	T. Wilks	0	1	R
H. Camnitz	0	1	R	J. Miljus	0	1	R	V. Willis	0	1	R
T. Carleton	0	1	R	P. Mikkelson	0	1	R	E. Wilson	0	1	R
S. Carlton	0	1	L	B. Miller	0	1	R	H. Wyse	0	1	R
G. Chalmers	0	1	R	R. Miller	0	1	R	E. Yde	0	1	L
T. Cloninger	0	1	R	W. Mizell	0	1	L	A. Brazle	0	2	L
A. Coakley	0	1	R	T. Morgan	0	1	R	R. Barney	0	2	R
J. Coates	0	1	R	B. Muncrief	0	1	R	V. Blue	0	2	L
C. Davis	0	1	R	B. O'Dell	0	1	L	A. Ditmar	0	2	R
A. Demaree	0	1	R	J. Odom	0	1	R	A. Downing	0	2	L
M. Dickson	0	1	R	F. Overmire	0	1	L	B. Feller	0	2	R
A. Donald	0	1	R	H. Parker	0	1	R	L. French	0	2	L
D. Donovan	0	1	R	C. Pascual	0	1	R	B. Friend	0	2	R
D. Ellis	0	1	R	E. Pfeffer	0	1	R	B. Grim	0	2	R
R. Fisher	0	1	R	H. Pollet	0	1	L	M. Harris	0	2	L
H. Gregg	0	1	R	N. Potter	0	1	R	L. Jansen	0	2	R
D. Hall	0	1	R	R. Prim	0	1	L	S. Jones	0	2	R
J. Hoerner	0	1	L	B. Purkey	0	1	R	B. Lee	0	2	R
D. Hughes	0	1	R	J. Quinn	0	1	R	S. Leever	0	2	R
T. Hughes	0	1	R	F. Rhem	0	1	R	L. Meadows	0	2	R
T. Hughson	0	1	R	A. Reinhardt	0	1	L	C. Melton	0	2	L
M. Garcia	0	1	R	E. Rixey	0	1	L	G. Nolan	0	2	R
S. Jakucki	0	1	R	R. Roberts	0	1	R	T. O'Brien	0	2	R
Ernie Johnson	0	1	R	B. Rush	0	1	R	J. O'Toole	0	2	L
B. Johnson	0	1	R	J. Russell	0	1	R	J. Santiago	0	2	R
S. Johnson	0	1	R	B. Schultz	0	1	R	G. Thompson	0	2	R
W. Kennedy	0	1	R	B. Shantz	0	1	L	W. Walker	0	2	L
R. Klinger	0	1	R	U. Shocker	0	1	R	F. Fitzsimmons	0	3	R
J. Konstanty	0	1	R	E. Siever	0	1	L	P. Malone	0	3	R
J. Lamabe	0	1	R	C. Simmons	0	1	L	C. Root	0	3	R
A. Leifield	0	1	L	K. Spooner	0	1	L	E. Watt	0	3	R
V. Lombardi	0	1	L	G. Staley	0	1	R	C. Williams	0	3	L
F. Marberry	0	1	R	W. Stewart	0	1	L	D. Newcombe	0	4	R
F. May	0	1	L	J. Turner	0	1	R	W. Sherdel	0	4	L
J. Mayer	0	1	R	B. Voiselle	0	1	R	E. Summers	0	4	R

48
Games Pitched Per Series

1903		1906		1908	
D. Phillippe	5	M. Brown	3	O. Overall	3
B. Dinneen	4	G. White	3	M. Brown	2
C. Young	4	N. Altrock	2	B. Donovan	2
S. Leever	2	O. Overall	2	E. Reulbach	2
T. Hughes	1	J. Pfeister	2	O. Summers	2
W. Kennedy	1	E. Reulbach	2	E. Killian	1
W. Thompson	1	E. Walsh	2	G. Mullin	1
F. Veil	1	F. Owen	1	J. Pfeister	1
				G. Winter	1

1907		1909	
B. Donovan	2		
G. Mullin	2	G. Mullin	4

1905		1907		1909	
C. Mathewson	3	O. Overall	2	B. Adams	3
C. Bender	2	E. Reulbach	2	H. Camnitz	2
J. McGinnity	2	M. Brown	1	B. Donovan	2
E. Plank	2	E. Killian	1	D. Phillippe	2
L. Ames	1	J. Pfeister	1	O. Summers	2
A. Coakley	1	E. Siever	1	R. Willett	2

V. Willis 2
A. Leifield 1
N. Maddox 1
R. Works 1

1910
M. Brown 3
J. Coombs 3
C. Bender 2
H. McIntire 2
L. Cole 1
O. Overall 1
J. Pfeister 1
E. Reulbach 1
L. Richie 1

1911
C. Bender 3
R. Marquard 3
C. Mathewson 3
L. Ames 2
J. Coombs 2
O. Crandall 2
E. Plank 2
G. Wiltse 2

1912
H. Bedient 4
J. Wood 4
C. Mathewson 3
J. Tesreau 3
R. Collins 2
C. Hall 2
R. Marquard 2
T. O'Brien 2
L. Ames 1
O. Crandall 1

1913
C. Bender 2
O. Crandall 2
R. Marquard 2
C. Mathewson 2
E. Plank 2
J. Tesreau 2
L. Bush 1
A. Demaree 1

1914
B. James 2
D. Rudolph 2
C. Bender 1
L. Bush 1
H. Pennock 1
E. Plank 1
B. Shawkey 1
G. Tyler 1
J. Wyckoff 1

1915
G. Alexander 2
G. Foster 2
J. Mayer 2
E. Shore 2
G. Chalmers 1
H. Leonard 1
E. Rixey 1

1916
E. Pfeffer 3
R. Marquard 2
C. Mays 2
E. Shore 2
L. Cheney 1
J. Coombs 1
W. Dell 1

G. Foster 1
H. Leonard 1
N. Rucker 1
B. Ruth 1
S. Smith 1

1917
U. Faber 4
E. Cicotte 3
W. Perritt 3
J. Benton 2
H. Sallee 2
F. Schupp 2
J. Anderson 1
D. Danforth 1
E. Russell 1
J. Tesreau 1
C. Williams 1

1918
G. Tyler 3
H. Vaughan 3
L. Bush 2
C. Mays 2
B. Ruth 2
P. Douglas 1
C. Hendrix 1
S. Jones 1

1919
E. Cicotte 3
C. Williams 3
H. Eller 2
R. Fisher 2
D. Kerr 2
A. Luque 2
J. Ring 2
W. Ruether 2

H. Sallee   2
R. Wilkinson   2
W. James   1
G. Lowdermilk   1
J. Mayer   1

1920

S. Coveleskie   3
B. Grimes   3
A. Mamaux   3
J. Bagby Sr.   2
L. Cadore   2
W. Mails   2
R. Marquard   2
S. Smith   2
G. Uhle   2
R. Caldwell   1
C. Mitchell   1
E. Pfeffer   1

1921

J. Barnes   3
P. Douglas   3
W. Hoyt   3
C. Mays   3
A. Nehf   3
B. Shawkey   2
F. Toney   2
H. Collins   1
H. Harper   1
W. Piercy   1
J. Quinn   1
T. Rogers   1

1922

L. Bush   2
W. Hoyt   2
S. Jones   2
A. Nehf   2
J. Barnes   1
C. Mays   1
H. McQuillan   1
W. Ryan   1
J. Scott   1
B. Shawkey   1

1923

L. Bush   3
H. Pennock   3
W. Ryan   3
J. Barnes   2
J. Bentley   2
C. Jonnard   2
H. McQuillan   2
A. Nehf   2
J. Scott   2
W. Hoyt   1
S. Jones   1
B. Shawkey   1
J. Watson   1

1924

F. Marberry   4
W. Johnson   3
H. McQuillan   3
A. Nehf   3
J. Bentley   3
J. Barnes   2
G. Mogridge   2
W. Ryan   2
T. Zachary   2

H. Baldwin   1
W. Dean   1
C. Jonnard   1
J. Martina   1
W. Ogden   1
A. Russell   1
B. Speece   1
J. Watson   1

1925

V. Aldridge   3
W. Johnson   3
R. Kremer   3
J. Morrison   3
N. Ballou   2
S. Coveleskie   2
A. Ferguson   2
F. Marberry   2
B. Adams   1
L. Meadows   1
J. Oldham   1
E. Yde   1
T. Zachary   1

1926

G. Alexander   3
J. Haines   3
H. Pennock   3
B. Shawkey   3
W. Hoyt   2
W. Sherdell   2
U. Shocker   2
M. Thomas   2
H. Bell   1
B. Hallahan   1
V. Keen   1
S. Jones   1
A. Reinhart   1

| F. Rhem | 1 |
| W. Ruether | 1 |

1927

M. Cvengros	2
J. Miljus	2
W. Moore	2
V. Aldridge	1
R. Dawson	1
C. Hill	1
W. Hoyt	1
R. Kremer	1
L. Meadows	1
H. Pennock	1
G. Pipgras	1

1928

G. Alexander	2
W. Hoyt	2
S. Johnson	2
W. Sherdell	2
J. Haines	1
C. Mitchell	1
G. Pipgras	1
F. Rhem	1
T. Zachary	1

1929

P. Malone	3
S. Blake	2
G. Bush	2
H. Carlson	2
G. Earnshaw	2
H. Ehmke	2
L. Grove	2
A. Nehf	2
C. Root	2
R. Walberg	2
J. Quinn	1
E. Rommel	1

1930

G. Earnshaw	3
L. Grove	3
B. Grimes	2
B. Hallahan	2
S. Johnson	2
J. Lindsey	2
H. Bell	1
J. Haines	1
J. Quinn	1
F. Rhem	1
W. Shores	1
R. Walberg	1

1931

P. Derringer	3
G. Earnshaw	3
L. Grove	3
B. Hallahan	3
S. Johnson	3
B. Grimes	2
J. Lindsey	2
R. Walberg	2
W. Hoyt	1
L. Mahaffey	1
F. Rhem	1
E. Rommel	1

1932

G. Bush	2
B. Grimes	2
J. May	2
H. Pennock	2
L. Tinning	2
L. Warneke	2
J. Allen	1
L. Gomez	1
P. Malone	1
W. Moore	1
G. Pipgras	1

C. Root	1
C. Ruffing	1
R. E. Smith	1

1933

J. Russell	3
A. Crowder	2
C. Hubbell	2
H. Schumacher	2
A. Thomas	2
H. Bell	1
F. Fitzsimmons	1
A. Luque	1
A. McColl	1
W. Stewart	1
M. Weaver	1
E. Whitehill	1

1934

T. Bridges	3
J. Dean	3
E. Hogsett	3
S. Rowe	3
E. Auker	2
T. Carleton	2
A. Crowder	2
P. Dean	2
F. Marberry	2
W. Walker	2
J. Haines	1
B. Hallahan	1
J. Mooney	1
D. Vance	1

1935

S. Rowe	3
L. Warneke	3
T. Bridges	2
L. French	2
B. Lee	2
C. Root	2

E. Auker	1
T. Carleton	1
A. Crowder	1
R. Henshaw	1
E. Hogsett	1
F. Kowalik	1

1936

D. Coffman	2
F. Fitzsimmons	2
F. Gabler	2
L. Gomez	2
H. Gumbert	2
C. Hubbell	2
P. Malone	2
C. Ruffing	2
H. Schumacher	2
C. Castleman	1
B. Hadley	1
J. Murphy	1
M. Pearson	1
A. Smith	1

1937

C. Melton	3
J. Brennan	2
D. Coffman	2
L. Gomez	2
H. Gumbert	2
C. Hubbell	2
A. Smith	2
I. Andrews	1
B. Hadley	1
J. Murphy	1
M. Pearson	1
C. Ruffing	1
H. Schumacher	1
K. Wicker	1

1938

L. French	3
J. Dean	2
B. Lee	2
C. Ruffing	2
J. Russell	2
C. Bryant	1
T. Carleton	1
L. Gomez	1
J. Murphy	1
V. Page	1
M. Pearson	1
C. Root	1

1939

P. Derringer	2
B. Walters	2
L. Gomez	1
L. Grissom	1
B. Hadley	1
O. Hildebrand	1
L. Moore	1
J. Murphy	1
M. Pearson	1
C. Ruffing	1
S. Sundra	1
G. Thompson	1

1940

P. Derringer	3
L. Moore	3
B. Newsom	3
S. Rowe	2
B. Walters	2
J. Beggs	1
T. Bridges	1
J. Gorsica	1
J. Hutchings	1
F. Hutchinson	1
A. McKain	1

E. Riddle	1
C. Smith	1
G. Thompson	1
D. Trout	1
J. Turner	1
J. Vandermeer	1

1941

J. Allen	3
H. Casey	3
L. French	2
J. Murphy	2
W. Wyatt	2
M. Breuer	1
E. Bonham	1
S. Chandler	1
C. Davis	1
A. Donald	1
F. Fitzsimmons	1
K. Higbe	1
C. Ruffing	1
M. Russo	1

1942

J. Beazley	2
E. Bonham	2
S. Chandler	2
M. Cooper	2
H. Gumbert	2
M. Lanier	2
C. Ruffing	2
H. Borowy	1
M. Breuer	1
A. Donald	1
H. Pollet	1
J. Turner	1
E. White	1

1943

H. Brecheen 3
M. Lanier 3
S. Chandler 2
M. Cooper 2
J. Murphy 2
E. Bonham 1
H. Borowy 1
A. Brazle 1
M. Dickson 1
H. Krist 1
M. Russo 1

1944

M. Cooper 2
B. Donnelly 2
D. Galehouse 2
J. Kramer 2
M. Lanier 2
B. Muncrief 2
N. Potter 2
T. Wilks 2
H. Brecheen 1
E. Byerly 1
A. Hollingsworth 1
S. Jakucki 1
A. Jurisich 1
F. Schmidt 1
A. Shirley 1

1945

H. Borowy 4
P. Erickson 4
A. Benton 3
P. Derringer 3
H. Newhouser 3
C. Passeau 3
H. Vandenburg 3
H. Wyse 3
R. Prim 2
D. Trout 2

V. Trucks 2
T. Bridges 1
G. Caster 1
B. Chipman 1
L. Mueller 1
F. Overmire 1
J. Tobin 1

1946

H. Brecheen 3
J. Dobson 3
T. Hughson 3
Earl Johnson 3
M. Dickson 2
D. Ferriss 2
M. Harris 2
H. Pollet 2
J. Bagby Jr. 1
J. Beazley 1
A. Brazle 1
Mace Brown 1
C. Dreisewerd 1
R. Klinger 1
G. Munger 1
M. Ryba 1
T. Wilks 1
B. Zuber 1

1947

H. Casey 6
H. Behrman 5
J. Hatten 4
J. Page 4
R. Barney 3
R. Branca 3
H. Gregg 3
F. Shea 3
F. Bevens 2
K. Drews 2

V. Lombardi 2
B. Newsom 2
V. Raschi 2
A. Reynolds 2
S. Chandler 1
J. Taylor 1
C. Wensloff 1

1948

W. Spahn 3
C. Barrett 2
G. Bearden 2
B. Feller 2
B. Lemon 2
N. Potter 2
J. Sain 2
B. Voiselle 2
V. Bickford 1
R. Christopher 1
S. Gromek 1
E. Klieman 1
B. Muncrief 1
S. Paige 1

1949

J. Banta 3
J. Page 3
C. Erskine 2
J. Hatten 2
D. Newcombe 2
V. Raschi 2
A. Reynolds 2
R. Barney 1
R. Branca 1
T. Byrne 1
E. Lopat 1
P. Minner 1
E. Palica 1
P. Roe 1

1950

J. Konstanty	3
R. Meyer	2
A. Reynolds	2
R. Roberts	2
T. Ferrick	1
W. Ford	1
R. Heintzelman	1
E. Lopat	1
B. Miller	1
V. Raschi	1

1951

L. Jansen	3
J. Hearn	2
B. Hogue	2
Sheldon Jones	2
M. Kennedy	2
D. Koslo	2
E. Lopat	2
V. Raschi	2
A. Reynolds	2
G. Spencer	2
E. Corwin	1
A. Konikowski	1
B. Kuzava	1
S. Maglie	1
T. Morgan	1
J. Ostrowski	1
J. Sain	1

1952

A. Reynolds	4
J. Black	3
C. Erskine	3
V. Raschi	3
P. Roe	3
B. Loes	2
E. Lopat	2

E. Blackwell	1
T. Gorman	1
B. Kuzava	1
K. Lehman	1
J. Rutherford	1
J. Sain	1
R. Scarborough	1

1953

C. Erskine	3
C. Labine	3
A. Reynolds	3
W. Ford	2
J. Sain	2
B. Wade	2
J. Black	1
J. Hughes	1
T. Gorman	1
B. Kuzava	1
B. Loes	1
E. Lopat	1
J. McDonald	1
R. Meyer	1
B. Milliken	1
J. Podres	1
V. Raschi	1
P. Roe	1
A. Schallock	1

1954

D. Mossi	3
J. Antonelli	2
M. Garcia	2
B. Lemon	2
D. Liddle	2
R. Narleski	2
H. Wilhelm	2
R. Gomez	1
M. Grissom	1
A. Houtteman	1

S. Maglie	1
H. Newhouser	1
E. Wynn	1

1955

C. Labine	4
D. Bessent	3
B. Grim	3
B. Turley	3
T. Byrne	2
W. Ford	2
J. Kucks	2
T. Morgan	2
J. Podres	2
K. Spooner	2
T. Sturdivant	2
G. Coleman	1
R. Craig	1
C. Erskine	1
D. Larsen	1
B. Loes	1
R. Meyer	1
D. Newcombe	1
E. Roebuck	1

1956

J. Kucks	3
E. Roebuck	3
B. Turley	3
D. Bessent	2
R. Craig	2
C. Erskine	2
W. Ford	2
C. Labine	2
D. Larsen	2
S. Maglie	2
T. Morgan	2
D. Newcombe	2
T. Sturdivant	2
T. Byrne	1

| D. Drysdale | 1 |
| M. McDermott | 1 |

1957

L. Burdette	3
Ernie Johnson	3
D. McMahon	3
B. Shantz	3
B. Turley	3
B. Buhl	2
T. Byrne	2
A. Ditmar	2
W. Ford	2
B. Grim	2
D. Larsen	2
W. Spahn	2
T. Sturdivant	2
G. Conley	1
J. Kucks	1
J. Pizarro	1
B. Trowbridge	1

1958

B. Turley	4
L. Burdette	3
R. Duren	3
W. Ford	3
D. McMahon	3
W. Spahn	3
M. Dickson	2
J. Kucks	2
D. Larsen	2
A. Ditmar	1
D. Maas	1
Z. Monroe	1
J. Pizarro	1
B. Rush	1
C. Willey	1

1959

L. Sherry	4
G. Staley	4
D. Donovan	3
T. Lown	3
B. Pierce	3
E. Wynn	3
R. Craig	2
S. Koufax	2
J. Podres	2
B. Shaw	2
C. Churn	1
D. Drysdale	1
J. Klippstein	1
C. Labine	1
R. Moore	1
S. Williams	1

1960

E. Face	4
T. Cheney	3
J. Coates	3
B. Friend	3
F. Green	3
C. Labine	3
V. Law	3
B. Shantz	3
G. Witt	3
A. Ditmar	2
R. Duren	2
W. Ford	2
J. Gibbon	2
H. Haddix	2
W. Mizell	2
B. Stafford	2
R. Terry	2
B. Turley	2
L. Arroyo	1
D. Maas	1

1961

J. Brosnan	3
L. Arroyo	2
B. Daley	2
W. Ford	2
B. Henry	2
J. Jay	2
J. O'Toole	2
B. Purkey	2
R. Terry	2
J. Coates	1
K. Hunt	1
K. Johnson	1
Sherman Jones	1
J. Maloney	1
B. Stafford	1

1962

W. Ford	3
D. Larsen	3
J. Sanford	3
R. Terry	3
B. Bolin	2
M. Bridges	2
J. Coates	2
S. Miller	2
B. O'Dell	2
B. Pierce	2
B. Daley	1
J. Marichal	1
B. Stafford	1

1963

H. Reniff	3
W. Ford	2
S. Koufax	2
J. Bouton	1
A. Downing	1
D. Drysdale	1
S. Hamilton	1
R. Perranoski	1
J. Podres	1

| R. Terry | 1 |
| S. Williams | 1 |

1964

P. Mikkelson	4
B. Schultz	4
B. Gibson	3
A. Downing	3
M. Stollemyre	3
J. Bouton	2
R. Craig	2
S. Hamilton	2
G. Richardson	2
R. Sadecki	2
R. Sheldon	2
C. Simmons	2
R. Taylor	2
W. Ford	1
B. Humphrey	1
H. Reniff	1
R. Terry	1

1965

J. Grant	3
J. Kaat	3
S. Koufax	3
D. Drysdale	2
J. Klippstein	2
J. Merritt	2
R. L. Miller	2
C. Osteen	2
J. Perry	2
R. Perranoski	2
H. Reed	2
A. Worthington	2
D. Boswell	1
J. Brewer	1
C. Pascual	1
B. Pleis	1

1966

| D. Drysdale | 2 |

D. McNally	2
R. Perranoski	2
P. Regan	2
W. Bunker	1
J. Brewer	1
M. Drabowsky	1
S. Koufax	1
R. L. Miller	1
J. Moeller	1
C. Osteen	1
J. Palmer	1

1967

G. Bell	3
B. Gibson	3
J. Lamabe	3
J. Lonborg	3
J. Santiago	3
R. Willis	3
K. Brett	2
N. Briles	2
J. Hoerner	2
D. Hughes	2
D. Morehead	2
D. Osinski	2
R. Washburn	2
G. Waslewski	2
J. Wyatt	2
S. Carlton	1
L. Jaster	1
L. Stange	1
J. Stephenson	1
H. Woodeshick	1

1968

P. Dobson	3
B. Gibson	3
J. Hoerner	3
M. Lolich	3
D. McLain	3
R. Willis	3

N. Briles	2
S. Carlton	2
D. McMahon	2
D. Patterson	2
R. Washburn	2
W. Granger	1
J. Hiller	1
D. Hughes	1
L. Jaster	1
F. Lasher	1
M. Nelson	1
J. Sparma	1
E. Wilson	1

1969

M. Cueller	2
J. Koosman	2
D. McNally	2
T. Seaver	2
R. Taylor	2
E. Watt	2
D. Cardwell	1
G. Gentry	1
D. Hall	1
D. Leonhard	1
J. Palmer	1
P. Richert	1
N. Ryan	1

1970

C. Carroll	4
D. Gullett	3
T. Cloninger	2
M. Cuellar	2
M. Drabowsky	2
W. Granger	2
G. Nolan	2
J. Palmer	2
M. Wilcox	2
D. Hall	1
M. Lopez	1

J. McGlothlin	1	D. Ellis	1	J. Horlen	1
D. McNally	1	D. Hall	1	B. Locker	1
J. Merritt	1	G. Jackson	1	J. McGlothlin	1
T. Phoebus	1	D. Leonhard	1		
P. Richert	1	P. Richert	1		
R. Washburn	1	B. Veale	1		
E. Watt	1	G. Walker	1		

1973

D. Knowles	7
R. Fingers	6
T. McGraw	5
R. Sadecki	4
K. Holtzman	3
P. Lindblad	3
J. Matlack	3
H. Parker	3
V. Blue	2
J. Hunter	2
J. Koosman	2
J. Odom	2
H. Pina	2
T. Seaver	2
G. Stone	2

1971

D. McNally	4
P. Dobson	3
D. Guisti	3
R. L. Miller	3
B. Moose	3
S. Blass	2
M. Cuellar	2
T. Dukes	2
B. Johnson	2
B. Kison	2
J. Palmer	2
E. Watt	2
N. Briles	1

1972

P. Borbon	6
R. Fingers	6
C. Carroll	5
V. Blue	4
R. Grimsley	4
T. Hall	4
J. Billingham	3
K. Holtzman	3
J. Hunter	3
D. Hamilton	2
G. Nolan	2
J. Odom	2
D. Gullett	1

49

Tabulation of Games Pitched

W. Ford	22	R. Terry	9	D. Knowles	7
A. Reynolds	15	J. Barnes	8	M. Lanier	7
B. Turley	15	G. Earnshaw	8	E. Lopat	7
C. Labine	13	L. Grove	8	G. Mullin	7
R. Fingers	12	S. Koufax	8	J. Page	7
W. Hoyt	12	J. Kucks	8	D. Phillippe	7
A. Nehf	12	F. Marberry	8	E. Plank	7
P. Derringer	11	C. Mays	8	E. Reulbach	7
C. Erskine	11	D. McMahon	8	V. Blue	6
R. Marquard	11	J. Murphy	8	P. Borbon	6
C. Mathewson	11	O. Overall	8	H. Borowy	6
V. Raschi	11	S. Rowe	8	L. Burdette	6
C. Bender	10	B. Shawkey	8	T. Byrne	6
D. Larsen	10	W. Spahn	8	S. Chandler	6
H. Pennock	10	G. Alexander	7	E. Cicotte	6
C. Ruffing	10	H. Brecheen	7	J. Coates	6
M. Brown	9	T. Bridges	7	J. Coombs	6
L. Bush	9	R. Craig	7	M. Cooper	6
C. Carroll	9	D. Drysdale	7	M. Cuellar	6
H. Casey	9	L. French	7	P. Dobson	6
B. Gibson	9	L. Gomez	7	B. Donovan	6
B. Grimes	9	B. Hallahan	7	H. Gumbert	6
D. McNally	9	S. Johnson	7	J. Haines	6

J. Hatten	6
C. Hubbell	6
W. Johnson	6
K. Holtzman	6
P. Malone	6
H. McQuillan	6
R. L. Miller	6
J. Palmer	6
J. Podres	6
C. Root	6
W. Ryan	6
R. Sadecki	6
J. Sain	6
B. Shantz	6
T. Sturdivant	6
J. Tesreau	6
R. Willis	6
H. Behrman	5
J. Bentley	5
D. Bessent	5
N. Briles	5
S. Coveleski	5
O. Crandall	5
A. Crowder	5
J. Dean	5
M. Dickson	5
A. Ditmar	5
R. Duren	5
B. Grim	5
J. Hoerner	5
J. Hunter	5
S. Jones	5
T. McGraw	5
T. Morgan	5
D. Newcombe	5
B. Newsom	5
R. Perranowski	5
J. Pfeister	5
B. Pierce	5
P. Roe	5
J. Russell	5
H. Schumacher	5
R. Walberg	5
L. Warneke	5
R. Washburn	5
E. Watt	5
B. Adams	4
V. Aldridge	4
J. Allen	4
L. Ames	4
R. Barney	4
H. Bedient	4
J. Black	4
E. Bonham	4
R. Branca	4
G. Bush	4
T. Carleton	4
D. Coffman	4
B. Dinneen	4
P. Douglas	4
A. Downing	4
P. Erickson	4
U. Faber	4
E. Face	4
F. Fitzsimmons	4
R. Grimsley	4
D. Gullett	4
T. Hall	4
E. Hogsett	4
J. Koosman	4
R. Kremer	4
B. Lee	4
B. Lemon	4
J. Lindsey	4
B. Loes	4
S. Maglie	4
R. Meyer	4
J. Odom	4
P. Mikkelson	4
L. Moore	4
H. Newhouser	4
G. Nolan	4
M. Pearson	4
E. Pfeffer	4
N. Potter	4
H. Reniff	4
F. Rhem	4
E. Roebuck	4
H. Sallee	4
B. Schultz	4
T. Seaver	4
W. Sherdel	4
L. Sherry	4
E. Shore	4
B. Stafford	4
G. Staley	4
O. Summers	4
R. Taylor	4
G. Tyler	4
B. Walters	4
C. Williams	4
J. Wood	4
E. Wynn	4
C. Young	4
T. Zachary	4
L. Arroyo	3
E. Auker	3
J. Banta	3
J. Beazley	3
G. Bell	3
H. Bell	3
A. Benton	3
J. Billingham	3
J. Bouton	3
J. Brosnan	3
S. Carlton	3
T. Cheney	3
B. Daley	3
J. Dobson	3
D. Donovan	3
M. Drabowsky	3
G. Foster	3
B. Friend	3
D. Guisti	3
W. Granger	3
J. Grant	3
H. Gregg	3
F. Green	3
B. Hadley	3
D. Hall	3
S. Hamilton	3
D. Hughes	3
T. Hughson	3
L. Jansen	3
Earl Johnson	3
Ernie Johnson	3
C. Jonnard	3
J. Kaat	3
J. Klippstein	3
J. Konstanty	3
B. Kuzava	3
J. Lamabe	3
V. Law	3
P. Lindblad	3
M. Lolich	3
J. Lonborg	3
T. Lown	3
A. Luque	3
A. Mamaux	3
J. Matlack	3
J. Mayer	3
D. McLain	3
C. Melton	3
J. Merritt	3
W. Moore	3

B. Moose	3	M. Cvengros	2	W. Mizell	2
J. Morrison	3	P. Dean	2	C. Mitchell	2
D. Mossi	3	A. Donald	2	G. Mogridge	2
B. Muncrief	3	B. Donnelly	2	D. Morehead	2
C. Osteen	3	K. Drews	2	R. Narleski	2
H. Parker	3	T. Dukes	2	T. O'Brien	2
C. Passeau	3	H. Ehmke	2	B. O'Dell	2
W. Perritt	3	H. Eller	2	D. Osinski	2
G. Pipgras	3	B. Feller	2	J. O'Toole	2
H. Pollett	3	A. Ferguson	2	D. Patterson	2
J. Quinn	3	D. Ferriss	2	J. Perry	2
P. Richert	3	R. Fisher	2	H. Pina	2
W. Ruether	3	F. Gabler	2	J. Pizarro	2
B. Ruth	3	D. Galehouse	2	R. Prim	2
J. Sanford	3	M. Garcia	2	B. Purkey	2
J. Santiago	3	J. Gibbon	2	H. Reed	2
J. Scott	3	T. Gorman	2	P. Regan	2
F. Shea	3	J. Gorsica	2	G. Richardson	2
A. J. Smith	3	H. Haddix	2	J. Ring	2
S. Smith	3	C. Hall	2	R. Roberts	2
M. Stottlemyre	3	D. Hamilton	2	E. Rommel	2
D. Trout	3	M. Harris	2	D. Rudolph	2
H. Vandenburg	3	J. Hearn	2	M. Russo	2
H. Vaughan	3	B. Henry	2	F. Schupp	2
G. White	3	J. Hiller	2	B. Shaw	2
T. Wilks	3	B. Hogue	2	R. Sheldon	2
G. Witt	3	B. James	2	U. Shocker	2
H. Wyse	3	L. Jaster	2	C. Simmons	2
N. Altrock	2	J. Jay	2	O. Spencer	2
J. Antonelli	2	B. Johnson	2	K. Spooner	2
J. Bagby Sr.	2	Sheldon Jones	2	G. Stone	2
N. Ballou	2	B. Kison	2	Al Thomas	2
C. Barrett	2	M. Kennedy	2	M. Thomas	2
G. Bearden	2	D. Kerr	2	G. Thompson	2
J. Bentley	2	E. Killian	2	L. Tinning	2
F. Bevens	2	D. Koslo	2	F. Toney	2
S. Blake	2	J. Kramer	2	V. Trucks	2
S. Blass	2	S. Leever	2	J. Turner	2
B. Bolin	2	H. Leonard	2	G. Uhle	2
A. Brazle	2	D. Leonhard	2	B. Voiselle	2
J. Brennan	2	D. Liddle	2	B. Wade	2
K. Brett	2	V. Lombardi	2	W. Walker	2
M. Breuer	2	D. Maas	2	E. Walsh	2
J. Brewer	2	W. Mails	2	G. Waslewski	2
M. Bridges	2	J. May	2	J. Watson	2
B. Buhl	2	J. McGinnity	2	M. Wilcox	2
L. Cadore	2	J. McGlothlin	2	H. Wilhelm	2
H. Camnitz	2	H. McIntire	2	R. Wilkinson	2
H. Carlson	2	L. Meadows	2	R. Willett	2
T. Cloninger	2	J. Miljus	2	S. Williams	2
R. Collins	2	S. Miller	2	V. Willis	2

| H. Woodechick | 1 | J. Wyckoff | 1 | B. Zuber | 1 |
| R. Works | 1 | E. Yde | 1 | | |

1973	50	1951	28	1909	22
1960	48	1953	28	1937	22
1972	48	1926	27	1917	21
1947	46	1952	27	1941	21
1967	41	1962	27	1954	21
1945	38	1940	26	1930	20
1971	38	1919	25	1932	20
1964	37	1923	25	1935	20
1968	37	1925	25	1942	20
1955	35	1931	25	1969	19
1957	35	1961	25	1903	19
1959	34	1912	24	1911	19
1924	32	1920	24	1933	18
1956	32	1921	24	1938	18
1958	31	1929	23	1943	18
1965	31	1936	23	1906	17
1946	30	1944	23	1916	17
1970	30	1948	23	1966	16
1934	28	1949	23	1908	15

1910	15	1922	14	1905	11
1918	15	1927	14	1914	11
1950	15	1939	14	1915	11
1963	15	1928	13		
1913	14	1907	12	TOTAL	1713

51
Most Times Leading in Games Pitched Per Series

G. Alexander	3		S. Johnson	2		E. Bonham	1
P. Derringer	3		C. Labine	2		P. Borbon	1
W. Hoyt	3		P. Malone	2		H. Borowy	1
M. Lanier	3		R. Marquard	2		T. Bridges	1
C. Mathewson	3		G. Mullin	2		J. Brosnan	1
D. McNally	3		A. Nehf	2		L. Burdette	1
H. Pennock	3		O. Overall	2		G. Bush	1
B. Turley	3		A. Reynolds	2		C. Carroll	1
C. Bender	2		S. Rowe	2		S. Chandler	1
H. Brecheen	2		C. Ruffing	2		E. Cicotte	1
M. Brown	2		L. Warneke	2		D. Coffman	1
L. Bush	2		R. Willis	2		J. Coombs	1
H. Casey	2		V. Aldridge	1		S. Coveleskie	1
M. Cooper	2		J. Allen	1		O. Crandall	1
G. Earnshaw	2		J. Banta	1		M. Cuellar	1
B. Gibson	2		J. Barnes	1		M. Cvengros	1
B. Grimes	2		J. Beazley	1		J. Dean	1
L. Grove	2		H. Bedient	1		J. Dobson	1
H. Gumbert	2		G. Bell	1		P. Dobson	1

B. Donnelly	1	J. Koosman	1	P. Regan	1
B. Donovan	1	S. Koufax	1	H. Reniff	1
P. Douglas	1	J. Kramer	1	E. Reulbach	1
D. Drysdale	1	R. Kremer	1	E. Roebuck	1
P. Erickson	1	J. Kucks	1	D. Rudolph	1
C. Erskine	1	J. Lamabe	1	J. Russell	1
U. Faber	1	D. Larsen	1	J. Sanford	1
E. Face	1	M. Lolich	1	J. Santiago	1
R. Fingers	1	J. Lonborg	1	B. Schultz	1
F. Fitzsimmons	1	A. Mamaux	1	H. Schumacher	1
W. Ford	1	F. Marberry	1	T. Seaver	1
G. Foster	1	J. May	1	B. Shantz	1
L. French	1	J. Mayer	1	B. Shawkey	1
F. Gabler	1	C. Mays	1	W. Sherdel	1
D. Galehouse	1	D. McLain	1	L. Sherry	1
L. Gomez	1	D. McMahon	1	E. Shore	1
J. Grant	1	C. Melton	1	W. Spahn	1
B. Hallahan	1	P. Mikkelson	1	G. Staley	1
J. Haines	1	J. Miljus	1	R. Taylor	1
J. Hoerner	1	L. Moore	1	R. Terry	1
E. Hogsett	1	W. Moore	1	J. Tesreau	1
C. Hubbell	1	J. Morrison	1	L. Tinning	1
T. Hughson	1	D. Mossi	1	G. Tyler	1
B. James	1	B. Muncrief	1	H. Vaughan	1
L. Jansen	1	B. Newsom	1	B. Walters	1
Earl Johnson	1	J. Page	1	E. Watt	1
Ernie Johnosn	1	R. Perranowski	1	G. White	1
W. Johnson	1	E. Pfeffer	1	T. Wilks	1
S. Jones	1	D. Phillippe	1	C. Williams	1
J. Kaat	1	N. Potter	1	J. Wood	1
J. Konstanty	1	E. Plank	1		

52
Leaders in Most Completed Games Per Series

1903		1909		1914	
D. Phillippe	5	B. Adams	3	D. Rudolph	2
		G. Mullin	3		
1905				1915	
C. Mathewson	3	1910		G. Alexander	2
		J. Coombs	3	G. Foster	2
1906				E. Shore	2
N. Altrock	2	1911			
M. Brown	2	C. Bender	3	1916	
				H. Leonard	1
1907		1912		B. Ruth	1
B. Donovan	2	C. Mathewson	3	E. Shore	1
G. Mullin	2			S. Smith	1
		1913			
1908		C. Bender	2	1917	
B. Donovan	2	C. Mathewson	2	E. Cicotte	2
O. Overall	2	E. Plank	2	U. Faber	2

1918

H. Vaughan	3

1919

E. Cicotte	2
H. Eller	2
D. Kerr	2

1920

| S. Coveleskie | 3 |

1921

W. Hoyt	3
C. Mays	3
A. Nehf	3

1922

J. Barnes	1
L. Bush	1
H. McQuillan	1
A. Nehf	1
J. Scott	1
B. Shawkey	1

1923

L. Bush	1
A. Nehf	1
H. Pennock	1

1924

| W. Johnson | 2 |

1925

| W. Johnson | 3 |

1926

| G. Alexander | 2 |
| H. Pennock | 2 |

1927

W. Moore	1
H. Pennock	1
G. Pipgras	1

1928

| W. Hoyt | 2 |

1929

G. Bush	1
G. Earnshaw	1
H. Ehmke	1
P. Malone	1

1930

G. Earnshaw	2
B. Grimes	2
L. Grove	2

1931

G. Earnshaw	2
L. Grove	2
B. Hallahan	2

1932

L. Gomez	1
C. Ruffing	1
L. Warneke	1

1933

| C. Hubbell | 2 |

1934

J. Dean	2
P. Dean	2
S. Rowe	2

1935

| T. Bridges | 2 |
| S. Rowe | 2 |

1936

F. Fitzsimmons	1
L. Gomez	1
C. Hubbell	1
M. Pearson	1
C. Ruffing	1
H. Schumacher	1

1937

| L. Gomez | 2 |

1938

| C. Ruffing | 2 |

1939

P. Derringer	1
M. Pearson	1
C. Ruffing	1
B. Walters	1

1940

| B. Newsom | 3 |

1941

| W. Wyatt | 2 |

1942

| J. Beazley | 2 |

1943

| S. Chandler | 2 |

1944

| D. Galehouse | 2 |

1945

| H. Newhouser | 2 |

1946

| H. Brecheen | 2 |

1947
F. Bevens   1
A. Reynolds   1
F. Shea   1

1948
J. Sain   2

1949
D. Newcombe   1
A. Reynolds   1
P. Roe   1

1950
V. Raschi   1
A. Reynolds   1
R. Roberts   1

1951
E. Lopat   2

1952
J. Black   1
C. Erskine   1
V. Raschi   1
A. Reynolds   1
P. Roe   1

1953
C. Erskine   1
E. Lopat   1
V. Raschi   1
P. Roe   1

1954
J. Antonelli 1
B. Lemon   1

1955
J. Podres   2

1956
S. Maglie   2

1957
L. Burdette   3

1958
W. Spahn   2

1959
None   0

1960
W. Ford   2

1961
W. Ford   1
J. Jay   1
B. Purkey   1

1962
R. Terry   2

1963
S. Koufax   2

1964
B. Gibson   2

1965
J. Grant   2
S. Koufax   2

1966
W. Bunker   1
D. Drysdale   1
D. McNally   1
J. Palmer   1

1967
B. Gibson   3

1968
B. Gibson   3
M. Lolich   3

1969
M. Cueller   1
J. Koosman   1
D. McNally   1
T. Seaver   1

1970
M. Cuellar   1
D. McNally   1

1971
S. Blass   2

1972
None   0

1973
None   0

53
Most Times Leading in Completed Games—Per Series

A. Reynolds	4	G. Mullin	2	H. Ehmke	1	D. Phillippe	1
C. Ruffing	4	M. Pearson	2	H. Eller	1	G. Pipgras	1
G. Earnshaw	3	S. Rowe	2	U. Faber	1	E. Plank	1
B. Gibson	3	E. Shore	2	F. Fitzsimmons	1	J. Podres	1
L. Gomez	3	B. Adams	1	G. Foster	1	B. Purkey	1
C. Mathewson	3	N. Altrock	1	D. Galehouse	1	R. Roberts	1
D. McNally	3	J. Antonelli	1	J. Grant	1	D. Rudolph	1
A. Nehf	3	J. Barnes	1	B. Grimes	1	B. Ruth	1
H. Pennock	3	J. Beazley	1	B. Hallahan	1	J. Sain	1
V. Raschi	3	F. Bevens	1	J. Jay	1	J. Scott	1
P. Roe	3	J. Black	1	D. Kerr	1	H. Schumacher	1
G. Alexander	2	S. Blass	1	J. Koosman	1	T. Seaver	1
C. Bender	2	H. Brecheen	1	H. Leonard	1	F. Shea	1
L. Bush	2	T. Bridges	1	B. Lemon	1	B. Shawkey	1
E. Cicotte	2	M. Brown	1	M. Lolich	1	S. Smith	1
M. Cuellar	2	W. Bunker	1	S. Maglie	1	W. Spahn	1
B. Donovan	2	L. Burdette	1	P. Malone	1	R. Terry	1
C. Erskine	2	G. Bush	1	C. Mays	1	H. Vaughan	1
W. Ford	2	S. Chandler	1	H. McQuillan	1	B. Walters	1
L. Grove	2	J. Coombs	1	W. Moore	1	L. Warneke	1
W. Hoyt	2	S. Coveleskie	1	D. Newcombe	1	W. Wyatt	1
C. Hubbell	2	J. Dean	1	H. Newhouser	1		
W. Johnson	2	P. Dean	1	B. Newsom	1		
S. Koufax	2	P. Derringer	1	O. Overall	1		
E. Lopat	2	D. Drysdale	1	J. Palmer	1	TOTAL	138

54
Most Times Pitching Completed Games—Total Series

C. Mathewson	10	B. Dinneen	4	W. Spahn	3	J. Haines	2
C. Bender	9	L. Gomez	4	B. Turley	3	D. Kerr	2
B. Gibson	8	B. Grimes	4	H. Vaughan	3	J. Koosman	2
C. Ruffing	8	L. Grove	4	B. Walters	3	R. Kremer	2
W. Ford	7	C. Hubbell	4	C. Young	3	B. Lemon	2
W. Hoyt	6	S. Koufax	4	V. Aldridge	2	H. Leonard	2
G. Mullin	6	D. McNally	4	N. Altrock	2	J. Lonborg	2
A. Nehf	6	H. Pennock	4	J. Beazley	2	S. Maglie	2
E. Plank	6	S. Rowe	4	S. Blass	2	R. Marquard	2
M. Brown	5	B. Adams	3	E. Bonhan	2	H. Newhouser	2
L. Bush	5	H. Brecheen	3	N. Briles	2	J. Pfeister	2
B. Donovan	5	P. Derringer	3	S. Chandler	2	G. Pipgras	2
G. Earnshaw	5	D. Drysdale	3	M. Cooper	2	J. Podres	2
W. Johnson	5	B. Hallahan	3	M. Cuellar	2	E. Reulbach	2
C. Mays	5	M. Lolich	3	J. Dean	2	D. Rudolph	2
D. Phillippe	5	E. Lopat	3	P. Dean	2	M. Russo	2
A. Reynolds	5	B. Newsom	3	P. Douglas	2	B. Ruth	2
G. Alexander	4	O. Overall	3	H. Eller	2	J. Sain	2
T. Bridges	4	M. Pearson	3	C. Erskine	2	H. Sallee	2
L. Burdette	4	V. Raschi	3	U. Faber	2	H. Schumacher	2
E. Cicotte	4	P. Roe	3	G. Foster	2	R. Terry	2
J. Coombs	4	E. Shore	3	D. Galehouse	2	L. Warneke	2
S. Coveleskie	4	S. Smith	3	J. Grant	2	J. Wood	2

W. Wyatt	2	A. Crowder	1	W. Mails	1	F. Schupp	1
T. Zachary	2	J. Dobson	1	P. Malone	1	J. Scott	1
J. Antonelli	1	H. Ehmke	1	J. Mayer	1	T. Seaver	1
E. Auker	1	B. Feller	1	J. McGinnity	1	B. Shawkey	1
J. Bagby Sr.	1	D. Ferriss	1	D. McLain	1	F. Shea	1
J. Barnes	1	F. Fitzsimmons	1	H. McQuillan	1	W. Sherdel	1
G. Bearden	1	L. French	1	W. Moore	1	B. Stafford	1
H. Bedient	1	S. Gromek	1	G. Munger	1	M. Stottlemyre	1
J. Bentley	1	B. James	1	D. Newcombe	1	T. Sturdivant	1
J. Benton	1	J. Jay	1	C. Osteen	1	J. Tesreau	1
F. Bevens	1	S. Jones	1	J. Palmer	1	D. Trout	1
J. Black	1	J. Kaat	1	C. Passeau	1	V. Trucks	1
H. Borowy	1	D. Koslo	1	B. Pierce	1	G. Tyler	1
J. Bouton	1	J. Kramer	1	H. Pollet	1	E. Walsh	1
W. Bunker	1	J. Kucks	1	B. Purkey	1	E. White	1
G. Bush	1	C. Labine	1	J. Ring	1	G. White	1
T. Byrne	1	D. Larsen	1	R. Roberts	1	E. Whitehill	1
G. Chalmers	1	S. Leever	1	W. Ruether	1	C. Williams	1
A. Coakley	1	N. Maddox	1	J. Sanford	1	TOTAL	382

55
Most Victories Per Season

1903		1909		1915	
D. Phillippe	3	B. Adams	3	G. Foster	2
B. Dinneen	3				
		1910		**1916**	
1905		J. Coombs	3	E. Shore	2
C. Mathewson	3				
		1911		**1917**	
1906		C. Bender	2	U. Faber	3
E. Walsh	2				
				1918	
1907		**1912**		C. Mays	2
M. Brown	1	J. Wood	3	B. Ruth	2
E. Pfeister	1				
O. Overall	1	**1913**		**1919**	
E. Reulbach	1	C. Bender	2	H. Eller	2
				D. Kerr	2
1908		**1914**		**1920**	
M. Brown	2	B. James	2	S. Coveleskie	3
O. Overall	2	D. Rudolph	2		

1921	**1930**	**1940**
J. Barnes 2	G. Earnshaw 2	P. Derringer 2
P. Douglas 2	L. Grove 2	B. Newson 2
W. Hoyt 2		B. Walters 2
	1931	
1922	B. Grimes 2	**1941**
H. McQuillan 1	L. Grove 2	E. Bonham 1
A. Nehf 1	B. Hallahan 2	J. Murphy 1
J. Ryan 1		C. Ruffing 1
J. Scott 1	**1932**	M. Russo 1
	L. Gomez 1	W. Wyatt 1
1923	W. Moore 1	
H. Pennock 2	G. Pipgras 1	**1942**
	C. Ruffing 1	J. Beazley 2
1924		
T. Zachary 2	**1933**	**1943**
	C. Hubbell 2	S. Chandler 2
1925		
V. Aldridge 2	**1934**	**1944**
W. Johnson 2	J. Dean 2	H. Brecheen 1
R. Kremer 2	P. Dean 2	M. Cooper 1
		B. Donnelly 1
1926	**1935**	D. Galehouse 1
G. Alexander 2	T. Bridges 2	J. Kramer 1
J. Haines 2	L. Warneke 2	M. Lanier 1
H. Pennock 2		
		1945
1927	**1936**	H. Borowy 2
W. Hoyt 1	L. Gomez 2	H. Newhouser 2
W. Moore 1		
H. Pennock 1	**1937**	
G. Pipgras 1	L. Gomez 2	**1946**
		H. Brecheen 3
1928	**1938**	
W. Hoyt 2	C. Ruffing 2	**1947**
		H. Casey 2
1929	**1939**	F. Shea 2
G. Earnshaw 1	B. Hadley 1	
H. Ehmke 1	J. Murphy 1	**1948**
E. Rommel 1	M. Pearson 1	B. Lemon 2
R. Walberg 1	C. Ruffing 1	
G. Bush 1		

1949	
E. Lopat	1
J. Page	1
V. Raschi	1
A. Reynolds	1
P. Roe	1

1950	
W. Ford	1
T. Ferrick	1
V. Raschi	1
A. Reynolds	1

1951	
E. Lopat	2

1952	
V. Raschi	2
A. Reynolds	2

1953	
C. Erskine	1
B. Loes	1
E. Lopat	1
J. McDonald	1
A. Reynolds	1
J. Sain	1

1954	
J. Antonelli	1
R. Gomez	1
M. Grissom	1
D. Liddle	1

1955	
W. Ford	2
J. Podres	2

1956	
W. Ford	1
D. Bessent	1
J. Kucks	1
C. Labine	1
D. Larsen	1
S. Maglie	1
T. Sturdivant	1

1957	
L. Burdette	3

1958	
W. Spahn	2
B. Turley	2

1959	
L. Sherry	2

1960	
W. Ford	2
H. Haddix	2
V. Law	2

1961	
W. Ford	2

1962	
R. Terry	2

1963	
S. Koufax	2

1964	
J. Bouton	2
B. Gibson	2

1965	
J. Grant	2
S. Koufax	2

1966	
W. Bunker	1
M. Drabowski	1
D. McNally	1
J. Palmer	1

1967	
B. Gibson	3

1968	
M. Lolich	3

1969	
J. Koosman	2

1970	
M. Cuellar	1
D. McNally	1
T. Phoebus	1
C. Carroll	1
J. Palmer	1

1971	
S. Blass	2
D. McNally	2

1972	
J. Hunter	2
R. Grimsley	2

1973	
K. Holtzman	2

56

Times Most Victories from 1903-1972, except 1904

W. Ford	5	J. Palmer	2	S. Chandler	1
A. Reynolds	4	G. Pipgras	2	J. Coombs	1
C. Ruffing	4	B. Adams	1	M. Cooper	1
L. Gomez	3	V. Aldridge	1	S. Coveleskie	1
W. Hoyt	3	G. Alexander	1	M. Cuellar	1
E. Lopat	3	J. Antonelli	1	J. Dean	1
D. McNally	3	J. Barnes	1	P. Dean	1
H. Pennock	3	J. Beazley	1	P. Derringer	1
V. Raschi	3	D. Bessent	1	B. Dinneen	1
C. Bender	2	S. Blass	1	B. Donnelly	1
H. Brecheen	2	E. Bonham	1	P. Douglas	1
M. Brown	2	H. Borowy	1	M. Drabowsky	1
G. Earnshaw	2	J. Bouton	1	H. Ehmke	1
B. Gibson	2	T. Bridges	1	H. Eller	1
L. Grove	2	W. Bunker	1	C. Erskine	1
S. Koufax	2	L. Burdette	1	U. Faber	1
W. Moore	2	G. Bush	1	T. Ferrick	1
J. Murphy	2	C. Carroll	1	G. Foster	1
O. Overall	2	H. Casey	1	D. Galehouse	1

R. Gomez	1	V. Law	1	D. Rudolph	1
J. Grant	1	B. Lemon	1	B. Ruth	1
B. Grimes	1	D. Liddle	1	M. Russo	1
R. Grimsley	1	B. Loes	1	W. Ryan	1
M. Grissom	1	M. Lolich	1	J. Sain	1
H. Haddix	1	S. Maglie	1	J. Scott	1
B. Hadley	1	C. Mathewson	1	F. Shea	1
J. Haines	1	C. Mays	1	L. Sherry	1
B. Hallahan	1	J. McDonald	1	E. Shore	1
K. Holtzman	1	H. McQuillan	1	W. Spahn	1
C. Hubbell	1	A. Nehf	1	T. Sturdivant	1
J. Hunter	1	H. Newhouser	1	R. Terry	1
B. James	1	B. Newsom	1	B. Turley	1
W. Johnson	1	J. Page	1	R. Walberg	1
D. Kerr	1	M. Pearson	1	E. Walsh	1
J. Kramer	1	E. Pfeister	1	B. Walters	1
R. Kremer	1	D. Phillippe	1	L. Warneke	1
J. Koosman	1	T. Phoebus	1	J. Wood	1
J. Kucks	1	J. Podres	1	W. Wyatt	1
C. Labine	1	E. Reulbach	1	T. Zachary	1
M. Lanier	1	P. Roe	1		
D. Larsen	1	E. Rommel	1	TOTAL	155

57
Pitchers Winning 3 Games Per Series

Pitcher	Pitch Style	Year	Club	W	L	G	Opponent
J. Coombs	R	1910	PhA	3 - 0		5	Ch C
C. Mathewson	R	1905	NY G	3 - 0		5	PhA
U. Faber	R	1917	Ch W	3 - 1		6	NY G
B. Adams	R	1909	P P	3 - 0		7	D
H. Brecheen	L	1946	St. L C	3 - 0		7	BRS
L. Burdette	R	1957	Mil	3 - 0		7	NY Y
S. Coveleskie	R	1920	CL	3 - 0		7	BR D
B. Gibson	R	1967	St. L C	3 - 0		7	BRS
M. Lolich	L	1968	D	3 - 0		7	St. L C
B. Dinneen	R	1903	BRS	3 - 1		8	P P
J. Wood	R	1912	BRS	3 - 1		8	NY G
D. Phillippe	R	1903	P P	3 - 2		8	BRS

58
Most Innings Pitched Per Season

1903	1905	1906	1907	1908
D. Phillippe 44	C. Mathewson 27	M. Brown 19 2/3	B. Donovan, 21	O. Overall 18 1/3

1909	1910	1911	1912	1913
G. Mullin 32	C. Bender 18 2/3	C. Mathewson 27	C. Mathewson 28 2/3	C. Mathewson E. Plank 19

1914	1915	1916	1917	1918
D. Rudolph 18	G. Foster 18	E. Shore 17 2/3	U. Faber 27	H. Vaughan 27

1919	1920	1921	1922	1923
E. Cicotte 21 2/3	S. Coveleskie 27	W. Hoyt 27	A. Nehf 16	H. Pennock 17 1/3

1924	1925	1926	1927	1928
W. Johnson 24	W. Johnson 26	H. Pennock 22	W. Moore 10 2/3	W. Hoyt 20

1929	1930	1931	1932	1933
G. Earnshaw 13 2/3	G. Earnshaw 25	L. Grove 26	L. Warneke 10 2/3	C. Hubbell 20

1934	1935	1936	1937	1938
J. Dean 26	S. Rowe 21	C. Hubbell 16	L. Gomez 18	C. Ruffing 18

1939	1940	1941	1942	1943
P. Derringer 15 1/3	B. Newsom 26	W. Wyatt 18	J. Beazley 18	S. Chandler 18

1944	1945	1946	1947	1948
D. Galehouse 18	H. Newhouser 20 2/3	H. Brecheen 20	F. Shea 15 2/3	J. Sain 17

1949	1950	1951	1952	1953
V. Raschi 14 2/3	J. Konstanty 15	E. Lopat 18	J. Black 21 1/3	C. Erskine 14

1954	1955	1956	1957	1958
B. Lemon 13 1/3	J. Podres 18	S. Maglie 17	L. Burdette 27	W. Spahn 28 2/3

1959	1960	1961	1962	1963
B. Shaw 14	V. Law 18 1/3	W. Ford 14	R. Terry 25	S. Koufax 18

1964	1965	1966	1967	1968
B. Gibson 27	S. Koufax 24	D. McNally 11 1/3	B. Gibson 27	B. Gibson M. Lolich 27

1969	1970	1971	1972	1973
J. Koosman 17 2/3	J. Palmer 15 2/3	S. Blass 18	J. Hunter 16	J. Matlack 16 2/3

Times Most Innings Pitched Per Season

C. Mathewson	4	B. Donovan	1	H. Newhouser	1
B. Gibson	3	C. Erskine	1	B. Newsom	1
G. Earnshaw	2	U. Faber	1	O. Overall	1
W. Hoyt	2	W. Ford	1	J. Palmer	1
C. Hubbell	2	G. Foster	1	D. Phillippe	1
W. Johnson	2	D. Galehouse	1	E. Plank	1
S. Koufax	2	L. Gomez	1	J. Podres	1
H. Pennock	2	L. Grove	1	V. Raschi	1
J. Beazley	1	J. Hunter	1	S. Rowe	1
C. Bender	1	J. Konstanty	1	D. Rudolph	1
J. Black	1	J. Koosman	1	C. Ruffing	1
S. Blass	1	V. Law	1	J. Sain	1
H. Brecheen	1	B. Lemon	1	B. Shaw	1
M. Brown	1	M. Lolich	1	F. Shea	1
L. Burdette	1	E. Lopat	1	E. Shore	1
S. Chandler	1	S. Maglie	1	W. Spahn	1
E. Cicotte	1	J. Matlack	1	R. Terry	1
S. Coveleskie	1	D. McNally	1	H. Vaughan	1
J. Dean	1	W. Moore	1	L. Warneke	1
P. Derringer	1	G. Mullin	1	W. Wyatt	1
		A. Nehf	1		
				TOTAL	72

Most Strikeouts Per Series

1903	1905	1906	1907	1908
B. Dinneen	C. Mathewson	E. Walsh	B. Donovan	O. Overall
28	18	17	16	15

1909	1910	1911	1912	1913
G. Mullin	J. Coombs	C. Bender	J. Wood	C. Bender
20	17	20	21	9

1914	1915	1916	1917	1918
D. Rudolph	G. Foster	R. Marquard E. Shore	E. Cicotte	H. Vaughan
15	13	9	13	17

1919	1920	1921	1922	1923
H. Eller	S. Coveleskie	J. Barnes W. Hoyt	J. Barnes L. Bush A. Nehf	H. Pennock
15	8	18	6	8

1924	1925	1926	1927	1928
W. Johnson	W. Johnson	G. Alexander	C. Hill L. Meadows J. Miljus	W. Hoyt
20	15	17	6	14

1929	1930	1931	1932	1933
G. Earnshaw 17	G. Earnshaw 19	G. Earnshaw 20	C. Ruffing 10	C. Hubbell 15

1934	1935	1936	1937	1938
J. Dean	S. Rowe	C. Ruffing	L. Gomez C. Ruffing	C. Ruffing
17	14	12	8	11

1939	1940	1941	1942	1943
P. Derringer 9	B. Newsom 17	W. Wyatt 14	C. Ruffing 11	M. Lanier 13

1944	1945	1946	1947	1948
M. Cooper	H. Newhouser	H. Brecheen	H. Gregg F. Shea	W. Spahn
16	22	11	10	12

1949	1950	1951	1952	1953
A. Reynolds	W. Ford A. Reynolds	A. Reynolds	V. Raschi A. Reynolds	C. Erskine
14	7	8	18	16

1954	1955	1956	1957	1958
J. Antonelli	W. Ford J. Podres	S. Maglie	L. Burdette	W. Spahn
12	10	15	13	18

1959	1960	1961	1962	1963
E. Wynn	W. Ford V. Law	W. Ford R. Terry	J. Sanford	S. Koufax
10	8	7	19	23

1964	1965	1966	1967	1968
B. Gibson	S. Koufax	M. Drabowsky	B. Gibson	B. Gibson
31	29	11	26	35

1969	1970	1971	1972	1973
M. Cuellar D. McNally	C. Carroll	J. Palmer	J. Odom	T. Seaver
13	11	15	13	18

Times Leading Most Strikeouts Per Series

C. Ruffing	5		J. Coombs	1		S. Maglie	1
W. Ford	4		M. Cooper	1		R. Marquard	1
A. Reynolds	4		S. Coveleskie	1		C. Mathewson	1
G. Earnshaw	3		M. Cuellar	1		D. McNally	1
B. Gibson	3		J. Dean	1		L. Meadows	1
J. Barnes	2		P. Derringer	1		J. Miljus	1
C. Bender	2		B. Dinneen	1		G. Mullin	1
W. Hoyt	2		B. Donovan	1		A. Nehf	1
W. Johnson	2		M. Drabowsky	1		H. Newhouser	1
S. Koufax	2		H. Eller	1		B. Newsom	1
W. Spahn	2		C. Erskine	1		J. Odom	1
G. Alexander	1		G. Foster	1		O. Overall	1
J. Antonelli	1		L. Gomez	1		J. Palmer	1
H. Brecheen	1		H. Gregg	1		H. Pennock	1
L. Burdette	1		C. Hill	1		J. Podres	1
L. Bush	1		C. Hubbell	1		V. Raschi	1
C. Carroll	1		M. Lanier	1		S. Rowe	1
E. Cicotte	1		V. Law	1		D. Rudolph	1

J. Sanford	1	R. Terry	1	W. Wyatt	1
T. Seaver	1	H. Vaughan	1	E. Wynn	1
F. Shea	1	E. Walsh	1		
E. Shore	1	J. Wood	1	**TOTAL**	84

62

15 or More Strikeouts Per Series

B. Gibson	35	1968	*	C. Mathewson	18	1905	*
B. Gibson	31	1964	*	V. Raschi	18	1952	*
S. Koufax	29	1965	*	A. Reynolds	18	1952	*
B. Dinneen	28	1903	*	T. Seaver	18	1973	*
B. Gibson	26	1967	*	W. Spahn	18	1958	*
S. Koufax	23	1963	*	G. Alexander	17	1926	*
H. Newhouser	22	1945	*	J. Coombs	17	1910	*
M. Lolich	21	1968		J. Dean	17	1934	*
J. Wood	21	1912	*	P. Douglas	17	1921	
C. Bender	20	1911	*	G. Earnshaw	17	1929	*
G. Earnshaw	20	1931	*	B. Newsom	17	1940	*
W. Johnson	20	1924	*	H. Vaughan	17	1918	*
G. Mullin	20	1909	*	E. Walsh	17	1906	*
D. Phillippe	20	1903		C. Young	17	1903	
G. Earnshaw	19	1930	*	J. Coombs	16	1911	
J. Sanford	19	1962	*	M. Cooper	16	1944	*
J. Barnes	18	1921	*	B. Donovan	16	1907	*
W. Hoyt	18	1921	*	C. Erskine	16	1953	*

***Denotes Series Leader**

W. Ford	16	1958		W. Johnson	15	1925 *
L. Grove	16	1931		S. Maglie	15	1956 *
R. Terry	16	1962		O. Overall	15	1908 *
D. Drysdale	15	1965		D. Rudolph	15	1914 *
H. Eller	15	1919 *		J. Tesreau	15	1912
C. Hubbell	15	1933		J. Palmer	15	1971 *
D. Galehouse	15	1944 *				

63
Times 15 or More Strikeouts Per Series

G. Earnshaw	3		H. Eller	1		J. Palmer	1
B. Gibson	3		C. Erskine	1		D. Phillippe	1
J. Coombs	2		W. Ford	1		V. Raschi	1
W. Johnson	2		D. Galehouse	1		A. Reynolds	1
S. Koufax	2		L. Grove	1		D. Rudolph	1
G. Alexander	1		W. Hoyt	1		J. Sanford	1
J. Barnes	1		C. Hubbell	1		T. Seaver	1
C. Bender	1		M. Lolich	1		W. Spahn	1
M. Cooper	1		S. Maglie	1		R. Terry	1
J. Dean	1		C. Mathewson	1		J. Tesreau	1
B. Dinneen	1		G. Mullin	1		H. Vaughan	1
B. Donovan	1		H. Newhouser	1		E. Walsh	1
P. Douglas	1		B. Newsom	1		J. Wood	1
D. Drysdale	1		O. Overall	1		C. Young	1
						TOTAL	49

No.	Year	G	Winning Pitcher	Pitch Style	Score				IP	R	H	BB	K	Losing Pitcher	Pitch Style
1	1905	1	C. Mathewson	R	NY–SFG	3	PH–OAK	0	9	0	4	0	6	E. Plank	L
2	1905	3	C. Mathewson	R	NY–SFG	9	PH–OAK	0	9	0	4	1	8	A. Coakley	R
3	1905	5	C. Mathewson	R	NY–SFG	2	PH–OAK	0	9	0	6	0	4	C. Bender	R
4	1913	2	C. Mathewson	R	NY–SFG	3	PH–OAK	0	9	0	8	1	5	E. Plank	L
5	1906	4	M. Brown	R	ChC	1	ChW	0	9	0	2	2	5	N. Altrock	L
6	1907	5	M. Brown	R	ChC	2	D	0	9	0	7	1	4	G. Mullin	R
7	1908	4	M. Brown	R	ChC	3	D	0	9	0	4	0	4	O. Summers	R
8	1960	3	W. Ford	L	NYY	10	PP	0	9	0	4	1	3	W. Mizell	L
9	1960	6	W. Ford	L	NYY	12	PP	0	9	0	7	1	5	B. Friend	R
10	1961	1	W. Ford	L	NYY	2	Cin	0	9	0	2	1	6	J. O'Toole	L
11	1957	5	L. Burdette	R	BB–Mil	1	NYY	0	9	0	7	0	5	W. Ford	L
12	1957	7	L. Burdette	R	BB–Mil	5	NYY	0	9	0	7	1	3	D. Larsen	R
13	1903	2	B. Dinneen	R	BRS	3	PP	0	9	0	3	2	11	S. Leever	R
14	1903	8	B. Dinneen	R	BRS	3	PP	0	9	0	4	2	7	D. Phillippe	R
15	1967	4	B. Gibson	R	StLC	6	BRS	0	9	0	5	1	6	J. Santiago	R
16	1968	1	B. Gibson	R	StLC	4	D	0	9	0	5	1	17	D. McLain	R
17	1930	3	B. Hallahan	L	StLC	5	PH–OAK	0	9	0	7	5	6	R. Walberg	L
18	1931	2	B. Hallahan	L	StLC	2	PH–OAK	0	9	0	3	7	8	G. Earnshaw	R
19	1965	5	S. Koufax	L	BR–LAD	7	Minn	0	9	0	4	1	10	J. Kaat	L
20	1965	7	S. Koufax	L	BR–LAD	2	Minn	0	9	0	3	3	10	J. Kaat	L
21	1921	8	A. Nehf	L	NY–SFG	1	NYY	0	9	0	4	5	3	W. Hoyt	R
22	1923	3	A. Nehf	L	NY–SFG	1	NYY	0	9	0	6	3	4	S. Jones	R
23	1949	1	A. Reynolds	R	NYY	1	BrD	0	9	0	2	4	9	D. Newcombe	R
24	1952	4	A. Reynolds	R	NYY	2	BrD	0	9	0	4	3	10	J. Black	R
25	1909	7	B. Adams	R	PP	8	D	0	9	0	6	1	1	B. Donovan	R

No.	Year	G	Winning Pitcher	Pitch Style	Score				IP	R	H	BB	K	Losing Pitcher	Pitch Style
26	1948	3	G. Bearden	L	CL	2	BB–Mil	0	9	0	5	0	4	V. Bickford	R
27	1904	2	C. Bender	R	PH–OAK	3	NY–SFG	0	9	0	4	3	9	J. McGinnity	R
28	1917	3	J. Benton	L	NY–SFG	2	ChW	0	9	0	5	0	5	E. Cicotte	R
29	1945	1	H. Borowy	R	ChC	9	D	0	9	0	6	5	4	H. Newhouser	L
30	1946	2	H. Brecheen	L	StLC	3	BRS	0	9	0	4	3	4	M. Harris	L
31	1966	3	W. Bunker	R	Balt	1	BR–LAD	0	9	0	6	1	6	C. Osteen	L
32	1943	5	S. Chandler	R	NYY	2	StLC	0	9	0	10	6	7	M. Cooper	R
33	1944	5	M. Cooper	R	StLC	2	StLB	0	9	0	7	2	12	D. Galehouse	R
34	1920	7	S. Coveleskie	R	CL	3	BrD	0	9	0	5	0	1	B. Grimes	R
35	1934	7	J. Dean	R	StLC	11	D	0	9	0	6	0	5	E. Auker	R
36	1963	3	D. Drysdale	R	BR–LAD	1	NYY	0	9	0	3	1	9	J. Bouton	R
37	1931	4	G. Earnshaw	R	PH–OAK	3	StLC	0	9	0	2	1	8	S. Johnson	R
38	1919	5	H. Eller	R	Cin	5	ChW	0	9	0	3	1	9	C. Williams	L
39	1946	3	D. Ferris	R	BRS	4	StLC	0	9	0	6	1	4	M. Dickson	R
40	1920	2	B. Grimes	R	BrD	3	CL	0	9	0	7	4	2	J. Bagby Sr.	R
41	1926	3	J. Haines	R	StLC	4	NYY	0	9	0	5	3	3	W. Ruether	L
42	1921	2	W. Hoyt	R	NYY	3	NY–SFG	0	9	0	2	5	5	A. Nehf	L
43	1914	2	B. James	R	BB–Mil	1	PH–OAK	0	9	0	2	3	8	E. Plank	L
44	1925	4	W. Johnson	R	W	4	PP	0	9	0	6	2	2	E. Yde	L
45	1919	3	D. Kerr	L	ChW	3	Cin	0	9	0	3	1	4	R. Fisher	R
46	1956	7	J. Kucks	R	NYY	9	BrD	0	9	0	3	3	1	D. Newcombe	R
47	1956	6	C. Labine	R	BrD	1	NYY	0	10	0	7	2	5	B. Turley	R
48	1956	5	D. Larsen	R	NYY	2	BrD	0	9	0	0	0	7	S. Maglie	R
49	1967	2	J. Lonborg	R	BRS	5	StLC	0	9	0	1	1	4	D. Hughes	R
50	1920	6	W. Mails	L	CL	1	BrD	0	9	0	3	2	4	S. Smith	L
51	1921	1	C. Mays	R	NYY	3	NY–SFG	0	9	0	5	0	1	P. Douglas	R
52	1905	4	J. McGinnity	R	NY–SFG	1	PH–OAK	0	9	0	5	3	4	E. Plank	L
53	1966	4	D. McNally	L	Balt	1	BR–LAD	0	9	0	4	2	4	D. Drysdale	R
54	1909	4	G. Mullin	R	D	5	PP	0	9	0	5	2	10	A. Leifield	L
55	1940	5	B. Newsom	R	D	8	Cin	0	9	0	3	2	7	G. Thompson	R
56	1965	3	C. Osteen	L	BR–LAD	4	Minn	0	9	0	5	2	2	C. Pascual	R
57	1908	5	O. Overall	R	ChC	2	D	0	9	0	3	4	10	B. Donovan	R
58	1966	2	J. Palmer	R	Balt	6	BR-LAD	0	9	0	4	3	6	S. Koufax	L
59	1945	3	C. Passeau	R	ChC	3	D	0	9	0	1	1	1	F. Overmire	L
60	1939	2	M. Pearson	R	NYY	4	Cin	0	9	0	2	1	8	B. Walters	R
61	1955	7	J. Podres	L	BrD	2	NYY	0	9	0	8	2	4	T. Byrne	L
62	1950	1	V. Raschi	R	NYY	1	PhP	0	9	0	2	1	5	J. Konstanty	R
63	1919	4	J. Ring	R	Cin	2	ChW	0	9	0	3	3	2	E. Cicotte	R
64	1949	2	P. Roe	L	BrD	1	NYY	0	9	0	6	0	3	V. Raschi	R
65	1918	1	B. Ruth	L	BRS	1	ChC	0	9	0	6	1	4	H. Vaughan	L
66	1948	1	J. Sain	R	BB–Mil	1	CL	0	9	0	4	0	6	B. Feller	R
67	1962	2	J. Sanford	R	NY–SFG	2	NYY	0	9	0	3	3	6	R. Terry	R
68	1917	4	F. Schupp	L	NY–SFG	5	ChW	0	9	0	7	1	7	U. Faber	R
69	1922	3	J. Scott	R	NY–SFG	3	NYY	0	9	0	4	1	2	W. Hoyt	R
70	1958	4	W. Spahn	L	BB–Mil	3	NYY	0	9	0	2	2	7	W. Ford	L
71	1962	7	R. Terry	R	NYY	1	NY–SFG	0	9	0	4	0	4	J. Sanford	R
72	1958	5	B. Turley	R	NYY	7	BB–Mil	0	9	0	5	3	10	L. Burdette	R
73	1918	5	H. Vaughan	L	ChC	3	BRS	0	9	0	5	1	4	S. Jones	R
74	1940	6	B. Walters	R	Cin	4	D	0	9	0	5	2	2	S. Rowe	R
75	1906	3	E. Walsh	R	ChW	3	ChC	0	9	0	2	1	12	J. Pfeister	L
76	1935	1	L. Warneke	R	ChC	3	D	0	9	0	4	4	1	S. Rowe	R
77	1942	3	E. White	L	StLC	2	NYY	0	9	0	6	0	6	S. Chandler	R
78	1933	3	E. Whitehill	L	W	4	NY–SFG	0	9	0	5	2	2	F. Fitzsimmons	R
79	1971	5	N. Briles	R	PP	4	Balt	0	9	0	2	2	2	D. McNally	L
80	1930	5	G. Earnshaw	R	PH–OAK	2	StLC	0	7	0	2	3	5		
			L. Grove *	L					2	0	1	1	2	B. Grimes	R
81	1958	3	D. Larsen *	R	NYY	4	BB–Mil	0	7	0	6	3	8		
			R. Duren	R					2	0	0	3	1	B. Rush	R
82	1959	1	E. Wynn *	R	ChW	11	BR–LAD	0	7	0	6	1	6		
			G. Staley	R					2	0	2	0	1	R. Craig	R

No.	Year	G	Winning Pitcher	Pitch Style	Score	IP	R	H	BB	K	Losing Pitcher	Pitch Style
83	1959	5	B. Shaw *	R	ChW 1 BR–LAD 0	7 1/3	0	9	1	1		
			B. Pierce	L		0	0	0	1	0		
			D. Donovan	R		1 1/3	0	0	0	0	S. Koufax	L
84	1961	4	W. Ford *	L	NYY 7 Cin 0	5	0	4	0	1		
			J. Coates	R		4	0	1	1	2	J. O'Toole	L
85	1969	3	G. Gentry *	R	NYM 5 Balt 0	6 1/3	0	3	5	1		
			N. Ryan	R		2 1/3	0	1	2	3	J. Palmer	R
86	1972	3	J. Billingham	R	Cin 1 PH–OAK 0	8	0	3	3	7	J. Odom	R
			C. Carroll	R		1	0	0	0	0		
87	1973	5	J. Koosman*	L	NYM 2 PhOak 0	6 1/3	0	3	4	4	V. Blue	L
			T. McGraw	L		2 2/3	0	0	3	3		

* Winning Pitcher

65

Pitchers Winning and Losing Shutouts

	W	L		W	L		W	L
C. Mathewson	4	0	B. James	1	0	E. White	1	0
M. Brown	3	0	W. Johnson	1	0	E. Whitehill	1	0
W. Ford	3	2	D. Kerr	1	0	C. Bender	1	1
B. Dinneen	2	0	J. Kucks	1	0	S. Chandler	1	1
B. Gibson	2	0	C. Labine	1	0	M. Cooper	1	1
B. Hallahan	2	0	J. Lonborg	1	0	D. Drysdale	1	1
A. Reynolds	2	0	W. Mails	1	0	G. Earnshaw	1	1
L. Burdette	2	1	C. Mays	1	0	D. Larsen	1	1
A. Nehf	2	1	B. Newsom	1	0	J. McGinnity	1	1
S. Koufax	2	2	O. Overall	1	0	G. Mullin	1	1
B. Adams	1	0	C. Passeau	1	0	D. McNally	1	1
G. Bearden	1	0	M. Pearson	1	0	C. Osteen	1	1
J. Benton	1	0	J. Podres	1	0	J. Palmer	1	1
H. Borowy	1	0	J. Ring	1	0	V. Raschi	1	1
H. Brecheen	1	0	P. Roe	1	0	J. Sanford	1	1
N. Briles	1	0	B. Ruth	1	0	R. Terry	1	1
W. Bunker	1	0	J. Sain	1	0	B. Turley	1	1
S. Coveleskie	1	0	F. Schupp	1	0	H. Vaughan	1	1
J. Dean	1	0	J. Scott	1	0	B. Walters	1	1
H. Eller	1	0	W. Spahn	1	0	B. Grimes	1	2
D. Ferriss	1	0	E. Walsh	1	0	W. Hoyt	1	2
J. Haines	1	0	L. Warneke	1	0	E. Wynn - G. Staley	1	0

	W	L		W	L		W	L
G. Earnshaw + L. Grove	1	0	B. Feller	0	1	W. Ruether	0	1
D. Larsen + R. Duren	1	0	R. Fisher	0	1	B. Rush	0	1
B. Shaw + B. Pierce - D. Donovan	1	0	F. Fitzsimmons	0	1	J. Santiago	0	1
W. Ford - J. Coates	1	0	B. Friend	0	1	S. Smith	0	1
G. Gentry - N. Ryan	1	0	D. Galehouse	0	1	O. Summers	0	1
J. Billingham - C. Carroll	1	0	M. Harris	0	1	G. Thompson	0	1
J. Koosman - T. McGraw	1	0	D. Hughes	0	1	R. Walberg	0	1
N. Altrock	0	1	S. Johnson	0	1	C. Williams	0	1
E. Auker	0	1	J. Konstanty	0	1	E. Yde	0	1
J. Bagby Sr.	0	1	S. Leever	0	1	E. Cicotte	0	2
V. Bickford	0	1	A. Leifield	0	1	B. Donovan	0	2
J. Black	0	1	S. Maglie	0	1	S. Jones	0	2
V. Blue	0	1	D. McLain	0	1	J. Kaat	0	2
J. Bouton	0	1	W. Mizell	0	1	D. Newcombe	0	2
T. Byrne	0	1	H. Newhouser	0	1	J. O'Toole	0	2
A. Coakley	0	1	J. Odom	0	1	S. Rowe	0	2
R. Craig	0	1	F. Overmire	0	1	E. Plank	0	4
M. Dickson	0	1	C. Pascual	0	1			
P. Douglas	0	1	D. Phillippe	0	1	TOTAL	87	87
U. Faber	0	1	J. Pfeister	0	1			

66
Clubs Involved in Shutouts

National League					American League				
Club	W	L	Tot	Margin	Club	W	L	Tot	Margin
NY — SFG	11	5	16	+ 6	NYY	16	13	29	+ 3
StLC	9	5	14	+ 4	BRS	5	3	8	+ 2
ChC	8	2	10	+ 6	ChW	4	5	9	− 1
BR - LAD	8	11	19	− 3	Balt	3	2	5	+ 1
BB - Mil	5	3	8	+ 2	CL	3	2	5	+ 1
Cin	4	5	9	− 1	PH - OAK	3	10	13	- 7
PP	2	6	8	− 4	W	2	0	2	+ 2
NYM	2	0	2	+ 2	D	2	10	12	− 8
PhP	0	1	1	- 1	StLB	0	1	1	− 1
					Minn	0	3	3	− 3
TOTAL	49	38	87	+ 11	TOTAL	38	49	87	- 11

67

Pitching Two or More Shutouts in the Same World Series

			First Game					Second Game					Third Game				
			IP	R	H	BB	K	IP	R	H	BB	K	IP	R	H	BB	K
C. Mathewson	3	1905	9	0	4	0	6	9	0	4	1	8	9	0	6	0	4
B. Dinneen	2	1903	9	0	3	2	11	9	0	4	2	7					
L. Burdette	2	1957	9	0	7	0	5	9	0	7	1	3					
W. Ford	2	1960	9	0	4	1	3	9	0	7	1	5					
S. Koufax	2	1965	9	0	4	1	10	9	0	3	3	10					

			10 Inning Shutout				
C. Labine	1	1956	10	0	7	2	5

68
First Game Shutouts

No.	Year	G	Score				Winning Pitcher	Style	Losing Pitcher	Style
1	1905	1	NYG	3	PhA	0	C. Mathewson	R	E. Plank	L
2	1918	1	Brs	1	ChC	0	B. Ruth	L	H. Vaughan	L
3	1921	1	NYY	3	NYG	0	C. Mays	R	P. Douglas	R
4	1935	1	ChC	3	D	0	L. Warneke	R	S. Rowe	R
5	1945	1	ChC	9	D	0	H. Borowy	R	H. Newhouser	L
6	1948	1	BBr	1	CL	0	J. Sain	R	B. Feller	R
7	1949	1	NYY	1	BrD	0	A. Reynolds	R	D. Newcombe	R
8	1950	1	NYY	1	PhP	0	V. Raschi	R	J. Konstanty	R
9	1959	1	ChW	11	Lad	0	E. Wynn	R	R. Craig	R
10	1961	1	NYY	2	Cin	0	W. Ford	L	J. O'Toole	L
11	1968	1	StLC	4	D	0	B. Gibson	R	D. McLain	R

Winning Pitcher		Losing Pitcher		Winning Club		Losing Club	
H. Borowy	1	R. Craig	1	NYY	4	D	3
W. Ford	1	P. Douglas	1	ChC	2	BR - LAD	2
B. Gibson	1	B. Feller	1	Brs	1	ChC	1
C. Mathewson	1	J. Konstanty	1	BBr	1	CL	1

Winning Pitcher		Losing Pitcher		Winning Club		Losing Club	
C. Mays	1	D. McLain	1	ChW	1	Cin	1
V. Raschi	1	D. Newcombe	1	NY SFG	1	NY SFG	1
A. Reynolds	1	H. Newhouser	1	StLC	1	PhP	1
B. Ruth	1	J. O'Toole	1			PhA	1
J. Sain	1	E. Plank	1				
L. Warneke	1	S. Rowe	1				
E. Wynn	1	H. Vaughan	1				
TOTAL	11	TOTAL	11	TOTAL	11	TOTAL	11

69
Last Game Shutouts

No.	Year	G	Score				Winning Pitcher	Style	Losing Pitcher	Style
1	1903	8	Brs	3	PP	0	B. Dinneen	R	D. Phillippe	R
2	1905	5	NyG	2	PhA	0	C. Mathewson	R	C. Bender	R
3	1907	5	ChC	2	D	0	M. Brown	R	G. Mullin	R
4	1908	5	ChC	2	D	0	O. Overall	R	B. Donovan	R
5	1909	7	PP	8	D	0	B. Adams	R	B. Donovan	R
6	1920	7	CL	3	BrD	0	S. Coveleskie	R	B. Grimes	R
7	1921	8	NyG	1	NYY	0	A. Nehf	L	W. Hoyt	R
8	1934	7	StLC	11	D	0	J. Dean	R	E. Auker	R
9	1955	7	BrD	2	NYY	0	J. Podres	L	T. Byrne	L
10	1956	7	NYY	9	BrD	0	J. Kucks	R	D. Newcombe	R
11	1957	7	Mil	5	NYY	0	L. Burdette	R	D. Larsen	R
12	1962	7	NYY	1	SFG	0	R. Terry	R	J. Sanford	R
13	1965	7	LAD	2	Minn	0	S. Koufax	L	J. Kaat	L
14	1966	4	Balt	1	LAD	0	D. McNally	L	D. Drysdale	R

Winning Pitcher		Losing Pitcher	
B. Adams	1	B. Donovan	2
M. Brown	1	E. Auker	1
L. Burdette	1	C. Bender	1
S. Coveleskie	1	T. Byrne	1
J. Dean	1	D. Drysdale	1
B. Dinneen	1	B. Grimes	1
S. Koufax	1	W. Hoyt	1
J. Kucks	1	J. Kaat	1
C. Mathewson	1	D. Larsen	1
D. McNally	1	G. Mullin	1
A. Nehf	1	D. Newcombe	1
O. Overall	1	D. Phillippe	1
J. Podres	1	J. Sanford	1
R. Terry	1		
TOTAL	**14**	**TOTAL**	**14**

Winning Club		Losing Club	
BR-LAD	2	D	4
ChC	2	BR-LAD	3
NY-SFG	2	NYY	3
NYY	2	Minn	1
Balt	1	PhA	1
BRS	1	PP	1
CL	1	NY-SFG	1
BB-Mil	1		
PP	1		
StLC	1		
TOTAL	**14**	**TOTAL**	**14**

70
Won and Lost Percentage

1903	1905	1906	1907	1908
B. Dinneen	C. Mathewson	E. Walsh	M. Brown	M. Brown
			J. Pfeister	O. Overall
			O. Overall	
			E. Reulbach	
3-1 .750	3-0 1.000	2-0 1.000	1-0 1.000	2-0 1.000

1909	1910	1911	1912	1913
B. Adams	J. Coombs	J. Coombs	R. Marquard	C. Bender
		O. Crandall		
3-0 1.000	3-0 1.000	1-0 1.000	2-0 1.000	2-0 1.000

1914	1915	1916	1917	1918
B. James	G. Foster	E. Shore	F. Schupp	B. Ruth
D. Rudolph				C. Mays
2-0 1.000	2-0 1.000	2-0 1.000	1-0 1.000	2-0 1.000

1919	1920	1921	1922	1923
H. Eller	S. Coveleskie	J. Barnes	H. McQuillan	H. Pennock
D. Kerr			A. Nehf	
			J. Ryan	
			J. Scott	
2-0 1.000	3-0 1.000	2-0 1.000	1-0 1.000	2-0 1.000

1924	1925	1926	1927	1928
T. Zachary	V. Aldridge	G. Alexander	W. Hoyt	W. Hoyt
		J. Haines	W. Moore	
		H. Pennock	G. Pipgras	
			H. Pennock	
2-0 1.000	2-0 1.000	2-0 1.000	1-0 1.000	2-0 1.000

1929	1930	1931	1932	1933
G. Bush	G. Earnshaw	B. Hallahan	L. Gomez	C. Hubbell
H. Ehmke		B. Grimes	W. Moore	
E. Rommell			G. Pipgras	
R. Walberg			C. Ruffing	
1-0 1.000	2-0 1.000	2-0 1.000	1-0 1.000	2-0 1.000

1934	1935	1936	1937	1938
P. Dean	T. Bridges	L. Gomez	L. Gomez	C. Ruffing
	L. Warneke			
2-0 1.000	2-0 1.000	2-0 1.000	2-0 1.000	2-0 1.000

1939	1940	1941	1942	1943
B. Hadley	B. Walters	E. Bonham	J. Beazley	S. Chandler
J. Murphy		J. Murphy		
M. Pearson		C. Ruffing		
C. Ruffing		M. Russo		
1-0 1.000	2-0 1.000	1-0 1.000	2-0 1.000	2-0 1.000

1944	1945	1946	1947	1948
H. Brecheen	C. Passeau	H. Brecheen	H. Casey	B. Lemon
B. Donnelly	V. Trucks		F. Shea	
J. Kramer				
M. Lanier				
1-0 1.000	1-0 1.000	3-0 1.000	2-0 1.000	2-0 1.000

1949	1950	1951	1952	1953
E. Lopat	T. Ferrick	E. Lopat	V. Raschi	C. Erskine
J. Page	W. Ford			B. Loes
A. Reynolds	V. Raschi			E. Lopat
P. Roe	A. Reynolds			J. McDonald
				A. Reynolds
				J. Sain
1-0 1.000	1-0 1.000	2-0 1.000	2-0 1.000	1-0 1.000

1954	1955	1956	1957	1958
J. Antonelli	W. Ford	D. Bessent	L. Burdette	D. Larsen
M. Grissom	J. Podres	J. Kucks		
R. Gomez		C. Labine		
D. Liddle		D. Larsen		
		T. Sturdivant		
1-0 1.000	2-0 1.000	1-0 1.000	3-0 1.000	1-0 1.000

1959	1960	1961	1962	1963
L. Sherry	W. Ford	W. Ford	D. Larsen	S. Koufax
	H. Haddix		B. Stafford	
	V. Law			
2-0 1.000	2-0 1.000	2-0 1.000	1-0 1.000	2-0 1.000

1964	1965	1966	1967	1968
J. Bouton	J. Grant	W. Bunker	B. Gibson	M. Lolich
	S. Koufax	M. Drabowsky		
		D. McNally		
		J. Palmer		
2-0 1.000	2-1 .667	1-0 1.000	3-0 1.000	3-0 1.000

1969	1970	1971	1972	1973
J. Koosman	M. Cuellar	S. Blass	J. Hunter	K. Holtzman
	D. McNally			
	J. Palmer			
	T. Phoebus			
	C. Carroll			
2-0 1.000	1-0 1.000	2-0 1.000	2-0 1.000	2-1 .667

71
Times Leading in Won and Lost Percentage

W. Ford	4	B. Adams	1	O. Crandall	1
C. Ruffing	4	V. Aldridge	1	M. Cuellar	1
L. Gomez	3	G. Alexander	1	P. Dean	1
D. Larsen	3	J. Antonelli	1	B. Dinneen	1
E. Lopat	3	J. Barnes	1	B. Donnelly	1
A. Reynolds	3	J. Beazley	1	M. Drabowsky	1
H. Pennock	3	C. Bender	1	G. Earnshaw	1
H. Brecheen	2	D. Bessent	1	H. Ehmke	1
M. Brown	2	S. Blass	1	H. Eller	1
J. Coombs	2	E. Bonham	1	C. Erskine	1
W. Hoyt	2	J. Bouton	1	T. Ferrick	1
S. Koufax	2	T. Bridges	1	G. Foster	1
D. McNally	2	W. Bunker	1	B. Gibson	1
W. Moore	2	L. Burdette	1	R. Gomez	1
J. Murphy	2	G. Bush	1	J. Grant	1
O. Overall	2	C. Carroll	1	B. Grimes	1
J. Palmer	2	H. Casey	1	M. Grissom	1
G. Pipgras	2	S. Chandler	1	H. Haddix	1
V. Raschi	2	S. Coveleskie	1	B. Hadley	1

B. Hallahan	1	R. Marquard	1	J. Sain	1
J. Haines	1	C. Mays	1	F. Schupp	1
K. Holtzman	1	J. McDonald	1	J. Scott	1
C. Hubbell	1	H. McQuillan	1	F. Shea	1
J. Hunter	1	A. Nehf	1	L. Sherry	1
B. James	1	J. Page	1	E. Shore	1
D. Kerr	1	C. Passeau	1	B. Stafford	1
J. Koosman	1	M. Pearson	1	T. Sturdivant	1
J. Kramer	1	J. Pfeister	1	V. Trucks	1
J. Kucks	1	T. Phoebus	1	R. Walberg	1
C. Labine	1	J. Podres	1	E. Walsh	1
M. Lanier	1	E. Reulbach	1	B. Walters	1
V. Law	1	P. Roe	1	L. Warneke	1
B. Lemon	1	E. Rommel	1	T. Zachary	1
D. Liddle	1	D. Rudolph	1		
B. Loes	1	M. Russo	1	TOTAL	135
M. Lolich	1	B. Ruth	1		
C. Mathewson	1	J. Ryan	1		

Pitching Records—by Club

New York Yankees

		BB-Mil	Br-LAD	ChC	Cin	NY-SFG	PhP	PP	StLC	NYM	Total
W. Ford	L	1-2	3-4	0-0	2-0	1-1	1-0	2-0	0-1	0-0	10-8
A. Reynolds	R	0-0	5-1	0-0	0-0	1-1	1-0	0-0	0-0	0-0	7-2
C. Ruffing	R	0-0	1-0	3-0	1-0	1-1	0-0	0-0	1-1	0-0	7-2
L. Gomez	L	0-0	0-0	2-0	0-0	4-0	0-0	0-0	0-0	0-0	6-0
W. Hoyt	R	0-0	0-0	0-0	0-0	2-2	0-0	1-0	3-1	0-0	6-3
H. Pennock	L	0-0	0-0	0-0	0-0	2-0	0-0	1-0	2-0	0-0	5-0
V. Raschi	R	0-0	3-2	0-0	0-0	1-1	1-0	0-0	0-0	0-0	5-3
M. Pearson	R	0-0	0-0	1-0	1-0	2-0	0-0	0-0	0-0	0-0	4-0
E. Lopat	L	0-0	2-1	0-0	0-0	2-0	0-0	0-0	0-0	0-0	4-1
B. Turley	R	3-1	0-2	0-0	0-0	0-0	0-0	1-0	0-0	0-0	4-3
C. Pipgras	R	0-0	0-0	1-0	0-0	0-0	0-0	1-0	1-0	0-0	3-0
D. Larsen	R	2-1	1-1	0-0	0-0	0-0	0-0	0-0	0-0	0-0	3-2
W. Moore	R	0-0	0-0	1-0	0-0	0-0	0-0	1-0	0-0	0-0	2-0
J. Murphy	R	0-0	1-0	0-0	1-0	0-0	0-0	0-0	0-0	0-0	2-0
M. Russo	L	0-0	1-0	0-0	0-0	0-0	0-0	0-0	1-0	0-0	2-0

		BB-Mil	Br-LAD	ChC	Cin	NY-SFG	PhP	PP	StLC	NYM	Total
F. Shea	R	0-0	2-0	0-0	0-0	0-0	0-0	0-0	0-0	0-0	2-0
J. Bouton	R	0-0	0-1	0-0	0-0	0-0	0-0	0-0	2-0	0-0	2-1
B. Hadley	R	0-0	0-0	0-0	1-0	1-1	0-0	0-0	0-0	0-0	2-1
J. Page	L	0-0	2-1	0-0	0-0	0-0	0-0	0-0	0-0	0-0	2-1
S. Chandler	R	0-0	0-1	0-0	0-0	0-0	0-0	0-0	2-1	0-0	2-2
R. Terry	R	0-0	0-0	0-0	0-1	2-1	0-0	0-2	0-0	0-0	2-4
L. Arroyo	L	0-0	0-0	0-0	1-0	0-0	0-0	0-0	0-0	0-0	1-0
H. Borowy	R	0-0	0-0	0-0	0-0	0-0	0-0	0-0	1-0	0-0	1-0
B. Daley	L	0-0	0-0	0-0	1-0	0-0	0-0	0-0	0-0	0-0	1-0
T. Ferrick	R	0-0	0-0	0-0	0-0	0-0	1-0	0-0	0-0	0-0	1-0
J. Kucks	R	0-0	1-0	0-0	0-0	0-0	0-0	0-0	0-0	0-0	1-0
J. McDonald	R	0-0	1-0	0-0	0-0	0-0	0-0	0-0	0-0	0-0	1-0
B. Stafford	R	0-0	0-0	0-0	0-0	1-0	0-0	0-0	0-0	0-0	1-0
T. Sturdivant	R	0-0	1-0	0-0	0-0	0-0	0-0	0-0	0-0	0-0	1-0
T. Zachary	L	0-0	0-0	0-0	0-0	0-0	0-0	0-0	1-0	0-0	1-0
T. Byrne	L	0-0	1-1	0-0	0-0	0-0	0-0	0-0	0-0	0-0	1-1
R. Duren	R	1-1	0-0	0-0	0-0	0-0	0-0	0-0	0-0	0-0	1-1
J. Sain	R	0-0	1-1	0-0	0-0	0-0	0-0	0-0	0-0	0-0	1-1
M. Stottlemyre	R	0-0	0-0	0-0	0-0	0-0	0-0	0-0	1-1	0-0	1-1
E. Bonham	R	0-0	1-0	0-0	0-0	0-0	0-0	0-0	0-2	0-0	1-2
B. Shawkey	R	0-0	0-0	0-0	0-0	1-1	0-0	0-0	0-1	0-0	1-2
L. Bush	R	0-0	0-0	0-0	0-0	1-3	0-0	0-0	0-0	0-0	1-3
C. Mays	R	0-0	0-0	0-0	0-0	1-3	0-0	0-0	0-0	0-0	1-3
F. Bevens	R	0-0	0-1	0-0	0-0	0-0	0-0	0-0	0-0	0-0	0-1
J. Coates	R	0-0	0-0	0-0	0-0	0-1	0-0	0-0	0-0	0-0	0-1
A. Donald	R	0-0	0-0	0-0	0-0	0-0	0-0	0-0	0-1	0-0	0-1
S. Jones	R	0-0	0-0	0-0	0-0	0-1	0-0	0-0	0-0	0-0	0-1
P. Malone	R	0-0	0-0	0-0	0-0	0-1	0-0	0-0	0-0	0-0	0-1
P. Mikkelson	R	0-0	0-0	0-0	0-0	0-0	0-0	0-0	0-1	0-0	0-1
T. Morgan	R	0-0	0-1	0-0	0-0	0-0	0-0	0-0	0-0	0-0	0-1
B. Newsom	R	0-0	0-1	0-0	0-0	0-0	0-0	0-0	0-0	0-0	0-1
J. Quinn	R	0-0	0-0	0-0	0-0	0-1	0-0	0-0	0-0	0-0	0-1
W. Ruether	L	0-0	0-0	0-0	0-0	0-0	0-0	0-0	0-1	0-0	0-1
B. Shantz	L	0-1	0-0	0-0	0-0	0-0	0-0	0-0	0-0	0-0	0-1
U. Shocker	R	0-0	0-0	0-0	0-0	0-0	0-0	0-0	0-1	0-0	0-1
A. Ditmar	R	0-0	0-0	0-0	0-0	0-0	0-0	0-2	0-0	0-0	0-2
A. Downing	L	0-0	0-1	0-0	0-0	0-0	0-0	0-0	0-1	0-0	0-2
B. Grim	R	0-1	0-1	0-0	0-0	0-0	0-0	0-0	0-0	0-0	0-2
TOTAL		7-7	27-21	8-0	8-1	23-19	4-0	7-4	15-13	0-0	99-65

Boston Red Sox

		BB-Mil	BR-LAD	ChC	Cin	NY-SFG	PhP	PP	StLC	NYM	Total
B. Ruth	L	0-0	1-0	2-0	0-0	0-0	0-0	0-0	0-0	0-0	3-0
B. Dinneen	R	0-0	0-0	0-0	0-0	0-0	0-0	3-1	0-0	0-0	3-1
E. Shore	R	0-0	2-0	0-0	0-0	0-0	1-1	0-0	0-0	0-0	3-1
J. Wood	R	0-0	0-0	0-0	0-0	3-1	0-0	0-0	0-0	0-0	3-1
G. Foster	R	0-0	0-0	0-0	0-0	0-0	2-0	0-0	0-0	0-0	2-0
H. Leonard	L	0-0	1-0	0-0	0-0	0-0	1-0	0-0	0-0	0-0	2-0
J. Lonborg	R	0-0	0-0	0-0	0-0	0-0	0-0	0-0	2-1	0-0	2-1
C. Mays	R	0-0	0-1	2-0	0-0	0-0	0-0	0-0	0-0	0-0	2-1
C. Young	R	0-0	0-0	0-0	0-0	0-0	0-0	2-1	0-0	0-0	2-1
H. Bedient	R	0-0	0-0	0-0	0-0	1-0	0-0	0-0	0-0	0-0	1-0
J. Dobson	R	0-0	0-0	0-0	0-0	0-0	0-0	0-0	1-0	0-0	1-0
D. Ferriss	R	0-0	0-0	0-0	0-0	0-0	0-0	0-0	1-0	0-0	1-0
E. Johnson	L	0-0	0-0	0-0	0-0	0-0	0-0	0-0	1-0	0-0	1-0
J. Wyatt	R	0-0	0-0	0-0	0-0	0-0	0-0	0-0	1-0	0-0	1-0
G. Bell	R	0-0	0-0	0-0	0-0	0-0	0-0	0-0	0-1	0-0	0-1
L. Bush	R	0-0	0-0	0-1	0-0	0-0	0-0	0-0	0-0	0-0	0-1
T. Hughes	R	0-0	0-0	0-0	0-0	0-0	0-0	0-1	0-0	0-0	0-1
T. Hughson	R	0-0	0-0	0-0	0-0	0-0	0-0	0-0	0-1	0-0	0-1
S. Jones	R	0-0	0-0	0-1	0-0	0-0	0-0	0-0	0-0	0-0	0-1
R. Klinger	R	0-0	0-0	0-0	0-0	0-0	0-0	0-0	0-1	0-0	0-1
T. O'Brien	R	0-0	0-0	0-0	0-0	0-2	0-0	0-0	0-0	0-0	0-2
M. Harris	L	0-0	0-0	0-0	0-0	0-0	0-0	0-0	0-2	0-0	0-2
J. Santiago	R	0-0	0-0	0-0	0-0	0-0	0-0	0-0	0-2	0-0	0-2
TOTAL		0-0	4-1	4-2	0-0	4-3	4-1	5-3	6-8	0-0	27-18

Philadelphia - Oakland Athletics

		BB-Mil	BR-LAD	ChC	Cin	NY-SFG	PhP	PP	StLC	NYM	Total
C. Bender	R	0-1	0-0	1-1	0-0	5-2	0-0	0-0	0-0	0-0	6-4
J. Coombs	R	0-0	0-0	3-0	0-0	1-0	0-0	0-0	0-0	0-0	4-0
L. Grove	L	0-0	0-0	0-0	0-0	0-0	0-0	0-0	4-2	0-0	4-2
G. Earnshaw	R	0-0	0-0	1-1	0-0	0-0	0-0	0-0	3-2	0-0	4-3
J. Hunter	R	0-0	0-0	0-0	2-0	0-0	0-0	0-0	0-0	1-0	3-0
K. Holtzman	L	0-0	0-0	0-0	1-0	0-0	0-0	0-0	0-0	2-1	3-1
E. Plank	L	0-1	0-0	0-0	0-0	2-4	0-0	0-0	0-0	0-0	2-5
H. Ehmke	R	0-0	0-0	1-0	0-0	0-0	0-0	0-0	0-0	0-0	1-0
P. Lindblad	L	0-0	0-0	0-0	0-0	0-0	0-0	0-0	0-0	1-0	1-0
E. Rommel	R	0-0	0-0	1-0	0-0	0-0	0-0	0-0	0-0	0-0	1-0

		BB-Mil	BR-LAD	ChC	Cin	NY-SFG	PhP	PP	StLC	NYM	Total
L. Bush	R	0-1	0-0	0-0	0-0	1-0	0-0	0-0	0-0	0-0	1-1
R. Walberg	L	0-0	0-0	1-0	0-0	0-0	0-0	0-0	0-1	0-0	1-1
R. Fingers	R	0-0	0-0	0-0	1-1	0-0	0-0	0-0	0-0	0-1	1-2
A. Coakley	R	0-0	0-0	0-0	0-0	0-1	0-0	0-0	0-0	0-0	0-1
W. Hoyt	R	0-0	0-0	0-0	0-0	0-0	0-0	0-0	0-1	0-0	0-1
J. Odom	R	0-0	0-0	0-0	0-1	0-0	0-0	0-0	0-0	0-0	0-1
B. Shawkey	R	0-1	0-0	0-0	0-0	0-0	0-0	0-0	0-0	0-0	0-1
V. Blue	L	0-0	0-0	0-0	0-1	0-0	0-0	0-0	0-0	0-1	0-2
TOTAL		0-4	-0-	8-2	4-3	9-7	0-0	0-0	7-6	4-3	32-25

Detroit Tigers

		BB-Mil	BR-LAD	ChC	Cin	NY-SFG	PhP	PP	StLC	NYM	Total
T. Bridges	R	0-0	0-0	2-0	1-0	0-0	0-0	0-0	1-1	0-0	4-1
M. Lolich	L	0-0	0-0	0-0	0-0	0-0	0-0	0-0	3-0	0-0	3-0
G. Mullin	R	0-0	0-0	1-2	0-0	0-0	0-0	2-1	0-0	0-0	3-3
H. Newhouser	L	0-0	0-0	2-1	0-0	0-0	0-0	0-0	0-0	0-0	2-1
B. Newsom	R	0-0	0-0	0-0	2-1	0-0	0-0	0-0	0-0	0-0	2-1
S. Rowe	R	0-0	0-0	1-2	0-2	0-0	0-0	0-0	1-1	0-0	2-5
V. Trucks	R	0-0	0-0	1-0	0-0	0-0	0-0	0-0	0-0	0-0	1-0
E. Auker	R	0-0	0-0	0-0	0-0	0-0	0-0	0-0	1-1	0-0	1-1
A. Crowder	R	0-0	0-0	1-0	0-0	0-0	0-0	0-0	0-1	0-0	1-1
D. McLain	R	0-0	0-0	0-0	0-0	0-0	0-0	0-0	1-2	0-0	1-2
D. Trout	R	0-0	0-0	1-1	0-1	0-0	0-0	0-0	0-0	0-0	1-2
B. Donovan	R	0-0	0-0	0-3	0-0	0-0	0-0	1-1	0-0	0-0	1-4
F. Overmire	L	0-0	0-0	0-1	0-0	0-0	0-0	0-0	0-0	0-0	0-1
E. Siever	L	0-0	0-0	0-1	0-0	0-0	0-0	0-0	0-0	0-0	0-1
E. Wilson	R	0-0	0-0	0-0	0-0	0-0	0-0	0-0	0-1	0-0	0-1
E. Summers	R	0-0	0-0	0-2	0-0	0-0	0-0	0-2	0-0	0-0	0-4
TOTAL		0-0	0-0	9-13	3-4	0-0	0-0	3-4	7-7	0-0	22-28

Chicago White Sox

		BB-Mil	BR-LAD	ChC	Cin	NY-SFG	PhP	PP	StLC	NYM	Total
U. Faber	R	0-0	0-0	0-0	0-0	3-1	0-0	0-0	0-0	0-0	3-1
E. Walsh	R	0-0	0-0	2-0	0-0	0-0	0-0	0-0	0-0	0-0	2-0
D. Kerr	L	0-0	0-0	0-0	2-0	0-0	0-0	0-0	0-0	0-0	2-0
E. Cicotte	R	0-0	0-0	0-0	1-2	1-1	0-0	0-0	0-0	0-0	2-3
N. Altrock	L	0-0	0-0	1-1	0-0	0-0	0-0	0-0	0-0	0-0	1-1
B. Shaw	R	0-0	1-1	0-0	0-0	0-0	0-0	0-0	0-0	0-0	1-1
G. White	L	0-0	0-0	1-1	0-0	0-0	0-0	0-0	0-0	0-0	1-1
E. Wynn	R	0-0	1-1	0-0	0-0	0-0	0-0	0-0	0-0	0-0	1-1
D. Donovan	R	0-0	0-1	0-0	0-0	0-0	0-0	0-0	0-0	0-0	0-1
G. Staley	R	0-0	0-1	0-0	0-0	0-0	0-0	0-0	0-0	0-0	0-1
C. Williams	L	0-0	0-0	0-0	0-3	0-0	0-0	0-0	0-0	0-0	0-3
TOTAL		0-0	2-4	4-2	3-5	4-2	0-0	0-0	0-0	0-0	13-13

Cleveland Indians

		BB-Mil	BR-LAD	ChC	Cin	NY-SFG	PhP	PP	StLC	NYM	Total
S. Coveleskie	R	0-0	3-0	0-0	0-0	0-0	0-0	0-0	0-0	0-0	3-0
B. Lemon	R	2-0	0-0	0-0	0-0	0-2	0-0	0-0	0-0	0-0	2-2
G. Bearden	L	1-0	0-0	0-0	0-0	0-0	0-0	0-0	0-0	0-0	1-0
S. Gromek	R	1-0	0-0	0-0	0-0	0-0	0-0	0-0	0-0	0-0	1-0
W. Mails	L	0-0	1-0	0-0	0-0	0-0	0-0	0-0	0-0	0-0	1-0
J. Bagby Sr.	R	0-0	1-1	0-0	0-0	0-0	0-0	0-0	0-0	0-0	1-1
R. Caldwell	R	0-0	0-1	0-0	0-0	0-0	0-0	0-0	0-0	0-0	0-1
M. Garcia	R	0-0	0-0	0-0	0-0	0-1	0-0	0-0	0-0	0-0	0-1
E. Wynn	R	0-0	0-0	0-0	0-0	0-1	0-0	0-0	0-0	0-0	0-1
B. Feller	R	0-2	0-0	0-0	0-0	0-0	0-0	0-0	0-0	0-0	0-2
TOTAL		4-2	5-2	0-0	0-0	0-4	0-0	0-0	0-0	0-0	9-8

St. Louis Browns

		BB-Mil	BR-LAD	ChC	Cin	NY-SFG	PhP	PP	StLC	NYM	Total
J. Kramer	R	0-0	0-0	0-0	0-0	0-0	0-0	0-0	1-0	0-0	1-0
D. Galehouse	R	0-0	0-0	0-0	0-0	0-0	0-0	0-0	1-1	0-0	1-1
S. Jakucki	R	0-0	0-0	0-0	0-0	0-0	0-0	0-0	0-1	0-0	0-1
B. Muncrief	R	0-0	0-0	0-0	0-0	0-0	0-0	0-0	0-1	0-0	0-1
N. Potter	R	0-0	0-0	0-0	0-0	0-0	0-0	0-0	0-1	0-0	0-1
TOTAL		0-0	0-0	0-0	0-0	0-0	0-0	0-0	2-4	0-0	2-4

Washington Senators

		BB-Mil	BR-LAD	ChC	Cin	NY-SFG	PhP	PP	StLC	NYM	Total
W. Johnson	R	0-0	0-0	0-0	0-0	1-2	0-0	2-1	0-0	0-0	3-3
T. Zachary	L	0-0	0-0	0-0	0-0	2-0	0-0	0-0	0-0	0-0	2-0
G. Mogridge	L	0-0	0-0	0-0	0-0	1-0	0-0	0-0	0-0	0-0	1-0
E. Whitehill	L	0-0	0-0	0-0	0-0	1-0	0-0	0-0	0-0	0-0	1-0
J. Ferguson	R	0-0	0-0	0-0	0-0	0-0	0-0	1-1	0-0	0-0	1-1
A. Crowder	R	0-0	0-0	0-0	0-0	0-1	0-0	0-0	0-0	0-0	0-1
F. Marberry	R	0-0	0-0	0-0	0-0	0-1	0-0	0-0	0-0	0-0	0-1
J. Russell	R	0-0	0-0	0-0	0-0	0-1	0-0	0-0	0-0	0-0	0-1
W. Stewart	L	0-0	0-0	0-0	0-0	0-1	0-0	0-0	0-0	0-0	0-1
M. Weaver	R	0-0	0-0	0-0	0-0	0-1	0-0	0-0	0-0	0-0	0-1
S. Coveleskie	R	0-0	0-0	0-0	0-0	0-0	0-0	0-2	0-0	0-0	0-2
TOTAL		0-0	0-0	0-0	0-0	5-7	0-0	3-4	0-0	0-0	8-11

Minnesota Twins

		BB-Mil	BR-LAD	ChC	Cin	NY-SFG	PhP	PP	StLC	NYM	Total
J. Grant	R	0-0	2-1	0-0	0-0	0-0	0-0	0-0	0-0	0-0	2-1
J. Kaat	L	0-0	1-2	0-0	0-0	0-0	0-0	0-0	0-0	0-0	1-2
C. Pascual	R	0-0	0-1	0-0	0-0	0-0	0-0	0-0	0-0	0-0	0-1
TOTAL		0-0	3-4	0-0	0-0	0-0	0-0	0-0	0-0	0-0	3-4

Baltimore Orioles

		BB-Mil	BR-LAD	ChC	Cin	NY-SFG	PhP	PP	StLC	NYM	Total
D. McNally	L	0-0	1-0	0-0	1-0	0-0	0-0	2-1	0-0	0-1	4-2
J. Palmer	R	0-0	1-0	0-0	1-0	0-0	0-0	1-0	0-0	0-1	3-1
M. Cuellar	L	0-0	0-0	0-0	1-0	0-0	0-0	0-2	0-0	1-0	2-2
W. Bunker	R	0-0	1-0	0-0	0-0	0-0	0-0	0-0	0-0	0-0	1-0
M. Drabowsky	R	0-0	1-0	0-0	0-0	0-0	0-0	0-0	0-0	0-0	1-0
T. Phoebus	R	0-0	0-0	0-0	1-0	0-0	0-0	0-0	0-0	0-0	1-0
D. Hall	R	0-0	0-0	0-0	0-0	0-0	0-0	0-0	0-0	0-1	0-1
E. Watt	R	0-0	0-0	0-0	0-1	0-0	0-0	0-1	0-0	0-1	0-3
TOTAL		0-0	4-0	0-0	4-1	0-0	0-0	3-4	0-0	1-4	12-9

New York – San Francisco Giants

		Balt	BRS	ChW	CL	D	Minn	NYY	Ph-Oak	StLB	W	Total
C. Mathewson	R	0-0	0-2	0-0	0-0	0-0	0-0	0-0	5-3	0-0	0-0	5-5
C. Hubbell	L	0-0	0-0	0-0	0-0	0-0	0-0	2-2	0-0	0-0	2-0	4-2
A. Nehf	L	0-0	0-0	0-0	0-0	0-0	0-0	3-3	0-0	0-0	1-1	4-4
W. Ryan	R	0-0	0-0	0-0	0-0	0-0	0-0	2-0	0-0	0-0	0-0	2-0
J. Barnes	R	0-0	0-0	0-0	0-0	0-0	0-0	2-0	0-0	0-0	0-1	2-1
P. Douglas	R	0-0	0-0	0-0	0-0	0-0	0-0	2-1	0-0	0-0	0-0	2-1
H. McQuillan	R	0-0	0-0	0-0	0-0	0-0	0-0	1-1	0-0	0-0	1-0	2-1
R. Marquard	L	0-0	2-0	0-0	0-0	0-0	0-0	0-0	0-2	0-0	0-0	2-2
H. Schumacher	R	0-0	0-0	0-0	0-0	0-0	0-0	1-2	0-0	0-0	1-0	2-2
J. Antonelli	L	0-0	0-0	0-0	1-0	0-0	0-0	0-0	0-0	0-0	0-0	1-0
O. Crandall	R	0-0	0-0	0-0	0-0	0-0	0-0	0-0	1-0	0-0	0-0	1-0
R. Gomez	R	0-0	0-0	0-0	1-0	0-0	0-0	0-0	0-0	0-0	0-0	1-0
M. Grissom	R	0-0	0-0	0-0	1-0	0-0	0-0	0-0	0-0	0-0	0-0	1-0
J. Hearn	R	0-0	0-0	0-0	0-0	0-0	0-0	1-0	0-0	0-0	0-0	1-0
D. Larsen	R	0-0	0-0	0-0	0-0	0-0	0-0	1-0	0-0	0-0	0-0	1-0
D. Liddle	L	0-0	0-0	0-0	1-0	0-0	0-0	0-0	0-0	0-0	0-0	1-0
A. Luque	R	0-0	0-0	0-0	0-0	0-0	0-0	0-0	0-0	0-0	1-0	1-0
F. Schupp	L	0-0	0-0	1-0	0-0	0-0	0-0	0-0	0-0	0-0	0-0	1-0
J. Benton	L	0-0	0-0	1-1	0-0	0-0	0-0	0-0	0-0	0-0	0-0	1-1
D. Koslo	L	0-0	0-0	0-0	0-0	0-0	0-0	1-1	0-0	0-0	0-0	1-1
J. McGinnity	R	0-0	0-0	0-0	0-0	0-0	0-0	0-0	1-1	0-0	0-0	1-1
B. Pierce	L	0-0	0-0	0-0	0-0	0-0	0-0	1-1	0-0	0-0	0-0	1-1
J. Scott	R	0-0	0-0	0-0	0-0	0-0	0-0	1-1	0-0	0-0	0-0	1-1
J. Sanford	R	0-0	0-0	0-0	0-0	0-0	0-0	1-2	0-0	0-0	0-0	1-2
J. Bentley	L	0-0	0-0	0-0	0-0	0-0	0-0	0-1	0-0	0-0	1-2	1-3
J. Tesreau	R	0-0	1-2	0-0	0-0	0-0	0-0	0-0	0-1	0-0	0-0	1-3
L. Ames	R	0-0	0-0	0-0	0-0	0-0	0-0	0-0	0-1	0-0	0-0	0-1
J. Anderson	R	0-0	0-0	0-1	0-0	0-0	0-0	0-0	0-0	0-0	0-0	0-1
A. Demaree	R	0-0	0-0	0-0	0-0	0-0	0-0	0-0	0-1	0-0	0-0	0-1
S. Maglie	R	0-0	0-0	0-0	0-0	0-0	0-0	0-1	0-0	0-0	0-0	0-1
B. O'Dell	L	0-0	0-0	0-0	0-0	0-0	0-0	0-1	0-0	0-0	0-0	0-1
L. Jansen	R	0-0	0-0	0-0	0-0	0-0	0-0	0-2	0-0	0-0	0-0	0-2
C. Melton	L	0-0	0-0	0-0	0-0	0-0	0-0	0-2	0-0	0-0	0-0	0-2
H. Sallee	L	0-0	0-0	0-2	0-0	0-0	0-0	0-0	0-0	0-0	0-0	0-2
F. Fitzsimmons	R	0-0	0-0	0-0	0-0	0-0	0-0	0-2	0-0	0-0	0-1	0-3
TOTAL		0-0	3-4	2-4	4-0	0-0	0-0	19-23	7-9	0-0	7-5	42-45

St. Louis Cardinals

		Balt	BRS	ChW	CL	D	Minn	NYY	Ph-Oak	StLB	W	Total
B. Gibson	R	0-0	3-0	0-0	0-0	2-1	0-0	2-1	0-0	0-0	0-0	7-2
H. Brecheen	L	0-0	3-0	0-0	0-0	0-0	0-0	0-1	0-0	1-0	0-0	4-1
J. Haines	R	0-0	0-0	0-0	0-0	0-0	0-0	2-1	1-0	0-0	0-0	3-1
B. Hallahan	L	0-0	0-0	0-0	0-0	0-0	0-0	0-0	3-1	0-0	0-0	3-1
J. Beazley	R	0-0	0-0	0-0	0-0	0-0	0-0	2-0	0-0	0-0	0-0	2-0
P. Dean	R	0-0	0-0	0-0	0-0	2-0	0-0	0-0	0-0	0-0	0-0	2-0
G. Alexander	R	0-0	0-0	0-0	0-0	0-0	0-0	2-1	0-0	0-0	0-0	2-1
J. Dean	R	0-0	0-0	0-0	0-0	2-1	0-0	0-0	0-0	0-0	0-0	2-1
M. Lanier	L	0-0	0-0	0-0	0-0	0-0	0-0	1-1	0-0	1-0	0-0	2-1
B. Grimes	R	0-0	0-0	0-0	0-0	0-0	0-0	0-0	2-2	0-0	0-0	2-2
M. Cooper	R	0-0	0-0	0-0	0-0	0-0	0-0	1-2	0-0	1-1	0-0	2-3
R. Craig	R	0-0	0-0	0-0	0-0	0-0	0-0	1-0	0-0	0-0	0-0	1-0
B. Donnelly	R	0-0	0-0	0-0	0-0	0-0	0-0	0-0	0-0	1-0	0-0	1-0
G. Munger	R	0-0	1-0	0-0	0-0	0-0	0-0	0-0	0-0	0-0	0-0	1-0
R. Sadecki	L	0-0	0-0	0-0	0-0	0-0	0-0	1-0	0-0	0-0	0-0	1-0
E. White	L	0-0	0-0	0-0	0-0	0-0	0-0	1-0	0-0	0-0	0-0	1-0
N. Briles	R	0-0	1-0	0-0	0-0	0-1	0-0	0-0	0-0	0-0	0-0	1-1
R. Washburn	R	0-0	0-0	0-0	0-0	1-1	0-0	0-0	0-0	0-0	0-0	1-1
S. Carlton	L	0-0	0-1	0-0	0-0	0-0	0-0	0-0	0-0	0-0	0-0	0-1
M. Dickson	R	0-0	0-1	0-0	0-0	0-0	0-0	0-0	0-0	0-0	0-0	0-1
J. Hoerner	L	0-0	0-0	0-0	0-0	0-1	0-0	0-0	0-0	0-0	0-0	0-1
D. Hughes	R	0-0	0-1	0-0	0-0	0-0	0-0	0-0	0-0	0-0	0-0	0-1
S. Johnson	R	0-0	0-0	0-0	0-0	0-0	0-0	0-0	0-1	0-0	0-0	0-1
J. Lamabe	R	0-0	0-1	0-0	0-0	0-0	0-0	0-0	0-0	0-0	0-0	0-1
H. Pollet	L	0-0	0-1	0-0	0-0	0-0	0-0	0-0	0-0	0-0	0-0	0-1
F. Rhem	R	0-0	0-0	0-0	0-0	0-0	0-0	0-0	0-1	0-0	0-0	0-1
A. Reinhart	L	0-0	0-0	0-0	0-0	0-0	0-0	0-1	0-0	0-0	0-0	0-1
B. Schultz	R	0-0	0-0	0-0	0-0	0-0	0-0	0-1	0-0	0-0	0-0	0-1
C. Simmons	L	0-0	0-0	0-0	0-0	0-0	0-0	0-1	0-0	0-0	0-0	0-1
T. Wilks	R	0-0	0-0	0-0	0-0	0-0	0-0	0-0	0-0	0-1	0-0	0-1
A. Brazle	L	0-0	0-1	0-0	0-0	0-0	0-0	0-1	0-0	0-0	0-0	0-2
P. Derringer	R	0-0	0-0	0-0	0-0	0-0	0-0	0-0	0-2	0-0	0-0	0-2
W. Walker	L	0-0	0-0	0-0	0-0	0-2	0-0	0-0	0-0	0-0	0-0	0-2
W. Sherdel	L	0-0	0-0	0-0	0-0	0-0	0-0	0-4	0-0	0-0	0-0	0-4
TOTAL		0-0	8-6	0-0	0-0	7-7	0-0	13-15	6-7	4-2	0-0	38-3

Brooklyn - Los Angeles Dodgers

		Balt	BRS	ChW	CL	D	Minn	NYY	Ph-Oak	StLB	W	Total
J. Podres	L	0-0	0-0	1-0	0-0	0-0	0-0	3-1	0-0	0-0	0-0	4-1
S. Koufax	L	0-1	0-0	0-1	0-0	0-0	2-1	2-0	0-0	0-0	0-0	4-3
D. Drysdale	R	0-2	0-0	1-0	0-0	0-0	1-1	1-0	0-0	0-0	0-0	3-3
L. Sherry	R	0-0	0-0	2-0	0-0	0-0	0-0	0-0	0-0	0-0	0-0	2-0
P. Roe	L	0-0	0-0	0-0	0-0	0-0	0-0	2-1	0-0	0-0	0-0	2-1
H. Casey	R	0-0	0-0	0-0	0-0	0-0	0-0	2-2	0-0	0-0	0-0	2-2
C. Erskine	R	0-0	0-0	0-0	0-0	0-0	0-0	2-2	0-0	0-0	0-0	2-2
C. Labine	R	0-0	0-0	0-0	0-0	0-0	0-0	2-2	0-0	0-0	0-0	2-2
D. Bessent	R	0-0	0-0	0-0	0-0	0-0	0-0	1-0	0-0	0-0	0-0	1-0
J. Coombs	R	0-0	1-0	0-0	0-0	0-0	0-0	0-0	0-0	0-0	0-0	1-0
S. Maglie	R	0-0	0-0	0-0	0-0	0-0	0-0	1-1	0-0	0-0	0-0	1-1
W. Wyatt	R	0-0	0-0	0-0	0-0	0-0	0-0	1-1	0-0	0-0	0-0	1-1
J. Black	R	0-0	0-0	0-0	0-0	0-0	0-0	1-2	0-0	0-0	0-0	1-2
R. Branca	R	0-0	0-0	0-0	0-0	0-0	0-0	1-2	0-0	0-0	0-0	1-2
R. Craig	R	0-0	0-0	0-1	0-0	0-0	0-0	1-1	0-0	0-0	0-0	1-2
B. Grimes	R	0-0	0-0	0-0	1-2	0-0	0-0	0-0	0-0	0-0	0-0	1-2
B. Loes	R	0-0	0-0	0-0	0-0	0-0	0-0	1-2	0-0	0-0	0-0	1-2
C. Osteen	L	0-1	0-0	0-0	0-0	0-0	1-1	0-0	0-0	0-0	0-0	1-2
S. Smith	L	0-0	0-1	0-0	1-1	0-0	0-0	0-0	0-0	0-0	0-0	1-2
L. Cadore	R	0-0	0-0	0-0	0-1	0-0	0-0	0-0	0-0	0-0	0-0	0-1
C. Davis	R	0-0	0-0	0-0	0-0	0-0	0-0	0-1	0-0	0-0	0-0	0-1
H. Gregg	R	0-0	0-0	0-0	0-0	0-0	0-0	0-1	0-0	0-0	0-0	0-1
V. Lombardi	L	0-0	0-0	0-0	0-0	0-0	0-0	0-1	0-0	0-0	0-0	0-1
E. Pfeffer	R	0-0	0-1	0-0	0-0	0-0	0-0	0-0	0-0	0-0	0-0	0-1
K. Spooner	L	0-0	0-0	0-0	0-0	0-0	0-0	0-1	0-0	0-0	0-0	0-1
R. Barney	R	0-0	0-0	0-0	0-0	0-0	0-0	0-2	0-0	0-0	0-0	0-2
R. Marquard	L	0-0	0-2	0-0	0-1	0-0	0-0	0-0	0-0	0-0	0-0	0-3
D. Newcombe	R	0-0	0-0	0-0	0-0	0-0	0-0	0-4	0-0	0-0	0-0	0-4
TOTAL		0-4	1-4	4-2	2-5	0-0	4-3	21-27	0-0	0-0	0-0	32-45

Chicago Cubs

		Balt	BRS	ChW	CL	D	Minn	NYY	Ph-Oak	StLB	W	Total
M. Brown	R	0-0	0-0	1-2	0-0	3-0	0-0	0-0	1-2	0-0	0-0	5-4
O. Overall	R	0-0	0-0	0-0	0-0	3-0	0-0	0-0	0-1	0-0	0-0	3-1
E. Reulbach	R	0-0	0-0	1-0	0-0	1-0	0-0	0-0	0-0	0-0	0-0	2-0
L. Warneke	R	0-0	0-0	0-0	0-0	2-0	0-0	0-1	0-0	0-0	0-0	2-1
H. Borowy	R	0-0	0-0	0-0	0-0	2-2	0-0	0-0	0-0	0-0	0-0	2-2
C. Passeau	R	0-0	0-0	0-0	0-0	1-0	0-0	0-0	0-0	0-0	0-0	1-0
G. Bush	R	0-0	0-0	0-0	0-0	0-0	0-0	0-1	1-0	0-0	0-0	1-1
G. Tyler	L	0-0	1-1	0-0	0-0	0-0	0-0	0-0	0-0	0-0	0-0	1-1
H. Vaughan	L	0-0	1-2	0-0	0-0	0-0	0-0	0-0	0-0	0-0	0-0	1-2
J. Pfeister	L	0-0	0-0	0-2	0-0	1-1	0-0	0-0	0-0	0-0	0-0	1-3
S. Blake	R	0-0	0-0	0-0	0-0	0-0	0-0	0-0	0-1	0-0	0-0	0-1
C. Bryant	R	0-0	0-0	0-0	0-0	0-0	0-0	0-1	0-0	0-0	0-0	0-1
T. Carleton	R	0-0	0-0	0-0	0-0	0-1	0-0	0-0	0-0	0-0	0-0	0-1
J. Dean	R	0-0	0-0	0-0	0-0	0-0	0-0	0-1	0-0	0-0	0-0	0-1
P. Douglas	R	0-0	0-1	0-0	0-0	0-0	0-0	0-0	0-0	0-0	0-0	0-1
F. May	L	0-0	0-0	0-0	0-0	0-0	0-0	0-1	0-0	0-0	0-0	0-1
H. McIntire	R	0-0	0-0	0-0	0-0	0-0	0-0	0-0	0-1	0-0	0-0	0-1
R. Prim	L	0-0	0-0	0-0	0-0	0-1	0-0	0-0	0-0	0-0	0-0	0-1
H. Wyse	R	0-0	0-0	0-0	0-0	0-1	0-0	0-0	0-0	0-0	0-0	0-1
L. French	L	0-0	0-0	0-0	0-0	0-2	0-0	0-0	0-0	0-0	0-0	0-2
B. Lee	R	0-0	0-0	0-0	0-0	0-0	0-0	0-2	0-0	0-0	0-0	0-2
P. Malone	R	0-0	0-0	0-0	0-0	0-0	0-0	0-0	0-2	0-0	0-0	0-2
C. Root	R	0-0	0-0	0-0	0-0	0-1	0-0	0-1	0-1	0-0	0-0	0-3
TOTAL		0-0	2-4	2-4	0-0	13-9	0-0	0-8	2-8	0-0	0-0	19-33

Pittsburgh Pirates

		Balt	BRS	ChW	CL	D	Minn	NYY	Ph-Oak	StLB	W	Total
B. Adams	R	0-0	0-0	0-0	0-0	3-0	0-0	0-0	0-0	0-0	0-0	3-0
D. Phillippe	R	0-0	3-2	0-0	0-0	0-0	0-0	0-0	0-0	0-0	0-0	3-2
S. Blass	R	2-0	0-0	0-0	0-0	0-0	0-0	0-0	0-0	0-0	0-0	2-0
H. Haddix	L	0-0	0-0	0-0	0-0	0-0	0-0	2-0	0-0	0-0	0-0	2-0
V. Law	R	0-0	0-0	0-0	0-0	0-0	0-0	2-0	0-0	0-0	0-0	2-0
V. Aldridge	R	0-0	0-0	0-0	0-0	0-0	0-0	0-1	0-0	0-0	2-0	2-1
R. Kremer	R	0-0	0-0	0-0	0-0	0-0	0-0	0-1	0-0	0-0	2-1	2-2

		Balt	BRS	ChW	CL	D	Minn	NYY	Ph-Oak	StLB	W	Total
N. Briles	R	1-0	0-0	0-0	0-0	0-0	0-0	0-0	0-0	0-0	0-0	1-0
B. Kison	R	1-0	0-0	0-0	0-0	0-0	0-0	0-0	0-0	0-0	0-0	1-0
N. Maddox	R	0-0	0-0	0-0	0-0	1-0	0-0	0-0	0-0	0-0	0-0	1-0
H. Camnitz	R	0-0	0-0	0-0	0-0	0-1	0-0	0-0	0-0	0-0	0-0	0-1
D. Ellis	R	0-1	0-0	0-0	0-0	0-0	0-0	0-0	0-0	0-0	0-0	0-1
B. Johnson	R	0-1	0-0	0-0	0-0	0-0	0-0	0-0	0-0	0-0	0-0	0-1
W. Kennedy	R	0-0	0-1	0-0	0-0	0-0	0-0	0-0	0-0	0-0	0-0	0-1
A. Leifield	L	0-0	0-0	0-0	0-0	0-1	0-0	0-0	0-0	0-0	0-0	0-1
J. Miljus	R	0-0	0-0	0-0	0-0	0-0	0-0	0-1	0-0	0-0	0-0	0-1
R. Miller	R	0-1	0-0	0-0	0-0	0-0	0-0	0-0	0-0	0-0	0-0	0-1
W. Mizell	L	0-0	0-0	0-0	0-0	0-0	0-0	0-1	0-0	0-0	0-0	0-1
V. Willis	R	0-0	0-0	0-0	0-0	0-1	0-0	0-0	0-0	0-0	0-0	0-1
E. Yde	L	0-0	0-0	0-0	0-0	0-0	0-0	0-0	0-0	0-0	0-1	0-1
B. Friend	R	0-0	0-0	0-0	0-0	0-0	0-0	0-2	0-0	0-0	0-0	0-2
S. Leever	R	0-0	0-2	0-0	0-0	0-0	0-0	0-0	0-0	0-0	0-0	0-2
L. Meadows	R	0-0	0-0	0-0	0-0	0-0	0-0	0-1	0-0	0-0	0-1	0-2
TOTAL		4-3	3-5	0-0	0-0	4-3	0-0	4-7	0-0	0-0	4-3	19-21

Boston - Milwaukee Braves

		Balt	BRS	ChW	CL	D	Minn	NYY	Ph-Oak	StLB	W	Total
L. Burdette	R	0-0	0-0	0-0	0-0	0-0	0-0	4-2	0-0	0-0	0-0	4-2
W. Spahn	L	0-0	0-0	0-0	1-1	0-0	0-0	3-2	0-0	0-0	0-0	4-3
B. James	R	0-0	0-0	0-0	0-0	0-0	0-0	0-0	2-0	0-0	0-0	2-0
D. Rudolph	R	0-0	0-0	0-0	0-0	0-0	0-0	0-0	2-0	0-0	0-0	2-0
J. Sain	R	0-0	0-0	0-0	1-1	0-0	0-0	0-0	0-0	0-0	0-0	1-1
V. Bickford	R	0-0	0-0	0-0	0-1	0-0	0-0	0-0	0-0	0-0	0-0	0-1
B. Buhl	R	0-0	0-0	0-0	0-0	0-0	0-0	0-1	0-0	0-0	0-0	0-1
E. Johnson	R	0-0	0-0	0-0	0-0	0-0	0-0	0-1	0-0	0-0	0-0	0-1
B. Rush	R	0-0	0-0	0-0	0-0	0-0	0-0	0-1	0-0	0-0	0-0	0-1
B. Voiselle	R	0-0	0-0	0-0	0-1	0-0	0-0	0-0	0-0	0-0	0-0	0-1
TOTAL		0-0	0-0	0-0	2-4	0-0	0-0	7-7	4-0	0-0	0-0	13-11

Cincinnati Reds

		Balt	BRS	ChW	CL	D	Minn	NYY	Ph-Oak	StLB	W	Total
H. Eller	R	0-0	0-0	2-0	0-0	0-0	0-0	0-0	0-0	0-0	0-0	2-0
R. Grimsley	L	0-0	0-0	0-0	0-0	0-0	0-0	0-0	2-1	0-0	0-0	2-1
P. Derringer	R	0-0	0-0	0-0	0-0	2-1	0-0	0-1	0-0	0-0	0-0	2-2
B. Walters	R	0-0	0-0	0-0	0-0	2-0	0-0	0-2	0-0	0-0	0-0	2-2
J. Billingham	R	0-0	0-0	0-0	0-0	0-0	0-0	0-0	1-0	0-0	0-0	1-0
W. Ruether	L	0-0	0-0	1-0	0-0	0-0	0-0	0-0	0-0	0-0	0-0	1-0
C. Carroll	R	1-0	0-0	0-0	0-0	0-0	0-0	0-0	0-1	0-0	0-0	1-1
J. Jay	R	0-0	0-0	0-0	0-0	0-0	0-0	1-1	0-0	0-0	0-0	1-1
J. Ring	R	0-0	0-0	1-1	0-0	0-0	0-0	0-0	0-0	0-0	0-0	1-1
H. Sallee	L	0-0	0-0	1-1	0-0	0-0	0-0	0-0	0-0	0-0	0-0	1-1
P. Borbon	R	0-0	0-0	0-0	0-0	0-0	0-0	0-0	0-1	0-0	0-0	0-1
T. Cloninger	R	0-1	0-0	0-0	0-0	0-0	0-0	0-0	0-0	0-0	0-0	0-1
R. Fisher	R	0-0	0-0	0-1	0-0	0-0	0-0	0-0	0-0	0-0	0-0	0-1
J. Merritt	L	0-1	0-0	0-0	0-0	0-0	0-0	0-0	0-0	0-0	0-0	0-1
B. Purkey	R	0-0	0-0	0-0	0-0	0-0	0-0	0-1	0-0	0-0	0-0	0-1
J. Turner	R	0-0	0-0	0-0	0-0	0-1	0-0	0-0	0-0	0-0	0-0	0-1
M. Wilcox	R	0-1	0-0	0-0	0-0	0-0	0-0	0-0	0-0	0-0	0-0	0-1
G. Nolan	R	0-1	0-0	0-0	0-0	0-0	0-0	0-0	0-1	0-0	0-0	0-2
J. O'Toole	L	0-0	0-0	0-0	0-0	0-0	0-0	0-2	0-0	0-0	0-0	0-2
G. Thompson	R	0-0	0-0	0-0	0-0	0-1	0-0	0-1	0-0	0-0	0-0	0-2
TOTAL		1-4	0-0	5-3	0-0	4-3	0-0	1-8	3-4	0-0	0-0	14-22

New York Mets

		Balt	BRS	ChW	CL	D	Minn	NYY	Ph-Oak	StLB	W	Total
J. Koosman	L	2-0	0-0	0-0	0-0	0-0	0-0	0-0	1-0	0-0	0-0	3-0
G. Gentry	R	1-0	0-0	0-0	0-0	0-0	0-0	0-0	0-0	0-0	0-0	1-0
T. McGraw	L	0-0	0-0	0-0	0-0	0-0	0-0	0-0	1-0	0-0	0-0	1-0
T. Seaver	R	1-1	0-0	0-0	0-0	0-0	0-0	0-0	0-1	0-0	0-0	1-2
J. Matlack	L	0-0	0-0	0-0	0-0	0-0	0-0	0-0	1-2	0-0	0-0	1-2
H. Parker	R	0-0	0-0	0-0	0-0	0-0	0-0	0-0	0-1	0-0	0-0	0-1
TOTAL		4-1	0-0	0-0	0-0	0-0	0-0	0-0	3-4	0-0	0-0	7-5

		Balt	BRS	ChW	CL	D	Minn	NYY	Ph- Oak	StLB	W	Total
G. Alexander	R	0-0	1-1	0-0	0-0	0-0	0-0	0-0	0-0	0-0	0-0	1-1
G. Chalmers	R	0-0	0-1	0-0	0-0	0-0	0-0	0-0	0-0	0-0	0-0	0-1
J. Konstanty	R	0-0	0-0	0-0	0-0	0-0	0-0	0-1	0-0	0-0	0-0	0-1
J. Mayer	R	0-0	0-1	0-0	0-0	0-0	0-0	0-0	0-0	0-0	0-0	0-1
R. Meyer	R	0-0	0-0	0-0	0-0	0-0	0-0	0-1	0-0	0-0	0-0	0-1
B. Miller	R	0-0	0-0	0-0	0-0	0-0	0-0	0-1	0-0	0-0	0-0	0-1
E. Rixey	L	0-0	0-1	0-0	0-0	0-0	0-0	0-0	0-0	0-0	0-0	0-1
R. Roberts	R	0-0	0-0	0-0	0-0	0-0	0-0	0-1	0-0	0-0	0-0	0-1
TOTAL		0-0	1-4	0-0	0-0	0-0	0-0	0-4	0-0	0-0	0-0	1-8

73

Individual Pitchers Winning 5 or More Victories—Total Series

Whitey Ford: Won 10, Lost 8

Year	G				Pitcher		Score				Decision
1950	4	W. Ford	L		B. Miller	R	NYY	5	PhP	2	Won
1953	4	W. Ford	L		B. Loes	R	BrD	7	NYY	3	Lost
1955	1	W. Ford	L		D. Newcombe	R	NYY	6	BrD	5	Won
1955	6	W. Ford	L		K. Spooner	L	NYY	5	BrD	1	Won
1956	1	W. Ford	L		S. Maglie	R	BrD	6	NYY	3	Lost
1956	3	W. Ford	L		R. Craig	R	NYY	5	BrD	3	Won
1957	1	W. Ford	L		W. Spahn	L	NYY	3	Mil	1	Won
1957	5	W. Ford	L		L. Burdette	R	Mil	1	NYY	0	Lost
1958	4	W. Ford	L		W. Spahn	L	Mil	3	NYY	0	Lost
1960	3	W. Ford	L		W. Mizell	L	NYY	10	PP	0	Won
1960	6	W. Ford	L		B. Friend	R	NYY	12	PP	0	Won
1961	1	W. Ford	L		J. O'Toole	L	NYY	2	Cin	0	Won
1961	4	W. Ford	L		J. O'Toole	L	NYY	7	Cin	0	Won
1962	1	W. Ford	L		B. O'Dell	L	NYY	6	SFG	2	Won
1962	6	W. Ford	L		B. Pierce	L	SFG	5	NYY	2	Lost
1963	1	W. Ford	L		S. Koufax	L	LAD	5	NYY	2	Lost

Year	G		Pitcher				Score				Decision
1963	4	W. Ford	L	S. Koufax	L		LAD	2	NYY	1	Lost
1964	1	W. Ford	L	R. Sadecki	L		StLC	9	NYY	5	Lost

Club Opponents

					W	L
W. Ford	L	vs	Br-LAD		3	4
W. Ford	L	vs	Cin		2	0
W. Ford	L	vs	PP		2	0
W. Ford	L	vs	PhP		1	0
W. Ford	L	vs	NY-SFG		1	1
W. Ford	L	vs	BB-Mil		1	2
W. Ford	L	vs	StLC		0	1
				Total	10	8

Pitching Opponents

					W	L	
W. Ford	L	J. O'Toole	L		2	0	Cin
W. Ford	L	R. Craig	R		1	0	Br-LAD
W. Ford	L	B. Friend	R		1	0	PP
W. Ford	L	B. Miller	R		1	0	PhP
W. Ford	L	W. Mizell	L		1	0	PP
W. Ford	L	D. Newcombe	R		1	0	Br-LAD
W. Ford	L	B. O'Dell	L		1	0	NY-SFG
W. Ford	L	K. Spooner	L		1	0	Br-LAD
W. Ford	L	W. Spahn	L		1	1	BB-Mil
W. Ford	L	L. Burdette	R		0	1	BB-Mil
W. Ford	L	B. Loes	R		0	1	Br-LAD
W. Ford	L	S. Maglie	R		0	1	Br-LAD
W. Ford	L	B. Pierce	L		0	1	NY-SFG
W. Ford	L	R. Sadecki	L		0	1	StLC
W. Ford	L	S. Koufax	L		0	2	Br-LAD
		Total			10	8	

Bob Gibson: Won 7, Lost 2

Year	G	Pitcher		Pitcher		Score				Decision
1964	2	B. Gibson	R	M. Stottlemyre	R	NYY	8	StLC	3	Lost
1964	5	B. Gibson	R	P. Mikkelson	R	StLC	5	NYY	2	Won
1964	7	B. Gibson	R	M. Stottlemyre	R	StLC	7	NYY	5	Won
1967	1	B. Gibson	R	J. Santiago	R	StLC	2	BRS	1	Won
1967	4	B. Gibson	R	J. Santiago	R	StLC	6	BRS	0	Won
1967	7	B. Gibson	R	J. Lonborg	R	StLC	7	BRS	2	Won
1968	1	B. Gibson	R	D. McLain	R	StLC	4	D	0	Won
1968	4	B. Gibson	R	D. McLain	R	StLC	10	D	1	Won
1968	7	B. Gibson	R	M. Lolich	L	D	4	StLC	1	Lost

Club Opponents					W	L
B. Gibson	R	vs	BRS		3	0
B. Gibson	R	vs	D		2	1
B. Gibson	R	vs	NYY		2	1
				Total	7	2

Pitching Opponents					W	L	
B. Gibson	R	J. Santiago	R		2	0	BRS
B. Gibson	R	D. McLain	R		2	0	D
B. Gibson	R	J. Lonborg	R		1	0	BRS
B. Gibson	R	P. Mikkelson	R		1	0	NYY
B. Gibson	R	M. Stottlemyre	R		1	1	NYY
B. Gibson	R	M. Lolich	L		0	1	D
		Total			7	2	

A. Reynolds: Won 7, Lost 2

Year	G	Pitcher		Score				Decision
1947	2	A. Reynolds	R	V. Lombardi	L	NYY 10	BrD 3	Won
1949	1	A. Reynolds	R	D. Newcombe	R	NYY 1	BrD 0	Won
1950	2	A. Reynolds	R	R. Roberts	R	NYY 2	PhP 1	Won
1951	1	A. Reynolds	R	D. Koslo	L	NYG 5	NYY 1	Lost
1951	4	A. Reynolds	R	S. Maglie	R	NYY 6	NYG 2	Won
1952	1	A. Reynolds	R	J. Black	R	BrD 4	NYY 2	Lost
1952	4	A. Reynolds	R	J. Black	R	NYY 2	BrD 0	Won
1952	7	A. Reynolds	R	J. Black	R	NYY 4	BrD 2	Won
1953	6	A. Reynolds	R	C. Labine	R	NYY 4	BrD 3	Won

Club Opponents				W	L
A. Reynolds	R	vs	Br-LAD	5	1
A. Reynolds	R	vs	PhP	1	0
A. Reynolds	R	vs	NY-SFG	1	1
			Total	7	2

Pitching Opponents					W	L	
A. Reynolds	R	vs	J. Black	R	2	1	Br-LAD
A. Reynolds	R	vs	C. Labine	R	1	0	Br-LAD
A. Reynolds	R	vs	V. Lombardi	L	1	0	Br-LAD
A. Reynolds	R	vs	S. Maglie	R	1	0	NY-SFG
A. Reynolds	R	vs	D. Newcombe	R	1	0	Br-LAD
A. Reynolds	R	vs	R. Roberts	R	1	0	PhP
A. Reynolds	R	vs	D. Koslo	L	0	1	NY-SFG
			Total		7	2	

Charles Ruffing: Won 7, Lost 2

Year G			Pitcher		Score		Decision
1932 1	C. Ruffing	R	G. Bush	R	NYY12	ChC 6	Won
1936 1	C. Ruffing	R	C. Hubbell	L	NYG 6	NYY 1	Lost
1937 2	C. Ruffing	R	C. Melton	L	NYY 8	NYG 1	Won
1938 1	C. Ruffing	R	B. Lee	R	NYY 3	ChC 1	Won
1938 4	C. Ruffing	R	B. Lee	R	NYY 8	ChC 3	Won
1939 1	C. Ruffing	R	P. Derringer	R	NYY 2	Cin 1	Won
1941 1	C. Ruffing	R	C. Davis	R	NYY 3	BrD 2	Won
1942 1	C. Ruffing	R	M. Cooper	R	NYY 7	StLC 4	Won
1942 5	C. Ruffing	R	J. Beazley	R	StLC 4	NYY 2	Lost

Club Opponents				W	L
C. Ruffing	R	vs	ChC	3	0
C. Ruffing	R	vs	Cin	1	0
C. Ruffing	R	vs	Br-LAD	1	0
C. Ruffing	R	vs	NY-SFG	1	1
C. Ruffing	R	vs	StLC	1	1
			Total	7	2

Pitching Opponents					W	L	
C. Ruffing	R	B. Lee	R		2	0	ChC
C. Ruffing	R	G. Bush	R		1	0	ChC
C. Ruffing	R	M. Cooper	R		1	0	StLC
C. Ruffing	R	C. Davis	R		1	0	Br-LAD
C. Ruffing	R	P. Derringer	R		1	0	Cin
C. Ruffing	R	C. Melton	L		1	0	NY-SFG
C. Ruffing X	R	J. Beazley	R		0	1	StLC
C. Ruffing	R	C. Hubbell	L		0	1	NY-SFG
		Total			7	2	

L. Gomez: Won 6, Lost 0

Year	G	Pitcher				Score				Decision
1932	2	L. Gomez	L	L. Warneke	R	NYY	5	ChC	2	Won
1936	2	L. Gomez	L	H. Schumacher	R	NYY	18	NYG	4	Won
1936	6	L. Gomez	L	F. Fitzsimmons	R	NYY	13	NYG	5	Won
1937	1	L. Gomez	L	C. Hubbell	L	NYY	8	NYG	1	Won
1937	5	L. Gomez	L	C. Melton	L	NYY	4	NYG	2	Won
1938	2	L. Gomez	L	J. Dean	R	NYY	6	ChC	3	Won

Club Opponents				W	L
L. Gomez	L	vs	NY-SFG	4	0
L. Gomez	L	vs	ChC	2	0
			Total	6	0

Pitching Opponents				W	L	
L. Gomez	L	J. Dean	R	1	0	ChC
L. Gomez	L	F. Fitzsimmons	R	1	0	NY-SFG
L. Gomez	L	C. Hubbell	L	1	0	NY-SFG
L. Gomez	L	C. Melton	L	1	0	NY-SFG
L. Gomez	L	H. Schumacher	R	1	0	NY-SFG
L. Gomez	L	L. Warneke	R	1	0	ChC
		Total		6	0	

C. Bender: Won 6, Lost 4

Year	G			Pitcher		Score					Decision
1905	2	C. Bender	R	J. McGinnity	R	PhA	3	NYG	0		Won
1905	5	C. Bender	R	C. Mathewson	R	NYG	2	PhA	0		Lost
1910	1	C. Bender	R	O. Overall	R	PhA	4	ChC	1		Won
1910	4	C. Bender	R	M. Brown	R	ChC	4	PhA	3		Lost
1911	1	C. Bender	R	C. Mathewson	R	NYG	2	PhA	1		Lost
1911	4	C. Bender	R	C. Mathewson	R	PhA	4	NYG	2		Won
1911	6	C. Bender	R	L. Ames	R	PhA	13	NYG	2		Won
1913	1	C. Bender	R	R. Marquard	L	PhA	6	NYG	4		Won
1913	4	C. Bender	R	A. Demaree	R	PhA	6	NYG	5		Won
1914	1	C. Bender	R	D. Rudolph	R	BBr	7	PhA	1		Lost

Club Opponents					W	L
C. Bender	R	vs		NYG	5	2
C. Bender	R	vs		ChC	1	1
C. Bender	R	vs		BBr	0	1
			Total		6	4

Pitching Opponents				W	L	
C. Bender	R	L. Ames	R	1	0	NYG
C. Bender	R	A. Demaree	R	1	0	NYG
C. Bender	R	R. Marquard	L	1	0	NYG
C. Bender	R	J. McGinnity	R	1	0	NYG
C. Bender	R	O. Overall	R	1	0	ChC
C. Bender	R	C. Mathewson	R	1	2	NYG
C. Bender	R	M. Brown	R	0	1	ChC
C. Bender	R	D. Rudolph	R	0	1	BBr
Total				6	4	

Waite Hoyt: Won 6, Lost 4

Year	G	Pitcher				Score				Decision
1921	2	W. Hoyt	R	A. Nehf	L	NYY	3	NYG	0	Won
1921	5	W. Hoyt	R	A. Nehf	L	NYY	3	NYG	1	Won
1921	8	W. Hoyt	R	A. Nehf	L	NYG	1	NYY	0	Lost
1922	3	W. Hoyt	R	J. Scott	R	NYG	3	NYY	0	Lost
1926	4	W. Hoyt	R	A. Reinhart	R	NYY	10	StLC	5	Won
1926	7	W. Hoyt	R	J. Haines	R	StLC	5	NYY	2	Lost
1927	1	W. Hoyt	R	R. Kremer	R	NYY	5	PP	4	Won
1928	1	W. Hoyt	R	W. Sherdel	L	NYY	4	StLC	1	Won
1928	4	W. Hoyt	R	W. Sherdel	L	NYY	7	StLC	3	Won
1931	5	W. Hoyt	R	B. Hallahan	L	StLC	5	PhA	1	Lost

Club Opponents				W	L
W. Hoyt	R	vs	StLC	3	2
W. Hoyt	R	vs	NY-SFG	2	2
W. Hoyt	R	vs	PP	1	0
			Total	6	4

Pitching Opponents					W	L
W. Hoyt	R	W. Sherdel	StLC	L	2	0
W. Hoyt	R	A. Nehf	NY-SFG	L	2	1
W. Hoyt	R	A. Reinhart	StLC	L	1	0
W. Hoyt	R	R. Kremer	PP	R	1	0
W. Hoyt	R	B. Hallahan	StLC	L	0	1
W. Hoyt	R	J. Haines	StLC	R	0	1
W. Hoyt	R	J. Scott	NY-SFG	R	0	1
			Total		6	4

J. Coombs: Won 5, Lost 0

Year	G			Pitcher		Score				Decision
1910	2	J. Coombs	R	M. Brown	R	Ph-Oak	9	ChC	3	Won
1910	3	J. Coombs	R	H. McIntire	R	Ph-Oak	12	ChC	5	Won
1910	5	J. Coombs	R	M. Brown	R	Ph-Oak	7	ChC	2	Won
1911	3	J. Coombs	R	C. Mathewson	R	Ph-Oak	3	NY-SFG	2	Won
1916	3	J. Coombs	R	C. Mays	R	Br-LAD	4	BRS	3	Won

Club Opponents					W	L
J. Coombs	R	vs	ChC		3	0
J. Coombs	R	vs	NY-SFG		1	0
J. Coombs	R	vs	BRS		1	0
			Total		5	0

Pitching Opponents				W	L	
J. Coombs	R	M. Brown	R	2	0	ChC
J. Coombs	R	H. McIntire	R	1	0	ChC
J. Coombs	R	C. Mathewson	R	1	0	NY-SFG
J. Coombs	R	C. Mays	R	1	0	BRS
		Total		5	0	

Herb Pennock: Won 5, Lost 0

Year	G			Pitcher		Score				Decision
1923	2	H. Pennock	L	H. McQuillan	R	NYY 4	NY-SFG	2		Won
1923	6	H. Pennock	L	A. Nehf	L	NYY 6	NY-SFG	4		Won
1926	1	H. Pennock	L	W. Sherdel	L	NYY 2	StLC	1		Won
1926	5	H. Pennock	L	W. Sherdel	L	NYY 3	StLC	2		Won
1927	3	H. Pennock	L	L. Meadows	R	NYY 8	PP	1		Won

Club Opponents					W	L
H. Pennock	L	vs	NY-SFG		2	0
H. Pennock	L	vs	StLC		2	0
H. Pennock	L	vs	PP		1	0
			Total		5	0

Pitching Opponents					W	L	
H. Pennock	L	vs	W. Sherdel	L	2	0	StLC
H. Pennock	L	vs	H. McQuillan	R	1	0	NY-SFG
H. Pennock	L	vs	A. Nehf	L	1	0	NY-SFG
H. Pennock	L	vs	L. Meadows	R	1	0	PP
			Total		5	0	

V. Raschi: Won 5, Lost 3

Year	G	Pitcher		Pitcher		Score				Decision
1949	2	V. Raschi	R	P. Roe	L	BrD	1	NYY	0	Lost
1949	5	V. Raschi	R	R. Barney	R	NYY	10	BrD	6	Won
1950	1	V. Raschi	R	J. Konstanty	R	NYY	1	PhP	0	Won
1951	3	V. Raschi	R	J. Hearn	R	NYG	6	NYY	2	Lost
1951	6	V. Raschi	R	D. Koslo	L	NYY	4	NYG	3	Won
1952	2	V. Raschi	R	C. Erskine	R	NYY	7	BrD	1	Won
1952	6	V. Raschi	R	B. Loes	R	NYY	3	BrD	2	Won
1953	3	V. Raschi	R	C. Erskine	R	BrD	3	NYY	2	Lost

Club	Opponents				W	L
V. Raschi	R	vs	Br-LAD		3	2
V. Raschi	R	vs	PhP		1	0
V. Raschi	R	vs	NYG		1	1
			Total		5	3

Pitching	Opponents				W	L	
V. Raschi	R	R. Barney	R		1	0	Br-LAD
V. Raschi	R	J. Konstanty	R		1	0	PhP
V. Raschi	R	D. Koslo	L		1	0	NY-SFG
V. Raschi	R	B. Loes	R		1	0	Br-LAD
V. Raschi	R	C. Erskine	R		1	1	Br-LAD
V. Raschi	R	J. Hearn	R		0	1	NY-SFG
V. Raschi	R	P. Roe	L		0	1	Br-LAD
		Total			5	3	

M. Brown: Won 5, Lost 4

Year	G			Pitcher		Score				Decision
1906	1	M. Brown	R	N. Altrock	L	ChW	2	ChC	1	Lost
1906	4	M. Brown	R	N. Altrock	L	ChC	1	ChW	0	Won
1906	6	M. Brown	R	G. White	L	ChW	6	ChC	3	Lost
1907	5	M. Brown	R	G. Mullin	R	ChC	2	D	0	Won
1908	1	M. Brown	R	E. Summers	R	ChC	10	D	6	Won
1908	4	M. Brown	R	E. Summers	R	ChC	3	D	0	Won
1910	2	M. Brown	R	J. Coombs	R	PhA	9	ChC	3	Lost
1910	4	M. Brown	R	C. Bender	R	ChC	4	PhA	3	Won
1910	5	M. Brown	R	J. Coombs	R	PhA	7	ChC	2	Lost

Club Opponents					W	L
M. Brown	R	vs	D		3	0
M. Brown	R	vs	ChW		1	2
M. Brown	R	vs	PhA		1	2
			Total		5	4

Pitching Opponents						W	L	
M. Brown	R	vs	E. Summers	R		2	0	D
M. Brown	R	vs	G. Mullin	R		1	0	D
M. Brown	R	vs	C. Bender	R		1	0	PhA
M. Brown	R	vs	N. Altrock	L		1	1	ChW
M. Brown	R	vs	G. White	L		0	1	ChW
M. Brown	R	vs	J. Coombs	R		0	2	PhA
			Total			5	4	

C. Mathewson: Won 5, Lost 5

Year	G		Pitcher		Score				Decision
1905	1	C. Mathewson R	E. Plank	L	NYG 3	PhA 0			Won
1905	3	C. Mathewson R	A. Coakley	R	NYG 9	PhA 0			Won
1905	5	C. Mathewson R	C. Bender	R	NYG 2	PhA 0			Won
1911	1	C. Mathewson R	C. Bender	R	NYG 2	PhA 1			Won
1911	3	C. Mathewson R	J. Coombs	R	PhA 3	NYG 2			Lost
1911	4	C. Mathewson R	C. Bender	R	PhA 4	NYG 2			Lost
1912	5	C. Mathewson R	H. Bedient	R	BRS 2	NYG 1			Lost
1912	8	C. Mathewson R	J. Wood	R	BRS 3	NYG 2			Lost
1913	2	C. Mathewson R	E. Plank	L	NYG 3	PhA 0			Won
1913	5	C. Mathewson R	E. Plank	L	PhA 3	NYG 1			Lost

Club Opponents				W	L
C. Mathewson	R	vs	PhA	5	3
C. Mathewson	R	vs	BRS	0	2
			Total	5	5

Pitching Opponents					W	L	
C. Mathewson	R	vs	C. Bender	R	2	1	PhA
C. Mathewson	R	vs	E. Plank	L	2	1	PhA
C. Mathewson	R	vs	A. Coakley	R	1	0	PhA
C. Mathewson	R	vs	J. Coombs	R	0	1	PhA
C. Mathewson	R	vs	H. Bedient	R	0	1	BRS
C. Mathewson	R	vs	J. Wood	R	0	1	BRS
			Total		5	5	

74

Top Ten Pitchers in Each Pitching Category

Most Games Pitched		Most Completed Games		Most Victories		Most Innings Pitched		Most Strikeouts	
W. Ford	22	C. Mathewson	10	W. Ford	10	W. Ford	196	W. Ford	94
A. Reynolds	15	C. Bender	9	B. Gibson	7	C. Mathewson	101 2/3	B. Gibson	92
B. Turley	15	B. Gibson	8	A. Reynolds	7	C. Ruffing	85 2/3	A. Reynolds	62
C. Labine	13	C. Ruffing	8	C. Ruffing	7	C. Bender	85	S. Koufax	61
W. Hoyt	12	W. Ford	7	C. Bender	6	W. Hoyt	83 2/3	C. Ruffing	61
A. Nehf	12	W. Hoyt	6	L. Gomez	6	B. Gibson	81	C. Bender	59
P. Derringer	11	G. Mullin	6	W. Hoyt	6	A. Nehf	79	G. Earnshaw	56
C. Erskine	11	A. Nehf	6	M. Brown	5	A. Reynolds	77 1/3	W. Hoyt	49
R. Marquard	11	E. Plank	6	J. Coombs	5	G. Earnshaw	62 2/3	C. Mathewson	48
C. Mathewson	11	M. Brown	5	C. Mathewson	5	L. Bush	60 2/3	B. Turley	46
V. Raschi	11	L. Bush	5	H. Pennock	5				
		B. Donovan	5	V. Raschi	5				
		G. Earnshaw	5						
		W. Johnson	5						
		C. Mays	5						
		D. Phillippe	5						
		A. Reynolds	5						

Most Shutouts		Most Bases on Balls		Lowest E. R. A. 50 or More Innings				Highest Won and Lost Percentage		
C. Mathewson	4	W. Ford	34	S. Koufax	57		0.95	L. Gomez	6-0	1.000
M. Brown	3	A. Nehf	32	C. Mathewson	101	2/3	1.15	J. Coombs	5-0	1.000
W. Ford	3	A. Reynolds	32	E. Plank	54	2/3	1.32	H. Pennock	5-0	1.000
L. Burdette	2	B. Turley	29	B. Turley	53	2/3	1.32	M. Pearson	4-0	1.000
B. Dinneen	2	P. Derringer	27	G. Earnshaw	62	2/3	1.58	B. Adams	3-0	1.000
B. Gibson	2	C. Ruffing	27	O. Overall	51	1/3	1.58	M. Lolich	3-0	1.000
B. Hallahan	2	B. Grimes	26	L. Grove	51	2/3	1.75	G. Pipgras	3-0	1.000
S. Koufax	2	W. Spahn	26	C. Hubbell	50	1/3	1.79	B. Ruth	3-0	1.000
A. Nehf	2	J. Palmer	25	W. Hoyt	83	2/3	1.83	T. Zachary	3-0	1.000
A. Reynolds	2	V. Raschi	25	B. Gibson	81		1.89			

21 Players with

2-0   1.000

75

Top Fifteen Pitchers: Times Leading in Various Pitching Categories

		Games	Comp. Games	Vict.	I. P.	Strike-Outs	Shutouts	Totals
1	W. Ford	1	2	5	1	4	3	16
2	A. Reynolds	2	4	4	0	4	2	16
3	B. Gibson	2	3	2	3	3	2	15
4	C. Mathewson	2	3	1	4	1	4	15
5	C. Ruffing	1	4	4	1	5	0	15
6	W. Hoyt	2	2	3	2	2	3	14
7	G. Earnshaw	2	3	2	2	3	1	13
8	D. McNally	3	3	3	1	1	1	12
9	S. Koufax	1	2	2	2	2	2	11
9	H. Pennock	2	3	3	2	1	0	11
11	M. Brown	2	1	2	1	0	3	9
11	L. Gomez	1	3	3	1	1	0	9
11	A. Nehf	2	3	1	1	0	2	9
11	V. Raschi	0	3	3	1	1	1	9
15	C. Bender	2	2	0	1	2	1	8

76
Overall Top Fifteen Pitchers in Various Categories

		Games	Comp. Games	Vict.	Inn. Pitch.	Strike-Outs	Shut-Outs	E.R.A.	Perc.	** Total Pts.
1	W. Ford	1	5	1	1	1	2*	0	0	55
2	C. Mathewson	7*	1	8*	2	9	1	2	0	47
3	B. Gibson	0	3*	2*	6	2	4*	10	0	39
4	A. Reynolds	2*	9*	2*	8	3	4*	0	0	38
5	C. Ruffing	0	3*	2*	3	5	0	0	0	31
6	W. Hoyt	5*	6*	5*	5	8	0	9	0	28
7	C. Bender	0	2	5*	5	6	0	0	0	27
8	S. Koufax	0	0	0	0	4	4*	1	0	24
9	A. Nehf	5*	6*	0	7	0	4*	0	0	22
10	B. Turley	2*	0	0	0	10	0	3*	0	18
11	L. Gomez	0	0	5*	0	0	0	0	1	16
12	J. Coombs	0	0	5*	0	0	0	0	2*	15
13	H. Pennock	0	0	5*	0	0	0	0	2*	15
14	M. Brown	0	9*	8*	0	0	2*	0	0	14
15	G. Earnshaw	0	9*	0	0	7	0	5*	0	12

* Tied

* * Points based upon 10 points for 1st place down to 1 point
for 10th place.

318

Part Five: World Series Miscellaneous Records

77

Series Games Won—Lost—Tied

American League	Series			Games			
	W	L	Margin	W	L	T	Margin
N.Y.Y.	20	9	+11	99	65	1	+34
Ph. Oak	7	3	+ 4	32	25	0	+ 7
BRS	5	2	+ 3	27	18	1	+ 9
D	3	5	− 2	22	28	1	− 6
ChW	2	2	Even	13	13	0	Even
Balt	2	2	Even	12	9	0	+ 3
CL	2	1	+ 1	9	8	0	+ 1
W	1	2	− 1	8	11	0	− 3
Minn	0	1	− 1	3	4	0	− 1
StLB	0	1	− 1	2	4	0	− 2
Total	42	28	+14	227	185	3	+42

	Series			Games			
National League	W L	Margin		W	L	T	Margin
StLC	8 4	+ 4		38	37	0	+ 1
NY SFG	5 10	− 5		42	45	2	− 3
Br LAD	4 9	− 5		32	45	0	−13
PP	4 2	+ 2		19	21	0	− 2
BB Mil	2 2	Even		13	11	0	+ 2
Cin	2 4	− 2		14	22	0	− 8
ChC	2 8	− 6		19	33	1	−14
NYM	1 1	Even		7	5	0	+ 2
PhP	0 2	− 2		1	8	0	− 7
Total	28 42	− 14		185	227	3	-42

78
Won—Lost—Tied Club Records by Game

| | Game 1 | Game 2 | Game 3 | Game 4 | Game 5 | Game 6 | Game 7 | Game 8 | |
	W L T	W L T	W L T	W L T	W L T	W L T	W L T	W L T	TOT
NYY	19-10-0	17-11-1	18-11-0	16-13-0	14- 8-0	10- 5-0	5- 6-0	0- 1-0	99-65-1
NY-SFG	9- 6-0	4- 9-2	9- 6-0	8- 7-0	6- 8-0	3- 6-0	2- 2-0	1- 1-0	42-45-2
StLC	4- 8-0	6- 6-0	7- 5-0	7- 5-0	4- 7-0	4- 5-0	6- 1-0	0- 0-0	38-37-0
BR-LAD	3-10-0	6- 7-0	9- 4-0	6- 7-0	3- 8-0	3- 5-0	2- 4-0	0- 0-0	32-45-0
Ph-Oak	7- 3-0	6- 4-0	4- 6-0	5- 5-0	4- 5-0	4- 1-0	2- 1-0	0- 0-0	32-23-0
BRS	4- 3-0	4- 2-1	3- 4-0	4- 3-0	6- 1-0	3- 2-0	1- 3-0	2- 0-0	27-18-1
D	1- 6-1	5- 3-0	3- 5-0	4- 4-0	4- 4-0	3- 3-0	2- 3-0	0- 0-0	22-28-1
PP	3- 3-0	1- 5-0	3- 3-0	3- 3-0	4- 1-0	1- 4-0	4- 1-0	0- 1-0	19-21-0
ChC	3- 6-1	4- 6-0	3- 7-0	4- 6-0	4- 4-0	1- 3-0	0- 1-0	0- 0-0	19-33-1
Cin	1- 5-0	3- 3-0	1- 5-0	3- 3-0	2- 3-0	2- 1-0	1- 2-0	1- 0-0	14-22-0
BB-Mil	3- 1-0	3- 1-0	1- 3-0	3- 1-0	2- 1-0	0- 3-0	1- 1-0	0- 0-0	13-11-0
ChW	3- 1-0	1- 3-0	2- 2-0	0- 4-0	3- 1-0	3- 1-0	1- 0-0	0- 1-0	13-13-0
Balt	4- 0-0	3- 1-0	2- 2-0	1- 3-0	1- 2-0	1- 0-0	0- 1-0	0- 0-0	12- 9-0
CL	1- 2-0	1- 2-0	1- 2-0	2- 1-0	1- 1-0	2- 0-0	1- 0-0	0- 0-0	9- 8-0
W	1- 2-0	1- 2-0	2- 1-0	2- 1-0	0- 3-0	1- 1-0	1- 1-0	0- 0-0	8-11-0
NYM	0- 2-0	2- 0-0	1- 1-0	2- 0-0	2- 0-0	0- 1-0	0- 1-0	0- 0-0	7- 5-0
Minn	1- 0-0	1- 0-0	0- 1-0	0- 1-0	0- 1-0	1- 0-0	0- 1-0	0- 0-0	3- 4-0
StLB	1- 0-0	0- 1-0	1- 0-0	0- 1-0	0- 1-0	0- 1-0	0- 0-0	0- 0-0	2- 4-0
PhP	1- 1-0	0- 2-0	0- 2-0	0- 2-0	0- 1-0	0- 0-0	0- 0-0	0- 0-0	1- 8-0

79
Overall Record on Wins, Losses and Ties

			4 Game Series Total									
Year	No.	Winner	Games	1	2	3	4	5	6	7	8	Loser
1914	1	BB Mil	4	W	W	W	W					Ph Oak
1927	2	NY Y	4	W	W	W	W					PP
1928	3	NY Y	4	W	W	W	W					StLC
1932	4	NY Y	4	W	W	W	W					ChC
1938	5	NY Y	4	W	W	W	W					ChC
1939	6	NY Y	4	W	W	W	W					Cin
1950	7	NY Y	4	W	W	W	W					PhP
1954	8	NY SFG	4	W	W	W	W					CL
1963	9	Br LAD	4	W	W	W	W					NY Y
1966	10	Balt	4	W	W	W	W					Br LAD
			5 Game Series									
1905	1	NY SFG	5	W	L	W	W	W				Ph Oak
1907	2	ChC	5	Tied	W	W	W	W				D
1908	3	ChC	5	W	W	L	W	W				D

Year	No.	Winner	Total Games	1	2	3	4	5	6	7	8	Loser
1910	4	Ph Oak	5	W	W	W	L	W				ChC
1913	5	Ph Oak	5	W	L	W	W	W				NY SFG
1915	6	BRS	5	L	W	W	W	W				PhP
1916	7	BRS	5	W	W	L	W	W				Br LAD
1922	8	NY SFG	5	W	T	W	W	W				NY Y
1929	9	Ph Oak	5	W	W	L	W	W				ChC
1933	10	NY SFG	5	W	W	L	W	W				W
1937	11	NY Y	5	W	W	W	L	W				NY SFG
1941	12	NY Y	5	W	L	W	W	W				Br LAD
1942	13	StLC	5	L	W	W	W	W				NY Y
1943	14	NY Y	5	W	L	W	W	W				StLC
1949	15	NY Y	5	W	L	W	W	W				Br LAD
1961	16	NY Y	5	W	L	W	W	W				Cin
1969	17	NY M	5	L	W	W	W	W				Balt
1970	18	Balt	5	W	W	W	L	W				Cin

<table><tr><td colspan="13" align="center">6 Game Series</td></tr></table>

Year	No.	Winner	Total Games	1	2	3	4	5	6	7	8	Loser
1906	1	ChW	6	W	L	W	L	W	W			ChC
1911	2	Ph Oak	6	L	W	W	W	L	W			NY SFG
1917	3	ChW	6	W	W	L	L	W	W			NY SFG
1918	4	BRS	6	W	L	W	W	L	W			ChC
1923	5	NY Y	6	L	W	L	W	W	W			NY SFG
1930	6	Ph Oak	6	W	W	L	L	W	W			StLC
1935	7	D	6	L	W	W	W	L	W			ChC
1936	8	NY Y	6	L	W	W	W	L	W			NY SFG
1944	9	StLC	6	L	W	L	W	W	W			StLB
1948	10	CL	6	L	W	W	W	L	W			BB Mil
1951	11	NY Y	6	L	W	L	W	W	W			NY SFG
1953	12	NY Y	6	W	W	L	L	W	W			Br LAD
1959	13	Br LAD	6	L	W	W	W	L	W			ChW

<table><tr><td colspan="13" align="center">7 Game Series</td></tr></table>

Year	No.	Winner	Total Games	1	2	3	4	5	6	7	8	Loser
1909	1	PP	7	W	L	W	L	W	L	W		D
1920	2	CL	7	W	L	L	W	W	W	W		Br LAD
1924	3	W	7	L	W	L	W	L	W	W		NY SFG
1925	4	PP	7	L	W	L	L	W	W	W		W
1926	5	StLC	7	L	W	W	L	L	W	W		NY Y
1931	6	StLC	7	L	W	W	L	W	L	W		Ph Oak

Year	No.	Winner	Total Games	1	2	3	4	5	6	7	8	Loser
1934	7	StLC	7	W	L	W	L	L	W	W		D
1940	8	Cin	7	L	W	L	W	L	W	W		D
1945	9	D	7	L	W	L	W	W	L	W		ChC
1946	10	StLC	7	L	W	L	W	L	W	W		BRS
1947	11	NY Y	7	W	W	L	L	W	L	W		Br LAD
1952	12	NY Y	7	L	W	L	W	L	W	W		Br LAD
1955	13	Br LAD	7	L	L	W	W	W	L	W		NY Y
1956	14	NY Y	7	L	L	W	W	W	L	W		Br LAD
1957	15	BB Mil	7	L	W	L	W	W	L	W		NY Y
1958	16	NY Y	7	L	L	W	L	W	W	W		BB Mil
1960	17	PP	7	W	L	L	W	W	L	W		NY Y
1962	18	NY Y	7	W	L	W	L	W	L	W		NY SFG
1964	19	StLC	7	W	L	L	W	W	L	W		NY Y
1965	20	Br LAD	7	L	L	W	W	W	L	W		Minn
1967	21	StLC	7	W	L	W	W	L	L	W		BRS
1968	22	D	7	L	W	L	L	W	W	W		StLC
1971	23	PP	7	L	L	W	W	W	L	W		Balt
1972	24	Ph Oak	7	W	W	L	W	L	L	W		Cin
1973	25	Ph Oak	7	W	L	W	L	L	W	W		NYM

			8 Game Series									
1903	1	BRS	8	L	W	L	L	W	W	W	W	PP
1912	2	BRS	8	W	T	L	W	W	L	L	W	NY SFG
1919	3	Cin	8	W	W	L	W	W	L	L	W	ChW
1921	4	NY SFG	8	L	L	W	W	L	W	W	W	NY Y

80
World Series Records on Games: Wins, Losses and Ties

Home Games		American League		National League	
1903	BRS *	L W L L W W W W	PP		W L W W L L L L
1905	Ph-OAK	L W L L L	NY-SFG *		W L W W W
1906	ChW *	W L W L W W	ChC		L W L W L L
1907	D	T L L L L	ChC *		T W W W W
1908	D	L L W L L	ChC *		W W L W W
1909	D	L W L W L W L	PP *		W L W L W L W
1910	Ph-OAK *	W W W L W	ChC		L L L W L
1911	Ph-OAK *	L W W W L W	NY-SFG		W L L L W L
1912	BRS *	W T L W W L L W	NY-SFG		L T W L L W W L
1913	Ph-OAK *	W L W W W	NY-SFG		L W L L L
1914	Ph-OAK	L L L L	BB-Mil *		W W W W
1915	BRS *	L W W W W	PhP		W L L L L
1916	BRS *	W W L W W	BR-LAD		L L W L L
1917	ChW *	W W L L W W	NY-SFG		L L W W L L
1918	BRS *	W L W W L W	ChC		L W L L W L
1919	ChW	L L W L L W W L	Cin *		W W L W W L L W
1920	CL *	W L L W W W W	BR-LAD		L W W L L L L
1921	**NYY	W W L L W L L L	NY-SFG *		L L W W L W W W
1922	**NYY	L T L L L	NY-SFG *		W T W W W
1923	NYY *	L W L W W W	NY-SFG *		W L W L L L
1924	W *	L W L W L W W	NY-SFG		W L W L W L L

Year		American League		National League
1925	W	W L W W L L L	PP *	L W L L W W W
1926	NYY	W L L W W L L	StLC *	L W W L L W W
1927	NYY *	W W W W	PP	L L L L
1928	NYY *	W W W W	StLC	L L L L
1929	Ph-OAK *	W W L W W	ChC	L L W L L
1930	Ph-OAK *	W W L L W W	StLC	L L W W L L
1931	PhOAK	W L L W L W L	StLC *	L W W L W L W
1932	NYY *	W W W W	ChC	L L L L
1933	W	L L W L L	NY-SFG *	W W L W W
1934	D	L W L W W L L	St.LC *	W L W L L W W
1935	D *	L W W W L W	ChC	W L L L W L
1936	NYY *	L W W W L W	NY-SFG	W L L L W L
1937	NYY *	W W W L W	NY-SFG	L L L W L
1938	NYY *	W W W W	ChC	L L L L
1939	NYY *	W W W W	Cin	L L L L
1940	D	W L W L W L L	Cin *	L W L W L W W
1941	NYY *	W L W W W	BR-LAD	L W L L
1942	NYY	W L L L L	StLC *	L W W W W
1943	NYY *	W L W W W	StLC	L W L L L
1944	**StLB	W L W L L	StLC *	L W L W W W
1945	D *	L W L W W L W	ChC	W L W L L W L
1946	BRS	W L W L W L L	StLC *	L W L W L W W
1947	NYY *	W W L L W L W	BR-LAD	L L W W L W L
1948	CL *	L W W W L W	BB-Mil	W L L L W L
1949	NYY *	W L W W W	BR-LAD	L W L L
1950	NYY *	W W W W	PhP	L L L L
1951	NYY *	L W L W W W W	NY-SFG	W L W L L L
1952	NYY *	L W L W L W W	BR-LAD	W L W L W L L
1953	NYY *	W W L L W W	BR-LAD	L L W W L L
1954	CL	L L L L	NY-SFG *	W W W W
1955	NYY	W W L L L W L	BR-LAD *	L L W W W L W
1956	NYY *	L L W W W L W	BR-LAD	W W L L L W L
1957	NYY	W L W L L W L	BB-Mil *	L W L W W L W
1958	NYY *	L L W L W W W	BB-Mil	W W L W L L L
1959	ChW	W L L L W L	BR-LAD *	L W W W L W
1960	NYY	L W W L L W L	PP *	W L L W W L W
1961	NYY *	W L W W W	Cin	L W L L L
1962	NYY *	W L W L W L W	NY-SFG	L W L W L W L
1963	NYY	L L L L	BR-LAD *	W W W W
1964	NYY	L W W L L W L	StLC *	W L L W W L W
1965	Minn	W W L L L W L	BR-LAD *	L L W W W L W
1966	Balt *	W W W W	BR-LAD	L L L L
1967	BRS	L W L L W W L	StLC *	W L W W L L W
1968	D *	L W L L W W W	StLC	W L W W L L L
1969	Balt	W L L L L	NYM *	L W W W W
1970	Balt *	W W W L W	Cin	L L L W L
1971	Balt	W W L L L W L	PP *	L L W W W L W
1972	Ph-OAK *	W W L W L L W	Cin	L L W L W W L
1973	Ph-OAK *	W L W L L W W	NYM	L W L W W L L

* World Series Winner

** Both Clubs in each league using same ball park

81
Won and Lost Records by Opponents

NYY / BRS

BY SERIES	W		L	BY GAME	W		L	T	BY SERIES	W		L	BY GAME	W		L	T
NYY	6	BR-LAD	2	NYY	27	BR-LAD	21	0	BRS	1	PP	0	BRS	5	PP	3	0
NYY	5	NY-SFG	2	NYY	23	NY-SFG	19	1	BRS	1	BR-LAD	0	BRS	4	BR-LAD	1	0
NYY	2	StLC	3	NYY	15	StLC	13	0	BRS	1	ChC	0	BRS	4	ChC	2	0
NYY	2	ChC	0	NYY	8	ChC	0	0	BRS	1	NY-SFG	0	BRS	4	NY-SFG	3	1
NYY	2	Cin	0	NYY	8	Cin	1	0	BRS	1	PhP	0	BRS	4	PhP	1	0
NYY	1	BB-Mil	1	NYY	7	BB-Mil	7	0	BRS	0	StLC	2	BRS	6	StLC	8	0
NYY	1	PP	1	NYY	7	PP	4	0									
NYY	1	PhP	0	NYY	4	PhP	0	0									
	20		9		99		65	1		5		2		27		18	1

StLC / NY-SFG

BY SERIES	W		L	BY GAME	W		L	T	BY SERIES	W		L	BY GAME	W		L	T
StLC	3	NYY	2	StLC	13	NYY	15	0	NY-SFG	2	NYY	5	NY-SFG	19	NYY	23	1
StLC	2	BRS	0	StLC	8	BRS	6	0	NY-SFG	1	Ph-OAK	2	NY-SFG	7	Ph-OAK	9	0
StLC	1	D	1	StLC	7	D	7	0	NY-SFG	1	W	1	NY-SFG	7	W	5	0
StLC	1	Ph-OAK	1	StLC	6	Ph-OAK	7	0	NY-SFG	1	CL	0	NY-SFG	4	CL	0	0
StLC	1	StLB	0	StLC	4	StLB	2	0	NY-SFG	0	BRS	1	NY-SFG	3	BRS	4	1
									NY-SFG	0	ChW	1	NY-SFG	2	ChW	4	0
	8		4		38		37	0		5		10		42		45	2

PH-OAK / BR-LAD

BY SERIES	W		L	BY GAME	W		L	T	BY SERIES	W		L	BY GAME	W		L	T
Ph-OAK	2	NY-SFG	1	Ph-OAK	9	NY-SFG	7	0	BR-LAD	2	NYY	6	BR-LAD	21	NYY	27	0

BY SERIES	W		L	BY GAME	W		L	T
Ph-OAK	2	ChC	0	Ph-OAK	8	ChC	2	0
Ph-OAK	1	StLC	1	Ph-OAK	7	StLC	6	0
Ph-OAK	1	Cin	0	Ph-OAK	4	Cin	3	0
Ph-OAK	0	BB-Mil	1	Ph-OAK	0	BB-Mil	4	0
Ph-OAK	1	NYM	0	Ph-OAK	4	NYM	3	0
	7		3		32		25	0
D	2	ChC	2	D	9	ChC	13	1
D	1	StLC	1	D	7	StLC	7	0
D	0	Cin	1	D	3	Cin	4	0
D	0	PP	1	D	3	PP	4	0
	3		5		22		28	1
PP	1	NYY	1	PP	4	NYY	7	0
PP	1	Balt	0	PP	4	Balt	3	0
PP	1	D	0	PP	4	D	3	0
PP	1	W	0	PP	4	W	3	0
PP	0	BRS	1	PP	3	BRS	5	0
	4		2		19		21	0
BB-Mil	1	Ph-OAK	0	BB-Mil	4	Ph-Oak	0	0
BB-Mil	1	NYY	1	BB-Mil	7	NYY	7	0
BB-Mil	0	CL	1	BB-Mil	2	CL	4	0
	2		2		13		11	0
ChW	1	ChC	0	ChW	4	ChC	2	0
ChW	1	NY-SFG	0	ChW	4	NY-SFG	2	0
ChW	0	BR-LAD	1	ChW	2	BR-Lad	4	0
ChW	0	Cin	1	ChW	3	Cin	5	0
	2		2		13		13	0
Balt	1	BR-LAD	0	Balt	4	BR-LAD	0	0
Balt	1	Cin	0	Balt	4	Cin	1	0
Balt	0	PP	1	Balt	3	PP	4	0
Balt	0	NYM	1	Balt	1	NYM	4	0
	2		2		12		9	0

BY SERIES	W		L	BY GAME	W		L	T
BR-LAD	1	ChW	0	BR-LAD	4	ChC	2	0
BR-LAD	1	Minn	0	BR-LAD	4	Minn	3	0
BR-LAD	0	CL	1	BR-LAD	2	CL	5	0
BR-LAD	0	BRS	1	BR-LAD	1	BRS	4	0
BR-LAD	0	Balt	1	BR-LAD	0	Balt	4	0
	4		9		32		45	0
CL	1	BR-LAD	0	CL	5	BR-LAD	2	0
CL	1	BB-Mil	0	CL	4	BB-Mil	2	0
CL	0	NY-SFG	1	CL	0	NY-SFG	4	0
	2		1		9		8	0
Cin	0	NYY	2	Cin	1	NYY	8	0
Cin	0	Balt	1	Cin	1	Balt	4	0
Cin	0	Ph-OAK	1	Cin	3	Ph-OAK	4	0
Cin	1	ChW	0	Cin	5	ChW	3	0
Cin	1	D	0	Cin	4	D	3	0
	2		4		14		22	0
ChC	2	D	2	ChC	13	D	9	1
ChC	0	Ph-OAK	2	ChC	2	Ph-OAK	8	0
ChC	0	BRS	1	ChC	2	BRS	4	0
ChC	0	ChW	1	ChC	2	ChW	4	0
ChC	0	NYY	2	ChC	0	NYY	8	0
	2		8		19		33	1
W	1	NY-SFG	1	W	5	NY-SFG	7	0
W	0	PP	1	W	3	PP	4	0
	1		2		8		11	0
NYM	1	Balt	0	NYM	4	Balt	1	0
NYM	0	Ph-OAK	1	NYM	3	Ph-OAK	4	0
	1		1		7		5	0

BY SERIES			BY GAME			
	W	L		W	L	T
			Minn			
Minn	0 BR-LAD	1	Minn	3 BR-LAD	4	0
	0	1		3	4	0
			StLB			
StLB	0 StLC	1	StLB	2 StLC	4	0
	0	1		2	4	0
			PhP			
PhP	0 BRS	1	PhP	1 BRS	4	0
PhP	0 NYY	1	PhP	0 NYY	4	0
	0	2		1	8	0

82
Winning and Losing Managers

	Winning Manager	Losing Manager
1903	Jim Collins	F. Clarke
1905	J. McGraw	C. Mack
1906	F. Jones	F. Chance
1907	F. Chance	H. Jennings
1908	F. Chance	H. Jennings
1909	F. Clarke	H. Jennings
1910	C. Mack	F. Chance
1911	C. Mack	J. McGraw
1912	J. Stahl	J. McGraw
1913	C. Mack	J. McGraw
1914	G. Stallings	C. Mack
1915	B. Carrigan	P. Moran
1916	B. Carrigan	W. Robinson
1917	C. Rowland	J. McGraw
1918	E. Barrow	F. Mitchell
1919	P. Moran	K. Gleason
1920	T. Speaker	W. Robinson

	Winning Manager	Losing Manager
1921	J. McGraw	M. Huggins
1922	J. McGraw	M. Huggins
1923	M. Huggins	J. McGraw
1924	S. Harris	J. McGraw
1925	B. McKechnie	S. Harris
1926	R. Hornsby	M. Huggins
1927	M. Huggins	D. Bush
1928	M. Huggins	B. McKechnie
1929	C. Mack	J. McCarthy
1930	C. Mack	G. Street
1931	G. Street	C. Mack
1932	J. McCarthy	C. Grimm
1933	B. Terry	J. Cronin
1934	F. Frisch	M. Cochrane
1935	M. Cochrane	C. Grimm
1936	J. McCarthy	B. Terry
1937	J. McCarthy	B. Terry
1938	J. McCarthy	G. Hartnett
1939	J. McCarthy	B. McKechnie
1940	B. McKechnie	D. Baker
1941	J. McCarthy	L. Durocher
1942	B. Southworth	J. McCarthy
1943	J. McCarthy	B. Southworth
1944	B. Southworth	L. Sewell
1945	S. O'Neill	C. Grimm
1946	E. Dyer	J. Cronin
1947	S. Harris	B. Shotten
1948	L. Boudreau	B. Southworth
1949	C. Stengel	B. Shotten
1950	C. Stengel	E. Sawyer
1951	C. Stengel	L. Durocher
1952	C. Stengel	C. Dressen
1953	C. Stengel	C. Dressen
1954	L. Durocher	A. Lopez
1955	W. Alston	C. Stengel
1956	C. Stengel	W. Alston
1957	F. Haney	C. Stengel
1958	C. Stengel	F. Haney
1959	W. Alston	A. Lopez
1960	D. Murtagh	C. Stengel

	Winning Manager	Losing Manager
1961	R. Hoak	F. Hutchinson
1962	R. Hoak	A. Dark
1963	W. Alston	R. Hoak
1964	J. Keane	Y. Berra
1965	W. Alston	S. Mele
1966	H. Bauer	W. Alston
1967	R. Schoendienst	D. Williams
1968	M. Smith	R. Schoendienst
1969	G. Hodges	E. Weaver
1970	E. Weaver	S. Anderson
1971	D. Murtagh	E. Weaver
1972	D. Williams	S. Anderson
1973	D. Williams	Y. Berra

83
Managers' Records

Manager		Series Won		Series Lost	Games		
					Win	Lost	Ties
J. McCarthy	7	1932-1936-1937-1938-1939-1941-1943	2	1929-1942	30	13	0
C. Stengel	7	1949-1950-1951-1952-1953-1956-1958	3	1955-1957-1960	37	26	0
C. Mack	5	1910-1911-1913-1929-1930	3	1905-1914-1931	24	19	0
W. Alston	4	1955-1959-1963-1965	2	1956-1966	19	16	0
M. Huggins	3	1923-1927-1928	3	1921-1922-1926	18	15	1
J. McGraw	3	1905-1921-1922	6	1911-1912-1913-1917-1923-1924	26	28	2
B. Carrigan	2	1915-1916	0	None	8	2	0
D. Murtagh	2	1960-1971	0	None	8	6	0
S. Harris	2	1924-1947	1	1925	11	10	0
R. Hoak	2	1961-1962	1	1963	8	8	0
D. Williams	2	1972-1973	1	1967	11	10	0
F. Chance	2	1907-1908	2	1906-1910	11	9	1
B. McKechnie	2	1925-1940	2	1928-1939	8	14	0
B. Southworth	2	1942-1944	2	1943-1948	11	11	0
E. Barrow	1	1918	0	None	4	2	0

Manager		Series Won		Series Lost	Games Win	Lost	Ties
H. Bauer	1	1966	0	None	4	0	0
L. Boudreau	1	1948	0	None	4	2	0
J. Collins	1	1903	0	None	5	3	0
E. Dyer	1	1946	0	None	4	3	0
F. Frisch	1	1934	0	None	4	3	0
F. Jones	1	1906	0	None	4	2	0
G. Hodges	1	1969	0	None	4	1	0
R. Hornsby	1	1926	0	None	4	3	0
J. Keane	1	1964	0	None	4	3	0
S. O'Neil	1	1945	0	None	4	3	0
C. Rowland	1	1917	0	None	4	2	0
M. Smith	1	1968	0	None	4	3	0
T. Speaker	1	1920	0	None	5	2	0
J. Stahl	1	1912	0	None	4	3	1
G. Stallings	1	1914	0	None	4	0	0
F. Clarke	1	1909	1	1903	7	8	0
M. Cochrane	1	1935	1	1934	7	6	0
F. Haney	1	1957	1	1958	7	7	0
P. Moran	1	1919	1	1915	6	7	0
R. Schoendienst	1	1967	1	1968	7	7	0
G. Street	1	1931	1	1930	6	7	0
L. Durocher	1	1954	2	1941-1951	7	8	0
B. Terry	1	1933	2	1936-1937	7	9	0
E. Weaver	1	1970	2	1969-1971	8	9	0
D. Baker	0	None	1	1940	3	4	0
D. Bush	0	None	1	1927	0	4	0
A. Dark	0	None	1	1962	3	4	0
K. Gleason	0	None	1	1919	3	5	0
G. Hartnett	0	None	1	1938	0	4	0
F. Hutchinson	0	None	1	1961	1	4	0
S. Mele	0	None	1	1965	3	4	0
F. Mitchell	0	None	1	1918	2	4	0
E. Sawyer	0	None	1	1950	0	4	0
S. Anderson	0	None	2	1970-1972	4	8	0
L. Sewell	0	None	1	1944	2	4	0
Y. Berra	0	None	2	1964-1973	6	8	0
J. Cronin	0	None	2	1933-1946	4	8	0
C. Dressen	0	None	2	1952-1953	5	8	0
A. Lopez	0	None	2	1954-1959	2	8	0
W. Robinson	0	None	2	1916-1920	3	9	0
B. Shotten	0	None	2	1947-1949	4	8	0
C. Grimm	0	None	3	1932-1935-1945	5	12	0
H. Jennings	0	None	3	1907-1908-1909	4	12	1

84

Managers versus Opponent Managers

New York Yankees

				Series		Game	
				W	L	W	L
C. Stengel	NY Y	C. Dressen	Br LAD	2	0	8	5
C. Stengel	NY Y	E. Sawyer	Ph P	1	0	4	0
C. Stengel	NY Y	B. Shotten	Br LAD	1	0	4	1
C. Stengel	NY Y	L. Durocher	NY SFG	1	0	4	2
C. Stengel	NY Y	W. Alston	Br LAD	1	1	7	7
C. Stengel	NY Y	F. Haney	BB Mil	1	1	7	7
C. Stengel	NY Y	D. Murtagh	PP	0	1	3	4
				7	3	37	26 + 11
J. McCarthy	NY Y	B. Terry	NY G	2	0	8	3
J. McCarthy	NY Y	C. Grimm	Ch C	1	0	4	0
J. McCarthy	NY Y	G. Hartnett	Ch C	1	0	4	0
J. McCarthy	NY Y	B. McKechnie	Cin	1	0	4	0
J. McCarthy	NY Y	L. Durocher	Br LAD	1	0	4	1
J. McCarthy	NY Y	B. Southworth	StLC	1	1	5	5
				7	1	29	9 + 20
M. Huggins	NY Y	D. Bush	PP	1	0	4	0

					Series		Game		
					W	L	W	L	
M. Huggins	NY Y	B. McKechnie	StLC		1	0	4	0	
M. Huggins	NY Y	R. Hornsby	StLC		0	1	3	4	
M. Huggins	NY Y	J. McGraw	NY SFG		1	2	7	11	1
					3	3	18	15	1 + 3
R. Hoak	NY Y	F. Hutchinson	Cin		1	0	4	1	
R. Hoak	NY Y	A. Dark	NY SFG		1	0	4	3	
R. Hoak	NY Y	W. Alston	Br LAD		0	1	0	4	
					2	1	8	8	
S. Harris	NY Y	B. Shotten	Br LAD		1	0	4	3	
					1	0	4	3	
Y. Berra	NY Y	J. Keane	StLC		0	1	3	4	
					0	1	3	4	
				Totals	20	9	99	65	1

Philadelphia - Oakland Athletics

					Series		Game		
					W	L	W	L	
C. Mack	Ph OAK	J. McGraw	NY SFG		2	1	9	7	
C. Mack	Ph OAK	F. Chance	Ch C		1	0	4	1	
C. Mack	Ph OAK	J. McCarthy	Ch C		1	0	4	1	
C. Mack	Ph OAK	G. Street	StLC		1	1	7	6	
C. Mack	Ph OAK	G. Stalling	BB Mil		0	1	0	4	
					5	3	24	19	
D. Williams	Ph OAK	S. Anderson	Cin		1	0	4	3	
D. Williams	Ph OAK	Y. Berra	NYM		1	0	4	3	
				Totals	7	3	32	25	

Detroit Tigers

					Series		Game		
					W	L	W	L	
H. Jennings	D	F. Chance	Ch C		0	2	1	8	1
H. Jennings	D	F. Clarke	PP		0	1	3	4	
					0	3	4	12	1
M. Cochrane	D	C. Grimm	Ch C		1	0	4	2	
M. Cochrane	D	F. Frisch	StLC		0	1	3	4	
					1	1	7	6	

				Series		Game		
				W	L	W	L	
S. O'Neill	D	C. Grimm	Ch C	1	0	4	3	
				1	0	4	3	
M. Smith	D	R. Schoendienst	StLC	1	0	4	3	
				1	0	4	3	
D. Baker	D	B. McKechnie	Cin	0	1	3	4	
				0	1	3	4	
			Totals	3	5	22	28	1

Boston Red Sox

				Series		Game		
				W	L	W	L	
B. Carrigan	BRS	P. Moran	Ph P	1	0	4	1	
B. Carrigan	BRS	W. Robinson	Br LAD	1	0	4	1	
				2	0	8	2	
J. Collins	BRS	F. Clarke	PP	1	0	5	3	
				1	0	5	3	
J. Stahl	BRS	J. McGraw	NY SFG	1	0	4	3	1
				1	0	4	3	1
E. Barrow	BRS	F. Mitchell	Ch C	1	0	4	2	
				1	0	4	2	
J. Cronin	BRS	E. Dyer	StLC	0	1	3	4	
				0	1	3	4	
D. Williams	BRS	R. Schoendienst	StLC	0	1	3	4	
				0	1	3	4	
			Totals	5	2	27	18	1

Cleveland Indians

				Series		Game		
				W	L	W	L	
T. Speaker	CL	W. Robinson	Br LAD	1	0	5	2	
				1	0	5	2	

					Series		Game	
					W	L	W	L
L. Boudreau	CL	B. Southworth	BB Mil		1	0	4	2
					1	0	4	2
A. Lopez	CL	L. Durocher	NY SFG		0	1	0	4
					0	1	0	4
			Totals		2	1	9	8

Chicago White Sox

					Series		Game	
					W	L	W	L
F. Jones	Ch W	F. Chance	Ch C		1	0	4	2
					1	0	4	2
C. Rowland	Ch W	J. McGraw	NY SFG		1	0	4	2
					1	0	4	2
K. Gleason	Ch W	P. Moran	Cin		0	1	3	5
					0	1	3	5
A. Lopez	Ch W	W. Alston	Br LAD		0	1	2	4
					0	1	2	4
			Totals		2	2	13	13

Baltimore Orioles

					Series		Game	
					W	L	W	L
E. Weaver	Balt	S. Anderson	Cin		1	0	4	1
E. Weaver	Balt	D. Murtagh	PP		0	1	3	4
E. Weaver	Balt	G. Hodges	NY M		0	1	1	4
					1	2	8	9
H. Bauer	Balt	W. Alston	Br LAD		1	0	4	0
					1	0	4	0
			Totals		2	2	12	9

Washington Senators

					Series		Game	
					W	L	W	L
S. Harris	W	J. McGraw	NY SFG		1	0	4	3

				Series		Game	
				W	L	W	L
S. Harris	W	B. McKechnie	PP	0	1	3	4
				1	1	7	7
J. Cronin	W	B. Terry	NY SFG	0	1	1	4
				0	1	1	4
			Totals	1	2	8	11

Minnesota Twins				Series		Game	
				W	L	W	L
S. Mele	Minn	W. Alston	Br LAD	0	1	3	4
			Totals	0	1	3	4

St. Louis Browns				Series		Game	
				W	L	W	L
L. Sewell	StLB	B. Southworth	StLC	0	1	2	4
			Totals	0	1	2	4

National League

St. Louis Cardinals

				Series		Game	
				W	L	W	L
B. Southworth	StLC	L. Sewell	StLB	1	0	4	2
B. Southworth	StLC	J. McCarthy	NY Y	1	1	5	5
				2	1	9	7
G. Street	StLC	C. Mack	Ph OAK	1	1	6	7
				1	1	6	7
R. Schoendienst	StLC	D. Williams	BRS	1	0	4	3
R. Schoendienst	StLC	M. Smith	D	0	1	3	4
				1	1	7	7
R. Hornsby	StLC	M. Huggins	NY Y	1	0	4	3
				1	0	4	3

				Series		Game	
				W	L	W	L
F. Frisch	StLC	M. Cochrane	D	1	0	4	3
				1	0	4	3
E. Dyer	StLC	J. Cronin	BRS	1	0	4	3
				1	0	4	3
J. Keane	StLC	Y. Berra	NY Y	1	0	4	3
				1	0	4	3
B. McKechnie	StLC	M. Huggins	NY Y	0	1	0	4
				0	1	0	4
			Totals	8	4	38	37

New York - San Francisco Giants

				Series		Game	
				W	L	W	L
J. McGraw	NY SFG	M. Huggins	NY Y	2	1	11	7
J. McGraw	NY SFG	C. Mack	Ph OAK	1	2	7	9
J. McGraw	NY SFG	J. Stahl	BRS	0	1	3	4
J. McGraw	NY SFG	S. Harris	W	0	1	3	4
J. McGraw	NY SFG	C. Rowland	Ch W	0	1	2	4
				3	6	26	28
B. Terry	NY SFG	J. Cronin	W	1	0	4	1
B. Terry	NY SFG	J. McCarthy	NY Y	0	2	3	8
				1	2	7	9
L. Durocher	NY SFG	A. Lopez	CL	1	0	4	0
L. Durocher	NY SFG	C. Stengel	NY Y	0	1	2	4
				1	1	6	4
A. Dark	NY SFG	R. Hoak	NY Y	0	1	3	4
				0	1	3	4
			Totals	5	10	42	45

Brooklyn - Los Angeles Dodgers

				Series		Game	
				W	L	W	L
W. Alston	Br LAD	R. Hoak	NY Y	1	0	4	0
W. Alston	Br LAD	A. Lopez	Ch W	1	0	4	2

				Series		Game	
				W	L	W	L
W. Alston	Br LAD	S. Mele	Minn	1	0	4	3
W. Alston	Br LAD	C. Stengel	NY Y	1	1	7	7
W. Alston	Br LAD	H. Bauer	Balt	0	1	0	4
				4	2	19	16
W. Robinson	Br LAD	B. Carrigan	BRS	0	1	1	4
W. Robinson	Br LAD	T. Speaker	CL	0	1	2	5
				0	2	3	9
B. Shotten	Br LAD	S. Harris	NY Y	0	1	3	4
B. Shotten	Br LAD	C. Stengel	NY Y	0	1	1	4
				0	2	4	8
C. Dressen	Br LAD	C. Stengel	NY Y	0	2	5	8
				0	2	5	8
L. Durocher	Br LAD	J. McCarthy	NY Y	0	1	1	4
				0	1	1	4
			Totals	4	9	32	45

Chicago Cubs

				Series		Game	
				W	L	W	L
F. Chance	Ch C	H. Jennings	D	2	0	8	1
F. Chance	Ch C	F. Jones	Ch W	0	1	2	4
F. Chance	Ch C	C. Mack	Ph-OAK	0	1	1	4
				2	2	11	9
C. Grimm	Ch C	J. McCarthy	NY Y	0	1	0	4
C. Grimm	Ch C	M. Cochrane	D	0	1	2	4
C. Grimm	Ch C	S. O'Neill	D	0	1	3	4
				0	3	5	12
F. Mitchell	Ch C	E. Barrow	BRS	0	1	2	4
				0	1	2	4
J. McCarthy	Ch C	C. Mack	Ph OAK	0	1	1	4
				0	1	1	4

					Series		Game		
					W	L	W	L	
G. Hartnett	Ch C	J. McCarthy	NY Y		0	1	0	4	
					0	1	0	4	
			Totals		2	8	19	33	1

Pittsburgh Pirates

					Series		Game	
					W	L	W	L
D. Murtagh	PP	C. Stengel	NY Y		1	0	4	3
D. Murtagh	PP	E. Weaver	Balt		1	0	4	3
					2	0	8	6
F. Clarke	PP	H. Jennings	D		1	0	4	3
F. Clarke	PP	J. Collins	BRS		0	1	3	5
					1	1	7	8
B. McKechnie	PP	S. Harris	W		1	0	4	3
					1	0	4	3
D. Bush	PP	M. Huggins	NYY		0	1	0	4
					0	**1**	**0**	**4**
			Totals		4	2	19	21

Cincinnati Reds

					Series		Game	
					W	L	W	L
B. McKechnie	Cin	D. Baker	D		1	0	4	3
B. McKechnie	Cin	J. McCarthy	NY Y		0	1	0	4
					1	1	4	7
P. Moran	Cin	K. Gleason	Ch W		1	0	5	3
					1	0	5	3
F. Hutchinson	Cin	R. Hoak	NY Y		0	1	1	4
					0	1	1	4
S. Anderson	Cin	E. Weaver	Balt		0	1	1	4
S. Anderson	Cin	D. Williams	Ph Oak		0	1	3	4
					0	2	4	8
			Totals		2	4	14	22

Boston - Milwaukee Braves

				Series		Game	
				W	L	W	L
G. Stallings	BB Mil	C. Mack	Ph OAK	1	0	4	0
				1	0	4	0
F. Haney	BB Mil	C. Stengel	NY Y	1	1	7	7
				1	1	7	7
B. Southworth	BB Mil	L. Boudreau	CL	0	1	2	4
				0	1	2	4
			Totals	2	2	13	11

New York Mets				Series		Game	
				W	L	W	L
G. Hodges	NY M	E. Weaver	Balt	1	0	4	1
				1	0	4	1
Y. Berra	NYM	D. Williams	Ph-OAK	0	1	3	4
				0	1	3	4
			Totals	1	1	7	5

Philadelphia Phillies				Series		Game	
				W	L	W	L
P. Moran	Ph P	B. Carrigan	BRS	0	1	1	4
				0	1	1	4
E. Sawyer	Ph P	C. Stengel	NY Y	0	1	0	4
				0	1	0	4
			Totals	0	1	1	8

85

Managers Who Participated in 6 or More World Series

*J. McCarthy 30-13-0 Games				C. Stengel 37-26-0 Games				C. Mack 24-19-0 Games		
Opp	Won	Lost	Tied	Opp	Won	Lost	Tied	Opp	Won	Lost	Tied
ChC	8	0	0	Br-LAD	19	13	0	NYG	9	7	0
NYG	8	3	0	BB-Mil	7	7	0	ChC	8	2	0
StLC	5	5	0	PhP	4	0	0	StLC	7	6	0
Cin	4	0	0	NYG	4	2	0	BB-Mil	0	4	0
Br-LAD	4	1	0	PP	3	4	0				
Ph-OAK *	1	4	0								
	30	13	0		37	26	0		24	19	0

W. Alston 19-16-0 Games				M. Huggins 18-15-1 Games				J. McGraw 26-28-2 Games		
Opp	Won	Lost	Tied	Opp	Won	Lost	Tied	Opp	Won	Lost	Tied
NYY	11	7	0	NYG	7	11	1	NYY	11	7	1
ChW	4	2	0	StLC	7	4	0	Ph-OAK	7	9	0
Minn	4	3	0	PP	4	0	0	BRS	3	4	1
Balt	0	4	0					W	3	4	0
								ChW	2	4	0
	19	16	0		18	15	1		26	28	2

* Won 29 and lost 9 in AL; Won 1 and lost 4 in NL

86
Managers in Four-Game World Series

1914	(1)	G. Stallings	BB-Mil	over	Ph-OAK	C. Mack
1927	(2)	M. Huggins	NYY	over	PP	D. Bush
1928	(3)	M. Huggins	NYY	over	StLC	B. McKechnie
1932	(4)	J. McCarthy	NYY	over	ChC	C. Grimm
1938	(5)	J. McCarthy	NYY	over	ChC	G. Hartnett
1939	(6)	J. McCarthy	NYY	over	Cin	B. McKechnie
1950	(7)	C. Stengel	NYY	over	PhP	E. Sawyer
1954	(8)	L. Durocher	NYG	over	CL	A. Lopez
1963	(9)	W. Alston	BR-LAD	over	NYY	R. Hoak
1966	(10)	H. Bauer	Balt	over	BR-LAD	W. Alston

Managers Winning and Losing Four-Game World Series

		W	L	By Club	W	L
(1)	J. McCarthy	3	0	NYY	6	1
(2)	M. Huggins	2	0	BB-Mil	1	0
(3)	G. Stallings	1	0	NY-SFG	1	0
(4)	C. Stengel	1	0	Balt	1	0
(5)	L. Durocher	1	0	BR-LAD	1	1

(6)	H. Bauer	1	0	Ph-OAK	0	1
(7)	W. Alston	1	1	PP	0	1
(8)	C. Mack	0	1	StLC	0	1
(9)	D. Bush	0	1	Cin	0	1
(10)	C. Grimm	0	1	PhP	0	1
(11)	G. Hartnett	0	1	CL	0	1
(12)	E. Sawyer	0	1	ChC	0	2
(13)	A. Lopez	0	1			
(14)	R. Hoak	0	1			
(15)	B. McKechnie	0	2			
		10	10		10	10

87

Managers with 2 or More Consecutive World Series Records

Two or More Consecutive World Series Wins

C. Stengel	5	NYY	1949 - 1950 - 1951 - 1952 - 1953
J. McCarthy	4	NYY	1936 - 1937 - 1938 - 1939
F. Chance	2	ChC	1907 - 1908
C. Mack	2	Ph-OAK	1910 - 1911
B. Carrigan	2	BRS	1915 - 1916
J. McGraw	2	NYG	1921 - 1922
M. Huggins	2	NYY	1927 - 1928
C. Mack	2	Ph-OAK	1929 - 1930
R. Hoak	2	NYY	1961 - 1962
D. Williams	2	Ph-OAK	1972 - 1973

Two or More Consecutive World Series Lost

H. Jennings	3	D	1907 - 1908 - 1909
J. McGraw	3	NYG	1911 - 1912 - 1913
M. Huggins	2	NYY	1921 - 1922
J. McGraw	2	NYG	1923 - 1924
B. Terry	2	NYG	1936 - 1937
C. Dressen	2	Br-LAD	1952 - 1953

88
New York Yankees World Series Records
from 1927 to 1941

Games

	W		L
NYY	8	ChC	0
NYY	8	NYG	3
NYY	4	PP	0
NYY	4	Cin	0
NYY	4	StLC	0
NYY	4	Br-LAD	1
	32		4

Series

	W		L
NYY	2	ChC	0
NYY	2	NYG	0
NYY	1	PP	0
NYY	1	Cin	0
NYY	1	StLC	0
NYY	1	Br-LAD	0
	8		0

Pitchers

	W	L
L. Gomez	6	0
C. Ruffing	6	1
M. Pearson	4	0
W. Hoyt	3	0
G. Pipgras	3	0
W. Moore	2	0
J. Murphy	2	0
B. Hadley	2	1
E. Bonham	1	0
H. Pennock	1	0
M. Russo	1	0
T. Zachary	1	0
S. Chandler	0	1
P. Malone	0	1
	32	4

Pitchers Opponents

		W	L
C. Hubbell	NYG	2	2
W. Wyatt	BR-LAD	1	1
H. Schumacher	NY-SFG	1	2
V. Aldridge	PP	0	1
G. Alexander	StLC	0	1
C. Bryant	ChC	0	1
G. Bush	ChC	0	1
C. Davis	BR-LAD	0	1
J. Dean	ChC	0	1
P. Derringer	Cin	0	1
J. Haines	StLC	0	1
R. Kremer	PP	0	1
F. May	ChC	0	1
L. Meadows	PP	0	1
J. Miljus	PP	0	1
C. Root	ChC	0	1
G. Thompson	Cin	0	1
L. Warneke	ChC	0	1
H. Casey	BR-LAD	0	2
F. Fitzsimmons	NY-SFG	0	2
B. Lee	ChC	0	2
C. Melton	NY-SFG	0	2
W. Sherdel	StLC	0	2
B. Walters	Cin	0	2
		4	32

From 1927 to 1932 Won 12 Straight Games
From 1927 to 1937 Won 20 Out of 23 Games
From 1927 to 1939 Won 28 Out of 31 Games
From 1927 to 1941 Won 32 Out of 36 Games

Year	G		Score			Winning Pitcher		Losing Pitcher		Decision
1927	1	NYY	5	PP	4	W. Hoyt	R	R. Kremer	R	Won
1927	2	NYY	6	PP	2	G. Pipgras	R	V. Aldridge	R	Won
1927	3	NYY	8	PP	1	H. Pennock	L	L. Meadows	R	Won
1927	4	NYY	4	PP	3	W. Moore	R	J. Miljus	R	Won
1928	1	NYY	4	StLC	1	W. Hoyt	R	W. Sherdell	L	Won
1928	2	NYY	9	StLC	3	G. Pipgras	R	G. Alexander	R	Won
1928	3	NYY	7	StLC	3	T. Zachary	L	J. Haines	R	Won
1928	4	NYY	7	StLC	3	W. Hoyt	R	W. Sherdell	L	Won
1932	1	NYY	12	ChC	6	C. Ruffing	R	G. Bush	R	Won
1932	2	NYY	5	ChC	2	L. Gomez	L	L. Warneke	R	Won
1932	3	NYY	7	ChC	5	G. Pipgras	R	C. Root	R	Won
1932	4	NYY	13	ChC	6	W. Moore	R	F. May	L	Won
1936	1	NY-SFG	6	NYY	1	C. Hubbell	L	C. Ruffing	R	Lost
1936	2	NYY	18	NY-SFG	4	L. Gomez	L	H. Schumacher	R	Won
1936	3	NYY	2	NY-SFG	1	B. Hadley	R	F. Fitzsimmons	R	Won
1936	4	NYY	5	NY-SFG	2	M. Pearson	R	C. Hubbell	L	Won
1936	5	NY-SFG	5	NYY	4	H. Schumacher	R	P. Malone	R	Lost
1936	6	NYY	13	NY-SFG	5	L. Gomez	L	F. Fitzsimmons	R	Won
1937	1	NYY	8	NY-SFG	1	L. Gomez	L	C. Hubbell	L	Won
1937	2	NYY	8	NY-SFG	1	C. Ruffing	R	C. Melton	L	Won
1937	3	NYY	5	NY-SFG	1	M. Pearson	R	H. Schumacher	R	Won
1937	4	NY-SFG	7	NYY	3	C. Hubbell	L	B. Hadley	R	Lost
1937	5	NYY	4	NY-SFG	2	L. Gomez	L	C. Melton	L	Won
1938	1	NYY	3	ChC	1	C. Ruffing	R	B. Lee	R	Won
1938	2	NYY	6	ChC	3	L. Gomez	L	J. Dean	R	Won
1938	3	NYY	5	ChC	2	M. Pearson	R	C. Bryant	R	Won
1938	4	NYY	8	ChC	3	C. Ruffing	R	B. Lee	R	Won
1939	1	NYY	2	Cin	1	C. Ruffing	R	P. Derringer	R	Won
1939	2	NYY	4	Cin	0	M. Pearson	R	B. Walters	R	Won
1939	3	NYY	7	Cin	3	B. Hadley	R	G. Thompson	R	Won
1939	4	NYY	7	Cin	4	J. Murphy	R	B. Walters	R	Won
1941	1	NYY	3	BR-LAD	2	C. Ruffing	R	C. Davis	R	Won
1941	2	BR-LAD	3	NYY	2	W. Wyatt	R	S. Chandler	R	Lost
1941	3	NYY	2	BR-LAD	1	M. Russo	L	H. Casey	R	Won
1941	4	NYY	7	BR-LAD	4	J. Murphy	R	H. Casey	R	Won
1941	5	NYY	3	BR-LAD	1	E. Bonham	R	W. Wyatt	R	Won